Culture and Containment

COLIN L. ANDERSON

Culture and Containment

Race, Geographic Mobility, and Popular Culture in Nineteenth-Century America

The University of North Carolina Press *Chapel Hill*

Set in Arno Pro by Westchester Publishing Services

Library of Congress Cataloging-in-Publication Data
Names: Anderson, Colin (Colin L.), author.
Title: Culture and containment : race, geographic mobility, and popular culture in nineteenth-century America / Colin Anderson.
Description: Chapel Hill : The University of North Carolina Press, [2026] | Includes bibliographical references and index.
Identifiers: LCCN 2026018190 | ISBN 9781469698113 (cloth) | ISBN 9781469698120 (paperback) | ISBN 9781469692296 (epub) | ISBN 9781469698137 (pdf)
Subjects: LCSH: Migration, Internal, in popular culture. | African Americans in popular culture. | Indigenous peoples in popular culture. | Popular culture—United States—History—19th century. | United States—Race relations. | BISAC: HISTORY / United States / 19th Century | SOCIAL SCIENCE / Ethnic Studies / American / Native American Studies
Classification: LCC E169.1 .A+
LC record available at https://lccn.loc.gov/2026018190

Cover art: *Top:* Jules Tavernier, *Gathering of the Clans, also known as Lakota Encampment (Red Cloud's Camp, Wyoming),* circa 1876. Oil on canvas, 41 × 69 inches. Collection of the Oakland Museum of California, The Kahn Collection. Photographer: Randy Dodson. *Bottom: Negro Life at the South,* ca. 1870, by Eastman Johnson. High Museum of Art.

Parts of chapter 2 and chapter 3 were previously published in Colin L. Anderson, "Segregation, Popular Culture, and the Southern Pastoral: The Spatial and Racial Politics of American Sheet Music, 1870–1900," *Journal of Southern History* 85, no. 3 (2019): 577–610. Part of chapter 5 was previously published in Colin L. Anderson, "Imagining Residential Segregation before the Ghetto: Representations of Black Urban Space and Mobility in the 'Darktown' Comics, 1877–1900," *Journal of Urban History* 50, no. 6 (2024): 1246–75.

This book will be made open access within three years of publication thanks to Path to Open, a program developed in partnership between JSTOR, the American Council of Learned Societies (ACLS), the University of Michigan Press, and the University of North Carolina Press to bring about equitable access and impact for the entire scholarly community, including authors, researchers, libraries, and university presses around the world. Learn more at https://about.jstor.org/path-to-open/.

To my parents

Contents

Acknowledgments

Support for this book has come from many different quarters. At George Washington University, I was incredibly lucky to have the amazing support and guidance of Tom Guglielmo, Gayle Wald, and Suleiman Osman. They were all dedicated to my growth as a scholar, and I learned so much from them. In particular, I could not have asked for a better primary advisor than Tom Guglielmo. His confidence in my academic work, thoughtful advice and guidance, and modeling of classroom teaching have all made me a better scholar. I am also extremely grateful for his deep engagement with multiple drafts of this manuscript—his feedback has been immensely helpful. Likewise, Gayle Wald and Suleiman Osman offered crucial insights on the chapter drafts, and their suggestions and encouraging words have been invaluable.

While I was an undergrad at Boston College, Davarian Baldwin first showed me the vital political stakes of history, and his classes sparked my interest in the field as well as changed my worldview. At NYU, Daniel Walkowitz taught me about the work and dedication needed to produce good historical writing, and at UPenn, Mary Frances Berry reaffirmed my belief that studying history is vital if one wants to truly understand the law. At GW, Libby Anker and Scott Larson were exemplars of undergraduate teaching—I strive to live up to their examples. I was also fortunate to be surrounded by amazing fellow graduate students in GW's American Studies department. Justin Mann, Julie Chamberlain, Thomas Dolan, Michael Horka, Sara Awartani, Vyta Pivo, Jackie Bolduan, and Zaynab Quadri all made the department a welcoming and stimulating intellectual community. Most of all they were great friends and a key source of advice and support.

I am also deeply thankful for the support of the University of Tampa's History, Geography, and Legal Studies department. I couldn't have asked for a kinder group of colleagues. Kelly Palmer, Spencer Segalla, Ed Pompeian, Andrew Grant, Elizabeth Littell-Lamb, Charles McGraw Groh, and Pat O'Brien have all made the department an incredibly welcoming environment, both socially and intellectually, and they have helped me feel at home at the university. Completing a book is a difficult task, but my colleagues at Tampa made it that much easier. Likewise, Andrew Winters at UNC Press was immensely helpful throughout the editorial process. He was flexible and communicative, and most of all he has been extremely supportive of the project. I am very grateful for all the work he has done in getting the book through the publication process.

This book has also benefitted from a number of sources of financial support. Funding from George Washington University, the Jeffrey C. Kasch Foundation, the Jacob M. Price Fellowship at the University of Michigan's Clements Library, the Mellon Scholar Program Fellowship at the Library Company of Philadelphia, and the Fred and Jeanette Pollock Research Grant all helped make this book possible. I am also grateful for financial assistance from the University of Tampa, which provided Faculty Travel and Professional Development grants.

Finally, I could not have completed this book without my family. While so much in life changes, they are the rock that remains constant. My siblings Austin, Emma, Marianne, and Natalie all remind me of the importance of family in life, and if I have them with me, everything will be all right. Their love and support keep me going and are at the core of who I am. Melissa VanSickle has been my best friend and an incredible source of joy in my life. I love our conversations about urban history and urban planning, and her humor and kindness make everyday life more enjoyable. Whether we're watching an English mystery or out on an adventure together, she reminds me of what's important in life, and I love her. Lastly, I owe everything to my parents. They have unconditionally supported me throughout this project and throughout my life. Even when I told them that I wanted to pursue a Ph.D. after graduating law school they never blinked an eye. All they want for me is my happiness and for that I am incredibly thankful. They taught me about the importance of justice, fairness, and compassion, and their love and belief in me have sustained me throughout this project. This book is dedicated to them because none of this would be possible without them.

Acknowledgments

Support for this book has come from many different quarters. At George Washington University, I was incredibly lucky to have the amazing support and guidance of Tom Guglielmo, Gayle Wald, and Suleiman Osman. They were all dedicated to my growth as a scholar, and I learned so much from them. In particular, I could not have asked for a better primary advisor than Tom Guglielmo. His confidence in my academic work, thoughtful advice and guidance, and modeling of classroom teaching have all made me a better scholar. I am also extremely grateful for his deep engagement with multiple drafts of this manuscript—his feedback has been immensely helpful. Likewise, Gayle Wald and Suleiman Osman offered crucial insights on the chapter drafts, and their suggestions and encouraging words have been invaluable.

While I was an undergrad at Boston College, Davarian Baldwin first showed me the vital political stakes of history, and his classes sparked my interest in the field as well as changed my worldview. At NYU, Daniel Walkowitz taught me about the work and dedication needed to produce good historical writing, and at UPenn, Mary Frances Berry reaffirmed my belief that studying history is vital if one wants to truly understand the law. At GW, Libby Anker and Scott Larson were exemplars of undergraduate teaching—I strive to live up to their examples. I was also fortunate to be surrounded by amazing fellow graduate students in GW's American Studies department. Justin Mann, Julie Chamberlain, Thomas Dolan, Michael Horka, Sara Awartani, Vyta Pivo, Jackie Bolduan, and Zaynab Quadri all made the department a welcoming and stimulating intellectual community. Most of all they were great friends and a key source of advice and support.

I am also deeply thankful for the support of the University of Tampa's History, Geography, and Legal Studies department. I couldn't have asked for a kinder group of colleagues. Kelly Palmer, Spencer Segalla, Ed Pompeian, Andrew Grant, Elizabeth Littell-Lamb, Charles McGraw Groh, and Pat O'Brien have all made the department an incredibly welcoming environment, both socially and intellectually, and they have helped me feel at home at the university. Completing a book is a difficult task, but my colleagues at Tampa made it that much easier. Likewise, Andrew Winters at UNC Press was immensely helpful throughout the editorial process. He was flexible and communicative, and most of all he has been extremely supportive of the project. I am very grateful for all the work he has done in getting the book through the publication process.

This book has also benefitted from a number of sources of financial support. Funding from George Washington University, the Jeffrey C. Kasch Foundation, the Jacob M. Price Fellowship at the University of Michigan's Clements Library, the Mellon Scholar Program Fellowship at the Library Company of Philadelphia, and the Fred and Jeanette Pollock Research Grant all helped make this book possible. I am also grateful for financial assistance from the University of Tampa, which provided Faculty Travel and Professional Development grants.

Finally, I could not have completed this book without my family. While so much in life changes, they are the rock that remains constant. My siblings Austin, Emma, Marianne, and Natalie all remind me of the importance of family in life, and if I have them with me, everything will be all right. Their love and support keep me going and are at the core of who I am. Melissa VanSickle has been my best friend and an incredible source of joy in my life. I love our conversations about urban history and urban planning, and her humor and kindness make everyday life more enjoyable. Whether we're watching an English mystery or out on an adventure together, she reminds me of what's important in life, and I love her. Lastly, I owe everything to my parents. They have unconditionally supported me throughout this project and throughout my life. Even when I told them that I wanted to pursue a Ph.D. after graduating law school they never blinked an eye. All they want for me is my happiness and for that I am incredibly thankful. They taught me about the importance of justice, fairness, and compassion, and their love and belief in me have sustained me throughout this project. This book is dedicated to them because none of this would be possible without them.

Culture and Containment

Introduction

That . . . is how the world moves: Not like an arrow, but a boomerang. (Beware of those who speak of the *spiral* of history; they are preparing a boomerang. Keep a steel helmet handy.)
—Ralph Ellison, *Invisible Man* (1952)

On February 23, 2020, Ahmaud Arbery, a twenty-five-year-old Black man, went on a run through the predominantly white neighborhood of Satilla Shores, in Brunswick, Georgia. As he was jogging on the street, he was spotted by three white residents. The three white men, two of them armed, chased after Arbery in vehicles. When Arbery refused their demands to stop, one of the men shot and killed him. The men justified the killing by claiming that they believed Arbery was a criminal fleeing after having committed a crime. In a 911 call made during the pursuit, one of the men simply told the dispatcher, "There's a Black male running down the street." At the ensuing trial, the prosecutor argued that the third white man, who had joined the pursuit later, "saw a Black guy running down the street being chased, and he figured the guy had to be a criminal. Instinct told him that Ahmaud must be a thief."[1]

These statements reveal how the simple act of running—of movement, or geographic mobility—conjured racist ideas about Black criminality. The link between movement and race has a long history, one that continues to influence our society in profound ways. Indeed, mobility is central to what are perhaps the two largest systems of racial control in our present era: mass incarceration and residential segregation, both of which are premised on confining and containing people of color. These systems and Arbery's murder testify to the important and enduring connections between race and geographic mobility, connections that are vital to understanding racial injustice in our current day.

This book examines the historical roots of these connections to shed light on the ideological and material processes underpinning our current racial landscape. Looking at the years 1845 to 1900, it traces the rise of a US nation-state and capitalist system founded on segregation and racial containment. Two historical developments underlie segregation's ascendance in this era: the rapid expansion of US settler colonialism into the West, and the end of formal enslavement in the South following the Civil War.[2] These two events were the twin catalysts of a transregional restructuring in the country—or what historians have labeled a "Greater Reconstruction"—that encompassed North, South, and West as the nation attempted to incorporate massive new western territories and reintegrate the rebellious Southern states. Both projects involved fundamental challenges to reigning white supremacist relations. Western expansion generated intense conflict with the Native peoples living in the West, and emancipation in the Civil War fundamentally altered Black-white relations in the country as Black Americans pressed for social and political rights.[3] In the face of these challenges, white Americans instituted the carceral relations of the Indian reservation and Jim Crow segregation to reassert their position atop the social hierarchy.

In this story of the country's racial reconstitution on the basis of segregation, popular culture played a significant role. *Culture and Containment* takes this role as its central focus, examining how the nexus of race, geographic mobility, and popular culture interacted with the development of both Jim Crow segregation and the segregation of Native Americans on reservations. Looking at representations of white Americans, African Americans, and Native Americans in an array of popular culture productions—including sheet music, lithographic prints, magazine stories, plantation reenactments, and Buffalo Bill's Wild West show—I make four main arguments. First, I argue that ideas about race and spatial mobility intimately informed nineteenth-century popular culture.[4] I demonstrate that representations of race and mobility were a core theme in popular culture and, in doing so, show that ideas about mobility were integral to racial ideology during this period. Popular culture is a site of everyday, hegemonic ideas that reflect Americans' most deeply held beliefs; the fact that representations of racial mobility suffused popular culture of the time testifies to the importance of mobility to nineteenth-century racial thought.

Second, I show that popular culture was a contested site, home to alternative visions of race and mobility. Whereas white cultural producers repeatedly presented nonwhite peoples with autonomous mobility as threats to white supremacy, Native Americans and African Americans used popular culture to speak back to such images and to emphasize the importance of mobility to freedom. Native and Black cultural producers thus seized on popular culture as a mechanism for resistance, injecting images and ideas that disrupted dominant white views of racial mobility into the cultural sphere. It is also imperative to note that African American and Native American agency and resistance were driving historical forces behind the structural and ideological shifts this book maps. Throughout, I not only analyze specific instances of Black and Native resistance in popular culture but also highlight the large-scale political efforts of Black and Native Americans that demanded a response from white Americans invested in white supremacy. Whether Black abolitionist activity and marronage, Native American military raids beyond the reservation, or Black migration in search of greater freedoms in the urban North, nonwhite actions fueled the dialectical history of race and mobility in the United States.

Third, I contend that the dominant popular culture imagery of this period not only reflected but also encouraged and reinforced the rise of the Indian reservation and Jim Crow segregation—which became the primary racial regimes governing Native Americans and African Americans, respectively, by the end of the nineteenth century. In addition to being a repository for white Americans' racial fantasies and desires, popular culture performed a pedagogical function, imparting the lesson that racial segregation was both natural and necessary. Portraying the autonomous mobility of Black and Native Americans as dangerous, disorderly, and a threat to white supremacy, while correspondingly associating Black and Native immobility with good order and white social control, dominant images conveyed that Native Americans and African Americans had to be spatially contained in order to maintain both social peace and white peoples' status atop the racial hierarchy. In other words, since restricted movement and spatial segregation are inextricably linked, these popular culture depictions actively encouraged the development of the Indian reservation and Jim Crow segregation, both of which relied on the spatial containment of nonwhite bodies.[5]

In particular, I assert that representations of Blackness, mobility, and urban space played an especially significant role in influencing the development of Jim Crow segregation.[6] Such representations were particularly pervasive in the last three decades of the nineteenth century, the years preceding Jim Crow's rise in the 1890s and 1900s. As white Americans confronted radically changed Black-white relations following emancipation in the Civil War, including the rapid growth of Black migration to urban centers across the North and West, nationally circulating popular culture images disseminated a powerful lesson to white audiences: Black bodies had to be confined in space in order to ensure white social dominance.

Thus, as whites sought a new racial regime to uphold white supremacy after the end of slavery, popular culture not only registered white desires for the spatial containment of African Americans but also promoted the implementation of that desire on the ground. It provided to millions of Americans, year after year, an ideological road map to white supremacy based on spatial containment and was thus a significant causal factor in the rise of Jim Crow in the 1890s and 1900s. While Jim Crow practices existed prior to these decades, the 1890s and 1900s saw Jim Crow segregation become the dominant form of Black oppression in the United States. In the 1890s, whites throughout the South passed a deluge of segregation laws, clamping down on Black movement in public spaces. Then, in the 1900s, whites across the country implemented large-scale urban residential segregation, or ghetto segregation. And once these Jim Crow practices were in motion, popular culture imagery further naturalized and armored them.

Of course, cultural representations were not the only factor in the development of Jim Crow practices. In terms of Southern Jim Crow laws, historians have named the growing assertiveness of the Black middle class, the threat to elites of interracial populist politics, white public discourse about Black men as sexual threats to white women, and the impersonal social relations of urbanization.[7] And as causes of residential segregation, scholars have pointed to white fears about growing Black urban migration, the general intensification of white racism in this "nadir" of Black-white relations, the emergence of racialized real estate practices that linked Black residents with declining property values, a growing discourse that cast African Americans as carriers of disease and a threat to public health, or some combination of these.[8] I would argue that all of these causes played a part in the emergence of large-scale residential segregation.

However, the scholarship on Jim Crow has omitted popular culture as a historical factor in Jim Crow segregation's consolidation at the turn of the twentieth century.[9] Again, popular culture was not the only cause of Jim Crow; it interacted with, and was influenced by, the other important factors historians have named. Likewise, cultural representations encouraging segregation did not predate racial segregation, the practice of which stretches back past the founding of the country. But such images did predate the solidification of Jim Crow segregation in the 1890s and 1900s. As the cultural arm of burgeoning Jim Crow segregation, the segregationist narratives in popular culture, consumed by millions of Americans, would have been a significant motivating force in the national development of Jim Crow. Popular culture therefore needs to be included in the history of Jim Crow segregation for the historical picture to be complete.[10]

My contention that popular culture influenced material practices applies historian Philip Deloria's argument that representations in popular culture create "expectations" that influence how audiences imagine and think about race and racial subjects.[11] Deloria himself develops his framework of "expectations" from the work of cultural theorist Stuart Hall, among others. As Hall has shown, popular culture is a crucial site for the study of ideology, including racial ideology.[12] As scholar Michael Omi puts it, "Popular culture has been an important realm within which racial ideologies have been created, reproduced and sustained."[13]

Since popular culture is deeply imbued with ideological significance, it produces material effects.[14] Once informed—either consciously or unconsciously—by the mental frameworks embedded in popular cultural, individuals act on those frameworks, giving representations their material dimension.[15] This insight demands that we connect the ideological developments around race and mobility in popular culture to historical developments on the ground. Because ideologies shape our social practices and material relations, popular culture is therefore an agent in the history of race and race relations. As Deloria writes, "Popular culture works to produce—and sometimes to compromise—racism" as a social practice.[16] Deloria's observation that popular culture sometimes undermines racism reveals culture to be a site of contestation, where counterhegemonic ideas challenge and destabilize prevailing ideologies and social structures. In the last half of the nineteenth century, popular culture was indeed a battleground, where African Americans, Native Americans, and white Americans all expressed competing ideas about race, mobility, and freedom, even if white supremacist ideas typically had the upper hand.

Greater Reconstruction

The book's fourth argument concerns the period known as Greater Reconstruction. First developed by historian Elliott West, Greater Reconstruction is a historical framework that expands the history of the Civil War and Reconstruction beyond North–South and Black–white axes to bring the West into the historical narrative. Encompassing the annexation of Texas in 1845 through the withdrawal of federal troops from the South and the culmination of the wars against the western Indians in 1877, Greater Reconstruction's geographical and chronological scope captures the transformations gripping the nation over the last half of the nineteenth century, including the addition of massive new western territories and the remaking of the Southern political economy after the Civil War. In particular, Greater Reconstruction highlights the multiregional, interrelated project of nation building and capitalist expansion and remodeling that was underway during this time.[17]

I build on prior Greater Reconstruction scholarship to argue that a fundamental trait of Greater Reconstruction was the installation of the Indian reservation and Jim Crow segregation as racial regimes designed to spatially contain Native and Black Americans.[18] These twin developments enshrined geographic containment as the dominant method of managing relations with Native Americans and African Americans in the United States. As scholars of carceral studies have stressed, both the Indian reservation and Jim Crow segregation implemented carceral relations, and both are part of a longer US history of carceral projects.[19] I draw on these insights to reframe our understanding of Greater Reconstruction by showing that containing the mobility of nonwhites was crucial to Greater Reconstruction's project of forging a modern white-supremacist nation.

While the Indian reservation and Jim Crow segregation existed prior to this period, these years saw them become the prevailing regimes governing Native Americans and Black Americans, respectively. As historian Nicholas Guyatt has shown, segregationist impulses can be traced to the early national period in the United States in the form of Indian removal and colonization schemes for free African Americans. Both of these policies demonstrate that white Americans have long sought spatial solutions to racial problems, and that racial separation was a national, rather than a regional preoccupation.[20]

Greater Reconstruction significantly altered the trajectory and shape of these segregationist impulses. In the decades prior to the 1850s, non–Indian Americans relied on the policy of Indian removal and its segregation of Native peoples across the Mississippi River to facilitate settler colonialism's expansion. But the movement of settler-colonists across the Mississippi after 1845 made removal no longer viable as the primary federal policy. In its place, white policymakers turned to the more intense containment of the reservation to manage US-Indian relations. Whereas removal involved pushing Native peoples beyond a border, thereby excising them from US society, the reservation enclosed and enveloped Native peoples within tightly policed borders surrounded by non-Indian settlement. More akin to a prison, the reservation and reservation officials subjected Native peoples' movement to intense scrutiny.

Likewise, in the antebellum era, the most popular antislavery scheme espoused by white Americans was colonization, which advocated the separation of free Black Americans by relocating them beyond the country's boundaries. Whites also imposed a regime of carceral immobility under slavery.[21] But both slavery and white hopes for colonization unraveled with large-scale emancipation in the Civil War. The dissolution of slavery engendered a profound escalation in white anxieties about Black mobility, and white Americans gradually re-created the carceral relations of slavery in the new guise of Jim Crow. Of course, Jim Crow altered the forms, practices, and institutions of containment, but the impetus to restrict Black movement remained.[22]

In making this argument, I expand Greater Reconstruction's chronology. Whereas previous scholarship has placed Greater Reconstruction's end date in the late 1870s or early 1880s, my contention that Jim Crow segregation was an essential facet of this era pushes its boundaries to the turn of the twentieth century, when Jim Crow solidified across the country.[23] While Jim Crow augments Greater Reconstruction's chronology, as a thoroughly national project it reaffirms the necessity of Greater Reconstruction's transregional lens. White fears about Black mobility played out in the South, North, and West in an interconnected process that ultimately led to Jim Crow's establishment across the nation.

Although the Indian reservation and Jim Crow had significant differences in structure and purpose—the reservation's primary goal was to acquire Native lands for white settlement, while Jim Crow segregation aimed to maintain a cheap labor source alongside white social dominance—they shared a fundamental focus on spatial containment. Placing the histories of the reservation and Jim Crow segregation alongside each other highlights this deep affinity, and their common objective of containing nonwhites testifies to the importance of mobility to race relations and white supremacy in the nineteenth century. Indeed, examining the two histories together reveals that spatial containment was a main feature of race in the period and that the two structures were integral to the larger process of US nation building and capitalist expansion.[24]

Histories of Race and Mobility

In addition to the work on Greater Reconstruction, this book adds to a burgeoning literature on the history of race and geographic mobility. In the last fifteen years or so, the field of geography has experienced a "mobilities turn," in which geographers have emphasized that spatial mobility is intimately intertwined with power relations. Building on the work of theorist Henri Lefebvre, they have shown that mobility—far from a neutral category that all individuals have equal access to—both constitutes and is constituted by social relations.[25] Recently, a number of historians have begun incorporating the insights of geographers into studies of the history of race and mobility in the United States. While historians have long studied racial migrations, especially international migrations, the new histories of race and mobility differ in that they make mobility a central analytic and treat it as a historical construct reciprocally related to racial categories. These works undertake a sustained analysis of mobility to plumb how movement is thought about and represented, how it is experienced by various racialized populations, and how conceptions and experiences of movement structure and change race itself.[26] Further, whereas most migration studies are concerned with global flows of peoples, the histories of race and mobility look at the everyday, more local transits and immobilities of populations as well.[27]

Culture and Containment contributes to this scholarship by uncovering the vital relationship between race, mobility, and popular culture imagery in the nineteenth-century United States. While some works have looked at how specific forms of popular culture reflected the intersection of race and mobility in the nineteenth century, none analyze the importance of race and mobility to popular culture in general, across multiple entertainment forms.[28] Not only did the interactions between race and mobility contour the material forms and institutions of popular culture industries, but they also consistently shaped popular culture's very content by engendering representations of racial movement. Such representations helped mold and reaffirm systems of racial immobility on the ground, demonstrating the importance of cultural representations of mobility to race and racial ideology. Indeed, the fact that ideas about race and mobility were so thoroughly interlaced with popular culture illustrates that mobility was a core component of racial ideology in the nineteenth century. That popular culture—the site of everyday, hegemonic ideas that simultaneously reflected and created commonsense notions of race among millions of Americans—so consistently trafficked in representations of racial movement testifies to the elementary place of mobility in nineteenth-century racial thought.

The importance of ideas about mobility to Indianness is well known in the field of Native American studies, which has long pointed out that Europeans have historically—and often inaccurately—viewed Indigenous peoples as nomadic and that this was a major justification for the expropriation of Native lands. However, historians have not paid enough attention to how white ideas about Indian mobility changed over the nineteenth century or how white people used these ideas to justify shifting federal Indian policies. I draw out these shifting relations in white views of Indian mobility over the last half of the nineteenth century, showing that the changing contexts and demands of settler colonialism produced derivations that met specific exigencies for specific groups of white Americans. Further, analyzing the history of ideas about Indianness and mobility alongside African American history reveals that the link between Indians and nomadism, while unique in many ways, was also part and parcel of a broader pattern of racial thinking in the nineteenth century.

Theoretical Groundings for Histories of Mobility

As is perhaps evident from the previous discussion, by "mobility" I mean simply the literal movement of a body or bodies across physical space; in other words, physical movement.[29] Crucially, the meaning and effects of mobility are relative based on geographical scale.[30] For example, slaves dancing the "cakewalk" certainly had mobility—dancing involves the movement of the body across physical space. But when we pull back to the scale of the Southern town, plantation district, or state, we see that the mobility of slaves was severely restricted. At various points in the book I use the term "(im)mobility" to explicitly highlight these relational dynamics, but often I use the more readable "mobility" or "immobility." But these designations, too, should always be understood as relational. It is by comparing relations and evaluating contexts that we can discern the distributions of power involved in racialized mobilities.

Attending to mobility as a historical construct unlocks valuable insights into the ideological and material structures of race. As scholar Genevieve Carpio, riffing on Stuart Hall, puts it, "Mobility is a key modality through which race is lived and contested."[31] Not only does uneven access to mobility constitute one of the material relations through which resources are unequally distributed across races, but geographic movement itself signals racial meanings. These insights apply just as much to the nineteenth century as to our current day. Whether a racial body moved, where it moved, and when it moved all affected the very racial meaning attached to that body. Ideas about mobility therefore informed how Americans understood Blackness, Indianness, and whiteness at a basic level, dictating whether particular racialized subjects were seen as dangerous, criminal, and savage, or as safe, progressive, and civilized.

Discussing the material and symbolic aspects of mobility, historian Cotten Seiler notes that because movement has often enabled or signaled the social mobility of nonwhites, "regimes of white supremacy have sought to control or curtail those forms and moments of nonwhite mobility that they could not instrumentalize for their own purposes."[32] Seiler's point is a vital one. Not only did white Americans often seek to stamp out autonomous nonwhite mobility in an effort to shore up whites' material advantages, but they also repeatedly reacted to the symbolic value of nonwhite mobility—spatial mobility as evidence of social mobility. This was particularly the case with free African Americans, whose ability to share space with whites—whether in a public theater, on a train, or in a city neighborhood—conveyed a sense of racial equality to white people.

Seiler's point also highlights that white supremacist structures have consistently attempted to curtail nonwhite movement that does not serve white interests. As this study repeatedly shows, the movement of nonwhite bodies was not per se problematic or threatening for white Americans. What whites so often perceived and cast as threatening was free and autonomous nonwhite movement. Nonwhite movement that fulfilled white desires or that was under white control was perfectly acceptable. Indeed, the coerced and controlled movement of nonwhites has historically been integral to the projects of white supremacy, settler colonialism, and racial capitalism.[33] Ultimately, in the nineteenth century, the white impetus to control Black and Native movement, and the identification of free nonwhite mobility as a threat to white supremacy, stemmed from the material and ideological demands of slavery and settler colonialism. Exploitation of Black labor and expropriation of Native land were the historical bedrocks on which the various manifestations of racial mobility arose over time.

Crucially, the categories of gender, sexuality, and class always mediated and structured the relationship between race and mobility in the nineteenth century. I trace the myriad ways these categories intersected in popular culture and emphasize that the movement of gendered and classed bodies could give rise to very different racial meanings and experiences. Popular culture representations not only reflected these differences but also consistently refracted white anxieties about race and mobility through gendered and classed lenses. In addition, as *Culture and Containment* emphasizes, the tastes and desires—or perceived tastes and desires—of middle-class women repeatedly shaped aspects of the cultural imagery portraying racial movement. Popular culture producers, hoping to appeal to the lucrative market of (white) middle-class women, made sure their productions matched the gender proprieties of the day and women's interests. I foreground the influential power that middle-class women audiences held over popular culture at various points throughout the book.

The chapters that follow move roughly chronologically, from the antebellum era through the end of the century. However, though the book's overarching organization is chronological and reveals a larger historical narrative, the chapters themselves are more episodic, presenting a series of case studies of different popular culture forms. While the case studies cover an array of forms, it is worth noting that sheet music figures prominently. Sheet music was one of the most popular forms of entertainment during the nineteenth century, if not the most popular. Often comprising not only musical notation and lyrics but also detailed cover illustrations, it is a rich source for historical analysis. Given both its popularity and textual richness, it makes an excellent source for examining representations of race and mobility.

Chapters 1 and 2 focus on antebellum sheet music and its representations of Black and Native movement. The chapters show that popular songs consistently cast free Black and Native movement as a deviant trait that was incompatible with social order and civilization, while conversely presenting immobile nonwhite bodies as natural and nonthreatening. Both chapters analyze the links between these images and the spatial relations of the Indian removal policy and slavery, while chapter 2 also delves into sheet music's gender politics and relation to the ideology of separate spheres.

Chapter 3 focuses on popular culture from 1850 to the mid-1880s and contextualizes it within two of Greater Reconstruction's foundational racial events: the mass influx of white settlers into the West and the end of slavery in the Civil War. First, it stays with sheet music to argue that heightened white anxieties about Black mobility after emancipation helped drive the explosive popularity of the Southern pastoral—the term historians use to refer to romantic images of the US South and its landscape—in popular culture. Southern pastoralism celebrated the rooted Black body, thus offering a blueprint for white supremacy based on Black immobility. While much great work has been done on the Southern pastoral, scholars have not identified this motif of Black rootedness and its spatial implications.[34] Next, the chapter examines how, following the rise of the reservation system in the 1850s, Ponca Chief Ma-chu-nah-zha, commonly known as Standing Bear, and Omaha citizen Susette La Flesche, or Inshtatheamba, used the popular lecture circuit, or lyceum, to contest the reservation system's ideologies and practices of confinement. The chapter ends with the convergence of these two strands in Southern pastoral music that referenced the Kansas Exodus, a mass migration of African Americans from the South to Kansas in the late 1870s. These songs trenchantly illustrate Greater Reconstruction's regional entanglements.

Chapter 4 analyzes the popular musical genre known as "coon songs" from the 1880s and 1890s, which portrayed urban African Americans with unfettered mobility as criminal and immoral. Together with the Southern pastoral, which remained prominent, the genres imparted the lesson that Black mobility had to be contained to ensure white social control, helping drive the proliferation of Southern Jim Crow laws and large-scale residential segregation across the country. However, Black popular entertainers continually resisted these racial scripts. The chapter shows that the Indianapolis *Freeman*, one of the country's preeminent Black newspapers, offered a counterforum to racist images of Black mobility by tracking and lauding the travels and successes of Black performers. In the pages of the *Freeman*, Black artists' movement became a symbol of race pride and triumph over segregation.

Chapter 5 details how late nineteenth-century popular culture presented exclusively Black urban neighborhoods as commonplace and natural, despite the fact that no such neighborhoods existed in US cities during the period. Looking at cultural representations of Thompson Street, New York City, and the Currier and Ives lithographic print series *Darktown* from 1877 to 1900, the chapter asserts that imagery of all-Black urban spaces portrayed segregation as correct, normal, and natural, thus helping to lay the ideological groundwork for ghettoization in the early twentieth century. Mobility remained a key motif in such images, with depictions of deviant Black movement flashing a warning about the need to segregate Black city space to ensure white safety.

Finally, chapter 6 studies two large outdoor performances of the 1880s and 1890s: Buffalo Bill's Wild West show and the plantation reenactment *Black America*. It contends that both were arenas in which competing ideas about race and mobility played out. In the Wild West show, the performance itself justified the reservation's carceral relations by foregrounding Native Americans' threatening mobility, but the show's Native actors consciously used it to escape the poverty and confines of the reservation, traveling the country and sometimes the world. Further, white reformers and Indian Bureau officials tried to prevent William "Buffalo Bill" Cody from hiring Native Americans off reservations, partly from the belief that traveling would rekindle Indian actors' racial tendency for nomadism—a tendency reformers wanted to stamp out. The Wild West show thus illustrates that late nineteenth-century popular culture was thoroughly enmeshed in political debates over federal Indian policy and the implementation of the reservation on the ground.

Similarly, a competing vision of racial mobility suffused *Black America*, staged in 1895 in Brooklyn, New York. The show's prevailing theme was Southern pastoralism, portraying Black Americans as content and naturally at home in the rural South. Yet during the show's musical portion, the show's Black manager, Billy McClain, inserted assertions of modern Black urbanity and professional respectability. The chapter also examines how McClain parlayed his success in the entertainment industry—including in *Black America*—into the creation of the Benevolent Order of Colored Professionals (BO of CP), a mutual aid society designed to further Black performers' careers. Through material aid and an insistence on Black artists' professionalism, the BO of CP pushed back against industry racism. Furthermore, with chapters in multiple US cities, it facilitated Black artists' interurban travels across the country, providing both a place to gather on the road and economic support. Just like the Wild West show, *Black America* was a staging ground for alternative visions of racial mobility.

CHAPTER ONE

Historical Groundings

Constructions of Racial Movement in Antebellum Popular Song

After opening to public passengers in the mid-1830s, several Massachusetts railroad companies instituted a policy of racial segregation on their trains. The companies forced Black riders to sit in the first railcar, the one closest to the soot of the engine and carrying all the train's luggage. Soon, white conductors came up with a nickname for this second-class car, one that would still be in use more than a century later: the Jim Crow car, after the extremely popular blackface minstrel song of the same name.[1] That the very name given to systematic racial segregation in the United States comes from one of the country's first popular culture phenomena speaks to the deep historical entanglements of popular culture and segregation. Indeed, a closer examination of the song itself reveals another important connection: that popular culture contained lessons about race and geographic mobility. In the song, the Black male narrator, Jim Crow, travels across the country, wreaking havoc as he goes. The tune portrays his movement—and, by extension, Black movement—as a source of social deviance and danger. The white conductors' nickname for segregation and the spatial containment it imposed was thus highly fitting. The Jim Crow car ensured that the phantom of disorderly Black movement that the song conjured would not disrupt white riders.

The focus on movement in the song "Jim Crow" was not an aberration. This chapter places antebellum sheet music and song sheets that portrayed African Americans side by side with those featuring Native Americans to show that representations of racial mobility were vital to both types. In particular, it compares images of African Americans in early blackface minstrel songs with songs about Native Americans to reveal that ideas about unfettered nonwhite movement were central to racial ideologies and popular culture of the period. This comparative analysis also demonstrates that popular songs consistently cast free Black and Native movement as a negative, deviant trait that was incompatible with social order and civilization.

This chapter further contends that the representations of Black and Native mobility in sheet music and song sheets had tangible effects on the ground. These hegemonic images not only reflected but also ideologically reinforced the relations of containment undergirding two of the primary racial structures of the period: slavery and the policy of Indian removal. Slavery as an institution relied on an elaborate set of practices designed to constrain and control the movement of the enslaved, and even in the free Northern states, white Americans influenced by practices forged in slavery continued to restrict free Black movement. Likewise, the then-ascendant removal policy called for the segregation and containment of Native peoples on a continental scale, walled off beyond the Mississippi River. By providing ideological ballast to these racial structures, popular song's attacks on free Black and Native movement connected to material practices restricting the mobility of Black and Native Americans across the country.

While analyzing early minstrel songs and songs about Native peoples alongside each other highlights the core theme of racial movement running through both, it also exposes crucial differences. These differences remind us of the importance of not flattening historical analyses of race and being attuned to the diversity of ways race can license and effect oppression and dispossession. This chapter elaborates on these differences below, but one worth noting up front is that minstrel songs featured a more brash racism, employing extremely denigrating and malicious images of Black Americans, while popular songs by and large romanticized Native Americans, painting them as innocent and noble, if inferior, figures. This romanticism of Native peoples was still laced with a violent racism of its own, as will be discussed, but it was less denigrating than minstrelsy's anti-Blackness. This difference stemmed largely from the intended audiences of the two genres. Songs about Native Americans targeted the middle class and thus featured more refined language and restrained imagery. They also were the product of two larger cultural movements then sweeping the middle class: romanticism and sentimentalism. Both of these cultural trends emphasized strong emotional experiences, and romanticized, tragic Native figures checked this box. In contrast, minstrelsy emerged from white working-class male contexts, which freed it from middle-class decorum and allowed more raucous and explicit content. Eventually, beginning in the mid-1840s, minstrel artists would gear minstrelsy toward the middle class as well, a shift that is examined in chapter 2. But in its early years, minstrelsy remained tethered to white working-class politics.

This difference is particularly important because sheet music's romanticism of Native peoples was related to a larger ambivalence in its racial politics. Of the forty-two songs primarily about American Indians published prior to 1860 that I have located in my research, eleven—slightly over 25 percent—depicted them as innately mobile. However, this stereotype, which was a pillar of racist claims of Native inferiority and licensed the expropriation of their lands under Enlightenment thought, also existed in popular song alongside overt critiques of white treatment of Indians. While historians have noted that popular music of the period heavily romanticized Native Americans and have correctly pointed out the racist trappings of this romantic imagery, they have overlooked the extent and depth of these critiques in sheet music and song sheets. This chapter contends that popular music was in fact a highly ambivalent space when it came to representing Native Americans, and it discusses both the subversive and repressive potential of popular song. While popular song's criticism of the seizure of Indigenous lands cut against the policy of Indian removal, imagery of wandering Indians simultaneously supported it, as the supposed nomadism of Native Americans was one of the primary justifications for the policy.[2]

Although early minstrelsy and songs about Native Americans had different primary audiences, it is important to note that there was still significant class overlap between the two forms. "Jim Crow," for example, was so popular that Americans of all classes knew and liked the song. The same is true of sheet music and song sheets (song sheets simply printed lyrics and named the tune to which they were to be sung; they had no musical notation). While antebellum publishers mainly geared sheet music toward middle-class audiences—especially middle-class women—and aimed the cheaper song sheets at working-class audiences, both often circulated across class and gender lines. Sheet music was relatively cheap, and one piece could reach numerous ears, as middle-class and working-class men and women regularly performed songs for group audiences in parlors or pubs. One therefore did not have to be literate to encounter the music and lyrics contained in sheet music. Indeed, some hit songs became so popular that it was difficult for Americans to avoid hearing them—people whistled them on the street and brass bands blared them to the public. Song sheets were even more affordable. While this chapter primarily discusses sheet music, it analyzes a number of song sheets as well. With their more boisterous and raunchy content, song sheets provide insight into the class differences mediating constructions of race, gender, and mobility. But the content of song sheets also overlapped a great deal with that of sheet music, and songs often appeared in both forms.[3]

Slavery and Black (Im)Mobility

The intense white anxieties about Black mobility that emerged in the 1830s and 1840s had their origins in a longer history of race and mobility that constructed Black movement as a threat to white supremacy. Crucially, the antebellum years did not produce a break with this prior history but an escalation in scale. Anxieties, conflicts, and discourse stemming from the nexus of race and mobility during this period represented an intensification of ideological and material struggles rather than a sharp rupture with the past.

Historian Steven Hahn's framework of "long emancipation," developed in his work on slavery, helps elucidate this point. Indeed, given the importance of slavery to the historical intersection of Blackness and mobility, Hahn's framework proves doubly useful. Rethinking traditional conceptual and chronological bounds of slave emancipation in the United States, Hahn asserts that emancipation should not be imagined as two discrete phases centered on the Revolutionary War and the Civil War but instead as a continuous, protracted process. Emancipation in Northern states following the Revolution was highly gradual and uneven, with many Black Americans remaining enslaved well into the nineteenth century. Those who did achieve freedom faced deep exclusion and repression. Hahn further notes that slavery exerted a tenacious grip on the country as a whole. Not only did it continue to exist in varying degrees throughout much of the United States during the antebellum period, but also many white Americans in the North and West supported Southern slavery. Emancipation in the Civil War was not, therefore, a discrete event but one connected to, and informed by, earlier emancipation struggles and processes that involved people, groups, and institutions throughout the nation.[4]

Ideas about Blackness and mobility and conflicts over Black mobility on the ground that intensified in the antebellum era similarly grew out of a protracted and national process, one integrally involving the history of slavery and emancipation. Stretching back to the colonial period, white fears about unrestrained Black mobility developed in reciprocal relation to the spatial arrangements necessary to uphold slavery. At its core, slavery relied on a "geography of containment" designed to constrain and control enslaved people's movement and thus yoke Black immobility to white profits. Historian Stephanie Camp's seminal work on the spatial relations of slavery and Black resistance shows the importance of white spatial control to the peculiar institution. Camp illustrates how slavery's geography of containment consisted of a set of spatial practices through which Southern slave owners rigidly restricted their slaves' mobility, including slave patrols, curfews, and laws requiring passes and banning meetings. In her analysis, Camp effectively demonstrates the link between spatial control and social control.[5]

However, slavery's demand for controlled slave mobility did not mean that slaveholders always imprisoned bondspeople on plantations. As historian Susan O'Donovan has noted, slave owners knew that confining their slaves to specific plantations as if they were prisons would hamper profits. Generating profits in the plantation economy required a mobile workforce to circulate both labor and goods. Historian Ryan A. Quintana corroborates this point in his detailed examination of slave mobility in colonial and early national South Carolina, demonstrating that slaveholders regularly put their slaves in motion to create profits and facilitate the expanding plantation economy. Enslaved people were crucial to transporting commodities and supplies, and they were often transferred and set to work on slaveholders' separate properties. White planters coerced and tracked their slaves' mobility in these instances using methods such as the slave pass system, slave patrols, and the state militia. Thus, many of the same practices that helped keep slaves incarcerated on the plantation also facilitated limited, strictly controlled slave movement.[6]

But while slavery did not completely deny enslaved mobility, it did deeply curtail, control, and surveil it. The (im)mobility Black slaves experienced under slavery was founded on coercion and designed to stamp out enslaved peoples' sovereignty over their own bodily movements. Despite the necessity of slave movement and slave owners' efforts to rigorously control it, whites still found enslaved mobility profoundly threatening. In part, this unease stemmed from the fact that Black slaves regularly resisted white domination and seized opportunities to freely exercise their mobility. Black slaves subverted efforts to dictate their movements by running away to safe havens in nearby swamps or woods, defying curfews and traveling to neighboring plantations to visit family and friends, and holding religious celebrations and community parties in the forest at night. Likewise, slaves with mobility were crucial to coordinating slave resistance and disseminating news about broader antislavery political developments, passing information on through covert communication networks that connected slave communities.[7]

This Black resistance provoked slaveholders to further clamp down on their slaves' movement and slaves to adapt their resistance in turn, sparking a dialectical struggle at the heart of slavery.[8] Such struggles over Black movement underlay white Americans' growing condemnation of Black mobility as a sign of social and racial disorder in the antebellum era. Quintana observes that despite their dependence on Black mobility, white Carolinians in the early national period increasingly viewed enslaved movement as indicative of criminal and insurrectionary motives.[9] Thus, while slavery demanded the circulation of Black bodies, it increasingly produced white desires for Black stasis and containment.

Slavery's tendency to produce white distrust of Black movement did not pertain solely to the South but informed Northern race relations as well. Slavery in the North had similarly regulated enslaved mobility and continued to influence white Americans in the Northern states after emancipation. Indeed, attempts by Northern white people to contain Black social and economic mobility in this period were conjoined to desires and attempts to contain Black spatial mobility. For example, even after instituting gradual emancipation in 1784, Connecticut required free African Americans to carry a pass testifying to their status and place of residency.[10] In her study of Black travelers in the antebellum North, historian Elizabeth Stordeur Pryor shows that white people repeatedly tried to control Black travel in a process she deems the "criminalization of black mobility."[11] Through a combination of private business policies, social codes, and physical violence, Northern whites increasingly subjected Black travelers to surveillance, segregation, and bodily harm. Meanwhile, Northern Black people recognized that access to modes of transportation and everyday mobility itself were vital aspects of American citizenship, and they consistently resisted limitations on their travel.[12] However, despite—and because of—Black resistance, Northern whites continued to see Black travel as a threat during the antebellum decades, both as a symbol of equality between the races and for its perceived connection to criminality and disorder.[13]

Conjoined to this very much national white trepidation over Black mobility was the colonization movement. Fundamentally rooted in the idea that free Black and white people could not live together in harmony, colonization was segregation on a continental scale. Thomas Jefferson was one of the first to advocate for colonization, which he saw as the most viable way to emancipate the slaves without compromising free white society, and in the early nineteenth century, it was the most popular form of white antislavery thought. With the founding of the American Colonization Society in 1816, colonization quickly became a mainstream and respectable policy among white Americans interested in ridding the United States of slavery or simply of free African Americans. It would continue to carry weight well into the antebellum years. Ultimately, colonization's appeal for white Americans emanated from their aversion to the idea of living with Black Americans outside the contained relations of slavery.[14]

Slavery and colonization would be the dominant frameworks informing Black-white relations during the antebellum era. For white Americans, colonization was one solution to the problem of how to control and police Black people outside the regime of slavery. Fundamentally, it expressed the interrelated white desires of establishing racial homogeneity and circumscribing Black mobility on a continental level. Colonization thus shared with slavery a deep focus on controlling Black mobility, though on a much larger scale than slavery's geography of containment.[15]

"I's Jist from Tuckyhoe": Race and Mobility in Early Minstrel Sheet Music

The dawning of the 1830s saw the emergence of one of the country's first culture industries: blackface minstrelsy. In part a cultural response to increased Black political agitation in the North, including Black abolitionism, blackface minstrelsy attempted to discursively contain this threat to the racial hierarchy through assertions of Black inferiority. Significantly, as part of its white supremacist lexicon, minstrelsy expressed white anxieties about Black mobility. Representations of Black movement were thus baked into US popular culture from the very beginning.[16]

Drawing on earlier strands of anti-Black racial imitation that circulated in British and American theater and print culture, blackface minstrelsy emerged on the American stage in the late 1820s and early 1830s.[17] Sonically, it was upbeat dance music that reworked traditional British folk dances such as reels and jigs.[18] In its early years, it reflected a working-class orientation and often contained raucous and raunchy themes deemed unsuitable for more respectable audiences. While minstrelsy nonetheless proved incredibly popular, and some songs became well known among all classes of Americans, its working-class inflection played a significant role in shaping its representations of Blackness and mobility. Always polyvalent, minstrelsy contained numerous social meanings, but Black inferiority was its foundation. Responding to rising Victorian and industrial norms that emphasized strict bodily comportment, economic frugality, self-discipline, and the repression of sexual desires, minstrelsy used Blackness as a cloak to license the enactment of increasingly prohibited behaviors and sensual pleasures. It also occasionally lampooned social elites and celebrated a working-class and frontier culture of rowdy, masculine fraternization and defiance. Minstrelsy performed these various social functions all while reaffirming Black inferiority and immutable racial difference.[19] Crucially, as a veiled outlet for white misbehavior, minstrelsy marshaled ideas about Blackness, mobility, and disorder in a way that conflated Black movement with criminality and social mayhem.

The breakthrough minstrel hit "Jim Crow," by blackface performer Thomas Dartmouth "T. D." Rice, epitomizes early minstrelsy's coupling of Black mobility with disorder.[20] Massively popular, "Jim Crow" became a social phenomenon that helped make minstrelsy the most popular form of entertainment in the antebellum era. Published circa 1832, the sheet music of "Jim Crow" features a litany of disorders, with the mobility of the Black narrator, Jim Crow, at their center. The entire song revolves around Jim Crow's journey across the country, as he leaps from city to city and from state to state. Whether Jim Crow is an escaped slave or a free person is unclear, but regardless of his status, he joyously partakes in unrestrained movement. Announcing in the first line that "I's jist from Tuckyhoe," Jim Crow tells of his travels that take him from Virginia to New Orleans, and then on to New York City. Once in New York, he visits Broadway before heading across the river to Hoboken. Showcasing his geographical dexterity, Jim Crow also mentions Philadelphia, Weehawken, and Brooklyn Heights before finally wrapping up his marathon, forty-four-verse narrative. Throughout his travels he repeatedly instigates fights, threatens violence against white people, and unabashedly chases women.[21]

Physically unrestrained, Jim Crow's incorrigible violence erupts again and again. Upon arriving in New Orleans, he "feel[s] so full of fight" that he is thrown in prison, only to immediately "hit a man" upon his release the next day. He also proudly states, "I struck a Jarsey niggar, / In de street de oder day," apparently for no reason at all. Then, in a scene laden with class valences, he relates a fight with a "Philadelphia niggar / Dress'd up quite nice and clean" who "[a]bused de Yorkers." Simultaneously expressing local pride, white working-class animosity to upper-class pretensions, and white hostility to the Black middle class, Jim Crow's violence against the "Philadelphia niggar" captures class and racial anger, all while deepening the ideological link between Black mobility and disorder. A similar dynamic occurs in the song's final stanza, which states, "An I caution all white dandies, / Not to come in my way, / For if dey insult me, / Dey'll in de gutter lay." As cover for white working-class resentments toward upper-class "dandies," Jim Crow's Blackness enables the expression of this unruly class desire but also explicitly conjures up the specter of Black-on-white violence. White people—granted, white "dandies"—face danger when impeding Jim Crow's "way." Thus, the song not only associates violent disorder with Black travel but also signals that autonomous Black movement can pose a direct threat to whites.

In addition to physical violence, "Jim Crow" casts Black mobility as producing sexual disorder. Moving effortlessly about the country, Jim Crow constantly pursues women. After going "down to de riber," he sees "so many galls [*sic*]" that he cannot leave. In Hoboken, he has "a promenade" and sees all "de pretty gals," and upon arriving in New York City he observes all the "Broadway bell[e]s" and begins to hunt for a wife with whom he, too, can stroll down Broadway. In all these scenarios, the lyrics connect Jim Crow's movement to access to women; in other words, going down to the river, promenading in Hoboken, and strolling down Broadway facilitate Black sexual desire. The song never overtly suggests interracial sex or sexual attraction, but neither does it specify that Jim Crow is interested only in Black women. Once again, the song's use of the Black body as a repository for white fantasies produces a haunting racial threat. In channeling the sexual anxieties and longings of white working-class men through the Black figure, "Jim Crow" simultaneously paints mobile Black masculinity as imperiling white male sexual prerogatives and flashes a warning about allowing the unchecked movement of Black men.

Crucially, much of the chaos in "Jim Crow" takes place in urban settings. Despite scholars' tendency to juxtapose the "plantation" Jim Crow with stereotypes of the "urban dandy" in their discussions of minstrelsy and its later variants, Jim Crow was intimately familiar with urban space from the beginning.[22] This original connection with the city is vital to mapping the development of ideas about Blackness and mobility in popular culture, as "Jim Crow" portrays Black mobility in urban space as particularly threatening. It is in New Orleans that Jim Crow's desire to fight gets him locked up in jail and where he hits a man upon his release, and it is in New York where he threatens white dandies and fights a Black man from New Jersey in the street. But while "Jim Crow" particularly inveighs against Black urbanity, it also features rural settings. Indeed, part of the song's disorder stems from Jim Crow's ability to move freely between rural and city spaces. Perambulating the country, Jim Crow's havoc knows no bounds. While not as great as his disruptions in urban spaces, Jim Crow's exploits in rural environments also portray him as an uncontrolled figure. He boasts, "I wip my weight in wildcats / I eat an Alligater, / And tear up more groud / Dan kifer 50 load of tater." He also "sit[s] upon a Hornet's nest" and ties a viper around his neck, immune to pain and unafraid of danger.

However, alongside these invocations of rural frontier braggadocio, the cover illustration to the sheet music of "Jim Crow" presents a more docile vision of the narrator, content in plantation slavery (see figure 1.1). Taking up nearly the full cover page, a large detailed drawing of Jim Crow shows him dancing with carefree joy, his head tilted upward to the sky, a huge smile on

FIGURE 1.1 Cover illustration to T. D. Rice, "Jim Crow" (New York: Firth and Hall, n.d., ca. 1832). Courtesy of the Lester S. Levy Sheet Music Collection, Johns Hopkins University.

his face, and limbs flailing ecstatically. His high spirits are undampened by his impoverished condition, which his tattered clothes and toeless shoes plainly indicate. The lower half of the image sketches out the plantation setting, evidenced by a row of slave cabins in the distance. The rendering of the landscape is sparse and unromanticized—the illustration focuses instead on Jim Crow's caricatured body, which ridicules Black humanity through its grotesque bodily exaggerations. But the image does feature one of the core components of what historians call the Southern pastoral (that is, the romanticism of the Southern landscape and rural Southern society): the idea of the contented slave. Unperturbed by the oppressions of slavery and its material degradations, Jim Crow is happy and carefree, cheerfully dancing the day away. This theme of the contented slave, while minor in early minstrel music, would become prevalent in sheet music romanticizing the South beginning in the late 1840s, as discussed in chapter 2. It is noteworthy, then, that the sheet music of "Jim Crow" contains the seeds of two dichotomous themes:

the Southern pastoral and the trope of deviant urban Blackness. Later sheet music and other forms of popular culture would elaborate and emphasize these themes, drawing inspiration from the racial typologies of the docile African American in bondage and the dangerous African American in freedom that were the ideological accretions of slavery.[23]

In many ways, the freewheeling geography of "Jim Crow," with its expansive coverage of both rural and urban settings, is not surprising given the spatial contexts from which T. D. Rice fashioned the song. Rice created and honed his famous act while traveling through the theaters of the frontier West, after which he headed to New York City in 1832 for a run of unprecedented success at the Bowery Theatre. The urban and rural content of "Jim Crow" reflects this cross-regional movement and the frontier and urban working-class makeup of Rice's audience. Imbued with the transregional Jacksonian ethos that aligned frontier and urban working-class whites against the "aristocracy" of the rich, the character Jim Crow not only resents the "white dandies" of Broadway but also channels frontier hero and politician Davy Crockett when he brags, "I wip my weight in wildcats, I eat an Alligater."[24]

The imagined disorderly Black mobility of "Jim Crow" thus emerged in part from Rice's relatively uninhibited movement through the expanding western and northeastern theater circuits, a movement Rice's whiteness and the growing leisure industry under industrial capitalism enabled. Touring through the West and then returning to his home of New York City, Rice circulated a song that warned that Black mobility was dangerous and that encouraged its curtailment, all while helping facilitate his own physical and economic mobility. The publication of "Jim Crow" as sheet music only magnified this spatial dynamic by further circulating the song's depiction of disorderly Black movement. And with its astounding success, the song demonstrated yet another way that race and anti-Blackness could produce white profits under capitalism.[25]

While Rice's mobility and the mobility of sheet music as a commodity made "Jim Crow" and its popularity possible, on a deeper historical level Black mobility played an equally important role in generating the song. Despite its claim of pure racial imitation, blackface minstrelsy was an extremely hybrid form, born out of the spatial proximity and social mixing of Black and white Americans, particularly members of the Black and white working classes. Appropriating and altering Black music and dance styles, white performers created minstrelsy not from observing Southern plantations but through contact with African Americans in the interracial markets, taverns, neighborhoods, and waterfronts of Eastern and Western cities. In the 1820s and 1830s, free Black communities grew in the North and West among white working-class neighborhoods and began to play a major role in mobilizing the abolitionist movement. This Black social progress and resistance to slavery catalyzed minstrelsy and its racism, which not only assuaged white fears about abolitionism but also relieved the racial anxieties of working-class whites worried about their physical and cultural proximity to Black people in the slums and commercial zones of burgeoning cities. Papering over its syncretic roots with claims of racial authenticity, blackface minstrelsy and its racist caricatures reassured the white working class that they were unquestionably superior to, and culturally distinct from, African Americans.[26]

Thus, the Black geographic mobility that produced these spatial and political conditions—whether that of escaped slaves fleeing to Northern Black communities, emancipated slaves in the North moving from the countryside to cities, or Black participation in the growing commercial circuits of capitalism—formed one of the structural bases for minstrelsy's development and articulation.[27] It was just such Black mobility that "Jim Crow" assailed.

Numerous other early minstrel songs also broadcast images of disorderly Black mobility, particularly Black male mobility. Indeed, the theme of the traveling Black male narrator, with various degrees of unruly and violent behavior, became common in the genre. Sheet music lyrics and cover art, such as those in "Sich a Gitting Upstairs" (ca. early 1830s), "Jim Brown" (1836), "Ginger Blue" (1841), "De Free Nigger" (1841), and "Old Dan Tucker" (1843) all linked Black mobility—especially urban mobility—to disorder, class inversion, interracial sex, and physical violence.[28]

But it was not only early minstrelsy that calumniated Black mobility in song. The song sheet for "Manners and Customs of Ann Street, or, A North End Frolic," published circa the early 1830s, reveals profound white anxieties about Black movement and presence in the city. As previously mentioned, song sheets simply printed lyrics with no musical notation, making them cheaper than sheet music, and publishers geared their content toward working-class consumers. As such, song sheets often contained more ribald and coarse material, and "Manners and Customs" is no exception. It strips away the Black veneer of minstrel songs and unabashedly indulges in white working-class riot, exposing the hypocrisy of minstrelsy's ascription of moral transgression to African Americans. Set in Boston, nearly the entire first half of the song recounts a white gang or mob chasing and attacking Black residents in the city streets with explicit detail. The initial stanzas set the tone:

> In the month of July of a Moon shiny night,
> We chanc'd with some negro's to have a hard fight,
> One negro he ran into C*****s [*sic*] old house,
> We leap'd through the door like a cat for a mouse.
> . . . .
> We search'd all around but could not him find,
> And if that we had we'd soon made him blind;
> We knock'd down the stairs and the bulkheads also,
> Stove the doors and the shutters likewise windows too,
> . . . .
> Then up in Ann Street for a negro did cruise,
> We found one and straight from his nose flew the juice;
> . . . .
> As I was walking down through Ann Street,
> A thundering negro I chanced for to meet;
> He strutted and travelled just like a Clown,
> You would have died laughing to see him knock'd down.

In this cornucopia of white violence, the lyrics ridicule Black mobility and mark it for physical punishment. The white narrator targets the "thundering" Black man who "strutted and travelled just like a Clown" precisely because he occupies and traverses urban space. This uncontained Black mobility implies racial equality and must be met with derision and the violent reassertion of white control. Physically knocking the Black man down and ending his threatening movement—both his physical movement and his symbolic crossing of racial boundaries to claim equality—thus produces white enjoyment and humor.[29]

Ironically, these lines unintentionally link white mobility with social disorder and destruction in the city. It is white men who "cruise" through the streets looking for African American victims, beating them up and threatening to make them "blind," all while destroying property as collateral damage. These escapades echo the many white mob attacks on African American communities that occurred across the North in the antebellum years, which themselves trenchantly illustrate the racial double standard around mobility and disorder in the period.[30] As "Manners and Customs" conveys, mobility was both symbolic of, and reserved for, whiteness.

However, not all songs venerated white mobility. The 1836 song "Billy Barlow," for example, points toward contemporary fears about poor white urban mobility, in particular over the figure of the vagabond. But these negative images of white mobility in popular song were relatively rare. "Billy Barlow" was one of the only songs that negatively portrayed white movement in the antebellum era. A tune in the rowdy minstrel vein, it deprecates poor white urban mobility, including by closely associating it with Blackness, but also refrains from the harsh condemnation reserved for Black mobility in minstrel songs. Rather than scenes of riotous disorder, it presents poor white mobility as generating more minor social disruptions. A version of the sheet music published in Philadelphia loosely connects Barlow—a vagabond character—with crime. He remarks, "They say there's been a robbery committed in town, / I dont [*sic*] know who could have done it but Canker the clown / I feel perfectly safe I'd have you to know / I should like to see a man try to rob Billy Barlow." Part of the joke is that Barlow owns no possessions, so of course he cannot be robbed. But the line also plays on the fact that Barlow himself is probably the thief in question, and so he is doubly unconcerned about the threat of robbery. This version also drives home Barlow's unrooted character, as he states, "I'm sure I was born, but where I cant [*sic*] tell, / My Mother never told me I know very well."[31] His transience is thus endemic; he is devoid of any fixity, past or present. As a self-deluded, lazy, and potentially criminal figure, his tale contains a sharp warning about poverty and urban mobility under its comic surface.

In addition to sly suggestions of criminality, the Philadelphia version associates poor white mobility with Blackness through its cover art (see figure 1.2). The figure of Billy Barlow takes up almost the entire page and is modeled on one of the most common sheet music cover images for "Jim Crow," the one in which Jim Crow strikes a dance pose (see figure 1.1). Indeed, as a result of the astounding success of "Jim Crow," the pose became synonymous with the Jim Crow character.[32] Barlow's stance is virtually the mirror image of this famous pose, and audiences would not have missed the visual allusion. At the same time, crucial differences between the two illustrations signal Barlow's racial distance from Jim Crow. Jim Crow is horrendously caricatured—he tilts his head back at an unnatural angle, wears a broad grin, and has an enormous rear end. His clothes are extremely tattered, with part of his left shoe missing and his toes poking out of the right, and he dances with his limbs splayed out from his body, one hand on his hip. Barlow, on the other hand, is hardly caricatured, if at all; he has a pleasant smile on his face and

FIGURE 1.2 Cover illustration to "Billy Barlow" (Philadelphia: J. G. Osbourn, 1836). Courtesy of the Lester S. Levy Sheet Music Collection, Johns Hopkins University.

looks directly at the viewer. His clothes are certainly patched and tattered, but not to the extent of Jim Crow's. And Barlow's bodily movements are far more staid; he merely gives a dainty lift of his right foot and places his left hand at his waist, well above his rear end. Finally, whereas Jim Crow raises his left arm in bodily abandon while dancing, Barlow's upraised right arm justifies itself by lifting his hat in a courteous greeting. The image of Barlow thus simultaneously proclaims his affinity with and distance from Blackness.[33]

So while "Billy Barlow" did, to a certain extent, question the racial status of poor mobile whites, it refrained from the level of condemnation that popular song reserved for African Americans and Black mobility. This tension in "Billy Barlow" reflects patterns in the treatment of the indigent under antebellum vagrancy laws. American officials and the public harshly criticized the white transient poor and punished them under vagrancy laws, but local authorities disproportionately arrested and convicted transient Black people.[34] Just as in "Billy Barlow," white itinerants benefited from their racial status, though their poverty and urban mobility remained highly suspect.

A more direct connection between racial practices and the content of popular song, as well as strong evidence that blackface minstrelsy's lessons about race and mobility were not lost on antebellum audiences, is white railroad conductors' application of the name "Jim Crow" to segregated railcars in Massachusetts. Soon after railroads began servicing Massachusetts in 1836, the railroad companies initiated a policy of segregating Black patrons to the "short car," a smaller railcar placed directly behind the engine. Exposed to the engine's smoke and fumes, the short car was dangerous and dirty, and it carried all those white passengers who could not afford a first-class ticket, as well as all the passengers' luggage. The relegation of African Americans to this cramped car—whether they could afford a first-class ticket or not—sent a clear racial message.

By 1838, white railroad workers had begun referring to this segregated car as the Jim Crow car, marking the first time "Jim Crow" was used as a name for racial segregation. That white Americans in Massachusetts first coined the name that would become indelibly linked with the Southern system of racial segregation implemented later in the century is a reminder that the history of segregation is a national one, and that a longer historical framework is integral to grasping the trajectory of race, mobility, and segregation over the nineteenth century. Not only did a Northern white man create the song "Jim Crow" and perform it for Northern white audiences, but Northern whites also applied that cultural representation to the practice of segregation. More broadly, the use of the term "Jim Crow" as a designation for segregation speaks to the importance of popular culture to the history of segregation. The enmeshment of blackface minstrelsy with segregationist practices on trains exposes the conduits between the ideological substance of sheet music and the material technologies and arrangements of Black containment. Just as in the lyrics for "Manners and Customs," white railroad conductors often used physical violence and verbal abuse to enforce segregation on trains. The danger that Black mobility posed to white supremacy, so ritualistically identified and enacted in early minstrel songs, was thus met with physical confinement to segregated railcars and white violence. While segregation on Massachusetts trains was brief, it ended only due to the strenuous resistance of Black and white abolitionists, who used lawsuits and public opinion campaigns to force railroad companies to abandon the policy in 1843.[35]

As white Americans were imbibing the lessons surrounding Black mobility in early minstrelsy, popular songs featuring Native Americans imparted a similar message to US audiences about the negative qualities of Native movement. Arising from the demands of settler colonialism for land expropriation, this negative construction of Native movement perpetuated a long-standing racial myth that Indians were nomadic hunters devoid of agriculture. Non–Indian Americans in the antebellum period mobilized this myth to justify the policy of Indian removal, which became the dominant means of securing Native land in these years. The next section briefly recounts the historical roots of the nomadic Indian myth and the rise of the removal policy, followed by a dive into Native American imagery in popular music.

Enlightenment Thought, Indian Mobility, and US Policy

By the nineteenth century, the stereotype of the roaming, hunting Indian had a long history. As early as 1625, the English writer Samuel Purchas, writing after the Powhatan peoples' attack on Jamestown in 1622, characterized the Indians as "more brutish than the beasts they hunt, more wild and unmanly than that unmanned wild countrey, which they range rather than inhabite."[36] Purchas's description reflected an emerging motif in European Enlightenment thought that categorized Indians as nomadic societies devoted to hunting. Aimed at justifying white colonists' expropriation of Indian lands, the idea that all Indian societies were nomadic and without sustained agriculture was deeply inaccurate. From the beginnings of European contact, Indians had extensive agriculture and fixed settlement. Even the Indian hunting practices that Europeans so quickly took to indicate a lack of agriculture and a nomadic lifestyle were in fact often rooted in the intensive management of forest lands to encourage game. But because the idea that Indians were wandering hunters served as a justification for European dispossession and settlement of Indian lands, the myth flourished and often overrode Europeans' direct exposure to conflicting evidence in their interactions with Native peoples.[37]

English philosopher John Locke expounded one of the earliest sustained articulations of this myth and its implication for land rights. In book 2 of his *Two Treatises of Government*, first published in 1689, Locke laid out his theory of how individuals acquire property. According to Locke, while God left the world and its resources to humans in common, an individual's labor belonged solely to them, and when they mixed their labor with the land through cultivation it became the individual's property.[38] This tenet held true provided that when the land was removed from the commons there remained enough left over for others.[39] Significantly, this caveat led Locke to state that the common lands in England could not be enclosed through individual labor, as there was not enough common land to allow conversion to private property without harming others. But in North America, the situation was different.

The presence of "inland, vacant places" meant that individual cultivation of the land would convert it to private property, as there would still be plenty left over for others.[40] With the stroke of a pen, Locke erased the widespread presence of Native Americans on the continent.

In fact, the "wild Indian, who knows no enclosure, and is still a tenant in common," played a central role in Locke's treatise, serving as both the theoretical staging ground and concrete evidence for his argument about the state of nature and property acquisition.[41] For Locke, America under Indian habitation was nothing but "wild woods and uncultivated waste," and since the Indians had failed to cultivate the land, they therefore did not possess a property right in it.[42] Furthermore, Locke insisted, Indians' lack of cultivation was detrimental to humankind because the cultivation of land increased its productivity and so added to society. And despite nature furnishing Native peoples "as liberally as any other people, with the material of plenty," they did not practice agriculture and so failed to build advance societies like that of England.[43] Seizure of Indian land was thus doubly justified—not only did Indians have no property rights to the land, but Europeans' cultivation was for the betterment of humankind.

Locke's work thus helped foster and amplify the myth that Indians did not practice agriculture and were therefore using the land wrong. Knowing "no enclosure," Indians merely ranged over the land as hunters rather than settling on it. Locke's writings were enormously influential with white American colonists, and by the Revolutionary War, his celebration of agriculture as the superior basis for society and the exclusion of Indians from that vision was accepted wisdom.[44] Nonetheless, such neat theoretical claims that Indians lacked ownership of the land did not transfer cleanly to practices on the ground. Colonists often recognized Indians' ownership rights, at least to a certain extent, in various transactions in which they purchased Native peoples' lands. However, they also often secured land through fraudulent purchases, outright force, or threat of force.[45]

Native nations resisted these settler-colonial encroachments through a variety of tactics.[46] One common strategy was traveling to Eastern Seaboard cities on diplomatic visits, especially to New York City and Philadelphia during each city's stint as capital during the early republic. Indians thus engaged in mobility, but in ways that directly contradicted the stereotype of the unsophisticated wandering hunter.[47] Indeed, they traveled to resist the territorial dispossession that such stereotypes helped authorize and abet.

When George Washington assumed the US presidency in 1789, he and his secretary of war, Henry Knox, instituted a "civilizing" policy to govern US relations with Native tribes. This policy favored purchasing Native lands rather than using the more expensive force of arms to secure Indian territory, as many exterminationists endorsed. It also advocated the slow spread of the white population around and among Native peoples after purchase, the idea being that Native Americans would gradually assimilate into US society where they were.[48] This policy would remain dominant well into the early nineteenth century, even as it failed to play out on the ground. Indian nations continued to resist assimilation and fought tenaciously—through warfare and diplomacy—to hold on to their territories. But at the beginning of the nineteenth century, federal officials began to shift their thinking to arrive at a different spatial solution to expropriating Indian lands. Increasingly, they saw spatial separation as the best way to facilitate US expansion. This new line of thought would culminate in the policy of removal.

Removal is most associated with Andrew Jackson and events of the 1830s, but the progenitor of the removal policy was Thomas Jefferson. During his presidency, Jefferson publicly supported and continued the civilization policy. However, the Louisiana Purchase of 1803 proved a turning point in his private thinking. It not only enlivened his vision of a vast "empire of liberty" for yeoman farmers but also presented a more immediate solution to the Indian resistance hampering white settlement east of the Mississippi River. With the massive new addition of territory, it was now feasible to relocate Indigenous nations onto lands across the Mississippi in exchange for their homelands on the eastern side. It was also increasingly apparent that the civilizing policy was not producing the desired results—recalcitrant Indian nations were clinging to their traditional ways and their territories. Removal thus offered an alternative path. While Jefferson continued to publicly advocate for Indian nations to adopt agriculture and amalgamate with the white population where they were, in private he increasingly pushed for removal. The idea continued to spread in policy circles, and by John Quincy Adams's presidency in the mid-1820s, voluntary removal was seen as the best and most benevolent option for resolving the seemingly perpetual conflicts between white Americans and Indians.[49] Thus, continuing white greed for Native lands and the steadfast military and cultural resistance of Native Americans impelled US policymakers to adapt their views on Indian-white relations and embrace removal.

A constant that bridged this shift was the racialization of Indians as inherently mobile hunters. White Americans continued to marshal the racial trope as a justification for US expansion, and it would remain fundamental to white conceptions of Indianness throughout the early decades of the nineteenth century. For example, in 1802, John Quincy Adams used the stereotype to bluntly justify expansion in a speech given at Plymouth, Massachusetts, commemorating the landing of the pilgrims. He rhetorically asked, "What is the right of a huntsman to the forest of a thousand miles over which he has accidentally ranged in quest of prey? . . . Shall the fields and vallies [*sic*], which a beneficent God has formed to teem with the life of innumerable multitudes, be condemned to everlasting barrenness?" The stereotype of the innately mobile Indian also deeply structured and influenced the landmark Supreme Court decision in *Johnson v. M'Intosh* (1823), which offered an extended meditation on Indian land rights. In his decision, Chief Justice John Marshall retroactively justified settler colonialism by construing Indians as hunters, declaring, "The tribes of Indians inhabiting this country were fierce savages, whose occupation was war, and whose subsistence was drawn chiefly from the forest. To leave them in possession of their country, was to leave the country a wilderness."[50]

Adams's and Marshall's racial distortions were only two prominent examples of what was a widespread view among white Americans that Native peoples were roaming hunters.[51] As removal emerged as the dominant federal policy in the late 1820s and early 1830s, the link between Indianness and mobility continued to license the expropriation of Native lands. Indeed, the administration of Andrew Jackson repeatedly and specifically used the notion of the transient Indian to justify removal. An escalating conflict in Georgia throughout the 1820s between white settlers and the southeastern Indian tribes, especially the Creek and the Cherokee, had brought removal to the fore of national politics. Stiff Creek and Cherokee resistance to Georgia's attempt to open Indian lands for white farmers and the expansion of plantation slavery led white Georgians to call for removal with increasing shrillness.[52] These calls met with a friendly ear in Jackson, who made plain his desire to forcibly expel the southeastern tribes to the other side of the Mississippi. After assuming the presidency in 1829, Jackson requested that Congress pass a removal bill. Despite strong political resistance, mostly from Native Americans and northeastern politicians and their constituents, Congress passed the Indian Removal Act in 1830.[53]

Jackson, like other proponents, wrapped his commitment to removal in a cloak of insincere humanitarianism. He claimed that the only way to prevent the extinction of the Indian tribes was to relocate them to the far west, where they would be safe from the corrupting influence of "bad" whites and free to practice their traditional ways undisturbed. At the heart of his rhetoric was the stereotype of the innately mobile Indian. In messages to the Creeks,

Jackson condemned them—inaccurately—for failing to abandon hunting and adopt agriculture, and portrayed resettlement as the only option for maintaining their traditional way of life.[54]

The Jackson administration's endorsement and eventual implementation of removal incited a significant backlash from white reformers, mostly in the Northern states. Indeed, the controversy over removal was perhaps the most prominent political issue of the late 1820s and 1830s.[55] This large resistance from white reformers occurred alongside strenuous Indian resistance and was in part the product of Indian leaders' exertions to drum up support among white Americans for their position.[56]

However, it is vital to note some caveats to white reformers' support for Indian land rights and their resistance to removal. First, many reformers took issue with the Jackson administration's removal efforts because the administration targeted the Cherokee Nation, which more than any other Indian tribe had demonstrated success in adopting "civilized" ways. The Cherokee had a written constitution, had embraced agricultural practices that comported with white notions, and had created their own written alphabet. For many white reformers, removal of the Cherokees was an egregious betrayal of US government promises that Cherokee land rights would be respected if they assimilated. But some of these reformers, while they criticized the removal of the Cherokees, in fact supported the policy of removal in general. They saw removal as the most expedient and benign way to save "non-civilized" Indians from annihilation, as it would encourage their eventual conversion to civilization away from the negative influence of "bad" frontier whites. Of course, plenty of white reformers did condemn removal in general, calling it both illegal and immoral. These reformers demanded that the United States and white Americans work with Indians where they were to convert them to Christianity and civilization. But this leads to the second caveat: White reformers protesting removal held the firm assumption that Native Americans had to adopt the "civilized" ways of US society. Support for Indigenous land rights did not translate into a support for Indigenous cultures and economies. Thus, while many reformers rejected the policy of removal outright, they nonetheless shared with supporters of that policy certain baseline racial assumptions about Native Americans.[57] White reformers' condemnation of removal thus had significant limits, limits that would shape the content of popular songs about Native Americans.

Despite the resistance to removal, it emerged as the dominant US policy for managing relations with the Indians in the 1830s and 1840s, completing the shift in spatial paradigms from the civilizing policy's white-Indian proximity model to removal's complete separation.[58] Ensconced beyond the Mississippi, expelled Indians would now be segregated from whites on a continental scale.[59] Crucially, ideas about race and mobility that cast Indians as inherently mobile were key to facilitating removal and the acquisition of Native lands.

Mobility, Racial Romanticism, and Ambivalence in Popular Songs About Indians

Just like early blackface minstrelsy, antebellum sheet music and song sheets about Native Americans prominently featured images of geographic movement. But whereas early minstrelsy focused on Black movement in urban areas and conflated it with unnatural disorder, violence, and the threat of interracial sex, songs featuring Native Americans equated Native movement with wild nature, painting Native peoples as undeveloped, untamed, and constantly mobile. At base, these representational differences stemmed from the differing historical and ideological contexts of slavery and settler colonialism. Since images of Black mobility emerged from and perpetuated slavery's function of seizing Black labor, they depicted African Americans within the bounds of US society. In contrast, settler colonialism's goal of land seizure and long-standing Enlightenment ideals about civilization and property rights focused imagery of Native peoples on the "wilderness" where white people imagined they lived. According to such songs, to be Indian was to be constantly desiring movement and roaming through the wilderness rather than settling down in a fixed place. This racial fabrication would be a steady theme in sheet music and song sheets between 1830 and 1855.

Popular song also consistently painted Indians, especially eastern Indians, as confined to the past—their customs, ways of life, and peoples lost to the sweeping tide of "civilization." In the antebellum years, this theme of the "vanishing Indian" reached the height of its popularity, becoming a regular occurrence not only in popular songs but also in other white cultural productions, like James Fenimore Cooper's novel *The Last of the Mohicans* (1826) and the hit play *Metamora* (1829).[60] While representations of Indians were not common in popular song prior to the antebellum era, beginning in the 1830s and continuing through the mid-1850s the vanishing Indian became prime fodder for the surging twin cultural movements of romanticism and sentimentalism. Both the romantic movement, which proliferated in literary circles of the period, and sentimentalism, which grew following the second Great Awakening and the rise of the cult of domesticity, encouraged a focus on emotions as a means to unlocking spiritual truths, and popular song conscripted images of Native Americans to meet audience desires for emotionally provocative content.[61]

As music scholar Jon Finson points out, the disappearing Indian motif made an excellent vehicle for the expression of romantic themes about tragically fated lovers and nostalgic loss. Indians came to stand in for "idealized love" as figures of "legendary beauty and fidelity." Heavily sentimentalized, Indians in sheet music and song sheets also epitomized the "noble savage" stereotype more broadly—they were uncivilized but morally pure and closer to nature. Depictions of wild nature and the Indians associated with it also appealed to Americans undergoing increased industrialization and urbanization during the period. Furthermore, as historian Robert Berkhofer observes, white conceptions of Indians as closer to the natural world meshed with the romantic movement's emphasis on sublime nature, and the cessation of large-scale military violence between whites and Indians in the eastern United States made it easier for white audiences in that region to romanticize Native Americans.[62]

In general, popular songs about Indians were written by an array of white, predominantly middle-class professional and amateur songwriters. Although mostly men, there were many women songwriters as well. Despite their often-sympathetic portrayal of Indians, they did not belong to a definable political movement or group, although some prominent reformers—such as Eliza Cook and Henry Clay Work—did author several songs. The lyrics of songs about Indians tended to feature ornate language in keeping with their romantic trappings, and the music for the most part ranged from light and melodic in tone to meditative and sad. Other than a number of instrumental songs invoking Indians in the title, they were almost never dance music.

Unlike other popular culture forms, such as plays and dime novels, antebellum popular songs predominantly featured romantic and sympathetic portrayals of Native Americans as opposed to more derogatory stereotypes and images of physical violence.[63] Popular music's focus on romantic images of Indians was due in large part to sheet music's primarily middle-class audience: descriptions of physical violence did not comport with the propriety and respectability to which sheet music aspired.

In addition, white reformers of the 1830s and 1840s opposed to removal were predominantly middle class, and their antiremoval sentiment undoubtedly helped spur the production of romantic imagery. However, it is important to note some limits to the causal link between rising removal protests and the romantic content of songs about Indians. As previously discussed, reformers often protested removal because they viewed the Cherokees and other southeastern tribes as having adopted "civilized" ways. As far as many reformers were concerned, the Cherokees threatened with removal under the Jackson administration bore little resemblance to the Indians running through the pages of sheet music. Additionally, as scholars have noted, while romantic songs about Indians often referenced past injustices, their persistent construction of Indians as naturally primitive, incapable of social change, and inevitably vanishing aligned with the language of removal.[64] It is thus vital to flag that while romantic images of Native peoples may have shied away from depictions of physical violence, they perpetuated and inflicted deep discursive violence.[65]

Evidencing the general importance of middle-class propriety to images of Indians in sheet music, antebellum song sheets, which more often targeted working-class consumers, had a more even balance between romantic and overtly negative images of Indians. Romantic themes were still in the majority, but only slightly.[66] A song like "Bold Northwestman" (ca. 1830), freed from the constraints of middle-class decorum, could indulge in more lurid descriptions of violence. The song overtly appeals to extermination, recounting the voyage of the ship *Lady Washington* to the Northwest and an ensuing clash with "blood-thirsty" Indians, who are all killed in "such slaughter" by the white crew. Such depictions of ruthless violence were incompatible with middle-class respectability, especially perceptions of middle-class women's more delicate and refined sensibilities.[67]

However, violence did creep into sheet music as well, if in a more restrained manner. "The Soldier and His Bride" (1841) dramatizes an actual event of the Revolutionary War, the death of a white American colonist named Jane McCrea. Colonists blamed members of the Wyandot Nation, charged with escorting McCrea to her husband, an officer in the British army, for her death, even though it was far from clear that they were responsible.[68] The song likewise condemns the Native Americans for her death. In it, after the Indians quarrel over who will get the reward for escorting McCrea, one "struck his tomahawk into her forehead, tore off her scalp and gashed her breast." As a result of this betrayal, "The frown of the Great Spirit fell / Upon the red men like a spell!" and now "O'er land and lake they roam accurst." The song thus neatly explains Indian mobility as a product of their own evil deeds.[69]

Scattered images of violence in antebellum sheet music aside, the vast majority of popular songs in the era romanticized Native Americans. As a prominent component of this romanticism, sheet music and song sheets repeatedly presented Indigenous peoples as inherently mobile and equated that mobility with the wilderness.[70] Sheet music often analogized Indians to wild animals, uncontained and ranging over unbounded territory. Thus, as with African Americans in early minstrelsy, uncontrolled mobility was a negative trait in Native Americans, signaling their wild primitivism and savage nature, even if it was often glazed in a sugary coat of romanticism.

Crucially, however, strong critiques of white treatment of Indigenous nations and the seizure of their land often accompanied romanticism of Indians and Indian mobility. "The Indian Hunter," written by the well-known British reformer Eliza Cook and published circa 1837, demonstrates how prominent these critiques could be. The lyrics are an indictment of white greed and the persecution of Native Americans, who are cast in the long-standing "noble savage" stereotype. "Oh why," one stanza begins, "does the white man follow my path, / Like the hound on the tiger's track, / Does the flush on my dark cheek waken his wrath[?]" The song chastises whites for possessing "riches" yet still coveting the land of "the sons of the wood." "Why," the song plaintively asks, "should he wrong the hunter one, / Who never did harm to him?" While the lyrics do refer to the Indian narrator as a hunter, reifying the myth of the nomadic Indian who lacks agriculture, the title of the song and the first stanza also reverse dominant constructions of white Americans by casting them first and foremost as hunters. Specifically, it is the white man who is "the Indian hunter," pursuing Native Americans out of greed and invading Indian territory despite already possessing an abundance of riches. Indians are the innocent victim of white "wrong[s]," and the song suggests racism motivates white actions.[71]

Despite the fairly transgressive characterization of white people as hunters, the remaining lyrics reproduce the dichotomy between hunting Indians and white agriculturalists:

> The Father above thought fit to give,
> The white man corn and wine;
> There are golden fields where they may live,
> But the Forest shades are mine.
>
> . . . .
>
> Then go back from the red mans [*sic*] track,
> For the hunters [*sic*] eyes grow dim.
> To find that the white man wrongs the one
> Who never did harm to him.

God has granted white society "corn and wine" and "golden fields," the fruits of settled agriculture, while to Indians he has left the "Forest shades." There is no condemnation of hunting here, but the song is unmistakable in its characterization of Indians as hunters who live in the uncultivated forest. Invoking the vanishing Indian theme at the end of the song, the "hunters [*sic*] eyes grow dim" with death, as white society encroaches further down the "track" into Indian territory. Thus, while the song overtly and directly critiques white Europeans' treatment of Native Americans and the seizure of their lands, it also reinforces the notion that Indians were nomadic hunters, indirectly contributing to the very ideology that greased the wheels of removal.[72]

"The Indian Hunter's Bride" (ca. 1850s–1860s), a sequel to "The Indian Hunter," revises these themes to make a similar point. In the song, an Indian woman tells her husband to be careful hunting and "beware the white man's track, / His rifle and his chains." The song not only repeats the original's depiction of white people as malicious hunters but also explicitly indicts white society with the captivity and enslavement of Indians, especially Indian women: "They say he loves his pale-faced bride, / Great spirit! can it be? / And yet he'd track the red skin's path, / And steal thy love from thee!" It thus alludes to the sexual violence of female Indian enslavement and calls out the hypocrisy of white men's professed love for their "pale-faced bride[s]." But like the original, the sequel levels all these critiques alongside a construction of Indians as hunters. Despite the dangers, the wife tells her husband, "Yet go—thy joy is in the woods, / Where roved thy fathers free." Freedom to "rove" the woods thus stands in direct contrast to the threat of white captivity, and while this freedom of movement in the wilderness is sentimentalized, it is also presented as natural and endemic. The Indian hunter repeats the mobility of his fathers, receiving his primary pleasure and "joy" from hunting in the forest.[73]

A number of other songs condemned white Americans for holding Indians in captivity and stifling their natural disposition to roam. Whether these songs referred to past practices of captivity from earlier eras or contemporary examples of captivity, such as in missionary schools, is often unclear. For example, the 1854 song "The Indian Captive, or, The Absent Lover" leaves the reason for the narrator's captivity unstated but offers a strong indictment of white practices. The male Indian captive pleads with the "White man" to "take me back to my home in the West," where his mother, father, and lover all mourn his absence. The lyrics also make it clear that incarceration suffocates the Native captive's inherent desire for mobility:

White man take me back where the buffaloes roam
    O'er their own native prairies so boundless and free,
I will join in the chase with the warrior's brave,
    For that life is the life for me:

Oh! yes take me back to my own native home
  Where an Indian spirit's as free as the air,
To the prairies and forests we still call our own
  White man take me back, take me there.

The song denounces white Americans' separation of Native children from their homelands and parents, and treats Native familial relations with sympathy and respect. But it also employs the stereotype of the wandering Indian to convey its criticism. The Indian captive wants to return to his home to partake in "the chase," where he will join the buffalo in "roam[ing]" over the "native prairies so boundless and free." According to the song, Native Americans in their homeland embody perpetual movement, as their "spirit" is "as free as the air." Thus, captivity's denial of this roaming lifestyle is its major moral evil alongside separation from loved ones.[74]

Whereas many songs used the notion of the morally pure Indian as a foil to critique white society, some songs presented more sophisticated and deeper criticisms, going so far as to justify and explain Indian violence against whites. "The Pequot Brave" (1844), set during the Pequot War of 1636–38, opens with an Indian woman encouraging her male lover as he readies for battle with "the pale face." She exhorts, "Let the ambush burst upon their ranks," and tells him, "the scalps thou bringest by thy side, / Shall claim for thee thy Pequot bride." What audiences at first could read as a rehash of simplistic stereotypes of Indian barbarity are quickly contextualized: White colonists have killed the Pequot man's father, and his future bride urges that "for every drop of thy father's blood, / Let a white heart bleed in the silent wood." Not only are the Pequot Indians in the song motivated by a prior white attack, but the lyric's ornate and refined language cuts against stereotypes of savagery. The Indians certainly take an aggressively militant stance, but the song justifies this militancy by depicting the Pequots as battling for their very existence. The woman exhorts, "Arm, for the hour is come," and explains that "our race from the wood may fade" unless the Pequots "sweep the strangers from the land." The verse thus subverts dominant tropes by resituating Indian violence as a fight against extinction at the hands of white settlers, casting it as justified and honorable.[75]

However, there are also sharp limits to the song's subversive potential. The Pequot War was a conflict safely ensconced in the past, making it easier to romanticize the Pequots' resistance. Further, the song implies that defeat will mean the end of the Pequots, playing on the trope of the vanishing Indian to suggest that the Pequots are gone—which was not, and still is not, the case.

Nevertheless, the song's sympathetic portrayal of Indian resistance, including violent resistance, to white land encroachment would have resonated with contemporary battles over removal.[76]

While popular songs contained some strong critiques of white society, it is important to note that some songs romanticizing Indians did heavily align with removal. "The Indian Warrior's Grave" (1850), for example, employed an extravagant version of the disappearing Indian theme to condone removal. "In the depths of the wildwood" where once he "rov'd," an Indian "brave" now lies buried after he "nobly" died "defending" his "wigwam." The song mentions that "the pale foe" and he "struggled together," but beyond this offers no discussion of the conflict. Instead, it merely concludes that "ere a moon" after the warrior's burial, "his tribe westward had hurried," leaving only a "rude cross" that "tells, 'the red warrior slumbers.'" Although the song describes the Indian warrior's resistance as noble, it offers no critique of white violence and evacuates all historical context around the dispossession of Indian lands. Removal becomes a voluntary action after defeat in war and a fait accompli; just like the Indian warrior who "slumbers" in his grave, removal is buried and put to rest as an issue. The Indians that once "rov'd" in their territory have moved westward to continue their nomadic ways. Songs such as this, however, were exceptions. More commonly, popular songs featuring Indians from 1830 through the mid-1850s offered strong, if in many ways limited, critiques of white society and its violations of Native land rights.[77]

One of the largest limitations to those critiques was popular song's persistent depiction of Indians as inherently mobile.[78] These images shored up one of the primary ideological and racial justifications for removal: that, as nomadic hunters constantly on the move, Indians were using the land wrong and lacked any meaningful property rights in their territories. Rather than producing cultivation and social development, Indians' mobility kept the country a wasteland. Thus, even as sheet music and song sheets often criticized white dispossession of Native lands, they simultaneously reinforced the racial logic that helped generate and license such outcomes.

Significantly, removal—and settler colonialism in general—also depended on a contradictory relationship between whiteness and mobility. In the nineteenth century, the idea of fixity was central to ideological constructions of whiteness—especially in relation to Indianness. It was white Americans' stationary, settled cultivation of the land and the "developed" society that followed that granted whiteness its claim to "civilization." However, at the same time, the entire discourse of US settlement paradoxically depended on white mobility. The celebrated white frontiersman who moved ever west, spreading civilization in his wake, underpinned the entire US narrative praising white development of empty western lands.[79]

This contradiction, in which white cultivation and establishment of fixed settlement relied on a celebrated white mobility and movement, passed unremarked and uninvestigated in Enlightenment thought. Of course, the fact that this white mobility was conceptually tied to future fixity palliated the contradiction and stemmed the need to question the implications of white mobility in general. But this incomplete logic, which failed to consider the ways in which white mobility not only thoroughly characterized European colonial and US society but also produced Indian mobility by pushing Native Americans off their land, was in fact fundamental to whiteness. White supremacy prioritizes resource extraction and accumulation over rationality and ideological coherence, and this contradiction is best understood not as an oversight or aberration in white racial ideology but as an essential feature enabling settler colonialism's seizure of Indigenous lands. In the end, whiteness had little concern for rationality; its prerogative was ignoring rationality in the interest of securing power.[80] So whereas Indian mobility was perpetual and reflected wild nature itself, white mobility produced civilization and fixity.

Whiteness thus had a privileged relationship to mobility. Enlightenment-based thought and ascendant narratives of US westward expansion and Manifest Destiny celebrated white mobility at the same time that they presented white Americans as settled and rooted. Yet certainly not all white mobility remained above suspicion and castigation. As the history of vagrancy laws and the treatment of white "vagabonds" in the nineteenth century show, the upper classes routinely cast poor white people as threats to the moral, social, and economic order. They pathologized poor white mobility and attributed it to personal failings rather than the dislocations of burgeoning industrial capitalism.[81] But middle- and upper-class white Americans, as well as frontier white settlers—who were depicted as the epitome of individual economic ambition and self-sufficiency—benefited from the racial and class ideology that lauded their mobility while portraying them as the bearers of fixed society.

This paradoxical and privileged construction of whiteness and mobility found expression and support in antebellum sheet music and song sheets. Popular song repeatedly glorified white men as dominating nature and bringing economic development and civilization to the vacant wilderness of the West. For example, "A Western Refrain: Westward Ho!" (1839) depicts white western expansion as the purview of men, with its call to "File o'er the mountains steady, boy's! [*sic*]" and head "westward ho! in legions, boys!" Once in the West, white men fulfill their Enlightenment mandate and possess the land through their labor as sovereign individual subjects: "When we've wood and prarie [*sic*] land, Won by our toil, / We'll reign like kings in fairy land, Lords of the soil!" In a hypocrisy exemplifying the deep contradictions involved in whiteness's favored relation to mobility, the song also celebrates white frontiersmen as hunters, pronouncing, "Log huts we'll rear, / While herds of deer and buffaloe [*sic*] Furnish the cheer!" and "For game afar / We have our rifles ready, boys!" These paeans to the white hunter throw in sharp relief the contradictions that characterized ideas about race and mobility, praising whites for hunting on land that whites saw as vacant and available because they considered Indians hunters.[82]

While popular song overwhelmingly portrayed white mobility as positive via the western pioneer narrative, it did not unanimously celebrate it. Denigration of white mobility did occur, as the above analysis of "Billy Barlow" illustrates, but it was few and far between.[83] On the whole, images of white mobility in antebellum sheet music and song sheets were positive and paradoxically linked to white fixity and social and economic development. They therefore stood in stark contrast to the castigations of Black and Native mobility that ran through songs of the period.

While antebellum songs consistently depicted Native Americans as innately mobile and equated them with the wilderness, songs featuring African Americans underwent a significant shift beginning in the mid-1840s. As blackface minstrelsy exploded in popularity, white performers and sheet music publishers attempted to increase their profits by growing their middle-class audiences. This shift in audience required shedding the more violent and suggestive content of minstrel music and replacing it with themes conforming to middle-class proprieties. This especially meant creating material considered appropriate for middle-class women, which would allow songs to reach the entire middle-class market. This concern for middle-class women then combined with growing political concerns about the stability of slavery to generate a major thematic change in antebellum minstrel sheet music: a rise in romantic imagery of the South and slavery. Chapter 2 analyzes this romanticism of the South—also known as the Southern pastoral—in minstrelsy alongside sheet music about Native American women to explore the intersection of gender, images of racial mobility, and structures of immobility on the ground.

CHAPTER TWO

Differing Natures

Representations of Gender, Racial Mobility, and Nature in Antebellum Sheet Music

A very brief but highly telling music review appeared in the January 1856 issue of the popular magazine *Frank Leslie's Illustrated*. The review was of four new sheet music titles, one of which was the maudlin Indian dirge "They Are Gone, They Are Gone, or The Red Man's Requiem," a typical rendition of the "vanishing Indian" theme so popular in the antebellum era. "We have received the above popular pieces from the enterprising [publishing] house of Horace Waters," the article announced, "got up in the best style of art." Having bestowed this high praise, the unnamed author wrapped up the short review by confidently asserting that the songs would form a "very desirable musical exercise for our lady readers."[1] This focus on women—specifically "ladies," with its class overtones—in the brief review speaks to the significance of middle-class women to sheet music in the antebellum years. Music publishers, songwriters, and the public at large widely understood middle-class women to be sheet music's primary audience, and publishers and songwriters geared much of their music toward women's perceived tastes in order to maximize profits. Gendered ideas and norms about what content was appropriate for, and desired by, middle-class women thus had a large impact on sheet music.[2]

This chapter takes the influence of gender norms and women audiences on sheet music as an organizing thread to tell two related stories about race and mobility in antebellum popular song. The first concerns the relationship between sheet music featuring images of Native American women and the mainly white middle-class women who made up its primary intended audience. As discussed in chapter 1, the middle class was experiencing a vogue for sentimentality in the antebellum era, one fostered by the rise of the romantic literary movement, the Second Great Awakening, and the emerging cult of domesticity, all of which emphasized emotional experience as a means of uncovering spiritual truths and achieving personal growth. Sheet music romanticizing Native peoples as "noble savages" who were fated to disappear in civilization's wake met this demand for emotional experiences.[3] Crucially, society also deemed such fare appropriate for delicate female audiences. But the images of Native mobility in romanticized sheet music had an unintended gendered effect. Not only did such sheet music help ideologically shore up the Indian removal policy, but it also intersected with another regime of immobility: the system of separate spheres that confined women to the home. I contend that sheet music romanticizing Indigenous mobility, especially a subset with Native American women as their main subject, would have appealed to middle-class white women partly for their depictions of unrestrained movement. Performing a "redface" function, these songs allowed white women stuck inside the home to act out desires for their own freedom of movement through racialized images of Native Americans.[4]

The second story is about a significant change in blackface minstrelsy's imagery of Black mobility that occurred in the late 1840s, a change partially shaped by gendered notions about middle-class women audiences. As detailed in chapter 1, early blackface minstrelsy emerged from working-class male contexts and contained rowdy and suggestive content. Even though some early minstrel songs such as "Jim Crow" were popular with the middle class, many of these early compositions remained rooted in themes deemed inappropriate for more "refined" audiences, especially women. But beginning in the early 1840s, minstrel performers increasingly sought to maximize their profits by attracting middle-class audiences, and women were key to this endeavor. As a result, minstrel songwriters began tailoring their lyrics to fit the strictures of middle-class feminine decorum.[5]

Critically, this shift helped encourage a major thematic change in minstrelsy: the rise of the Southern pastoral, with its sentimental and romantic themes. But while desires to appeal to female audiences were one factor spurring the Southern pastoral—the term scholars use to describe romanticism of the US South and its landscape—a bigger engine of its popularity, with both men and women, was a sharp escalation in white anxieties about the stability of slavery.[6] Beginning in the late 1840s and continuing through the 1850s, sectional tensions generated by US western expansion and more aggressive abolitionism translated into heightened white fears about the repercussions of any large-scale emancipation, including the mass Black mobility it might unleash.[7]

I posit that, as a response to white concerns about free Black movement, the Southern pastoral consistently depicted African Americans as physically fixed within the Southern landscape and constructed white social dominance as dependent on the immobile Black body. This Black fixity was a core theme in the Southern pastoral and fundamental to its resonance for white audiences. Indeed, as discussed in chapter 1, while representations of Blackness and mobility surfaced in early blackface minstrelsy, songs featuring the Southern pastoral evidenced a significantly increased focus on Black movement and a deeper investment in the defense of slavery.

Thus, while the goal of attracting female consumers set the parameters for minstrelsy's anti-Blackness, guiding it toward the Southern pastoral's innocuous respectability, broader concerns about emancipation and Black movement drove its popularity in sheet music of the late 1840s and 1850s. I also contend that the representations of Black immobility in Southern pastoral sheet music interacted with racial structures on the ground. As with early blackface minstrelsy, these hegemonic images not only reflected but also ideologically reinforced slavery's practices of Black containment, which were discussed in chapter 1. By presenting Black immobility as commonsense, natural, and integral to white social control, Southern pastoral songs helped shore up the carceral practices of human bondage. But Southern pastoral imagery also bolstered the rationale behind a new anti-Black practice that was proliferating across the North and West in the 1850s: state legislation designed to restrict free Black migration. Southern pastoral sheet music thus spoke to practices restricting the mobility of African Americans in all regions of the country.

Analyzing sheet music featuring Native Americans alongside Southern pastoral minstrelsy provides a number of insights. First, it illuminates the key role that images of nature played in the construction of race in antebellum popular song. Both categories of sheet music linked Black and Native bodies with nature, a connection vital to their assertions of racial inferiority. But even though both employed depictions of nature, they did so in different ways. Whereas popular music associated Black Americans with nature through pastoral images of immobility, it linked Indians with romantic, untamed wilderness and unrestrained mobility. These differences mapped the dictates of settler colonialism and slavery. To seize Native territories, settler-colonial ideology construed Natives as having no attachment to the land—they disappeared with the wilderness, forever roaming over the landscape and never tying themselves down within or as part of it. In contrast, enslaved Black people and their labor formed yet another natural resource white Americans could tap to produce profits and enjoyment.

Comparing the two types of sheet music also shows the power of middle-class women as consumers of music. Dominant ideas about feminine, middle-class strictures proved a strong force shaping the contours of both minstrel sheet music and songs about Native Americans over the antebellum decades, with blackface minstrelsy undergoing a profound shift in content due in large part to songwriters and publishers competing for the market of middle-class women. However, despite this shift, portrayals of nonwhite mobility remained central to both minstrelsy and songs about Indians. Indeed, even as minstrel content morphed to meet changing class and audience demands, its focus on Black movement only intensified. Examining the two categories together therefore also demonstrates that ideas about nonwhite movement were a fundamental racial preoccupation of the era.

Playing Indian Music

Gender played a central organizing role in the romanticism that gripped popular songs about Indians, as such songs often made Native women their primary subject and held them up as symbols of beauty untainted by European society's corruption.[8] The sentimental and romantic ideals that Indians represented—lost innocence, victims of white rapacity—fit better on the body of Native American women. Whereas Indian men could connote war and violence, Indian women invoked gendered ideas about the need for protection and guardianship that echoed reformers' larger views about the moral and political obligations white society owed to Indian nations, which Supreme Court Chief Justice John Marshall famously labeled "domestic dependent nations."[9] Of the songs overtly representing Indians as mobile, over half featured peripatetic women as the main subject.[10]

So while the imagery of the Indian as nomadic hunter carried masculine overtones, popular music demonstrates that the racialization of Native Americans as mobile resolutely applied to Native American women as well. Take, for example, one of the most popular sheet music songs of the nineteenth century, "The Blue Juniata" (1844). Taking its title from the Juniata River in Pennsylvania, the song's very first lines state: "Wild rov'd an Indian girl, / Bright Alfarata, / Where sweep the waters / Of the blue Juniata." The lyrics thus immediately equate the Indian woman, Alfarata, with a "wild," roaming mobility. Indeed, movement characterizes the entire song. Alfarata is "swift as an Antelope," again linking Indians with nature and wild animals, whose speed and mobility she mimics "thro' the forest," her hair "flowing." She also travels "swift" down the "rapid" Juniata River, which perpetually "sweep[s]." The song soon makes clear that it memorializes the past, as the "fleeting" years have likewise swiftly borne Alfarata away. Death thus constitutes her last journey in a typical rendition of the "vanishing Indian" trope, which was a central theme in cultural imagery of Native Americans and vital to sanitizing and legitimizing settler-colonial land seizures. The song makes clear that, as a part of wild nature, Indian women and Indian societies are transient, both in their physical habits and in that they are destined to exit the stage of history.[11]

Another song invoking the movement of Indian women was "Dark Eyed Ulalee, or Indian Maiden of Echo Lake" (1855), which focuses on an Indian woman's expansive movement in her canoe and links this movement with freedom: "And her father loved his maiden, / Dark eyed Ulalee. / With her tresses flower-laden, / And her wild song free." The phrase "wild song free" indicates a deep connection between freedom and the wilderness, both of which the Indian woman embodies, as she "roams" the lake with her hair "flower-laden." The song then gestures toward the hereditary quality of Indian mobility, with the woman's father teaching her to "rove" "fearlessly" in her canoe. This transfer of generational knowledge also grants Native American women an equality with men, as the father consciously inducts his daughter into the tradition of free-spirited movement. While the fact that the father "taught" these traits to his daughter could suggest that Indian mobility is a learned practice and not innate, the constant equations of the Native woman and her roving with nature foreclose this reading. The lyrics end with the standard allusion to the disappearing Indian, averring, "Now no longer roams the maiden / . . . O'er the lake, the breezes sighing / Chant her elegy." Nature mourns the loss of its companion, the Native woman who "no longer roams," and her unexplained absence telegraphs the larger inevitability of Native American extinction.[12]

Another rendering of freedom through wild mobility comes in one of the more interesting sheet music songs about Native Americans, "Cora: The Indian Maiden's Song," published in 1851. The tune was original composed in 1847 as part of the burletta *The Wigwam*, which employed base stereotypes of Indians as backward savages capable of only mindless violence, drunkenness, and theft.[13] Yet in the midst of this assassination of Native American civil society, the main female Indian character, Cora, sings a plaintive song that has all the hallmarks of typical romantic Indian fare. Its contrast with the comic and demeaning content of the play is jarring, but the sheet music version sheds the play's contexts and fits seamlessly into the general romanticism of popular song.[14] Perhaps this turn to sentimentalism was intentionally done with an eye toward the sheet music market. Regardless, the publication of the sheet music version adds to popular song's more sympathetic treatment of Native Americans. But again, deep racializations course beneath this sympathetic portrait, as the song celebrates Indians for their freedom but predicates that freedom on the equation of Indians with the wilderness. It opens with the line, "Oh! the wild free wind is a Spirit kind, and it loves the Indian well," establishing the affiliation between Indians and nature. This "wild free wind," which is defined by movement, is at the Indian maiden's command, as after she "implor'd its aid" the "wild free wind is there, / And it speeds her dart to the red deer's heart / As he bounds from his secret lair." Mobility suffuses and unites all the imagery in this scene—the Indian woman is included in the myth of the nomadic Indian hunter, and she is capable of harnessing the speed and motion of the wind to take down her "bound[ing]" prey. So constituted, she embodies the freedom of movement the wind symbolizes.[15]

The most direct articulation of female Indian mobility and its integral relationship to a wild freedom comes in the 1835 song "The American Indian Girl." The sheet music provides a short preface to the musical notation and lyrics, which reads: "An American Indian girl residing in one of the early settlements, upon being asked in the course of her education whether she did not think her present situation and prospects more happy than when wandering in ignorance among the woods, replied in the following strain of feeling and pathos." The lyrics then relate the Indian girl's rejection of white education and society. Over music directed to be played "with simplicity," she pleads,

> O give me back my forest shade,
>   Where once I roam'd so blithe and gay,
> . . . .
> They told me in the white man's home,
>   I'd soon forget my woodlands wild;
> And never wish again to roam, The simple native forest child.
> And never wish again to roam, The simple, native, forest child.

The word "roam" appears repeatedly, and roaming brought the girl happiness when she lived in the "forest shade." But whites, presumably white missionaries ("they" also tell her of Christian heaven), have told her that in the "white man's home," such desires would fade. The song defends Indian mobility and the "simple," natural life of which it is a part, critiquing by implication whites' coercive placement of Indian children in educational institutions. According to the song, freedom for the Indian girl lies in the "woodlands wild." But it makes this point by reifying the notion that Indians are inherently mobile; not even white education and society can stamp out Indians' proclivity for wandering. The song reaffirms this immutable racial trait in the final stanza, as "Each rustling of the forest tree" conveys to the girl visions of her "native land," where she once "roam'd so blithe and gay." Highlighting Indians' connection with nature, the forest calls to the girl and awakens her desire to roam.[16]

The song ultimately offers an ambivalent critique of white actions. While it can be read as a criticism of the separation of Indian children from their families and homes, it also presents this separation as well-intended though misguided: Indians are simply incapable of assimilation and mastering white education. Although set in the "early settlements," the song would have had resonance for contemporary debates about removal as well. While it potentially cut against pro-removal arguments by depicting Native peoples as attached to their homes and their land, it also reduced this home to a generic forest, such that one forest could easily be substituted for another. Likewise, by asserting that Indians were incapable of assimilation, it aligned with removal supporters' argument that Indians had failed to adopt civilized ways. And of course, once again, the racialization of Native Americans as mobile shored up one of the major ideological justifications for removal.

The racialization of Indian women as inherently mobile had implications for a spatial structure besides removal. The female redface images flitting across the pages of sheet music also held significant potential meanings for white middle-class women in relation to the ideology of separate spheres and, more specifically, the space of the parlor. As the increasing circulation of commodities under industrial capitalism in the mid-nineteenth century sent more and more sheet music zipping around the country, it often came to a halt in middle-class parlors for the entertainment of women—predominantly white women—who at the same time saw their mobility shrinking as gender norms increasingly consigned them to those parlors.

A thoroughly classed and gendered construction that shadowed the rise of the middle class, the ideology of separate spheres relegated women to the domestic realm. To fortify its rearrangement of gender relations, it advanced the contrivance—masquerading as natural difference—that women were spiritually and morally purer than men but also more delicate and less intelligent. As such, it assigned them the role of keepers of the home, preserving for men the rough-and-tumble universe of public life and economic competition. With women's "proper" sphere designated as the private life of the home, they soon found their mobility curtailed in myriad ways. However, the ability to conform to these norms was available only to those households that could afford to have women abstain from paid work. Working-class families, which depended on the income of their women members, did not have the luxury of performing such gender roles. Conformity to the strictures of separate spheres thus became both a reflection and a marker of class status.[17]

As women became increasingly confined to the home, the parlor room emerged as a vital space in which middle-class women demonstrated their family's class credentials. The larger Victorian ethos of restraint and respectability heavily structured the decorum of the parlor, and sheet music publishers and songwriters tailored the content of sheet music to meet these requirements. While sheet music certainly circulated outside the parlor and the middle class, in the mid-nineteenth century the parlor remained the primary site of sheet music performance and consumption, and music publishers strove to keep the content of their songs respectable in order to reach their largest consumer base. Crucially, the parlor was also a heavily gendered space. As the focal point of the household, the parlor was the locus of feminine domesticity. It was the space in which the women of the household most prominently performed their refinement and demonstrated their adherence to the gender and class norms of separate spheres. Music was intimately caught up in this gendered performance—pianos were invariably located in the parlor—and it played a large role in women's socialization. Sheet music in turn reflected the importance of middle-class women to the music industry's consumer base, as publishers and songwriters produced songs they envisioned as appropriate for, and appealing to, female consumption.[18]

The convergence of the parlor, sheet music, and women's gender roles under the confines of separate spheres opened up subversive possibilities around the images of Indian women in sheet music. In her work on blackface minstrel sheet music, historian Stephanie Dunson argues that antebellum minstrelsy's raucous antics, which were so appealing to the white working class during an age of increased industrial discipline and repressive Victorian mores, would have appealed just as powerfully to those encountering minstrel sheet music in the parlor. Dunson states that white parlor audiences gained "a kind of psychic space" through their encounters with minstrel sheet music, as the music became a space providing momentary but significant escape from middle-class behavioral norms. The release that minstrelsy provided certainly extended to middle-class white men, but Dunson contends that it would have been doubly powerful for white women in the parlor. Whereas mid-nineteenth-century class and gender norms held middle-class men to increasingly strict moral and behavioral standards, they placed even higher standards on women and policed them more sharply. Furthermore, unlike men, middle-class women had fewer outlets for expressing prohibited urges.[19]

Dunson's point that minstrel sheet music supplied a special reprieve for middle-class white women in the parlor prompts consideration of the ways sheet music featuring Indians may have held particular meaning for them as well. As scholar Robin D. G. Kelley observes, constructions of the "noble savage" could perform functions similar to blackface minstrelsy; as the epitome of preindustrial freedom, stereotyped Indians could provoke envy and a desire to emulate within white Americans, even as they simultaneously evoked hatred.[20] The "noble savage" stereotype that so pervasively stalked the pages of sheet music about Indians certainly conjured such conflicting emotions as well.

Sheet music featuring mobile Native American women would have especially sparked these contradictory emotions in white women confined to their parlors, with potentially transgressive and disciplinary effects. Just as blackface minstrelsy provided a "psychic space" for white women to escape the confines of middle-class propriety and behavioral proscriptions, so, too, did sheet music with Native American women constitute a "psychic space" to imaginatively escape the *physical* confines of the parlor and the broader system of separate spheres. Dunson's point about sheet music as an imaginary space providing emotional release must be extended to address the spatial contexts—both ideological and material—in which sheet music circulated and was performed. Images of Indian women with unfettered, autonomous mobility, roaming the natural landscape and in charge of their own bodies, would have been highly attractive to middle-class white women experiencing increased restrictions on their own movement, independence, and freedom. Such images would have operated as a form of redface, encouraging white women to explore and express their stifled desires for movement and independence, especially given their shared position as women.

As part of wild nature itself, moving over the land with ease and speed, Indian women in sheet music represented the antithesis of domesticity and domestic space.[21] They therefore unintentionally stood as romanticized representatives of an alternative femininity built on uncontained movement, their very sentimental rendering inciting empathy. Through sheet music, white women could enact an imagined connection to bodily mobility through space, one without restraint and uncontained by the ideology of separate spheres. This romanticized mobile femininity, then, constituted a potential locus of ideological resistance to separate spheres, linking mobility with freedom and sustaining white women's desires for geographic movement and escape from the confines of the parlor.

However, race always mediated these redface images and would have militated against any subversive effects. Thus, mid-nineteenth-century sheet music about Indian women offers an example of "playing Indian" that was specific to women, and one that had a similar dynamic of subversive potential crosscut by deeply limiting racism.[22] The constant reminder that unrooted mobility was a fundamental aspect of Indianness implicitly relayed the message that to be a "civilized" white woman meant rejecting such mobility. Indian women had mobility, but white women did not. Fully endorsing and celebrating these images of mobility would have therefore required white women to renounce their whiteness, at least to an extent, which was a powerful disincentive.

Indeed, these redface images of Native women potentially allowed white women to express longings for freedom of movement without feeling that they were transgressing the racial and gender demands of separate spheres. Furthermore, in providing an outlet for white women's desires for unlimited mobility, sheet music helped release pressures and dissatisfaction that confinement under separate spheres may have generated, thus dissipating potential energy for resistance. Imaginatively enacting freedom of mobility under sheet music's racial cover was a safer way for white women to release any oppositional impulses they might have had. Thus, while sheet music about Native American women contained the seeds of resistance to separate spheres, its countervailing racism and potential function as an outlet for women's desires for mobility simultaneously eased and helped facilitate the transition to separate spheres and the spatial containment of the parlor. Sheet music depicting Indian women therefore intersected in deep but ambivalent ways with the ideological and material structures of separate spheres.[23]

The potentially immobilizing effects of redface sheet music both found support in and worked hand in hand with popular music's representations of white women. Songs circumscribing women to the domestic sphere by associating them with the home and homelife were legion.[24] A single example will suffice. The cover illustration to the sheet music for "Home, Sweet Home!" (1830), perhaps the most popular song of the nineteenth century, thoroughly conflates women with domestic space (see figure 2.1). The illustration occupies the top third of the first page of musical notation and shows a charming rural scene, with a lake surrounded by lush trees and vegetation, and a cottage by the shore half-hidden in greenery. In the distance, the tall buildings and spires of a nearby town peek over the trees. Directly in the foreground center is a figure of a white woman wearing a dress and a broad-brimmed hat, her hands clasped in a gesture of prayer as she stares out at the viewer with a serious yet serene expression. That the woman occupies center stage in the image suggests she is interchangeable with home itself, either as the matron of the house ready to welcome back the absent viewer or as a woman who has returned to her home and is so grateful to be back, she has

FIGURE 2.1 Cover illustration to Henry Bishop and John Howard Payne, "Home, Sweet Home!" (New York: Firth and Hall, 1830). Courtesy of The University of North Carolina.

brought her hands together in a prayer of thanks. Either way, the image reinforces the association of women with domesticity and the home. The woman's prominence, her body positioned toward the house (notably, facing away from the public space of the town), and the absence of men make the link abundantly clear. Whether she has never left or she has been traveling, a woman's ideal place is in the home, a home racialized as normatively white.[25]

Sheet music also promoted the immobility of white women by consistently analogizing them to flowers and songbirds. In a move that echoes the Southern pastoral's reduction of African Americans to landscape, imagery in lyrics and cover art associating or equating women with flowers and songbirds divested them of mobility. Rendered as plants, women became objects for men to pick and then protect, providing them with the sustenance they required. As songbirds, they became pieces of nature that provided entertainment and pleasure for (male) admirers. Songbirds, of course, were often locked in cages to ensure such enjoyment. This symbolism in sheet music is merely one outcropping of what was a larger cultural pattern in Anglo-American society of associating women with the landscape. As literary scholar Annette Kolodny has demonstrated, since colonial times Anglo-American literature has repeatedly employed femininity and women as metaphors for the American landscape. Likewise, geographer Gillian Rose has shown how geographic discourse and European landscape paintings have equated women with the landscape, echoing dominant understandings of women as property.[26] As the separate-spheres ideology intensified middle-class white women's enclosure in the home, the circulation of images likening women to flowers and songbirds in sheet music bolstered this spatial confinement by presenting women as naturally rooted and immobile.

Sheet music's equation of white women with nature differed from its depiction of Native Americans as wild nature, mirroring in some ways the difference between African Americans and Native Americans in popular song. Rather than present white women as wilderness, as it did Indians, sheet music associated them with the pastoral—they were cultivated, tended, and controlled. Flowers and songbirds served the (male) observer of nature by providing aesthetic pleasure, and they both connoted the space of the garden rather than the wilderness. Similarly, imagery of women and nature differed from the Southern pastoral's treatment of African Americans, although there were also large parallels. One key difference is that images of women and nature were more geographically generic. To the extent flowers and songbirds invoked any specific location, it was simply the generic home, including the spaces of the garden and the house. In contrast, the Southern pastoral's spatiality of containment was centered on the South, linking African Americans with the Southern environment and the plantation specifically, and constructing ideas about race and mobility on a regional scale.

Finally, despite parallels, it is important to mention that the different historical contexts surrounding images of race, gender, and mobility in sheet music encouraged different meanings for audiences and conscripted them toward different social purposes. As historian Melani McAlister puts it, "a cultural product, be it a novel or a painting or a film, cannot be understood solely through 'immanent' analyses that stay within the text itself."[27] The ideological currents of nineteenth-century white supremacy, in addition to spurring whites to create Southern pastoral images in the first place, channeled the meaning of those racial images and their spatiality of containment in certain directions, reinforcing the spatial arrangements of slavery and racial separation. Likewise, nineteenth-century race and gender ideologies pushed audiences to decipher portrayals of white women and nature in sheet music through the lens of gendered domesticity.

To be clear, teasing out the potentially adverse effects of sheet music about Indians on white women does not mean that white women constituted the primary victims of such popular songs. Native Americans bore the brunt of the genre's violent effects. As examined above, popular song's construction of Indians as inherently mobile, while mainly cloaked in romanticism and appended to some fairly strong critiques of white society, nonetheless fortified and perpetuated one of the foundational ideological justifications for removal. While songs about romanticized Indians continued to appear in the early 1850s, a new type of blackface minstrel songs increasingly satiated white demand for romanticism: those employing Southern pastoralism.

Growing Fears: The Roots of the Southern Pastoral

As the 1840s progressed, a shift occurred in minstrel sheet music as songs featuring African Americans in urban settings, discussed in chapter 1, became increasingly less common, and instead the plantation South emerged as the standard backdrop for minstrel tunes. While songs set in the rural South had been a part of minstrelsy from the beginning, by the end of the 1840s such songs would predominate. Furthermore, while the pastoral theme of the contented slave had existed in sheet music since at least the publication of "Bonja Song" around 1811, sheet music of the late 1840s and 1850s witnessed a significant intensification of Southern pastoralism.[28]

Before analyzing the Southern pastoral in sheet music, it is helpful to contextualize its emergence in popular music by tracing its longer roots as a theme in American culture writ large. The term "Southern pastoral" refers broadly to any imagery celebrating the Southern landscape as aesthetically stunning and/or portraying the social organization of the rural South as idyllic. The pastoral as a theme, Southern or otherwise, has always been about more than just an articulation of aesthetically pleasing space—it is a tool to express social meaning. As cultural historian Leo Marx explains, the pastoral expresses a "yearning for a simpler, more harmonious style of life, an existence 'closer to nature,'" and reflects an urge to escape a perceived negative development in society. Pastoral descriptions of America stretch all the way back to the beginnings of colonialism, with Europeans employing the pastoral in their conceptions of America as a "New" world free from the contamination of the "Old."[29]

Pastoral descriptions of the South likewise date to the early colonial period, appearing in English propaganda tracts that portrayed Virginia as an Edenic land of plenty in order to encourage migration. Initially not unique or separate from the American pastoral at large, the Southern pastoral developed into a distinctive strand by the end of the eighteenth century. A prime example is Thomas Jefferson's *Notes on the State of Virginia* (1785), which described Virginia's abundant landscape alongside a panegyric on its superior socioeconomic organization.[30]

As the early decades of the nineteenth century progressed, the growth of slavery in the South and the spread of emancipations in the North contributed to the further distinction of the Southern pastoral. Slavery's essential role in Southern society demanded that the Southern pastoral account for its presence. Primarily a literary tradition until its emergence in sheet music in the late 1840s, the Southern pastoral became fraught territory for Southern white authors. In fact, the expanding scale of the peculiar institution in the first half of the nineteenth century touched off a minor literary crisis in the South. As scholar Lewis P. Simpson shows, Southern white authors struggled to reconcile the increasingly undeniable market logics of antebellum slavery with the pastoral vision. While some authors jettisoned slavery altogether and identified it as a flaw in the social order of the South, others struggled to include it in the Southern pastoral. Those including slavery in the pastoral often resorted to ideological contortions and gave a full-throated defense of the institution.[31] However, for whites living in the North who did not have to confront the realities of Southern slavery in person, its expansion posed no barrier to pastoral imaginings of the South. Thus, when minstrel artists—overwhelmingly from the North—introduced the Southern pastoral into their music, they included slavery without qualms.

The rise of the Southern pastoral in sheet music of the late 1840s and 1850s was connected to three historical shifts. First, as numerous scholars have shown, the popularity of the pastoral—including the Southern pastoral—in literature and popular culture grew as a response to the dislocations of industrialism and urbanization.[32] As industrial capitalism took off in the antebellum period and more Americans began working and living in cities, romantic images of the rural South offered a nostalgic, escapist vision of agrarian nature. Through the Southern pastoral, audiences could glimpse the preindustrial world that economic changes were swiftly eradicating. Second, beginning in the early 1840s, theater managers and minstrel artists attempted to clean up minstrelsy and make it more "respectable" in order to reach a wider middle-class audience. Minstrel artists purged the genre of much of its sexual innuendo, rowdy content, and class critiques and instead focused on absurd humor, physical buffoonery, and, increasingly, sentimental themes and love songs. These new motifs offered a racism more palatable to middle-class sensibilities. In particular, minstrel artists turned to the Southern pastoral as a safely respectable theme that was well-suited to the sentimental material they increasingly peddled to the middle class.

Finally, heightened white fears about the potential end of slavery made the Southern pastoral extremely appealing to white audiences. The United States's acquisition of massive western territory following its victory in the Mexican-American War (1846–48) sparked widespread white trepidation about slavery's future. The Wilmot Proviso, introduced in Congress by antislavery Democrat David Wilmot in 1846, called for a complete ban on slavery in the territories acquired from Mexico and unleashed a political firestorm as the nation debated slavery's future role in the country. Many Northern whites were unconcerned with abolishing slavery where it existed and simply wanted to contain it as an institution, which they felt undermined free white labor. The proviso became a rallying point for those who saw the restriction of slavery as a means to reserve the resources of the western territories for whites. But while the proviso may have galvanized some Northern whites against the extension of slavery—reflected in the creation of the Free-Soil Party—it also spurred a backlash among those who perceived the proviso as an assault on slavery generally. Many whites in the North and South decried the proviso as unnecessary government interference in the slavery question, and Southern whites in particular saw it as an attack on the sanctity of the peculiar institution. Neither the Democrats nor the Whigs endorsed the proviso in their 1848 presidential platforms, and supporters of both parties deployed racist attacks against the Free-Soilers, labeling them race traitors and enemies of white supremacy.[33]

As the new decade arrived, the controversy over slavery only deepened, as the struggle over slavery's future dominated national politics in the 1850s. Furthermore, political efforts to repair the sectional rift through compromise stimulated abolitionist activities and rhetoric. The Fugitive Slave Law of 1850, passed as a concession to Southern slaveholders, triggered highly visible abolitionist resistance. Most Northern whites saw this resistance as irresponsible lawlessness and remained firmly opposed to any abolitionist sentiment they felt might upset delicate sectional relations. Nonetheless, as the 1850s progressed, antislavery agitation and rhetoric increased, with abolitionists becoming more militant in their political stance and actions. Even those arguing merely for the restriction of slavery stepped up their invective against human bondage. The amazing success of Harriet Beecher Stowe's 1852 novel *Uncle Tom's Cabin* and the violent resistance of John Brown were prime accelerants fueling the fire of white anxieties about the stability of slavery—and the nation. Throughout the 1850s, the looming clouds of abolition gathered increasingly on the political horizon and seemed to threaten slavery not only in the territories but also in the South.[34] This heightened conflict helped spark the

emergence of the Southern pastoral in minstrelsy and sheet music, as Southern pastoral images ameliorated white anxieties about slavery's status. Thus, the conflict over slavery joined desires for agrarian imagery and sentimental material as prime drivers of the Southern pastoral's growth.

The Southern Pastoral in Antebellum Sheet Music

Not only did Southern pastoral imagery become far more frequent in the late 1840s and 1850s, but songwriters began accentuating the Southern landscape and describing it in ever more elaborate terms. In the face of proliferating challenges to slavery's authority, popular song reinforced the claim that slavery merely reflected the natural racial order by conscripting images of nature itself. The Southern pastoral presented slavery as part of an idyllic Southern environment, linking slavery with images of nature. It thus portrayed Black bondage as organic and immutable. As cultural theorist Stuart Hall observes, "The hope of every ideology is to naturalize itself out of History and into Nature, and thus to become invisible, to operate unconsciously."[35] The Southern pastoral exposes this process in a particularly trenchant manner, for the Southern pastoral mobilizes images of nature precisely to naturalize ideology.

Popular song's focus on the rural South did not mean an end to its preoccupation with Black mobility. On the contrary, with escalating white fears about slavery's potential demise came deepened anxieties about unfettered Black mobility, and Southern pastoral sheet music expressed these anxieties in a new, and in many ways more insidious, form: felicitous and idyllic scenes of nature that rendered Black bodies rooted in space as part of their pleasing aesthetics. As scholars have pointed out, works featuring the Southern pastoral inserted African Americans into the landscape, reducing them to just another aspect of the romanticized terrain.[36] However, scholars have failed to recognize and address the larger spatial implications of this reduction to landscape. On a fundamental level, the Southern pastoral portrays white social control as dependent on the immobilization of Black bodies in space by depicting African Americans as part of the landscape, physically fixed within a harmonious racial society.[37] The Southern pastoral thus celebrates the immobile Black body and casts the containment and rootedness of Black people as the blueprint for white supremacy.

As with earlier minstrel songs, the images of Black immobility embedded in the Southern pastoral emerged in tandem with representations of gender and sexuality. Easing white concerns about Black male mobility—and the threat of interracial sex it conjured—remained a primary objective. But as minstrel artists attempted to transform the genre into a middle-class entertainment, the working-class impulses that drove early minstrelsy's masculine rowdiness disappeared, swept away in a flood of sentimentalism and romanticism. Rather than portraying the riotous dangers of uncontained Black male mobility, Southern pastoral songs presented the opposite—the demure, effeminate, loyal, and subjugated Blackness that followed from the physically fixed Black body. This new manifestation of white unease over Black mobility arose because such images not only passed the test of middle-class respectability but also enabled the solemn sentimentalism that middle-class audiences craved. Thus, minstrelsy's changing class contexts produced a significant shift in its gendered representations of Black mobility.

As rural settings for minstrel songs became more common in the mid-1840s, the first romantic images of the South outside the contented slave trope began to spring up in lyrics and cover art. These initial forays contained only minor pastoral imagery, which speaks to the inchoate nature of the Southern pastoral as a theme in sheet music at this early stage. These early songs provided a slapdash defense of slavery rather than a more streamlined one.[38] However, after the onset of the Mexican-American War (1846), sheet music began featuring a more coherent and consistent Southern pastoralism. The South became the primary setting of minstrel songs in the late 1840s, and with the Southern pastoral's maturation came its reduction of African Americans to landscape.

"My Lovely Virginia Gal" (1847), sung by the famous Christy's Minstrels, illustrates this trend.[39] A sentimental song about an aged Black man pining for his former lover named Virginia, it opens with a description of the Southern setting:

> One night just at the close ob day,
> On de ribber bank I chanc'd to stray,
> Some darkies did on de banjo play,
>   For my sweet lub, Virginia:
> Dey danc'd and sung away all night,
> By de stars and de bright moon's silv'ry light;
> Dey kept it up 'till broad daylight,
> For de sake ob my Virginia.

This dreamy depiction not only casts slavery as leisurely and undemanding, with Black slaves inexhaustibly dancing all night in the "silv'ry" moonlight, but also makes the frolicking slaves a key aspect of the Southern scene. Their carefree celebration becomes just one more element establishing the idealized Southern setting, a part of the landscape the audience surveys along with the riverbank and starry sky. Equating the Black bodies with the natural environment, the song divests them of mobility—they are naturally, and happily, fixed as part of the plantation's ambiance. The narrator of the song, whose "hairs are turning gray," also reflects another emerging motif in Southern pastoral sheet music: the use of an older Black man as narrator, especially in sentimental songs. The older Black male narrator made a safe vehicle for the peaceful and romantic imagery of the Southern pastoral, eliding the threatening sexuality and potential violence associated with younger Black men, an association minstrelsy itself encouraged through the vigorous, if denigrated, Black masculinity of Jim Crow and his brethren.[40]

Another popular Southern pastoral song from 1847 was "De Floating Scow of Old Virginia," alternatively titled "Carry Me Back to Old Virginia."[41] The song also features an aged Black narrator and initiated what would be another long-standing and common theme in Southern pastoral sheet music: songs about a former slave or, in the postbellum period, a former Black laborer, who had left their old plantation but now longed to return. These songs were often referred to as "carry-me-backs."[42] In the lyrics, the "old and feeble" narrator recounts brighter days from his past, when he worked on "De floating scow [sailing dinghy] ob ole Virginia" as an oyster fisher. Rather than producing hardship or pain, the narrator says oyster fishing "was but play," suggesting that African Americans enjoy manual labor. But despite the ease of his labor, the narrator proclaims he is now too old to work and pitifully pleads, "Oh! carry me back to ole Virginia, To ole Virginia shore." While the song is unclear as to whether the narrator is free or enslaved, it unequivocally conveys that Black Americans want nothing more than to stay in the South and perform menial labor.[43]

Of course, the song advocates the movement of the narrator insofar as he must return to "Virginia shore." But this return is mobility that conforms to white desires. In other words, it is not the free Black movement so troubling to whites but rather mobility that promises to fulfill the white fantasy of the Black body that will wander no more. Interestingly, the song never specifies where the narrator currently is or why he left Virginia's shore. This ambiguity potentially heightened the song's emotional power and appeal for white audiences, allowing them to more easily identify any of their own personal feelings of loss and nostalgia with the narrator's sorrow.[44]

Although the elderly Black male narrator emerged as a theme in antebellum plantation pastorals, such songs did feature younger Black men—and sometimes Black women—as narrators. For example, in "I Hab Leff Alabama" (1849), an enslaved woman serves as the mouthpiece for African Americans' desires to remain on the plantation. Having run away out of trivial jealousy because "de galls all would kiss" her "true lub," she quickly realizes her error. Not only does she immediately miss her lover, but she also reports that her lover and her "ole massa" have both "gone crazy becase dey can't find me." In the face of the distress she has caused herself, her lover, and her white master, she promises in the chorus, "I's gwine to go back to Alabama agen. . . . / And if eber I lib till de sun rise tomorrow, / I's a gwine to go back to Alabama agen." This affirmation of Black longing for geographic stasis is coupled with a testimony to the benevolent nature of white slave owners, as the narrator states that on her return her "massa will smile and be glad to receibe me." This image of the generous and forgiving white master profoundly erases the violence—including sexual violence—that enslaved Black women suffered at the hands of their white owners. The song's account of Black love disturbed only by petty jealousy also presents a picture of secure Black familial relations, covering up the cruelty of the slave trade's separation of Black families and loved ones. In "I Hab Leff Alabama," it is not white slave owners who generate (forced) Black mobility and separate lovers but the foolish decisions of African Americans themselves. The song assured listeners that Black people immediately regretted such decisions and wanted to return to their kindly masters.[45]

Such praise of white slaveholders represented a new trend in minstrel sheet music. For all its proslavery rhetoric, early minstrelsy did not regularly highlight or celebrate the kindhearted white master in such overt terms. But as the 1850s dawned, Southern pastoral sheet music repeatedly indulged in this myth. Perhaps the apotheosis of the theme came in 1852 with Stephen Foster's enormous hit, "Massa's in de Cold Ground." Not only does the song elevate the figure of the white slaveholder to nearly divine status, it also, from its very first lines, reduces African Americans to landscape in its focus on the plantation scenery: "Round de meadows am a ringing / De darkeys' mournful song, / While de mockingbird am singing, / Happy as de day am long." The lyrics continue to reiterate both the environment and the slaves' sorrow, stating, "Down in de cornfield / Hear dat mournful sound: / All de darkeys am a weeping / Massa's in de cold, cold ground." As scholars have noted, such pastoral constructions of the Southern environment as preternaturally abundant erased the slave labor that produced and maintained the landscape of the plantation.[46] Further, this erasure naturalized white supremacist race relations. Devoid of any scenes of coercion, the Southern pastoral presents racial hierarchy as an organic, immutable order.[47] Accordingly, "Massa's in de Cold Ground" equates the Black body with this natural terrain. Portraying the slaves' song as "ringing" through the meadows and their weeping as echoing in the cornfield, the lyrics relegate the slaves' cries to the natural landscape. Just as the mockingbird and its songs constitute a part of the plantation environment, so do the slaves and their singing.

The song's final stanzas continue to invoke the natural beauty of the South: "Now de orange trees am blooming / On de sandy shore, / Now de summer days am coming, / Massa nebber calls no more." The most serene of race relations reign in this blossoming landscape, as "Massa made de darkeys love him, / Cayse he was so kind, / Now dey sadly weep above him, / Mourning cayse he leave dem behind." White superiority produces the deepest of love between the slaves and their master, converting the plantation from a site of economic extraction and exploitation to one of familial cooperation. Indeed, so deep is the slaves' love of their kindly master and their attachment to the space of the plantation that the only movement the slaves desire is that of death, so they can follow their master who has left "dem behind."[48] It is difficult to overstate the popularity of "Massa's in de Cold Ground," which sold seventy-five thousand copies in 1852. Indeed, a number of the songs Foster wrote in the 1850s, some discussed later in the chapter, proved incredibly influential and popular.[49] Foster's paean to Southern white masters struck a chord with white Americans and further inscribed the link between Black bodies and the Southern terrain in sheet music.[50]

While "Massa's in de Cold Ground" exemplifies the dominant representation of white slave owners in Southern pastoral sheet music, not all minstrel songs presented such a rosy view. As scholars Robert Nowatzki and Sarah Meer have shown, minstrelsy in the 1850s had significant ideological overlaps with abolitionist views. While minstrelsy as a genre was decidedly anti-Black and proslavery, numerous songs nonetheless presented antislavery ideas and encouraged sympathy for enslaved individuals. Nowatzki in particular shows how minstrel artists offered antislavery critiques that could appeal to abolitionists while refraining from overtly critiquing slavery as a whole, thus increasing the potential audience for their songs and performances. A common tactic was for minstrel songs to critique the slave trade for separating Black families and loved ones, portraying white slaveholders as emotionally callous and profit oriented. An especially weak spot in Southern defenses of slavery as a paternalistic and beneficial system, minstrel artists seized on ambivalence around the slave trade. In converting the emotional terror of the slave trade into sentimentalism, minstrel composers walked a fine line between appealing to abolitionists and general middle-class sentimentalism and not offending those with proslavery views.[51]

However, even minstrel sheet music that called the slave trade into question often reaffirmed the Southern pastoral's overall logic of containment. Indeed, some Southern pastoral songs indicted the forced mobility of the slave trade for interrupting the harmonious relations of the plantation. For example, in "The Little White Cottage, or Gentle Nettie Moore" (1857), a slave trader from "Louisiana bay" destroys a pastoral paradise where "the trees are ever green, / And the climbing roses blossom by the door" when he buys the enslaved narrator's lover, leaving the plantation "dreary." Such songs updated the carry-me-back theme to include the forced mobility of slavery, critiquing it only to the extent that it disrupts African Americans' own desire to remain rooted to the plantation.[52]

Perhaps the best and most important example of the Southern pastoral's ability to incorporate ambivalence and antislavery themes while still presenting its essential vision of Black immobility is Stephen Foster's 1853 song "My Old Kentucky Home, Good Night," one of the best-known tunes of the nineteenth century. In fact, Foster used Harriet Beecher Stowe's *Uncle Tom's Cabin* as the basis for the song, demonstrating how minstrelsy could co-opt abolitionist themes and ideas and transcribe them within larger proslavery representations.[53] Foster's song also demonstrates the increased focus on the landscape in sheet music of the 1850s. The opening lyrics proclaim that "The sun shines bright in the old Kentucky home, / 'Tis summer, the darkies are gay, / The corn top's ripe and the meadow's in bloom / While the birds make music all the day." This first stanza immediately establishes a synthesis between nature and African Americans. Inserting the "gay darkies" between descriptions of the landscape, the song constructs the Black body as just one more feature of the Southern terrain and implicitly ties Black emotion to the rhythms of nature, their happiness blooming with the summer. Within this idyl, all the slaves are "happy and bright."

But "sorrow" soon steals over the plantation "when the darkies have to part." Now "they hunt no more for the possum and the coon / On the meadow, the hill and the shore, / They sing no more by the glimmer of the moon, / On the bench by the old cabin door." Foster's description of the landscape casts the South as a land of abundance. The removal of African Americans from the "old Kentucky Home" disrupts the pastoral, replacing the "bright" sunlight with "shadow." The sentimentality of the song thus operates not simply through the idea of a lost pastoral but through the removal of the Black figure from the pastoral landscape. "Part[ed]" from the physical surroundings, Black Americans' natural joviality ceases and they "sing no more by the glimmer of the moon."

Significantly, as the remaining lyrics make clear, the removal the song speaks of is the sale of the slaves to a sugarcane plantation farther South, most likely in Louisiana or Texas, though the song does not specify. There, they "tote the weary load" until death ends their suffering. Foster's song therefore critiques the interstate slave trade and plantations of the Deep South. Nonetheless, the lyrics still engage the Southern pastoral to glorify border-state slavery and reify Black Americans as closer to nature. Even as one form of slavery causes a problematic mobility, bringing hardship "wherever the darkey may go," the other delivers happiness in conjunction with the rooted, immobile Black body. Thus, while "My Old Kentucky Home, Good Night" complicates the Southern pastoral, it never transgresses or contests the larger spatiality of containment that underwrote slavery.[54]

Foster also contributed to the rising number of "carry-me-backs" published in the 1850s. His song "Old Folks at Home," written in 1851, was another massive hit that became a popular music standard in the nineteenth century.[55] Along with "My Old Kentucky Home, Goodnight" and "Massa's in de Cold Ground," the success of "Old Folks at Home" speaks to the growing importance of the Southern pastoral in sheet music and popular culture more generally—and, of course, Foster's ability to capitalize on the trend. "Old Folks at Home" also illustrates the intensifying focus on the Southern landscape and the growing white ventriloquism of Black desires for immobility that characterized songs of the decade. It begins with a Black narrator reminiscing, "Way down upon de Swanee ribber, / Far, far away, / Dere's wha my heart is turning ebber, / Dere's wha de old folks stay." The narrator has, for an unspecified reason, left his old plantation and now "sadly . . . roam[s]," "longing for de old plantation." The narrator makes his distress abundantly clear, proclaiming, "All de world am sad and dreary, / Ebery where I roam." Expressing a longing for "de old folks," the song captures a common sentiment among white audiences in an increasingly urbanizing country—missing one's family and home.

However, Foster's song routes such longings through the blackface mask and couples them to the rooted Black body. More than just missing family, the Black narrator of the song is "longing for de old plantation" and the peaceful serenity of its environs. The narrator misses his "little hung among de bushes" and wonders, "When will I see de bees a humming, / All round de comb? / When will I hear de banjo tumming / Down in my good old home?" The simple natural pleasures of the hut "among de bushes" and the humming bees contrast sharply with the despair engendered by the narrator's "roam[ing]." With his heart and mind "turning ebber" to his former plantation on the "Swanee" river—Foster's dialect perversion of the Suwannee River in Florida—the Black narrator cannot escape the plantation's pull. Of course, this inexorable force emanates from his own wish to return rather than from the architecture of immobility propping up slavery, and the narrator's misery testifies to the emotional futility of leaving the plantation. The song thus expresses a profound desire to see African Americans safely ensconced within the space of the Southern plantation. That this desire was hitched to, and played on, white desires for their own familial homes does not mitigate the power of the former or the song's racial lessons about Black immobility and peaceful race relations. Always multivocal, minstrelsy wove numerous strands in its ideological cloth.[56]

The success of "Old Folks at Home" spawned spin-offs that echoed the original's articulation of Black stasis and pastoral beauty, including the songs "Old Folks Are Gone" (1852), "'I Long for My Home in Kentuck'" (1852), and the not-so-creatively titled "Young Folks at Home" (1852).[57] And as the 1850s progressed, renunciations of Black movement in carry-me-backs grew more adamant. Songs began to explicitly dismiss freedom as unimportant or counterproductive to Black happiness. Others went a step further to paradoxically claim that Black freedom could only be found on the slave plantation. In "Old River Farm, or the Darkey's Regret" (1853), the Black narrator decries freedom as merely a ruse, saying, "Freedom once craved is a name at the best," and the song suggests that he is now "mournfully roam[ing]" in the North, though his location is a bit hazy. Regardless, he yearns for "the old fields with their gold waving grain" and states, "My thoughts must still cling round the cool mossy spring, / When [*sic*] the grapevine I planted so leafly entwined." As the title unmistakably conveys, the former slave regrets leaving home and bondage. Instead, his thoughts and desires remain tied to the landscape of slavery, with the mobile Black body once again violating African Americans' natural attachment to the plantation terrain.[58]

By 1861, the Southern pastoral was so popular that the massive minstrel hit "I Wish I Was in Dixie's Land" made it to the White House. Published the previous year, the song and its emphatic Southern pastoralism took the nation by storm. It soon became one of Abraham Lincoln's favorite songs, and during the White House reception for his first inauguration in 1861, the band played a rendition of the hit.[59] Composed by blackface performer Dan Emmett, the song later became synonymous with the Confederate cause in the Civil War. However, before Southern whites forged this connection, it appealed to white audiences throughout the nation. Not only did it have an infectious tune, but it also had a racial message that whites on both sides of the Mason-Dixon Line appreciated.[60] Lincoln is an excellent example. Despite authoring the Emancipation Proclamation, he held some bedrock racist views. A committed advocate of Black colonization outside the United States well into the Civil War, Lincoln shared some of the fears that white Americans across the country had about emancipation.[61]

These fears found expression in Emmett's song and its Southern pastoral imagery. The song's Black narrator, having inexplicably wandered north, professes to having made a major mistake: "I wish I was in de land ob cotton, / Old times dar am not forgotten, / . . . Away, Away, Away down south in Dixie." Repeatedly stating his wish to return to the South, the narrator casts his return journey as inevitable, proclaiming, "To Dixie's land I'm bound to trabble." Replacing the bindings of slavery's shackles with the blackface conceit that African Americans steadfastly desired to remain in slavery, the song presents Black Americans in the North as naturally "bound" to return to the South and their subordinate social position. The laws of racial nature compel this return, and the Black narrator will soon travel back to his Southern home, where he will rejoin the cotton crop as another fixed, rooted object. In this way, "I Wish I Was in Dixie's Land" reflected white anxieties about Black mobility—anxieties its racial fictions aimed to placate.[62]

As part of its larger cultural and ideological defense of slavery, the Southern pastoral made images of Black immobility a key feature in its imagined racial landscape. The representations of Black fixity circulating in popular song helped naturalize, and thus reinforce, the geography of containment underwriting slavery. Immensely popular throughout the nation, Southern pastoral songs reflected the mounting anxieties of whites across the country about the specter of mass Black mobility as the fate of slavery grew increasingly uncertain. These concerns about free Black movement embedded in the Southern pastoral lend support to historian Steven Hahn's point that slavery was a national, not a regional, investment during the period.[63] They also indicate the foundational role of ideas about mobility to anti-Black racial ideology in the United States during the antebellum era.

Indeed, the emergence of the Southern pastoral and its spatiality of containment was one of a panoply of Northern white responses to the threat of potential Black mobility in the years leading up to the Civil War. Throughout the late 1840s and 1850s, a string of states across the Midwest and West passed laws banning Black in-migration. In 1848, Illinois ratified a new state constitution that called for legislation regulating free Black migration. The Illinois legislature then followed through in 1853 by passing a law that barred free Black people from entering the state. Similarly, in 1851, Indiana adopted a new state constitution that explicitly banned further free Black settlement; and in 1852, the legislature passed another law to help enforce the constitutional provision. In 1851, Iowa also promulgated a law that prohibited free Black in-migration by establishing a two-dollar-a-day fine for any new Black resident. And in 1854, state legislators in Minnesota proposed and considered a law designed to discourage Black settlement, though it failed to pass. Oregon rounded out the list of Midwestern and Western states enacting restrictions with the most complete ban of all, adopting a constitution prohibiting all Black in-migration, free or enslaved, in 1859. While many of these laws were only sporadically enforced, and Iowa repealed its restriction in 1860, this spurt of legislation nonetheless spoke to the rising anxieties of white Americans in the North and West about Black movement.[64] Indeed, during Illinois's 1847 constitutional convention, a state legislator announced that if a law preventing free Black in-migration was not passed to protect the southern part of the state "from being overrun by these swarms of free negroes . . . the people of the south [southern Illinois] would take the matter into their own hands, and commence a war of extermination."[65]

In 1862, with the Civil War pushing white fears of a Black "invasion" of the North to an even higher pitch, Abraham Lincoln referenced these migration laws in his annual message to Congress to reassure Northern whites skittish about Black mobility. After acknowledging that many white Americans "dreaded that the freed people will swarm forth and cover the whole land," Lincoln attempted to assuage this concern both by arguing that African Americans would stay in the South if they were paid wages and by making another plea for colonization. Then, to round out his argument, he posed the rhetorical question, "In any event, cannot the north decide for itself whether to receive them [the freed slaves]?"[66] He thus suggested that Northern states could solve the problem of Black migration simply by passing restrictive legislation. Lincoln's comments therefore attest to the prevalence and strength of white fears about Black mobility following any large-scale emancipation, as well as to the link between these fears and state migration restrictions.[67]

Critically, Southern pastoral sheet music's imagery of Black immobility not only registered the deep white anxieties about Black movement motivating such laws but also fortified the laws' rationale and encouraged their spread. And this process was encouraged by economic changes. The Southern pastoral's hegemonic vision of immobile Blackness increasingly traversed the nation in the 1850s through industrial capitalism's expanding networks of commodity production and exchange. The decade saw sixty-six new music publishing houses spring up, nearly double the amount of the 1840s. Transportation improvements, especially the growth of railroads, were also key. Railroads linked the country as never before, greatly speeding the transport of goods, including sheet music and song sheets. Furthermore, publishers began adding full-page advertisements of their song inventories to their sheet music. One piece of Southern pastoral sheet music now delineated numerous other Southern pastoral songs that might appeal to customers. Thus, as representations of Black fixity emerged in Southern pastoral sheet music, those images increasingly crisscrossed the nation through the circuits of capitalism, helping encourage and ossify structures of Black immobility on the ground.[68]

When the Civil War did break out, white concerns about Blackness and mobility only escalated further. These concerns would continue to build in the postbellum period following emancipation, and precepts about race and mobility forged in slavery would remain central to the era's racial developments. Sheet music reflected this escalation, as themes of Blackness and mobility further intensified in the second half of the nineteenth century.

Crossings

In looking at images of Native and Black mobility in popular song, it becomes apparent that antebellum sheet music enacted a hierarchy that positioned Indianness above Blackness. Sheet music did serious damage to views of Indians and Black Americans, but it at least accorded Indian mobility a modicum of dignity and respect. At the same time that Indian mobility signaled uncivilized culture and economic backwardness, it also conveyed a steadfast independence and freedom. So while romantic images of Indians often ultimately presented Indian mobility and Indian society as uncivilized and primitive, they also expressed a degree of admiration for that mobility by refusing to caricature it and lamenting its loss. In contrast, sheet music and song sheets overwhelmingly refused even the slightest respect for Black mobility. Early blackface minstrel songs featured vicious stereotypes, and even the romanticized Southern pastoral songs employed base dialect and malapropisms.[69]

However, this relationship would change slightly beginning in the mid-1850s, as sheet music ceased romanticizing Native Americans in the overwhelming proportions of prior decades. A spate of songs adapting Henry Wadsworth Longfellow's poem "The Song of Hiawatha" marked the last spasms of this trend.[70] In general, the number of songs about Indians declined significantly, and those that were published took a decidedly more negative turn, often emphasizing Native violence.[71] So while the Southern pastoral grew in popularity, songs about Native Americans withered.

The diverging paths of these two song types were in fact linked. Songs romanticizing Indigenous peoples petered out in part because songwriters and music publishers alighted on another thematic vehicle for peddling sentimentality and romanticism to audiences: the Southern pastoral. Likewise, white reformers—now over twenty years out from the onset of the removal debate—were turning their energies to the gathering crisis over slavery and the increasingly visible abolitionist movement. As the Southern pastoral steadily climbed in popularity, songs about Indians receded. Finally, the decrease also coincided with the advent of large-scale white migration beyond the Mississippi River in the late 1840s and 1850s. This white encroachment produced a sharp escalation in physical violence and conflict in the following years, as settlers and the US Army embarked on a campaign to eradicate Native life and land ownership. The ecological, economic, and armed assault on Native peoples was comprehensive, and Native nations often resisted by taking up arms.[72] Warfare with western Indigenous nations made white Americans' empathy for Indians harder to sustain, especially as Indians' military resistance signaled defiance of not just land seizure but also reformers' assimilation efforts.[73] As a result, sentimental images of Indians evaporated from the pages of sheet music. And since violent themes were still considered inappropriate for sheet music, songs about Indians simply dwindled rather than push more martial narratives, though, again, these did arise on occasion.

Though Native Americans faded from the pages of sheet music, they did not fade from popular culture in general. The mid-1850s saw the reservation emerge as the new dominant means of managing US relations with Indigenous nations, and it instituted an even more intense regime of spatial containment.[74] Alongside the Civil War and its accentuation of white anxieties about Black mobility, the growth of the reservation system formed a fundamental feature of what historians have labeled the Greater Reconstruction period. Chapter 3 examines this period and its core politics of racial containment through the lens of popular culture. In particular, it looks not only at how sheet music indexed the intensification of white anxieties about Black mobility after the Civil War but also at how two Native Americans—Chief Standing Bear of the Ponca Nation and Susette La Flesche of the Omaha Nation—harnessed the popular culture form of the lecture circuit to push back against the reservation's confines.

CHAPTER THREE

Reconstructions

Westward Expansion, Emancipation, and Images of Racial Mobility in Popular Culture, 1850–1885

In 1879, a mass Black migration to Kansas arose in response to resurging white oppression in the South. The migration attracted national attention and became known in popular parlance as the Kansas Exodus. Interestingly, while many African Americans across the country supported the exodus, the famed Black abolitionist and leader Frederick Douglass came out against it. While Douglass understood that white violence and oppression in the South were the root causes of the mass migration, he nonetheless maintained that African Americans should stay in the South and fight for their political rights. He perceived the exodus as a surrender and felt it sent the message that whites could deny Black rights without any repercussions. Tellingly, Douglass stated that he did not want African Americans to develop "the habit of roaming place to place" and claimed that Anglo-Saxons had become hardy by enduring struggle and hardship. According to Douglass, to succeed on the path to freedom, African Americans would need to do the same.[1]

Not only did Douglass thus repeat and reinforce the link between white fixity and settlement found in Enlightenment thought and the frontier myth, but he also echoed and invoked the trope of the uncivilized, nomadic Indian in his warning about the "habit of roaming."[2] His criticism therefore speaks to the power of dominant ideas about race, fixity, and mobility, and it illustrates how ideas about Black movement formed in tandem with notions of white and Indigenous mobilities. What is more, the Kansas Exodus itself reveals the larger racial and regional entanglements of the Greater Reconstruction period. As African Americans fled the racial violence of the South for Kansas, they contributed to the ongoing seizure of Native American territory in the West. With the exodus, Greater Reconstruction's project of incorporating western territories under US settlement intersected with the upheavals generated by its project of reintegrating the US South as a non-slave society and economy.

Douglass's focus on mobility was especially apropos. An integral aspect of Greater Reconstruction was the reconstitution of structures of racial immobility. As US settler migration to the West grew in the 1850s, the Indian reservation replaced removal as the dominant US federal policy for managing relations with Native nations. Whereas removal enforced containment on a continental scale, the reservation instituted more intense carceral relations. The notion that Indians were wandering hunters remained crucial to US policymakers' thinking during this transition. Another fundamental element of Greater Reconstruction was the demise of slavery in the Civil War. Emancipation triggered an escalation in white anxieties about free Black movement across the North, West, and South. Eventually, white Americans around the country would reconstruct slavery's geography of containment under the new guise of Jim Crow segregation in the 1890s and 1900s. In the intervening decades, concerns about Black movement remained a central preoccupation of white Americans.

In the book's remaining chapters, I trace this twin reconstitution and associated ideas about racial mobility through the lens of post-1860 popular culture. The current chapter focuses on two examples of popular culture appearing between 1860 and the mid-1880s. First, it picks up where chapter 2's analysis left off by looking at Southern pastoral sheet music from 1860 to the mid-1880s. I contend that heightened white anxieties about Black mobility after emancipation helped drive the immense and increased popularity of the Southern pastoral in the last half of the nineteenth century.[3] These increased fears also resulted in more elaborate images of Black immobility in the Southern pastoral. Circulating prominently in popular culture, the Southern pastoral's advocacy of rooted Black bodies offered a blueprint for white supremacy based on Black immobility, and it would form part of the ideological groundwork for Jim Crow segregation's national emergence in subsequent decades.

Next, the chapter examines the 1879–1880 lecture tour of Ponca Chief Ma-chu-nah-zha, commonly known as Standing Bear, and Omaha citizen Susette La Flesche, or Inshtatheamba, which protested the federal government's treatment of the Ponca Nation. The chapter contextualizes the tour within the reservation's ascension to policy dominance to show that Standing Bear and La Flesche contested the reservation system and its ideologies and practices of confinement—first through a legal court case and then through the cultural form of the lecture circuit. The lecture circuit, or lyceum, was one of the most popular forms of entertainment in the late nineteenth century, and Americans saw attending lectures as both edifying and entertaining. Standing Bear and La Flesche's tour was highly popular and widely publicized in the press, which rebroadcast their lecture content to even larger audiences.

The chapter ends by returning to the Kansas Exodus, looking at how Southern pastoral sheet music incorporated the exodus into its romantic narratives of the South. These songs are a trenchant example of how Greater Reconstruction's historical imbrications manifested in popular culture. As US settler expansion into the West had the unintended effect of opening up possibilities for Black flight from the South, the Southern pastoral adapted in an attempt to conceptually contain the exodus's threat to the racial order. In a sense, songs about the Kansas Exodus are where the Southern pastoral and Standing Bear and La Flesche meet. But the connections between the two in fact run much deeper. Perhaps most basically, they intersect around the politics of racial mobility. Placing the two alongside each other demonstrates that practices and ideologies of racial mobility remained fundamental to postbellum American society and popular culture. It also reveals the changes that were occurring to formations of Black and Native immobility on the ground. Examined together, the Southern pastoral and Standing Bear and La Flesche's lecture tour provide a vantage point from which to survey Greater Reconstruction's broader transformations.

"A Very Great Aversion": Sheet Music and White Fears of Black Migration During the Civil War

White Americans' sense of crisis over Black mobility after emancipation in the Civil War shines through clearly in both the political statements and popular culture of the time. Consternation about the potential for large-scale, unrestricted Black movement had been rising among whites throughout the late 1840s and 1850s, but the outbreak of the Civil War and the Union's eventual commitment to emancipation in the South brought fears to a new pitch. White Democrats howled most fiercely about the threat of Black migration to the North, but they were hardly alone. Many white Republicans expressed trepidation over Black freedom in general, epitomized by Abraham Lincoln's support for colonization well into the war. In August 1861, the pro-Republican *Chicago Tribune* testified to the important role Black migration played in these worries when it stated that white fears about freed slaves heading north in droves to become "roaming, vicious vagabonds" posed the largest obstacle to support for emancipation. Republican Senator Lyman Trumbull, also a supporter of colonization, corroborated the prevalence of these views that same year, remarking, "There is a very great aversion in the West . . . against having free negroes come among us. Our people want nothing to do with the negro."[4]

Northern Democrats attempted to turn such aversion to their political advantage, harping constantly on what they portrayed as Republicans' support of Black people at the expense of the white population.[5] In an 1862 speech to Congress, which was then published as a broadside to be bought and sold alongside the song sheets of the day, Democratic Congressman Samuel S. Cox from Ohio charged the Republicans in Congress with enabling a dangerous Black mobility. In apocalyptic language, he stated, "Weary in watching its [Congress's] mad designs of revolution—and its crazy crotchets of black freedom—and for the self preservation [*sic*] of my native State and the North from the black immigration with which it is threatened, I shall go to my home and ask the ballot to speak its denunciation." He claimed that upon seeing "the fate of thirty-four white commonwealths in peril," Congress had merely "babbled of the Negro!" In the broadside, the word "Negro!" stands alone in the center of the sheet in enlarged and bolded text, while directly below it sits a small illustration of an African American man in a running pose with a stick and handkerchief slung over his shoulder. The only image on the page, it underscores the threat of Black immigration, painting free Black mobility as a dangerous specter shadowing Republican policies.[6] Cox's words did not fall on deaf ears, at least not in his home state. Many Ohio Democrats echoed his message of Black invasion from the South, and in response, the Ohio House of Representatives initiated a detailed census in 1863 to count every Black resident in the state and ascertain their place of birth.[7]

So strong were white apprehensions about the Black mobility that emancipation might unleash that one abolitionist song sheet went out of its way to refute the notion that freed slaves would migrate to the North. "The New Jim Crow Song, About the Darkies and the War" was published in 1862 in Ohio and is a parody of the massive minstrel hit from the 1830s. It keeps the original song's chorus but devotes all the quick two-line verses to countering many of the proslavery arguments put forth by the Confederacy and its supporters. The song is long, with over forty of these short rhymes, and it provides numerous antislavery and antiracist arguments, as well as recounts recent Union victories in the war. Of these verses, four focus exclusively on rebutting the notion that freed Black people would migrate north, citing everything from African Americans' supposed aversion to cold weather and new types of work, to Southern planters' need for Black labor—whether free or slave. However, in mobilizing these antislavery arguments, the song refused to confront whites' racist animosity to free Black mobility. In doing so, it implicitly confirmed the idea that Black mobility was in fact something to be avoided.[8]

Harriet Beecher Stowe, author of *Uncle Tom's Cabin,* perhaps best summed up the distress over free Black movement when she observed in 1862 that "many well-meaning people can form no idea of immediate emancipation but one full of dangers and horrors. They imagine the blacks free from every restraint of law, roaming abroad a terror and nuisance to the land."[9] Her statement attests to the direct link many whites drew between unrestrained Black mobility and Black criminality. As historian Leslie A. Schwalm has shown in her study of Reconstruction in the upper Midwest, white anxiety about job competition from newly freed African Americans was a significant aspect of fears about Black migration to the North. But as Schwalm also notes—and as Stowe's quote demonstrates—white Americans saw former slaves' mobility as a harbinger of shifting race relations.[10] Black mobility was thus an emblem of broader changes in the racial order, evoking images of uncontrolled Black criminality and social disorder.

The specter of free Black mobility looming over white Americans heavily inflected popular music of the period. As discussed in chapter 2, tensions over slavery's future in the late 1840s and 1850s spurred the growth of the Southern pastoral as a theme in antebellum sheet music. With the racial tumult of the Civil War, Southern pastoral imagery intensified further, and assertions of both natural Black inferiority and Black desires to remain in the South became even more strenuous. Exemplifying this trend was minstrel performer Dan Emmett's "I'm Going Home to Dixie" (1861), a sequel to his colossal hit "I Wish I Was in Dixie's Land." The song was a carry-me-back—a common subgenre that emerged in the 1850s in which a wandering Black narrator professes their longing to return to their former plantation—and it demonstrates a heightened focus on African Americans' supposed desire to remain in the South. A written preface to the song explains that "with the southern negroes, Dixies [*sic*] Land is but another name for Home. Hence it is fair to conclude, that all south of Mason's and Dixons [*sic*] line is the true 'Dixies Land.'" By conflating the South with Southern African Americans' "home," this definition suggests that Black people had no desire to leave the region.[11]

The Black narrator of the song then corroborates this definition, announcing, "Freedom to me will never pay!" and happily chanting, "I'm going home to Dixie! Yes! I am going home." The song thus ironically reverses the remunerative relations of slavery and the wage labor system: African Americans do not desire and need no economic reimbursement for their labor—the affective bonds of the South are "pay" enough. The epitome of the contented slave myth, the free Black narrator pines for the comforts of slavery and placates white fears about Black social and economic ambitions.

In addition to returning the Black body to its proper social place—the relations of slavery—"I'm Going Home to Dixie" sends the Black body back to its proper spatial relations. Emmett's song celebrates an ideal that sees Blackness submerged within the landscape. After describing the South as "a land where milk and honey flows," the narrator proclaims, "In Dixie Land the fields do bloom / And color'd men have welcome room!" This "welcome room" that the South offers Black Americans is not room to spread out over the region but rather room to reenter the controlled relations of slavery. Rejecting freedom, the Black narrator assumes his proper place among the fields that "bloom," as the song conjures an image of slaves at work among plantation fields all over the region. Black bodies are thus fundamental to the portrait of the South in "I'm Going Home to Dixie," constituting a core feature of the Southern scenery as fixed objects within the landscape. Certainly, the song advocates the movement of the narrator insofar as he must return to the relations of slavery. But this return is mobility that conforms to white desires; in other words, it is not the free Black movement so troubling to whites but a mobility that promises to fulfill the white fantasy of immobile Blackness rooted to the plantation South. The pastoral imagery therefore not only violently confines the Black body to social subordination but also confines it in space.

This ventriloquism of Black desires to return to the South and then remain there, rooted to the landscape, echoed the pervasive white anxieties about Black mobility and migration in the wake of emancipation. While Emmett's 1861 "I'm Going Home to Dixie" could only hope to discourage any future emancipation, songs published later in the war, or directly after it, responded to emancipation as an unfolding reality. "Carry Me Back to Tennessee, or, Ellie Rhee" (1865), for example, finds its Black male narrator relating a tale of tragedy brought on by "dis cruel war," which has separated him from his lover, Ellie Rhee. The lyrics reveal that this separation is due to the narrator's decision to run away, a decision he now regrets: "Oh why did I from day to day, / Keep wishing to be free, / And from my massa run away, / And leave my Ellie Rhee." The song thus neatly shifts the violence of slavery's family separation onto emancipation and the misguided decisions of African Americans themselves. In a typical example of the Southern pastoral's reduction to landscape, the narrator pleads, "Carry me back to Tennessee, / Back where I long to be / Among the fields of yellow corn; / To my darling Ellie Rhee." He thus longs for both his lover and the landscape, wishing to resume his place among the Southern terrain and crops. The narrator then pledges that if he makes it back to slavery, "I'll nebber run away." This manufactured Black rejection of emancipation and freedom of movement would have been highly attractive to white Americans anxious about Black mobility, as would have the promise of Black stasis attending the narrator's felicitous merger with the "yellow corn."[12]

Though incredibly common, proslavery themes did not have a monopoly on popular song during the 1860s. Antislavery and pro-Union sentiment galvanized by the war resulted in the publication of numerous songs that trumpeted abolitionist ideas and themes. In some cases, these songs presented Black mobility as a positive good for the Union and the cause of freedom, usually in the form of slaves running away to Union lines.[13] These compositions offered a counterbalance to proslavery minstrel songs, some of which exceeded Emmett's songs and "Carry Me Back to Tennessee" in their anti-Black and proslavery content.[14] And as late as 1870, with Reconstruction underway, support for Southern Black rights appeared in the song "Get Along Old Mule, or, 'Plowing the Field Where the Sugar Cane Grew.'" As alluded to in the title, the song is about a freed slave who now owns his own farm on land formerly belonging to his old master's sugarcane plantation. Employing minimal dialect, the lyrics render the Black male farmer respectfully and paint slavery as evil, stating, "O the sad times are gone, may they never come again, / For heavy was the trouble of the poor slave then."[15]

However, such articulations of Black respectability and economic independence were sparse in sheet music of the postbellum period. Overwhelmingly, sheet music continued minstrelsy's tradition of thoroughly denigrating Black Americans, and the Southern pastoral and its imagery of Black immobility remained a major theme. In fact, in the postbellum period, sheet music became the primary venue for racist songs, as the 1870s marked the beginning of a long decline for the minstrel show. Although it continued well into the early twentieth century, the minstrel show receded in popularity as new forms of entertainment supplanted it, foremost among them the variety acts of vaudeville (though vaudeville shows did often incorporate minstrel skits into their programs).[16]

While these transitions in the music business were underway, the Southern pastoral exploded in popularity in the 1870s and 1880s, especially in the North. It cropped up in many forms of popular culture besides music, including plays, magazine stories, local color literature, and novels. Southern writers such as Joel Chandler Harris, Sidney Lanier, and Thomas Nelson Page produced hugely popular books glorifying the "Old South" throughout the 1880s. Their nostalgic accounts fashioned a narrative that praised slavery as benevolent and erased its history of racial violence.[17] However, sheet music continued to be one of the primary transmitters of the Southern pastoral, with most songs written by Northern composers eager to exploit the market for romantic depictions of the South.

Many structural and political forces gave the Southern pastoral new valences for white audiences after 1865 and in turn contributed to its rise in popularity. Numerous scholars have argued that the growing desire among white Americans for an amicable reunion between North and South after the end of federal Reconstruction drove demand for Southern pastoralism. For such scholars, white Americans' eagerness to put the racial sins of the South out of their minds and stitch the wounds of sectional division led them to consume such images voraciously.[18] And of course the Lost Cause ideology and desires to vindicate a defeated South certainly motivated Southern writers like Page and Harris in the first place.[19]

In addition, scholars have reached a broad consensus that the intertwined processes of urbanization and industrialism fueled the Southern pastoral's popularity. Both accelerated in the North in the last half of the nineteenth century and, in later decades, began to transform the South as well.[20] Americans experiencing the upheavals and pressures of modernity sought out pastoral escapisms that gave a glimpse of nature and reminded them of their rural pasts.[21] All of these social contexts contributed to the Southern pastoral's increased popularity and wider circulation in the postbellum era. But alongside these factors, the Southern pastoral continued to reflect deep anxieties about Black mobility, anxieties exacerbated by emancipation.

"I'll Never Come Away": Emancipation and the Triumph of the Carry-Me-Back

Amplified white fears about Black movement following emancipation produced a corresponding intensification in Southern pastoral imagery during the final decades of the century. Beginning in the 1870s and continuing through the 1880s, sheet music lyrics and cover art featured more elaborate depictions of the Southern landscape. The change was especially noticeable in cover art, which displayed larger and more eye-grabbing illustrations of Southern scenes across the front pages of sheet music. The period also saw the carry-me-back become far and away the favorite template for songs romanticizing the South. And carry-me-backs themselves underwent an important shift, as the aged Black male narrator became almost universal. In part, this development occurred because the older character symbolized a connection to the former relations of slavery. Having spent a lifetime in bondage, the older Black male narrator became the ideal mouthpiece for white assertions that slavery had been a gentle and beneficial institution for Black people. But this figure also circumvented white concerns about Black male sexual and social energy in an era when African Americans widely pushed for inclusion in US civic life. Gender and sexuality thus fundamentally configured the Southern pastoral's racio-spatial imagery. That said, carry-me-backs with Black women and younger Black men as their narrators, and non-carry-me-back Southern pastorals, did exist as well.[22] But in all these various forms, representations of Black immobility remained a common thread.

"The Old Home Ain't What It Used to Be" (1872) illustrates how carry-me-backs linked the aged Black narrator to slavery. The song confronts the listener with a pastoral devastated by the end of slavery. Directed to be played andante (moderately slow) and dolce (sweetly, softly), the music sets a tragic mood as the aged Black male narrator explains, "Great changes have come to the poor colored man, / But this change makes him sad and forlorn, / For no more we hear the darkies singing, / Among the sugar cane and corn." Emancipation has irrevocably shattered the pastoral, and the plantation is not "what it used to be." The old man mourns the absence of the children who "used to play" by his cabin and who "are scattered now, and o'er the world . . . roam," never to return. In the final stanza, the song suddenly shifts to the third person to offer a sweeping picture of freedom's effect on the South: "Now the old man would rather lived and died, / In the old home here his children were born, / But when freedom came to the colored man, / He left the cotton field and corn." Emancipation, and not slavery, thus stands as the primary oppression in Black lives, and its main evil is that of Black mobility. Having "scattered" Black bodies and sent them "roam[ing]," emancipation snuffs out the pastoral and its harmonious relations. The narrator, who has been sufficiently tempered by slavery's relations, knows that life was better before the war, while the younger generations errantly take to the road.[23]

The song's cover illustration displays the flip side of this errant Black movement, articulating the pleasing conditions that attend the immobile Black body (see figure 3.1). It shows an elderly bespectacled Black man, white hair fringing his bald head, sitting placidly on a fallen log. He wears a serene and contented look on his face as lush tropical vegetation ensconces him from all sides, practically subsuming him. Behind him runs a calm river with a steamboat off in the distance, while halfway up the riverbank, also nestled in greenery, sits a somewhat rickety-looking wood cabin. The Southern terrain is thus the primary subject of the illustration, and the Black man, so thoroughly immersed in the vegetation, just one more aspect of the scenery. Thus rooted to the landscape, the Black man and his immobility both constitute and enable the serenity of the scene.

FIGURE 3.1 Cover illustration to C. A. White, "The Old Home Ain't What It Used to Be" (Boston: White, Smith, 1872). Courtesy of the California Sheet Music Collection, University of California Berkeley Library.

One of the most popular songs of 1874, "Trabling Back to Georgia," also demonstrates the increased focus on the landscape in Southern pastorals of the postbellum period. Again an older Black man expresses the standard carry-me-back themes, proclaiming, "I'se trabling back to Georgia, dat good ole land to see, / The place I left to wander, the day that I was free." Now "tired of roaming," the narrator heads back to the plantation where he was born "among the fields of cotton / The sugar cane and corn." The lyrics thus cast him as simply another product of the fields. In this bucolic idyll, his happiness derived from the agricultural labor of "hoe[ing] the corn and cotton," performed for the benefit of whites on the "old plantation." Crucially, the narrator's detachment from the fields produces profound unhappiness, his mobility engendering only unfulfilling "wandering" and "roaming." Pleasure returns only when he plants himself firmly back on Southern ground, his natural environment. Given the song's subtext of rootedness, the line "I'll never come away" acquires a particularly literal resonance that encapsulates its racial and spatial promise.[24]

The popularity of carry-me-backs with an aged Black male narrator proved to be extraordinary throughout the 1870s. For example, in 1874, the same year that "Trabling Back to Georgia" became a smash hit, the highly similar "I'se Gwine Back to Dixie" also achieved massive popularity, selling over 500,000 copies. Its renunciations of Black mobility are equally strong: "I'se gwine back to Dixie, / No more I'se gwine to wander, / My heart's turned back to Dixie, / I can't stay here no longer, / I miss de ole plantation, . . . / My heart's turned back to Dixie, / And I must go." Demand for this fare was seemingly insatiable.[25]

Amid this popularity, cover illustrations to carry-me-backs broadcast the Southern pastoral's logics of Black containment as never before. The cover to "Dem Good Ole Times" (1877) depicts the joys of plantation life for African Americans (see figure 3.2). In the lyrics, the aged Black male narrator fondly recalls his youthful days on a plantation in Louisiana, from which he is now separated for unspecified reasons. In those golden years, he would play with the other children and "blow de horn at noon, for de work hands all to come," bringing in the "many happy darkies" from the fields. Now, old and gray, he is "trabblin' back again, all thro' de winds and snow and rain" to see his old plantation. That he travels through snow suggests he is currently in, and fed up with, the North.[26]

The cover illustration provides a full-page vision of this plantation paradise. An aged Black man crowned with white hair sits in the foreground while behind him is an expansive view of the plantation's cotton fields, with numerous African American figures, male and female, working waist-deep in the white crop. Their features indistinct and their bodies half-submerged in the field, they meld into the panoramic view to become simply one aspect of the picturesque Southern environment, static and unmoving. Whether this image is set during slavery or afterward is both unclear and irrelevant. Its figuration of Black immobility and subservience as blissfully natural applies irrespective of time period.

The theme of construing Black bodies as part of the Southern panorama and thus reducing them to the landscape was not unique to "Dem Good Ole Times" but appeared consistently in sheet music cover illustrations of the time.[27] Some cover images went even further and explicitly contrasted the welcoming space of the plantation South with the dangers and disappointments of the city for African Americans. The cover to "My Old Home in Mississippi" (1879) visually captures the theme of the ex-slave yearning to return

FIGURE 3.2 Cover illustration to Henry Newman, "Dem Good Ole Times" (Boston: White, Smith, 1877). Courtesy of the Lester S. Levy Sheet Music Collection, Johns Hopkins University.

to the plantation (see figure 3.3). The print shows an aged forlorn Black man sitting on a chair in a sparsely furnished room. Cracks in the walls and the man's ragged clothes and bedsheets indicate his impoverished state, while a small window reveals a cityscape through its frame. A banjo lying silent across his knees conveys his dejected mood. An image in a cloud bubble at the top of the print reveals the object of his thoughts: a bucolic scene with broad fields and tall rows of corn in the foreground and a grand mansion in the distance nestled at the foot of a mountain range. In the fields, Black figures work diligently, their features ill-defined, while the crop—most likely cotton—engulfs their lower bodies. The illustration thus constructs a racial narrative of Black Americans as out of place in the city but at home when rooted to the landscape of the plantation. Once again, the idealized vision of the plantation reduces the Black laborers to a single component of a larger panoramic in

FIGURE 3.3 Cover illustration to James Bland, "My Old Home in Mississippi" (Boston: John F. Perry, 1879). Courtesy of the Lester S. Levy Sheet Music Collection, Johns Hopkins University.

which the landscape is the main character. Literally half-embedded in the fields and without distinguishing features, the Black laborers merge with the terrain and become one more prop contributing to the aesthetic beauty of the fantasy.[28]

Echoing this upsurge in elaborate Southern pastoral cover art, song lyrics more intensely focused on the Southern landscape during this period. James Bland's "Carry Me Back to Old Virginny," published in 1878 and perhaps the most popular song of the decade, exemplifies this trend.[29] Bland himself was a Black Northerner, and he was one of the first Black artists to have success in the popular-music business. But he wrote many songs with racist stereotypes to survive in an industry that demanded such themes at the time. "Carry Me Back to Old Virginny" heavily employs the Southern pastoral:

> Carry me back to old Virginny,
> There's where the cotton and the corn and tatoes grow,
> There's where the birds warble sweet in the springtime,

There's where the old darke'ys [*sic*] heart am long'd to go,
There's where I labor'd so hard for old massa,
Day after day in the field of yellow corn,
No place on earth do I love more sincerely,
Than old Virginny, the state where I was born.
Carry me back to old Virginny,
There's where the cotton and the corn and tatoes grow,
There's where the birds warble sweet in the springtime,
There's where this old darkey's heart am long'd to go.

It is worth noting that Bland's song contains a measure of resistance to the prevailing racist themes of the day. The lines emphasizing the "hard" labor performed "day after day" contrast sharply with the images of enjoyable labor found in other carry-me-backs of the period. Reading this language as a veiled critique of slavery lends an air of satire to the following lines about the narrator's "sincere" love for the land he left. Further, in the second verse, the narrator reminisces, "Long by the old Dismal Swamp have I wandered." This reference to Virginia's Great Dismal Swamp cuts against the pastoral, as slaves often used swamps as safe havens when escaping from bondage, including the Great Dismal Swamp, which was noted for its maroon communities. It also invokes Harriet Beecher Stowe's second antislavery novel, *Dred: A Tale of the Great Dismal Swamp* (1856).[30] Bland thus inserted a coded allusion to illicit Black mobility under the noses of his white audience, covertly undermining the Southern pastoral's racist romanticism.[31]

Yet the subversive moments in Bland's song are buried among a litany of archetypal pastoral celebrations, and white audiences clearly reacted to the song's romantic qualities. Once again, the nonthreatening older Black man acts as a conduit for the Southern pastoral. The song associates the "old darkey" with the "cotton and the corn and tatoes" and the "warbl[ing]" birds as the narrator professes his deep wish to return to Virginia and resume his life among its natural bounty. The narrative is thus one of return to the landscape in the most literal sense—the Black body returning to take its place among "the field of yellow corn" and the other natural features of the environment. Therefore, while Bland offered some subversive resistance, his song also reinforced the Southern pastoral's dominant myths and helped circulate its imagery of Black containment.

The carry-me-back was legion throughout the 1870s and 1880s.[32] But songwriters also produced many non-carry-me-back Southern pastorals, which likewise celebrated Black immobility. "Down Among De Sugar Cane"

(1875) avers that African Americans want nothing more than to inhabit the crop fields of the South in the most literal way: "Ole Marsa says foreber with him I shall remain, / And when I'm dead he'll lay me down among de sugar cane. / Dar let me rest, / Dar let me rest, neber to wake again, / Dar'll be no care or trubble, / Down among de sugar cane." Taking a different tack, "My Mississippi Home" (1882) offered a requiem for slavery, paradoxically asserting that before the Civil War, "the darkies liv'd so happy gay and free." But now Black people have disappeared from "the canes" and "the fields where [they] used to plant the cotton, rice and corn." Perhaps the epitome of racial ideology's penchant for irrationality and contradiction, the song's configuration of slavery as freedom marks the apogee of the Southern pastoral's racial forgery. In the song, it is the blight of emancipation that eradicates the pastoral and its felicitous relations of Black containment.[33]

The Rise of the Indian Reservation in the West

As the Southern pastoral was blooming in the minds of white Americans, US Indian policy was changing. Beginning in the 1850s, federal policymakers turned from removal to the reservation as the reigning method for governing relations with Native Americans. While many historical works discuss the Indian reservation as if its definition were self-evident, it is helpful to explicitly state the differences between the reservation system and the policy of removal, as they shared a number of common features. Both involved white promises to Indian nations of land that would remain free from US settlement, and both enforced, to varying degrees, the geographical separation of whites and Indians. The most commonsense understanding of the difference between the two—that removal created an Indian territory envisioned as beyond US settlement and that reservations are circumscribed Indian land surrounded by US settlement—goes a long way toward capturing the crucial divergence between them, yet more is involved than this basic demarcation.

Historian Robert Trennert offers further clarification. Removal established a boundary between whites and Native Americans, but it did not impose any surveillance or geographic restrictions on the tribes in Indian country, nor did it involve drawing boundaries between the tribes themselves. In contrast, the term "reservation" refers to land set aside by colonial-era governments—or, later, the US federal government—that was far more restricted and well-defined and often geared toward the coercive assimilation of Indigenous peoples into "civilization." The reservation system thus involved the concentration of Native Americans onto smaller areas of territory around which white settlement advanced. It also entailed far more surveillance and restriction of Native movement, often including prohibitions against Native peoples leaving designated territories. Furthermore, many policymakers explicitly understood the reservation's increased geographic concentration of Native Americans as enabling more effective educational and assimilationist efforts.[34]

As a structure and form, the Indian reservation in Anglo-America has long roots that stretch back to the colonial period. Historian Yasu Kawashima has shown that an early example of the reservation developed in colonial Massachusetts with the "praying towns" of the early seventeenth century. Initially granting the Native inhabitants a degree of municipal control over their communities, the colony passed an act in 1677 after King Philip's War mandating that all Indians living within the colony—regardless of religious status—be confined to one of the four praying towns, excepting only Indian children and servants living with English colonists. Though colonists did not employ the term "reservation" at the time, these lands set aside for the use and occupancy of Native Americans within the colony's borders represent the origins of the reservation system.[35]

Similarly, articulations of the reservation concept occasionally surfaced among federal officials in the early national period.[36] Nonetheless, as discussed in chapter 1, the policy of securing Native lands through white proximity and, beginning in the 1820s, the removal policy would remain the dominant federal strategies for governing relations with the Indian tribes. But beginning in the late 1840s, the United States's acquisition of extensive new western territories and the expansionist ideology of Manifest Destiny forced white Americans to find a new method for managing relations with Native peoples in the West. As historians Elliott West and Robert Trennert have shown, these changes led white Americans to confront the question of how to deal with Native Americans as a spatially internal group. As West observes, expansion precipitated a "racial crisis" that posed the question of whether Indigenous peoples in the West should be brought inside the US polity and, if so, how. As white settlers streamed West—many of them heading across the plains for California and Oregon—it became increasingly clear to government officials and elected representatives that the removal policy was no longer adequate for administering Indian affairs in the western territories. White settler expansion appeared inevitable, and many felt federal action was necessary to stave off violent conflict with Native Americans and facilitate the advance of "civilization" into the West.[37]

US officials landed on the reservation system as the solution to the problems raised by the specter of an "internal" Native American population. As early as 1845, field agents in the Office of Indian Affairs were suggesting that the federal government move the plains Indians away from white emigration routes to the Pacific to allow whites to pass unmolested. Commissioner of Indian Affairs William Medill turned these initial suggestions into a larger strategy. In 1848, Medill outlined the beginnings of a reservation policy in the West. He proposed the creation of two "colonies," one northern and one southern, with a large corridor of land between them for white passage and settlement. The plan had all the hallmarks of the reservation system: The United States would expropriate the desirable lower Platte and Kansas valleys for whites and relegate Native Americans to smaller, circumscribed, and clearly defined lands from which they would be prohibited to leave. Mobilizing established ideas about nomadic Native Americans and the superiority of settled agricultural societies, Medill asserted that restricting Indians to smaller tracts of land would force them to give up their traditional reliance on hunting and take up agriculture. Furthermore, schools for manual labor would impose a civilizing education on the now restricted Indian tribes.[38] Thus, enduring ideas about Indianness and mobility were baked into the first detailed federal proposal for a reservation system.

While Medill couched his reservation plan in humanitarianism, it deeply aligned with the political and economic interests of white settlers. Even though Medill never implemented his plan as laid out in 1848, powerful material interests within the federal government and white society at large—namely desires for land for white settlement and railroads—gave it an impetus that would make it influential in succeeding years.[39] Subsequent commissioners were committed to the reservation idea, and in 1851, Congress responded to calls for a reservation system by enlarging the Office of Indian Affairs in that year's Indian Appropriations Act, thus providing the bureaucratic resources required to implement the system. While the powerful plains tribes were able to resist reservations until the late 1860s, in 1853 and 1854 the United States succeeded in forcing the Indian nations bordering Missouri and Iowa onto reservations, opening up most of what is now eastern Nebraska and Kansas for white settlement. Thus, as the removal policy failed to meet the exigencies of white westward migration, what emerged from the crucible of an altered US geography was a policy that confined Native peoples to restricted and well-defined areas.[40]

This new racial regime, with its fundamental focus on the spatial confinement of Native Americans, would shape the landscape of the West with accelerating speed in the 1860s. Even during the Civil War, conflicts with Native nations in the West remained crucial to US policy, and the war years saw both warfare with Indian tribes and white massacres in what was very much a "three-cornered war."[41] The reservation policy remained a cornerstone of the Office of Indian Affairs throughout the 1860s and was widely accepted and imposed by military leaders in the army.[42] In 1867 and 1868, the United States secured two major treaties with some of the largest plains nations, which saw the tribes agree to designated reservations in exchange for certain US concessions, such as removing forts from Indian territories. However, warfare soon sprang up again between Native peoples and frontier whites. The US military succeeded in defeating most of the Native nations that had taken up arms, but Native peoples would withdraw to their reservations merely as an interlude, during which they regained their strength for future military resistance. It was not until 1877 that the army defeated the last major armed resistance of Native peoples, finally overcoming bands of the powerful Sioux Nation and, in what Elliott West has called "the last Indian war," a group of Nez Perce who refused to accept reservation confinement.[43]

Throughout the 1860s and 1870s, US military leaders, civilian officials, and white philanthropists justified the reservation system by consistently invoking the imperative of restraining Indian mobility. For military commanders, Native American movement outside reservation boundaries was taken as indisputable proof of hostile intentions. Commenting in 1868 on the necessity of the reservation system, General William Tecumseh Sherman maintained that "to labor with their own hands, or even to remain in one place, militates with all the hereditary pride of the Indian, and *force* must be used to accomplish the result."[44] General John Schofield, commander of the Pacific region, advised his troops that "every Indian found off his reservation without permission . . . will be regarded and treated as hostile."[45]

Civilian officials and white reformers also concentrated on the dangers of Indian mobility, but many professed more humanitarian concerns.[46] White philanthropist William Welsh, writing in 1869, claimed paternalistically that "the time has arrived when our Indians are to be gathered into reservations" so that they could be "trained in the habits of civilized people, that the Christian Church may exert its holy influences over them."[47] Welsh saw containing the movement of Indians as fundamental to the reservation system and its purpose of assimilating Native peoples. For Welsh and other reformers, attempts to spread "the saving influence of the Christian religion to the Indians in their nomadic condition" had failed.[48] Commissioner of Indian Affairs Francis Amasa Walker struck a similar note in 1873. In support of the reservation system, Walker repeatedly referenced Indians' supposed racial penchant to wander. He argued it was vital to keep Native peoples "upon the reservation assigned to them, and to arrest and return such as may, from time to time, wander away." Unless contained on reservations, Indians' "old roving spirit" would prevent their assimilation into US society.[49]

Throughout the postbellum period, white Americans employed a variety of tactics to uphold the carceral relations of the reservation, some of which resonated with those designed to control Black mobility under slavery. The threat of military action remained the strongest method of controlling Native mobility, and military campaigns and surveillance from forts throughout the West echoed the slave patrols of the US South. Another strategy more directly bridged slavery and the reservation: the pass system. Acting for the federal government, US Indian agents on many reservations required Native peoples wishing to travel to visit friends or communities on other reservations to carry and present a pass that physically described the bearer, stated where they were headed and why, and confirmed they were of trustworthy character. Often, travel permits were authorized as a reward for good behavior, particularly economic industriousness (as white officials perceived it). Even when granted a pass, Native individuals often had to travel with a police escort. Yet another way US officials on reservations enforced Native immobility was through daily roll calls. These ensured that Indigenous peoples, especially raiding parties, could not leave the reservation for significant periods of time without federal authorities being aware.[50]

Through the reservation system and its containment of Indian movement, white Americans advanced the Greater Reconstruction project of incorporating the western territories into the capitalist settler-colonial state. But spatial containment was not just a useful method for expropriating Native lands and enabling assimilation efforts in the post-1845 landscape. It also dovetailed with, and seemingly addressed, long-standing racial ideas about Indianness and mobility. Ironically, despite white Americans' relentless focus on the problem of Indian mobility and the inadequacies of a hunting economy, it was *white* migration and hunting that were disrupting Native societies and that necessitated the reservation policy in the first place. White migrants moving across the plains to reach the Pacific territories hunted as they traveled, reducing the game on which the tribes of the trans-Mississippi West depended. And, of course, it was the enormous scale of white migration into the western territories that produced the reservation policy and its land cessions. Furthermore, in the 1870s, whites in the West engaged in an industrial slaughter of buffalo to procure their hides, dealing a crippling blow to Native economies just as consequential as US military power in forcing Native Americans to accept reservation life.[51] The contradiction of chastising Native peoples for their supposedly savage nomadism while simultaneously celebrating white migration as the font of civilization escaped white Americans. But as discussed in chapter 1, this paradox around mobility was central to the power of whiteness and the privileges it afforded.

Lessons in Freedom and Liberty: Standing Bear and Susette La Flesche's Lecture Tour

The story of Ponca Chief Standing Bear and Omaha Nation citizen Susette La Flesche's lecture tour showcases both the carceral relations of the reservation and the steadfast Native resistance to those relations. The tour had its roots in the experience of the Ponca Nation, a smaller Native nation that lived on the plains west of the Mississippi River in the nineteenth century. In 1858, a treaty between the Ponca and the United States relegated the Ponca to a reservation in what is now called Nebraska. However, in 1868, a treaty between the Sioux and the United States ending the powerful Sioux Nation's armed resistance to settler-colonial encroachment included—apparently mistakenly—a provision that granted a major portion of the Ponca's land to the Sioux. The Sioux thereafter laid claim to the land and repeatedly raided Ponca settlements. These raids—primarily carried out by Brule Sioux but sometimes by Oglala Sioux—continued into the mid-1870s, placing the Ponca in constant fear.[52]

Aware of this situation but unwilling to antagonize the powerful Sioux, US federal agents arranged to move the Ponca from their current reservation to a reservation in Indian Territory, or what is now called Oklahoma. US impetus for the move lay not just in "humanitarian" considerations for the Ponca but also in the fact that it would enable US agencies better access to the more lucrative Sioux trade. The Ponca in general remained adamantly against the move to Indian Territory, but federal officials in Washington insisted. A minority of the Ponca did voluntarily leave with US agents in April 1877, but the majority remained. In response, the US government sent in federal troops, and the remaining group of over five hundred Ponca finally left in May in the face of this clear threat of force. Indeed, in the run-up to removal, troops arrested Standing Bear, who was outspoken in his opposition, and confined him at Fort Randall to prevent organized resistance.[53]

The Ponca suffered terribly on the monthslong journey; many got sick and died, including Standing Bear's daughter. Many more died after finally arriving on their new reservation in Indian Territory, as US officials had not made proper preparations for food and shelter. The Ponca eked out an existence as they tried to reestablish themselves, but conditions remained incredibly harsh, and approximately one hundred to two hundred died between 1877 and 1880.[54]

The experience of the Ponca reveals that even with the ascendancy of the reservation system, removals continued to occur. However, instead of removal to an undefined, amorphous territory west of the Mississippi River, the Ponca's removal was from one clearly defined reservation to another. And it was the more intense and systematic containment of the reservation that would most directly motivate Standing Bear and La Flesche's lecture tour. In January 1879, Standing Bear violated reservation policy by leading a group of twenty-nine Ponca members off the reservation in the middle of the night without permission from the reservation's agent. Their intention was to return to their homelands in Nebraska. Standing Bear's son had recently died, and he was determined to bury him in the Ponca's traditional lands. After an arduous journey, the band of fugitives eventually reached the Omaha reservation in early March, where the friendly Omaha tribe offered them land to resettle on.[55]

But the reservation system's carceral apparatus quickly caught up with the group. Word of their flight reached the secretary of the interior, who requested that the military arrest and then return the rogue Ponca to the Indian Territory reservation. Members of the Ninth Infantry duly arrested the Ponca and held them at Fort Omaha while preparing their return. But at this point, the Ponca's incarceration garnered the attention of a white journalist in Omaha, Thomas Tibbles. Tibbles interviewed the Ponca and, after hearing their story, took it upon himself to find them legal aid. He located two attorneys willing to take the Ponca's case, and they filed a petition for a writ of habeas corpus in federal court.[56]

The resulting court case, *Standing Bear v. Crook*, is a landmark in federal Indian law. The federal government strenuously defended the policy of confining Native peoples to their reservations. A key point of contention was Standing Bear's group's claim that they had severed their connection with the Ponca tribe and that, as such, the government could not keep them on a reservation. In other words, they were no longer members of a Native nation subject to the reservation. At trial, Standing Bear provided moving testimony about the Ponca's hardships and desire to return home. Highlighting the essential questions of movement involved in the case, he addressed Judge Elmer Dundy and said, "A man bars the passage [home]. . . . If he says that I cannot pass, I cannot." Standing Bear then paused, and concluded, "You are that man."[57]

Judge Dundy's subsequent decision on May 12, 1879, freed the Ponca from federal custody and established that Native peoples had a right to separate from their Native nations. Once separated, the US government could not confine them on reservations.[58] The case thus undercut the reservation system's carceral relations. Crucially, Native historical agency and mobility underlay this legal victory—it was the courageous decision of Standing Bear and his fellow Ponca to flee their designated reservation that was the catalyst for Dundy's decision.[59]

However, the victory had sharp limits. For one, the decision only licensed free Native movement off the reservation for Native people who formally renounced their Indian nationhood. The mobility of Native people still claiming affiliation with their tribe remained curtailed. Second, while Dundy found that the government had no right to send the Ponca back to Indian Territory, it still had the right to arrest and remove from a reservation any individuals deemed detrimental to the welfare of Native residents. Thus, the government could legally eject the Ponca from the Omaha reservation. And since US law still designated the Ponca's traditional homeland part of the Sioux reservation, Standing Bear and his compatriots had no legal right to live on or even enter it. The reservation's structure of containment therefore continued to constrain their movement.

This continued exclusion of the Ponca from their homelands sparked Standing Bear and La Flesche's lecture tour. Tibbles, the white journalist who helped publicize the Ponca's cause, suggested a lecture tour of the United States to Standing Bear with the goal of securing federal reinstatement of the Ponca's homelands. Standing Bear agreed to the tour, and Susette La Flesche, an Omaha citizen who had studied at the Elizabeth Institute for Young Ladies in New Jersey and was currently teaching at an Omaha reservation school, agreed to act as his translator. But La Flesche did not just translate—she became a regular speaker herself. Her uncle was a Ponca Nation citizen who had undergone removal, so she had a personal connection to the Ponca's plight. She quickly joined Standing Bear as a star attraction on the tour.[60]

The lecture tour, or lyceum, was a highly popular form of entertainment and education in the nineteenth century, and Standing Bear and La Flesche used the form to great effect. The lecture tour emerged as a recognized form in the 1830s, and by the 1850s, an estimated four hundred thousand people per week attended lectures across the country, both in large cities and in small towns, on a diverse range of topics. While audiences were predominantly, though not exclusively, white and middle class, newspapers regularly covered lecture circuit talks, thus spreading their content to a wider reading public. Indeed, Americans understood lectures as designed for popular audiences and educational self-improvement, although by the late nineteenth century it had also become a profitable commercial entertainment. La Flesche and Standing Bear sought to capitalize on this popular form to educate white audiences on the injustices done to the Ponca.[61]

Standing Bear and La Flesche's lecture tour subverted the reservation system's policies and practices of Native immobility in multiple ways. First, with the assistance of sympathetic whites, Standing Bear and La Flesche used the mobility of the lecture circuit to travel across the United States and build national support for the Ponca's cause. This movement both undermined the conceptual links between "savagery" and Native movement and defied the reservation's physical confinement. Additionally, Standing Bear and La Flesche's speeches called attention to and criticized the reservation's carceral features, overtly pushing back against their logic. These critiques reached wide audiences—the talks were well attended and the tour made a splash in the papers, which covered the lectures and rebroadcast Standing Bear and La Flesche's words to even larger audiences. Indeed, Standing Bear and La Flesche's success at generating public support directly overturned Secretary of the Interior Carl Schurz's prediction that if the *Standing Bear v. Crook* decision "should result in spreading among the Indians the impression that they can leave their places of abode and roam about at pleasure, the effect would only be disastrous to them."[62]

The tour kicked off in Chicago on October 19, 1879, before moving on to longer stints in Boston, New York City, and Philadelphia. In his speeches, Standing Bear exposed the federal government's coercive control of Native movement. Speaking in Boston, he said, "Soldiers force [*sic*] me from the land at the point of the bayonet. . . . 158 of my people died. . . . What crime did I commit that the soldier should make me go? You walk around and have perfect liberty. I should like to do the same." Standing Bear thus linked freedom of movement with freedom itself. Further, in rhetorically asking what "crime" the Ponca had committed, he also highlighted the carceral function of the reservation. Elaborating on this theme in the same speech, he stated, "When I fled from the Indian Territory the Government sent soldiers after me and arrested me on the Omaha reserve. Now I should like to know what I have done to deserve all this." He then closed with a metaphor capturing the reservation's carceral relations: "When we ask you for your help we wish you to open the door and set us free. You have the key."[63]

Standing Bear repeated these points in various forms throughout the lecture circuit. He also foregrounded the violence of reservation confinement with another vivid and personal anecdote. While on the lecture tour, soldiers shot and killed Standing Bear's brother, Big Snake, when he resisted arrest. The incident stemmed from a conflict over Big Snake leaving his reservation without a pass. His death starkly underscored the limits of the *Standing Bear v. Crook* decision. In his speeches, Standing Bear not only pointed out the brutal absurdity of the killing but also relayed the longer history of his brother's encounters with reservation confinement. Speaking in New York City, Standing Bear explained, "When I left the West I had a brother and sister. I thought as much of them, perhaps, as you do of yours. My brother was twice put in jail for trying to get back to his own home. Since we have been in the East he was shot by the soldiers, by the order of the agent, for trying to escape." Standing Bear's use of the word "escape" unmistakably identifies the reservation as a carceral space, one, in the Ponca's case, preventing their return home. He thus highlighted the violence of the reservation's carceral policies and the urgent need to dismantle them. "It is time," he pleaded, "such wrongs were righted quickly."[64]

La Flesche also publicized and condemned the reservation's spatiality of containment. She made it clear that, throughout the tour, she was haunted by the fear that the federal government would forcibly return her to the Omaha reservation. In an interview with the *Chicago Inter-Ocean*, La Flesche argued that the Fourteenth Amendment granted Native Americans basic civil rights, but that the federal government did not recognize this. To make her point, she asked her interviewer, "Have the United States authorities the legal privilege to come right into this room, arrest me, put me under guard of a soldier, and send me back to my reservation?" The interviewer found the suggestion ridiculous and laughed, but La Flesche admonished that the threat was real and "she did more than half expect to be turned over to a soldier, to be taken back before the day was over."[65]

La Flesche also emphasized the carceral aspects of the reservation system in her lectures. Her talks offered a plethora of critiques of US Indian policy, touching on the government's failure to uphold treaties, white settlers' greed for land, and the inhumane treatment of the Ponca. But a significant portion of her speeches attacked the reservation system and its enclosures. Reservation policy, La Flesche explained, told Native peoples "you must not pass beyond this line without the permission of this man, your agent, whom we place over you." Employing heavy sarcasm, she told audiences that this incarceration was "a lesson in freedom and liberty"—indeed, it was the "first lesson in the art of civilization." Like Standing Bear, she called attention to the absurd level of force upholding the reservation's boundaries. "It sounds like some strange story," she observed, that the powerful US government would send "its armed forces" to arrest and return Standing Bear's small group of Ponca men, women, and children. Yet this is exactly what federal officials did, employing such disproportionate force simply because the Ponca had "fled from that strange land, which meant death to [them], without permission from [their] master." Her words highlighted the inhumanity of reservation policy and the government's extreme dedication to upholding the impermeability of the reservation's borders.[66]

While on the lecture tour, La Flesche also penned an introduction to a book published by Tibbles on the government's dealings with the Ponca. In it, she wrote that Native Americans "ask for their liberty, and law is liberty." An article in the *New York Tribune* discussing the lecture tour and the forthcoming book reported that Tibbles was so taken with this line that he asked La Flesche how she came to it. La Flesche's answer highlighted the centrality of freedom of movement to her thinking on federal reservation policy and freedom in general. Sitting by a window, La Flesche gestured to the people below and said, "I see all people coming and going as they like; they can go to Europe if they like; that is being free; and it is because they have law to take care of them that they can go." Equating freedom of movement with the rule of law, La Flesche portrayed unrestricted movement as essential to justice and freedom and implicitly critiqued Indian peoples' captivity on the reservation.[67]

La Flesche's comments about the law and the extensions of its protections to Native peoples point to an important aspect of her political views. She was a stern critic of US Indian policy, but she also supported many assimilationist ideas. Her father, Joseph La Flesche, was an Omaha tribal leader who had embraced Christianity and saw providing a Western education for his children as vital to his family's survival in a changing world. As a result, Susette attended a missionary school on her reservation before going on to study at the Elizabeth Institute in New Jersey. This travel through assimilationist circuits, to the Eastern Seaboard and back, underlay La Flesche's later travels on the lecture tour. Constrained though it was by settler colonialism, her earlier travel provided skills—especially written and spoken command of English—that she later used to critique federal Indian policy. At the same time, La Flesche's education led her to embrace many aspects of assimilationism, which she subsequently advocated for in her lectures. In particular, she called for US citizenship for Native Americans and allotment of tribal lands to Native individuals. She felt that citizenship would secure the protection of the law and civil rights for Native peoples, alleviating their oppression and exploitation, and she saw individual ownership of land, with its attendant property rights under US law, as the best way to guarantee Native land possession. These views aligned with those of a growing number of white reformers, a development discussed in chapter 6.[68]

Nonetheless, for all her assimilationist impulses, La Flesche recognized the value of Indian culture and desired to preserve aspects of it. In 1883, she translated a number of Omaha childhood legends into English for the children's magazine *Wide Awake*, and in the introduction to the stories she lamented the potential loss of Indian culture.[69] Also, despite La Flesche's assimilationist trappings, the lecture tour offered incisive and radical critiques of US Indian policy. These critiques proved quite successful in achieving significant, though by no means complete, governmental redress. As a result of the publicity Standing Bear and La Flesche generated, Congress launched an investigation into the government's dealings with the Ponca. In particular, the lectures so moved Massachusetts Senator Henry Dawes, who had attended them in Boston, that he spearheaded calls for the federal investigation. Following congressional hearings, at which both Standing Bear and La Flesche testified in February 1880, marking the end of their tour, Congress provided $165,000 to the Ponca as restitution for their hardships and negotiated with the Sioux to allow the Ponca to reinhabit their traditional homelands.[70]

While Standing Bear and La Flesche's lecture tour circulated incisive critiques of the reservation's incarceration of Native peoples and helped the Ponca move back onto their former territory, it did not disrupt the reservation system's carceral relations in general. As chapter 6 shows, spatial containment remained central to the reservation throughout the nineteenth century, and Native Americans continued to resist its fetters. In fact, even as Standing Bear's court case got underway in 1879, a large movement of Americans from the South headed west to resettle in Kansas—the land Standing Bear's group of Ponca crossed in their escape back home—and it was settler colonialism and the reservation that made this movement possible. But because these Americans were Black, their western migration engendered intense white anxieties—anxieties that the Southern pastoral would help mediate.

Kansas Fever: Southern Pastoral Sheet Music and the Kansas Exodus

While the Southern pastoral's popularity reflected a nationwide angst among white Americans about free Black mobility, whites did not experience and express this angst in uniform ways. Responses to the Kansas Exodus—a Black migration movement from the South to Kansas in the late 1870s and early 1880s—exemplify the multivalent nature of white concerns about Black mobility. The exodus arose as a response to racial oppression in the South at the end of Reconstruction and triggered vigorous resistance from Southern whites, especially white planters. Demeaning the Black migration as "Kansas fever," Southern whites panicked at the thought of their labor supply suddenly disappearing into the West and tried to staunch the movement. Meanwhile, many Northern white republicans approved of the migration and reveled in Southern planters' agonized fretting, even as they themselves were far from eager to support Black migration to the North. But many Northern whites, especially white democrats, joined Southern whites in labeling the exodus irrational and misguided. Whites in Kansas itself remained, for the day, progressively ambivalent about the exodus.[71]

With the end of federal Reconstruction in 1877, Southern whites were able to accelerate their campaign to reassert white supremacy. Whites could now deploy extralegal violence to intimidate African Americans and prevent their political participation with less fear of federal reprisal. White Democratic legislators also passed laws granting planters greater control over the Black labor force. The sharecropping system, which came to predominate in Southern agriculture after the war, also kept African Americans economically subservient through perpetual indebtedness, and planters tightened the system's exploitative screws as Black political protections evaporated following the North's abandonment of Reconstruction. In addition, a racist system of convict leasing arose throughout the South that doled out the labor of Black prisoners arrested under vagrancy laws or falsely convicted of crimes.[72]

In the face of this resurging racial oppression, many rural African Americans began contemplating migration out of the South. What contemporaries termed the exodus and what generated the most public attention were the Black migrations to Kansas in the years 1879–80, involving roughly six thousand African Americans.[73] Crucially, white efforts to clamp down on Black mobility following the end of Reconstruction helped precipitate this grassroots movement. Alongside poor labor conditions, racial violence, and exploitative wages, the reestablishment of the pass system motivated support for the exodus among African Americans in Louisiana, where, in 1878, a number of parishes in the state began to again require African Americans to carry passes when traveling on public roads. Local Black communities perceived this reinstatement of the pass system as a clear sign that whites intended to revive slavery, and it galvanized their efforts to leave and head for Kansas.[74]

Once the exodus was underway, Southern whites attempted to sabotage and impede it at every turn. To dissuade those still in the South from migrating, white newspapers reported that Kansas politicians did not want the migrants in their state—an untrue claim, since, as previously noted, Kansas officials were ambivalent about the migrants—and printed letter after letter from supposed Black migrants in Kansas who were unhappy with their lot. The white press also ridiculed the Exodusters, as they were called, portraying them as ignorant about conditions in Kansas and pointing out that many of them could not afford to pay for the journey. Taking more direct action, planters also paid Black recruiters to infiltrate migrant camps and talk up their plantations in an attempt to entice migrants to stay.[75]

In addition to subterfuge, Southern whites used physical violence to intimidate migrants and prevent them from leaving. However, the tactic that most effectively broke the exodus's momentum ended up being the refusal of steamboat companies to carry migrants up the Mississippi River. Following the companies' ban on ferrying migrants in April 1879, Exodusters began piling up on the shores of the Mississippi, at times in camps of 150 to 300 people. Colluding in the effort to stop the exodus, white merchants refused to sell the migrants food, and white officials harassed and disbanded the camps. With migrants slowly starving on the banks of the Mississippi, the exodus largely subsided by the summer, despite the fact that steamboat companies once more began to offer migrants passage after Republican officials threatened lawsuits under the Civil Rights Act of 1875.[76] These drastic coordinated efforts by Southern whites, especially white planter elites, reveal the profound anxieties Black mobility could engender and the integral role labor demands played in these worries in the South.

Indeed, the event's racial tremors were large enough to extend to popular culture. The Kansas Exodus became the subject of a number of songs, which incorporated the exodus into Southern pastoral narratives, discursively containing the migration's subversive movement and illustrating the Southern pastoral's flexibility and sensitivity to events unfolding on the ground. For example, "Going from de Cotton Fields" (1879) perverted the causes of the migration, rendering it a mournful undertaking forced on Black participants by tough economic times. The Black male narrator of the song informs the audience that "I's gone and jined de 'Exodus' dats making for de norf," but confesses, "I's going from de cotton fields, / And oh! it makes me sigh." Having heard that Black people received better pay in Kansas, he feels he must try his luck there, since "de times hab got so hard." The song fully absolves whites of racial violence—the narrator tends to his former master's grave and worries about its neglect in his absence. While the narrator feels he must leave, his wife wishes to stay, saying she "don't believe" the stories about the work and pay. The song thus complicates the Southern pastoral, showing a South of agricultural languish rather than superabundance. Nonetheless, it maintains the myth of the South as a racial paradise and suggests African Americans were unadvisedly migrating based on unsubstantiated rumors. Its main thrust is thus against Black movement, and the opening line "I's going from de cotton fields, I's going from de cane" makes it clear that the uprooting of the Black body from the landscape is the primary source of sorrow in the song.[77]

In contrast to "Going from de Cotton Fields," the images of incompetent Black mobility in the 1880 song "Am Dis Kansas?" offered no such complications. The younger Black male narrator of the song has left his home in Alabama, where he "spent a many bright and happy day," to travel to Kansas. But he soon regrets his decision. Left "lonely tramping on de prairie," he gets lost and has to ask the white people he passes, "Tell me, white man, am dis Kansas, / Where de darkies come to play?" The song's implication that African Americans are emigrating to Kansas "to play" reaffirms Black laziness and evacuates the political, economic, and racial calculations that informed Black migration. The narrator ends up destitute on the prairie, where he "plow[s] up de ground among de stubble." In iconic carry-me-back fashion, he pines for the Southern terrain, saying, "How I long to see de blooming fields again, / And de mansion where old Massa used to dwell, / But 'tis now in dreams alone I see de places." The dream of Kansas now deflated and replaced by dreams of home, his existence on the plains is bleak. Other songs about the exodus reinforced these themes.[78]

These cultural eruptions stemming from the Kansas Exodus highlight the extensive geographic bounds of white anxieties about Black mobility. Again, it is important not to overstate Northern white concerns about the exodus—many Republicans came out in support of the Exodusters, although they were motivated in large part by political considerations involving white repression of African American voters in the South, who were overwhelmingly Republican.[79] But Northern white Democrats remained highly critical of the Black migrants, and the appearance of songs belittling the movement reflects the widespread acceptance of such views among Northern white audiences.[80]

The Kansas Exodus and its perversion in sheet music also attest to the importance of approaching issues of race and mobility in the nineteenth century through a transregional lens. It was the dispossession of Native American lands on the western plains that enabled African Americans to use westward migration as a tool for resisting white oppression in the South. Thus, as white supremacy reasserted itself in the South after emancipation, African Americans migrating to Kansas participated in the settler-colonial process eroding Native sovereignty and land rights in the West. This migration then reverberated throughout the North, surfacing in the content of sheet music. The Exoduster movement thus compactly exposes the dense historical entanglements existing between events occurring in the South, West, and North in this Greater Reconstruction period.[81]

Placing postbellum Southern pastoral sheet music alongside Chief Standing Bear and Susette La Flesche's lecture tour shows that Greater Reconstruction's racial upheavals and structural changes registered in popular culture of the era. It also shows that popular culture was a contested site that various visions of racial mobility struggled over, as Standing Bear and La Flesche used popular culture to resist and critique the reservation's carceral relations, whereas Southern pastoral sheet music reflected white fears about free Black movement in a postemancipation society. Indeed, while federal officials had firmly adopted the reservation system as the country's dominant Indian policy by the 1860s, white Americans were just beginning to deal with the aftermath of slavery's dissolution in the South and the possibilities of Black movement it engendered. But the imagery of Black stasis in Southern pastoral songs of the 1870s and 1880s helped lay the ideological groundwork for white Americans' reworking of slavery's relations of containment into the national structure of Jim Crow segregation in the 1890s and 1900s.

And the Southern pastoral would not be alone in telegraphing that white supremacy and social order depended on the immobile Black body. The book's remaining chapters detail multiple forms of popular culture that arose post-1880 to assault the idea of free Black movement. One was a new genre of sheet music called the "coon song." Exploding into the most popular form of music in the 1890s, "coon songs" emphasized in starkly racist terms the dangers of unfettered Black movement, particularly in the city. However, as chapter 4 also shows, African Americans consistently spoke back to such representations, seizing the circuits of the popular culture industry to demonstrate their professionalism and talent, and to foster their own geographic movement.

CHAPTER FOUR

Consolidation and Contestation

Popular Culture, Segregation, and Black Resistance, 1880–1900

On Christmas Eve, 1898, the Indianapolis *Freeman*, a leading Black newspaper, reprinted a rousing message from Clifford D. Brooks, a Black musician touring with John Vogel's Mastodon Minstrels. "Mr. Lawrence Chenault, J. Gibson, Geo. Bailey, Gil Garay, H. La She, Chas. B. Tyler and Clifford Brooks [made] a flying trip to New York City Wednesday eve. the 6th," Clifford's missive began. They were "on mere pleasure bent and all had a high old time." After visiting "several places of note," they "all went to the Douglass Club where they met some of the members of the [entertainment] profession and . . . had a hearty shaking of the hand." "You can guess the rest," Brooks stated slyly, "as we did not go home until morning." He then quickly trumpeted the show's successes, remarking, "Master Willie Shields is making a big hit with his gun spinning at each performance," and "the daily papers at Troy, spoke very highly of Mr. Lawrence Chenault, tenor soloist." He ended with a playful "The boys send regards to Dooley Alexander."[1]

Part gossip, part advertising, and part lighthearted fun, Brooks's letter may, at first glance, appear to be merely a creative way of publicizing a musical act. However, as a historical document it reveals far more, speaking to the ways that popular culture created avenues for Black geographic and economic mobility in a rapidly industrializing United States. Allowed a limited participation in the music and theater industries of the late nineteenth century, Black performers made the most of these opportunities, forming professional networks that, like their travels, spanned the country.

But even as African Americans made inroads into the entertainment industry, new forms of popular culture emerged to undermine Black equality and freedom of movement. While Southern pastoral music remained incredibly popular in the last two decades of the nineteenth century, its spatial lesson was being echoed in the new musical genre known as "coon songs," which sprang up in the mid-1880s. I argue that the songs in this genre represent the reverse side of the mobility coin, portraying unrestrained Black mobility—particularly in urban settings—as producing sexual and criminal disorder. In this way, coon songs reinvigorated and updated the themes of disorderly

Black mobility found in early blackface minstrelsy. While on their surface coon songs and Southern pastorals appear highly dissimilar—coon songs with their tales of explicit violence and moral laxity, and Southern pastorals with their imagery of demure Blackness—they were in fact highly complementary. One showed the racial and social chaos attending the mobile Black body, while the other showed the harmonious, white supremacist relations attending the rooted Black body. Circulating alongside each other, they offered white Americans a powerful lesson about the need to constrain Black mobility in order to ensure white social control.

This double-barreled racial lesson was linked to a major shift in Black-white relations occurring at the turn of the twentieth century. As white Americans in the 1890s and early 1900s enacted Jim Crow laws in the South and began to institute large-scale residential segregation in all regions of the country, nationally circulating—and primarily Northern-authored—Southern pastoral and coon song sheet music helped spark and then reinforce this rising Jim Crow segregation.[2] Another centerpiece of Greater Reconstruction's racial project, Jim Crow segregation renovated slavery's geography of containment and joined the Indian reservation as a system clamping down on nonwhite mobility. Popular music both helped produce this development and provided a lens onto the white anxieties driving its emergence.

At the same time that popular music helped generate the turn toward Jim Crow, Black musicians and performers in the last decades of the nineteenth century harnessed newly available opportunities in the popular music industry to subvert and contest racist images and ideas about Black mobility. While Black musicians and performers had to engage in racist stereotypes to survive in an industry largely beholden to the demands of white audiences, publishing companies, and theater owners, they nonetheless consciously cast their participation in the entertainment industry as a direct refutation of white ideas about Black inferiority. Paradoxically, white desires to see Black performers enacting racist stereotypes that ridiculed Black movement created opportunities for African Americans to put themselves in motion through the circuits of capitalism and consumer culture.

In this chapter, I demonstrate that the Black popular press seized on popular music to fashion a counternarrative that emphasized and celebrated the geographic mobility of Black musicians and actors. Examining the Indianapolis *Freeman*—one of the largest Black newspapers of the period—I show that one of its recurring sections, titled "The Stage," provided consistent and detailed coverage of the extensive travels and economic successes of Black musical shows.[3] It also provided a forum for Black entertainers themselves to write about and report on their movements and latest professional triumphs. The *Freeman* thus crafted an alternative spatial narrative to the invective against Black mobility found in Southern pastorals and coon songs, a narrative that then circulated via the *Freeman*'s national distribution network. This national reach makes the *Freeman* an ideal source for examining the impact of the Black press and Black artists on constructions of racial mobility. Even though Black musicians and artists often contributed to the spread of the Southern pastoral and coon songs by performing and producing such works in concession to white expectations, the *Freeman*'s coverage created a spatial imaginary that made the mobility of Black cultural producers a communal experience and a point of race pride. My work here thus adds to existing scholarship showing that African Americans leveraged the mass culture industry to further their economic and social advancement and were intimate participants in a cosmopolitan, capitalist modernity.[4]

Evolutions

In the late nineteenth century, ideas about segregation in popular culture spread with increased speed and volume thanks to advances in the production and distribution of sheet music. Technological improvements drove this increase, as expanding railroads in the postbellum era facilitated greater distribution, while faster printing presses and cheaper paper drove down prices. The drop in sheet music prices meant the demise of song sheets, as sheet music became more affordable for all classes. Cheaper color printing also made sheet music even more desirable to consumers, as publishing companies rolled out greater numbers of attractive, eye-catching cover illustrations. Likewise, innovations in advertising enlarged the market for sheet music. In one particularly effective method, songwriters and publishers began selling their material to popular minstrel and vaudeville artists, who, thanks to improved railroad connections, would then tour the country popularizing the songs and generating demand for sheet music versions.[5]

As demand for popular songs rose, music retailers, who before sold sheet music as just one of their musical wares, increasingly began to sell it exclusively. Furthermore, in order to increase readership, newspapers in the 1890s began publishing sheet music as inserts, making it even more accessible and widespread. The 1890s also saw the music publishing industry consolidate on Twenty-Eighth Street in New York City, spawning what became known as Tin Pan Alley. A veritable factory of popular music hits, Tin Pan Alley companies focused on more standardized musical styles and lyrical content to maximize the appeal of their songs. This centralizing of the music industry was accompanied by a rise in the number of American homes with pianos, especially in the 1890s, when piano sales grew 5.6 times as fast as the country's population.[6] On all these material bases, the ideologies of Black (im)mobility found in sheet music spread, paradoxically promoting the containment of Black bodies on the ground.

Meanwhile, throughout the 1880s and 1890s, the Southern pastoral continued to be a major theme in sheet music. Many new songs were published during the decade, and old minstrel favorites were repeatedly performed and still widely known. Changes did occur in the Southern pastoral's presentation. The carry-me-back that had been so dominant receded in popularity by the mid-1880s. It was replaced by the Southern lullaby song, which also initiated an increased focus on Black women, especially through the character of "mammy," and Black children. Like the prior focus on the aged Black man, these images offered safe visions of the intraracial nuclear Black family, defusing white concerns about interracial sex and circumventing the threatening connotations—both sexual and political—of younger Black men. Throughout these changes, the Southern pastoral's theme of Black containment remained constant.

For example, the smash hit "Little Alabama Coon," written in 1893, takes a Black child as its subject. In stereotypical dialect, the child announces, "I's a little Alabama Coon! / And I has'nt been born very long; / I 'member seein' a great big round moon! / . . . When dey tote me down to de cotton field, / Dar I roll and I tumble in de sun! / While my daddy pick de cotton, mammy watch me grow." The lyrics tap into Americans' yearnings to be closer to nature through the infantilized pleasure of "roll[ing]" and "tumbl[ing]" in "de sun," and simultaneously affiliate the Black infant with the surrounding landscape. The Black child's first memories are of nature, from a "big round moon" to playing in the cotton fields, and his comfort and pleasure in the fields suggests a natural fluency with the Southern environment. Deepening the link, his "mammy" watches him "grow" under the sun while his father picks cotton. Just another natural outcropping, he is fated to live out life in his native environment. Alongside this naturalization, the nuclear Black family takes center stage in the narrative and similarly assumes a quality of fate, with the child proclaiming that once grown up, "I's gwine to wed a yellow gal, / Den we'll hab picaninnys ob our own!" Born within the bounds of proper Black sexuality, the infant will never stray from those bounds, as he grows up to re-create the intraracial nuclear family in an automatic and natural cycle.[7]

"Little Alabama Coon" also features the key figure of mammy. As scholar Tara McPherson explains, "mammy" could be a highly contradictory figure in American culture. Sometimes whites presented her as beastly, while at other times she embodied motherhood writ large, facilitating white fantasies of a return to childhood.[8] Southern pastoral sheet music most often mobilized the mammy stereotype in the latter sense.[9] In the pastoral contexts, mammy also provided an ideal vehicle for conveying the claim of harmonious race relations produced by the rooted Black body. Focusing on mammy allowed songwriters not only to elide Black male sexuality but also to imbue compositions with a broad sense of safety through the motherly figure. "Mammy's Carolina Twins (Southern Lullaby)," published in 1899, illustrates this role:

> It was down in South Car'lina,
> Where the Southern moon was shining,
> And the mocking birds sing sweetly in the trees:
> In an ivy cover'd cottage,
> Whar de honeysuckle's creeping,
> Lives Aunt Jennie and her Carolina Twins.
> It was four o'clock dat morning,
> When de roosters, they were crowing,
> And de silv'ry moon had gone to rest;
> It was dar dem twins were born,
> Just befo' de break of dawn, in dere Mammy's Southern nest.

The central character in this lullaby is the Southern environment itself. The initial lines are devoted solely to limning the setting, and they reiterate the beauty of the terrain. Nature has reclaimed the "ivy cover'd cottage" with its "creeping" honeysuckle, and the description of the cottage as a "nest" reinforces this naturalization. Within this litany of scenic descriptions, the song announces the birth of the "Carolina twins," suggesting that the Black children are but one of the Southern fauna—they will grow in their "nest" and remain in their habitat under the nurturing eye of mammy. The scene also quietly evacuates Black fatherhood and Black male sexuality.[10]

Again, avoidance of younger Black men was not an absolute rule in Southern pastoral songs. While such tunes certainly displayed a tendency to circumvent Black male sexuality through the figures of the older Black man and mammy, young Black men were not beyond the Southern pastoral's pacifying reach. For example, the cover illustration to the instrumental dance number "Honey in the Cornfield" (1899) broadcasts one of the more explicit visions of the Black body as landscape (see figure 4.1). It shows a Black man sitting in

FIGURE 4.1 Cover illustration to G. M. Blandford, "Honey in the Cornfield" (Boston: Vivian, 1899). Courtesy of the Sixto Campano Collection, Broward County Library.

front of a log cabin, strumming a banjo and smiling at a Black woman standing in a cornfield off to the right. She is the "honey in the cornfield," and she gazes impassively back at the man. She wears a long skirt that reaches all the way to the ground, and its large yellow-and-black plaid pattern makes it identical to a shucked ear of corn. With her white apron intervening at the waist, it appears as if the woman's top half has sprouted directly out of a large piece of corn stuck upright in the earth. The woman's shirt continues the allusion with its yellow-on-white plaid design. She reaches out and rests her hand lightly on a nearby cornstalk, telegraphing her equivalence with the crops, and her blank expression reinforces her static condition. The Black man, too, is affiliated with the landscape, though not in as extreme a manner. He is dressed entirely in yellow, and his plaid pants, like the woman's outfit, invoke an ear of corn. Intraracial Black sexual desires are thus once again tethered to immobile Black bodies.[11]

Old standards romanticizing the South remained well known and continued to be performed in the 1890s as well. Newspaper articles from across the country that covered society parties, Civil War veteran reunions, theatrical performances, and other public events demonstrate the steadfast popularity of past Southern pastoral hits—especially those of Stephen Foster.[12] In one particularly revealing episode, the New York Southern Society, a group formed by Southern whites living in New York City to foster community and "southern culture," printed a program for its ninth annual dinner in 1895 that included the lyrics to Foster's 1853 song "My Old Kentucky Home, Good Night." Significantly, the program printed only the first two verses of the song, excising the third verse that complicated the Southern pastoral with its indictment of the slave trade, as discussed in chapter 3. The program thus revised the iconic standard in a way that enhanced its Southern pastoralism.[13]

The New Jim Crow: Coon Songs, Criminality, and the Condemnation of Urban Black Mobility

While the Southern pastoral continued to evolve, a new genre of sheet music emerged that was to become the most popular form of music over the last decade of the nineteenth century: the coon song. Referring to songs that predominantly used the term "coon" in conjunction with Black caricatures of all types, coon songs began appearing in significant numbers in the mid-1880s before exploding into a full-fledge phenomenon in the 1890s.[14] Music companies published thousands of the songs, and some sold copies in the millions.[15] Coon songs were in fact not entirely distinct from the Southern pastoral; many coon songs were also Southern pastorals, as the song "Little Alabama Coons" illustrates.[16]

However, many other coon songs reinvigorated early minstrel sheet music's lampooning of Black men—especially the urban dandy figure, with his class pretensions. While rooted in the blackface minstrel tradition, coon songs featured an intensified racist imagery that set them apart from their cultural forebears. Indeed, coon songs represent the height of racist vitriol in sheet music. In this regard, they index the larger shift in white supremacy in this period toward more extreme racism, or what Joel Williamson has termed "Racial Radicalism." Heavily informed by the rise of scientific racism, this increased anti-Blackness led historian Rayford W. Logan to label the late 1880s and 1890s the "nadir" of race relations.[17] In keeping with this historical shift, coon songs took minstrelsy to new lows. As historian James H. Dormon details, coon songs showed African Americans as gamblers, drunks, lascivious degenerates, and "razor-wielding savages" susceptible to outbursts of violence at any moment.[18] While Black women faced these stereotypes, Black men bore the brunt of them. As music scholar Sam Dennison remarks, "The relentless attack on Black manhood [in coon songs] was seemingly endless."[19]

Coon songs constitute the reverse side of the containment coin, the geographic, gender, and racial mirror of the Southern pastoral's controlled social relations. Non-Southern pastoral coon songs were primarily set in urban spaces, and it is in the city, the songs suggest, that the latent violence and criminality in Blackness emerge. In particular, coon songs portray unrestricted Black movement within the city as producing and enabling Black violence and criminality. The urban Black (male) body that slips the bounds of containment is a racial threat that must be put back in its proper social place and space through ridicule and discursive violence.

In their excoriation of urban Black mobility, coon songs reanimated early blackface minstrelsy's concern with Black male movement (examined in chapter 1) and took such fears to obsessive new heights. In the 1840s, minstrel acts had largely abandoned raucous imagery of Black urban disorder to conform to middle-class standards of propriety and thus broaden their consumer base. Minstrel shows and sheet music publishers then avoided such unruly themes for much of the next four decades. But by the late nineteenth century, the strictures of Victorian morality had begun to soften.[20] Further, while women remained the primary audience for sheet music, it became much more common for middle-class men to learn and play the piano, divorcing sheet music from its associations with Victorian femininity. Certainly, coon songs did not avoid scandal—a debate played out in magazines and newspapers of the day about their appropriateness and merit. But on the whole, Americans of all classes and genders proved quite willing to purchase and play them.[21]

One of the new violent motifs that coon songs introduced was the stereotype of the razor-wielding African American. The stereotype coalesced in part from the association of Black men with barbering.[22] But razors also made an ideal weapon for the urban tales of coon songs—they were easy to conceal and cheap to purchase. The razor would become the choice method for enacting fantasies of punishing the unrestrained Black body in coon songs. For example, the 1885 song "De Coon Dat Had de Razor" gives a voyeuristic account of violence inflicted on the Black male body:

I went to a ball de other night,
At Susie Simpkin's hut,
Where dem coons all carry razors;
And how dem niggers cut.
Ole Horace Jinks got in a row with slew foot John-y Frazier.
. . . .
He carved poor Johny's coat tail off,
Den cut him to de fat:
He cut his ear clear off his head,
Den cut his beaver hat.
Aunt Hannah said, "for gracious sake you'll kill poor Johny Frazier."
But de coon he didn't notice her,
But slashed on wid de razor.
. . . .
De coons came flying down de stairs,
De gals all hollored murder
Den Johny Frazier he fell down
He couldn't go no furder
Den Horace started for de mokes,
And ole policeman Haiser said "I 'aint gwine to touch dat coon,
For he has got a razor."

Here, Black pretense to the high-society customs of a "ball" and wearing "coat tails" meets with brutal derision, as Black society collapses under its own violence.[23]

The song's cover illustration emphasizes the danger Black masculinity poses in the urban environment (see figure 4.2). The image shows a city street with a Black man in the foreground glaring menacingly at the viewer in a stance of defiance. In his right hand shines a massive razor, open and ready for use. The cover mocks Black aspiration to social refinement by portraying the man in the dandy stereotype: his flashy striped pants, garish bow tie, and overly high collar all convey absurdity. Paired with the razor, the caricature reminds viewers that African American men, no matter their class pretensions, never escape their violent nature. Driving home the pervasiveness of Black violence, even the words of the title are formed by razors. In the background, a group of Black men flee in panic across an urban street in one direction, while a white police officer turns and runs in the other. The inability of

FIGURE 4.2 Cover illustration to William F. Quown and Sam Lucas, "De Coon Dat Had de Razor" (Boston: White, Smith, 1885). Courtesy of the James Francis Driscoll Collection of American Sheet Music, The Newberry Library.

the police to maintain order and punish Black transgression suggests to listeners that urban Black deviance requires some form of social control beyond the normal institutions, and the cover image makes plain that Black men threaten public safety and upset authority. In their presence, city streets become a site of danger rather than civility.

The street constituted a key locus in coon songs, acting invariably as a setting for Black deviance.[24] "I'm the Toughest, Toughest Coon" typifies the theme:

> I'm the toughest, toughest coon that walks the street,
> You may search the wide, wide world my equal never meet;

I got a razor in my boot, I got a gun with which to shoot,
I'm the toughest, toughest coon that walks the street.

"Walk[ing] the street" lies at the nexus of the threat the Black man poses here. His unchecked mobility is integral to the atmosphere of danger, generating an unpredictability that drives the fear and fascination of the lyrics. "May Irwin's 'Bully' Song," one of the most popular coon songs of the 1890s, similarly finds Black movement at the heart of the narrative:

I's gwine down the street with my ax in my hand,
I'm lookin' for dat bully and I'll sweep him off dis land,
I'm a lookin' for dat bully and he must be found.
I'll take 'long my razor, I'se gwine to carve him deep,
And when I see dat bully, I'll lay him down to sleep.
I'm lookin' for dat bully and he must be found.

The dangerous Black male roaming "down the street" and "lookin'" for a fight embodies moral and social disorder, and his unpredictable and uncontrolled movements are instrumental to the song's underlying racial fear.[25]

May Irwin, one of a cadre of white female "coon shouters" who burst onto the vaudeville stage in the 1890s, played a large role in the success of the song. Impersonating the Black narrator without blackface, Irwin captivated white audiences through the juxtaposition between her white female body and her performance of Black masculinity, which both fascinated and amused her spectators.[26] An 1898 review of Irwin's performance in the *New York Times* succinctly captures these elements and illuminates the key role of the urban street as a qualifier for Blackness: "The spectacle of a plump, good-natured, blonde (or light-haired) woman in evening dress transforming herself, without aid of make-up or accessories, into a wicked colored person of the streets, is as startling and, seemingly, as gratifying to the public taste as ever."[27]

It was also on the street that the oversexed Black female flourished. The 1893 song "On the Sunny Side of Thompson Street (Away Down Town)" invokes the racial anarchy of miscegenation through the "yellow" sexually promiscuous mixed-race woman:

Now white folk, keep on the shady side when you're trav'ling around;
Don't talk lo[u]d, but keep your eye on the crow'd on the Sunny side
 of Thompson Street, away down town.
Oh, it's there you'll find a razor with a nigger on the handle,
Day and night he's full of fight, you can't [keep] him down;

A yellow wench sits on a bench a making all the scandal,
On the sunny side of Thompson Street, away down town.

In the song, sexual "scandal" accompanies Black dominance of the street. Significantly, the lyrics overtly state the need for spatial distance between the races to ensure the physical and moral safety of whites. The "crow'd" of African Americans, with their disorderly and uncontrolled behavior, have taken over city space and must therefore be segregated to protect whites from Black danger. The song conveys a sense of loss of control over urban space, with the sexually unrestrained mixed-race woman and the violent young Black man as the beachheads of Black urban disorder.[28]

The national popularity of coon songs stemmed from a number of sources. For one, images of free Black deviance meshed with the racist narratives that Southern whites spun to justify their reassertion of white supremacy in the postbellum era. But more specifically, white fears about Black Americans in urban areas spiked at the end of the nineteenth century. Black migration to urban areas had been growing ever since the Civil War, but the 1890s saw a large increase in Northern Black urbanization, with some 174,000 African Americans leaving the South during the decade, and 197,000 following from 1900 to 1910.[29] As African Americans traveled north to take advantage of the industrial job market and escape violent oppression in the South, race relations strained between white and Black residents in cities across the North. Also beginning in the 1890s, Northern industrialists began using African Americans as strikebreakers in conflicts with white labor unions, a tactic that greatly exacerbated race relations. Most of this competition over labor occurred with newly arriving Eastern and Southern European immigrants, themselves subject to intense questioning of their racial fitness.[30]

The spike in Black migrants to Northern urban centers in the 1890s greatly affected Northern whites' racial views. As historian Marcy Sacks demonstrates in her study of New York City, these early African American newcomers to the urban North—and the specter of future Black migration they conjured—sparked fears in white communities about Black migration and its threat to white social dominance.[31] Likewise, Southern whites also had concerns about Black migration. For Southern elites, these primarily involved the loss of Black labor, as chapter 3's analysis of the Kansas Exodus highlighted. But Southern cities also saw their Black populations grow significantly in the last two decades of the century, and this rising urban Black population deeply troubled Southern whites as well.[32] Coon songs about urban African Americans thus reflected these nationwide white anxieties.[33]

Furthermore, just as with the Southern pastoral, coon songs about urban African Americans also registered white fears about free Black movement, particularly in the city. In fact, the logic of coon songs set in urban spaces worked in tandem with the Southern pastoral to produce a powerful lesson for white audiences: Black bodies had to be spatially contained to generate peaceful race relations—that is, white social control. Thus, the seemingly contradictory images of demure African Americans in Southern pastorals and sexually and criminally deviant African Americans in coon songs in fact harbored a deeply complementary and coherent racial and spatial message. Where the Southern pastoral testified that the immobile Black body produced harmonious racial hierarchy, coon songs about urban African Americans implied that the mobile Black body led to social and sexual breakdown. Indeed, this dyad simply updates in more elaborate terms the linked minstrel figures of the contented slave and the unfit-for-freedom urban dandy. It also echoes the symbiotic relationship between images of Black Americans as children under slavery and savages outside it that historian George M. Fredrickson has identified in proslavery ideology.[34]

The explosion in popularity of both Southern pastorals and coon songs in the late nineteenth century occurred at a critical juncture in the history of segregation in the West, North, and South. In the South, the 1890s saw Jim Crow laws coalesce and gain constitutional sanction with the Supreme Court's 1896 decision in *Plessy v. Ferguson*. Across the West and North, racial tensions mounted steadily in the face of sharply rising Black migration, eventually triggering whites to implement large-scale ghetto segregation at the start of the twentieth century. These developments were not preordained. Although segregationist practices predate the Civil War, in the interregnum between the end of slavery and the consolidation of Jim Crow at the turn of the century, Black-white race relations were open to alternative arrangements.[35] Throughout this transitional period, the Southern pastoral's naturalization of the immobile Black body worked to reaffirm and point the ideological way toward Jim Crow segregation laws and ghettoization, both of which imposed spatial containment. The Southern pastoral not only reflected white concerns about Black mobility but also broadcast and disseminated the notion that white supremacist relations followed Black immobility. Meanwhile, the dangerous mobility imputed to urban African Americans in coon songs only sharpened the Southern pastoral's spatial lesson. Thus, these two genres of sheet music offered an ideological blueprint that simultaneously gestured toward and buttressed efforts at segregation. This is of course not to argue that sheet music was the sole cause of segregation; rather, it is to contend that in an era when Jim Crow segregation and ghettoization were far from inevitable, sheet music constituted one site where Americans encountered and acquired ideas about race and mobility, helping produce the turn to Jim Crow across the country.[36]

Black Routes: Representations of Popular Music and Black Movement in the Indianapolis *Freeman*

While late nineteenth-century popular music undermined Black mobility by amplifying white fears and encouraging the development of Jim Crow segregation, it also paradoxically opened up avenues for Black movement. As sheet music production and distribution networks expanded in the final decades of the nineteenth century, zipping images endorsing Black immobility around the country as never before, African American artists commandeered and repurposed these networks to facilitate their geographic, as well as social and economic, movement. They also joined a conversation arising in the pages of the Black press to publicly cast their success in the entertainment industry as a point of racial pride and as evidence refuting assertions of Black inferiority.

This was particularly the case in the Indianapolis *Freeman*, one of the largest Black newspapers of the period. The editors of the *Freeman* and Black artists themselves crafted a racial counternarrative that highlighted Black artists' geographic mobility, making it an implicit aspect of a larger claim that African American entertainers were active participants in modern American society. By creating a public forum that presented Black mobility as respectable and pervasive, the *Freeman* fostered a spatial imaginary that allowed all members of the Black community to identify with, and take pride in, the movements of Black artists as if they were their own. This communal vision of Black mobility then itself traversed the nation through the *Freeman*'s extensive distribution network.

Examining representations of Black entertainers in the *Freeman*'s reoccurring series "The Stage," this section adds to the work of scholars who have demonstrated that African Americans were vital contributors to late nineteenth-century US cultural life. Far from being premodern, as the prevailing racial thought of the times asserted, African Americans were thoroughly modern subjects.[37] Examining "The Stage" also reveals that many African Americans recognized the subversive and transgressive potential of Black artists' travels, and the *Freeman* recorded and then hitched those movements to an antiracist, antisegregationist politics.

Following the closure in 1823 of New York City's Black-owned African Grove Theater, a venture that garnered a large white following but also met with repeated white violence, African Americans found themselves ejected—with some minor exceptions—from mainstream entertainments in the antebellum era.[38] Instead, white men masquerading as African Americans held a monopoly on representations of Blackness in popular music. Shortly after the Civil War, Black performers made inroads into the popular music business when white-managed minstrel shows began to hire Black performers in order to market their acts as more authentic. This move toward authenticity in minstrelsy opened the door for African American musicians and performers, but only at the cost of their participation in blackface stereotypes. In the late 1870s and early 1880s, James Bland, discussed in chapter 3, became the first Black songwriter to achieve large-scale success, and while he did insert subversive content into his songs, he was also beholden to many of the racist strictures of the day. Other Black minstrel performers, such as Billy Kersands, also achieved success, but they likewise had to conform to the racist demands of white audiences. Black musicians and performers would face the same dilemma throughout the late nineteenth century: While popular entertainment offered an escape from the menial, low-wage jobs that the racist labor market so often shunted African Americans into, it also required them to perpetuate racial stereotypes.[39]

As the 1880s and 1890s arrived, Black artists became more numerous and commonplace, with not only Black men but also Black women achieving success in popular music and theater. Figures such as Sam Lucas, Ernest Hogan, Sissieretta "Black Patti" Jones, Ada Overton Walker, Bob Cole, J. Rosamond Johnson, James Weldon Johnson, George Walker, and Bert Williams were all part of a growing list of successful Black entertainers of the period. And Black artists did not simply roll over to racist white demands. As a number of outstanding scholarly works have demonstrated, Black musicians and performers regularly included coded, subversive content in their songs that was discernible to Black audiences but illegible to white ones. They were thus able to covertly build in resistance to racism while still appeasing white audiences and industry gatekeepers.[40] As scholar David Krasner writes, "Countercodes, innuendos, and subtle shifts in emphasis" were the means by which African American entertainers "play[ed] against the grain of restrictive racial codes."[41]

One song that scholars have discussed for its resistant double meaning but that bears further analysis here given its commentary on Black movement and segregation is Bob Cole and Billy Johnson's "No Coons Allowed!" (1897).

Billed as comedy, the song was part of Cole and Johnson's musical *A Trip to Coontown*, offering white audiences what on the surface appeared to be a farcical story about a Black man's inflated social expectations:

There's a dead swell gentleman of color
Saved up all the money he could find
He call'd one night and said to his baby
"My Lulu gal we'll go and cut a shine"
He put her in a cab and told the driver
"To drive us to the swellest place in town
I'm gwine to buy my gal a fine supper
So I want the finest place that can be found"
To a swell restaurant the driver took them
With his Lulu gal he started in so proud
But that coon almost went blind
When he saw a great big sign up o'er the door which read
"No coons allowed."
[chorus]
"No coons allowed, No coons allowed
This place is meant for white folks that's all
We don't want no kinky-head kind,
So move on darky down the line
No coons allow'd in here at all."
So this coon got mighty offended
Commenc'd to swearing vengeance by the yard
To be thrown down in the presence of his baby
'Deed it hurt this darky's feelings mighty hard
So he rush'd on down town to a lawyer
And told him bout the sign that he had seen
He said "Boss can't you sue the firm for damage
'Case I think that I've been tre[a]ted mighty mean"
So the lawyer took the coon to the courthouse
And they started in the courthouse with a crowd
But his head began to swim
When he saw that sig[n] again o'er the courthouse door which read
"No coons allowed."

Paired with upbeat music directed to be played allegro, the lyrics tell a humorous tale about a Black man who has foolishly forgotten his social and racial station and gets overly excited when confronted with segregation. On the sheet music cover, beneath a photograph of Cole and Johnson in outlandish costumes, there is a smaller drawn inset of half a watermelon with two open razors and a set of dice perched on top. A chicken pokes its head out from behind the watermelon, while a bottle of gin stands in front. This compilation of stereotypes serves as a badge certifying African Americans' social limitations and reinforcing a demeaning reading of the lyrics.[42]

But heard from another angle, the lyrics to "No Coons Allowed" provide a heartbreaking account of segregation's emotional toll on African Americans. They also offer an incisive social critique. Keeping derogatory dialect to a minimum, the lyrics capture the pain and anger of being denied access to the "swellest" places in society, unable to simply buy a "fine supper." Gender mediates the song's account of segregation, as the Black male narrator is particularly incensed and hurt at being "thrown down in the presence of his baby." The song further suggests that segregation prevents Black men from fulfilling the dominant masculine role of provider, as the narrator cannot even take his female lover out to dinner. Attempting to seek justice for this harm, the narrator then finds that even the courts have barred him. Published in 1897, just one year after the Supreme Court's *Plessy v. Ferguson* decision, the song slyly critiques the court's legal blessing of segregation, showing that segregation is an injustice that runs throughout the country's political, legal, and social institutions.

Cole and Johnson's song also provides a different picture of Black urban mobility than that of typical coon songs. Here, Black mobility is repeatedly checked by white racism. Far from unrestrained and rampant, Black men are denied access to the city's most prestigious and fundamental spaces. The Black narrator is able to get a cab but is then prevented from entering the restaurant at the door. He is able to approach the courthouse, a spectacle that, by itself, draws "a crowd," but is then repelled from this quintessential space of governance. Instead of recounting autonomous Black movement, the lyrics show that whites repeatedly tell Black Americans to "move on . . . down the line," as segregation constrains and blocks Black mobility, funneling it away from white space. Furthermore, rather than link Black movement in the city with violence and criminality, "No Coons Allowed!" shows it as geared toward respectable and ordinary ends. The Black male narrator has "saved up" money and merely wants to go out on the town for a nice dinner. When refused at the restaurant, he "rush'd on down town"—not to break the law but to get a lawyer and appeal to it. The song thus overturns the dominant representations of Blackness and mobility found in most coon songs.

Although Black artists slipped subversive meanings into their music, coon songs in general were a controversial subject in Black communities, just as they were in white communities. Many African Americans denounced coon songs as racist travesties with vulgar and inappropriate language and themes. An 1899 article in the Black newspaper the *Iowa State Bystander* decried the fact that the "public has been flooded both upon the stage and on the streets with lots of nigger foolishness, coon songs, cake walking, and buck and wing dancing, until it has lowered the race, [and] lessen[ed] the respect for us; especially among our white friends and well wishers." An editorial in the *Plaindealer*, a Black newspaper based in Topeka, Kansas, concurred, stating, "There is nothing elevating or ennobling in the 'coon song' and 'rag-time music.'" However, neatly encapsulating Black communities' division over coon songs, the theater section in the very same newspaper regularly reported on Black coon song creators and performers without a hint of condemnation.[43]

Indeed, some African Americans celebrated coon songs and Black minstrel performers in general as emblems of racial pride. In response to a controversy involving Al Field's minstrel show, an article in the Black *Leavenworth Herald* praised Black minstrel troupes. Announcing that "Al G. Field's genuine Negro minstrels" were scheduled to perform that night, the unnamed author went on to relate that "these Negro minstrels were once united with Al Field's white minstrels, but as the stars of the white minstrels were afraid that their talents would be obscured by measuring arms with the stars of the Negro minstrels, and as Field did not have backbone enough to keep them together despite the protestations of the white minstrels, they were separated." But, the author assured readers, "the show which appears here tonight is superior in every respect to the one under the personal supervision of Field. You can bet on that." Attributing segregation to white fears of Black success, the author cast Black minstrelsy as a site of Black achievement and triumph over white competition. The author capped their argument by asserting, "There [is] really no good Negroe [*sic*] minstrelsy unless there are genuine Negroes to produce it."[44]

Many African Americans especially saw coon songs as a symbol of racial progress. For one, coon songs were heavily associated with the Black musical innovation of ragtime. Indeed, so many coon songs were set to ragtime melodies that in the parlance of the time, the terms "coon song" and "ragtime" were often interchangeable. Thus, many Black critics saw the entire genre of coon songs as representative of modern Black music. Also, by the late 1890s, so many Black artists and songwriters had achieved success in the entertainment business through their creation and performance of coon songs that the genre was deeply linked with Black artists in a way that minstrelsy, with its long tradition of white performance, was not.

An article in the Black *New York Age*, reprinted in Kansas City's *American Citizen*, illustrates the positive symbolism coon songs could hold. Focusing on the music and dismissing the lyrics, the author reported, "I heard some 'coon songs' recently. The chorus was beautifully balanced and some of the songs, put to farci[c]al words, were rich in harmony and so uplifting in the orchestration as to be worthy of a grand opera." R. C. Ransom, a Black minister at Bethel AME Church in Chicago, argued that the pervasive popularity of coon songs was a preview of what was to come from Black musicians in the future. Writing in the Indianapolis *Freeman*, he exuberantly pointed out that "five hundred Negroes are upon the American stage to-day entertaining the public successfully, and winning great applause," and asserted that "this peculiar form of music [coon songs] is scarcely a faint prophecy of the immortal master pieces [*sic*] . . . to be given to the world within the next century, by the great Negro composers who are to be the master musicians of the world." Likewise, another piece in the *Freeman* proclaimed, "'Coon Songs,' now famous the world over, are here to stay. They carry a sweeping force with them that compels some acknowledgements from all who come in contact with them."[45]

Such celebrations of Black musicianship advanced a starkly different conception of Blackness than that of the stereotypes in the coon songs themselves. Highlighting Black musical success, many African Americans characterized Black talent as professional and highly sought after by white Americans. In contrast to Southern pastoral songs, this view situated Black Americans firmly at the center of modern urban and cultural life, portraying Black entertainers as innovators and drivers of cultural progress.

This vision of modern Blackness found regular expression in the Indianapolis *Freeman*'s entertainment section, "The Stage." Founded in 1884 and published weekly, the Indianapolis *Freeman* became a leading Black newspaper when Edward E. Cooper acquired it in 1888 and devoted its coverage to national news he deemed of interest to African Americans. Due to this expansive coverage, the *Freeman* soon developed a national circulation, with the paper claiming that it was read in every US state and territory. In 1891, the African American cultural critic Garland Penn pronounced it the country's leading Black publication, characterizing it as the *Harper's Weekly* of the Black community.[46]

"The Stage" reflected this national focus. It began as a smaller column in 1889, but as more and more Black artists broke into the mainstream entertainment business it expanded to half a page, and occasionally an entire page, in the mid-1890s. It featured reviews and snippets of news on the latest Black plays, musicals, songs, and minstrel shows from across the country. J. Harry Jackson was the main editor of "The Stage" for most of the 1890s, during which time he gathered and presented this information. But information also came from the paper's official correspondents in various cities and from Black musicians and performers themselves. The paper often printed excerpts of the letters it received from artists about their shows' latest happenings and triumphs. A mixture of reportage, gossip, and criticism, "The Stage" offered a collective cultural space that kept readers abreast of the latest developments in Black popular entertainment.

In particular, "The Stage" spotlighted Black entertainers' travels in its collation of popular culture news. For example, the November 29, 1890, column alerted readers in rapid-fire succession that "McCabe and Young's Minstrels did an excellent business during a week in New Orleans"; "the Jingler Singers including the Jingler Quartette have been doing excellently in Illinois"; "W. A. Turner's Dramatic Company appeared Nov. 20th at the Providence Baptist church, Chicago"; and "Prof. Symons, the champion bass soloist, and Mr. Henry Tate, the wonderful soprano singer, will appear in a concert at Liberty Baptist church, Wednesday, Dec. 3d, Washington, DC." Similarly, another column from 1891 reported in clipped bulletins that "the Fisk University Singers are in Ohio"; "the New Orleans University Jubilee Singers are in Philadelphia"; "Mme. Flora Batson Bergen sings at Cooper Union hall, New York, Nov. 17th"; "the Olympian Quartette, comedians and vocalists, are making a great hit in Texas"; "Mme. Lizzie Pugh-Dugan is touring the East"; and "Harry Clark, the commedian [*sic*] late of McCabe and Young's minstrels[,] is managing a company playing in San Antoni[o], Texas." These numerous snippets, typical of "Stage" columns throughout the decade, underscored not only the national scope of Black musical and cultural performance but also the movement of the artists, emphasizing their tours through cities, states, and regions. The last bulletin, about Harry Clark, also alluded to the business side of popular music performance. Black artists left shows to join others and had a hand in "managing" performances rather than simply reenacting natural, "authentic" behavior.[47]

Likewise, an 1892 column demonstrates an almost laser focus on the movement of Black artists and their successes. It rattled off updates: "The Fisk singers are in Kansas"; "Mme. Slika was in Pittsburg last week"; "J. H. Fiddler, the humorist[,] is in Milwaukee"; "Mme. Sissieretta Jones was in New York recently"; "Lew Johnson's minstrels are in the State of Washington"; "W.

Owens King performed at New Haven, Conn., June 21st"; "Mme. Flora Batson has taken permanent residen[ce] in Chicago"; "Mme. Lizzie Pugh Dugan scored a success in Cincinnati recently"; "Lulu Vere Childers, who is studying in the Oberlin Conservatory of Music, is considered its best contralto"; and "Miss Rachel L. Walker of Cleveland appeared with great success at the Indianapolis Musical festival." The article thus traced the expansive and frequent movement of Black musicians and performers, compiling a larger picture of African Americans on the move and excelling in the cultural field.[48]

Black women in particular played a prominent part in this presentation of Black mobility, many of them—Sissieretta Jones, Marie Selika Williams, Flora Batson Bergen, and Lizzie Pugh Dugan, for example—classical concert singers. A brief vogue for Black female concert singers gripped white audiences in the 1880s and early 1890s, but it subsided by the mid-1890s as the novelty wore off and Black vaudeville performers gained more fame. Nevertheless, in the pages of "The Stage," they represented a counterpoint to white stereotypes about Black mobility, moving with great acclaim and respectability through the circuits of mainstream, modern cultural life.[49]

In the mid- and late 1890s, "The Stage" expanded its coverage of Black popular entertainment as African Americans made more inroads into the industry. It began to feature short exposés on leading Black musical stars, giving brief biographies of their work and touting their accomplishments. In 1897, for example, a long paragraph on vaudeville star Billy McClain—complete with a dignified illustration of him in formal dress—listed his many plays and songs as well as his multiple production jobs on various shows. Making sure to note that McClain "was the first colored man to write and successfully star in his own plays," the article lauded him for having "gained great proficiency in his work, a distinction that he has gained by his conscientious work and finished acting." Other gleanings highlighted Black musicians' successes in more sensational ways. "George Bailey, trombone soloist, of 'Darkest America,'" one article relayed, "is playing upon one of the finest trombones ever turned out of the factory of Whaley Royce and Co., of Toronto, Canada. The instrument is silver-plated, with gold raised flowers all over the bell, also gold lining, at a cost of $85.00."[50]

Alongside this expanded coverage and more diverse content, reports of Black artists' movements remained just as frequent and became more detailed. An 1896 article filled readers in on not just Black artists' travels between cities but also their transits within the industry, listing in standard bulletin fashion that "the Georgia Graduates are touring North Dakota"; "Sam T. Jack's Creoles are playing to big business in Buffalo, N.Y., this week";

"Miss Mayme Bohee, late of Black Patti's Troubadours, has joined Sam T. Jack's Creoles"; and "James DeCosta, late of South Before the War company, joined Sam T. Jack's Creoles in Columbus, O." The article also went into greater detail about a number of acts, reporting, "Black Patti's Troubadours, headed by Mme. Sissieretta Jones, made their metropolitan debut at the Star Theatre, New York City . . . and, in spite of the decidedly inclement weather, the heralded merit of the organization drew out a well filled house"; "Richard & Pringle's Georgia Minstrels succeeded in drawing to the Auditorium, Memphis, Tenn., Sept. 10., in the neighborhood of 5,000 people—4,000 Negroes and 1,000 whites, the largest indoor paid audience ever known in that city"; and "Miss Rachel Walker has signed a contract with Mr. Hammerstein, the vaudeville king, to sing in the principal cities of the country. Her engagement with Mr. Hammerstein is for 25 weeks, and at the close she will return to the Paris conservatory to complete her studies." In "The Stage," Black popular entertainers were cosmopolitan professional figures connected to a wider industry network through which they traversed the country and even continents. Rachel Walker performed on vaudeville stages but also studied in Paris.[51]

An 1897 article further captured Black artists' international voyages, informing readers that the famous Black vaudeville stars Williams and Walker had "just returned from Europe, [and] made their appearance May 31, at Koster & Bials' [in New York City] and found themselves as popular as ever." Another, from 1898, noted that the popular singer, songwriter, and performer Sam Lucas and his wife "are playing with their usual big success on the Castle circuit, which includes, Olympic Theater, Chicago Opera House, Haymarket, and others; thence to the Puget Sound and Orpheum circuit, it is stated, at the highest salary ever paid to colored artists. From there they go to England, where they have contracts for three solid months, when[ce] they will return to America."[52]

"The Stage" also drew attention to the geographical diversity of Black minstrel troupe members, a fact that exposed the artifice of minstrelsy's common claim to Southern Black authenticity. Speaking of John W. Vogel's *Darkest America*, "The Stage" reported that "the various members of the company were notified to report for rehearsals at the High Street Theatre, Columbus, O., on a certain date. Inasmuch as these people came from all quarters of the globe, there is no absolute certainty that all will report, disappointments being frequent." "The Stage" further stripped minstrel shows' veneer of Black authenticity by consistently focusing on the musical and acting dexterity of Black entertainers, indicating that these were performances involving cultivated talent and not unvarnished anthropological displays. It also concentrated on the economic and social successes of the Black performers, rather than the content of the shows themselves. One article that explicitly mentioned a minstrel show's Southern pastoral content did so only in the context of highlighting the show's overall success: "The Lew Johnson Minstrels appeared recently at the opera house to a good sized audience, and it was easily the best colored company seen in Duluth, Minn., for some time. The singing was far above average. The scenery and sketches of the south before the war were just as advertised. The Dixie choruses and marches brought down the house."[53]

Another article, also once again foregrounding Black artists' mobility, played up the talent and economic achievement of Mahara's Minstrels. Announcing that the Black group had just closed a highly successful run in Chicago and "toured the entire West the past season," it apprised readers that "among the many prominent artists with the attraction were Billy Young, Leroy Bland, George Moxley, Dan Avery, Rube Brown and Hillard Brewer." It also stressed that these Black artists were traversing the country in style, stating that in the next season the show members would be "traveling in their own private Pullman cars, and the coming tour will cover the entire country, lasting two years."[54]

Black musicians and performers themselves contributed to the vision of success and expansive Black movement coalescing in the pages of "The Stage." Writing letters from their various tours and engagements across the country, which "The Stage" then reprinted verbatim, they trumpeted the popularity of their shows and the talent of their musicians and actors. These letters also updated readers on the current location of the shows and their recent travels. Each article in "The Stage" was thus an assemblage of multiple entertainers' journeys, experiences, and triumphs. The November 19, 1898, edition of "The Stage" is a case in point. A member of Leon W. Washburn's Double Minstrels reported, "We are still playing to [our] usual big business, and the show is improving greatly. In Binghamton, N.Y., each member of the company recurred himself a fresh top-buttoner. . . . The show spent Sunday in Wilkesbarre [*sic*], Pa. While there Messres. G. A. Hillman, Harry Allen and Paul C. Floyd were royally entertained by Mr. and Mrs. Overton." Similarly, W. T. Cary, of the Canadian Jubilee Singers, wrote in to share, "We have been in the States of New York, Pennsylvania, and Ohio. Miss Daisy Underwood, the 'Black Melba,' never fails to please the audiences, scoring two and three encores nightly." And the letter of Ollie Hall, manager and singer in "The Original Imperial Concert Company," directly addressed readers of the *Freeman* in the third person: "Our company numbers ten people, headed by America's greatest descriptive baritone, Ollie C. Hall, assisted by Mme. Devar. Mr. Hall is negotiating for a trip to Australia and the fair at Paris. The company send regards to their many friends and readers of The Freeman. We will tour California, Arizona and New Mexico during the winter."[55]

Musician Fred W. Simpson's missive in another edition demonstrates that Black cultural producers' travels included the urban spaces of the Deep South, despite the intensification of Jim Crow in the 1890s. Simpson, touring with Oliver Scott's Refined Negro Minstrels, wrote, "We have about completed our Southern tour, of Alabama, Tenn., and Kentucky and business was far beyond expectations, considering that several colored shows have preceeded [*sic*] us. Never-the-less the Scott's minstrels have made a name in the South as the cleanest up-to-date, first-class minstrel show that has visited the several cities we have played in for several years." Of course, the movement of Black popular entertainers was never completely unrestricted. Black musicians and performers regularly encountered racism in their travels, which curtailed their mobility—especially in the South, where not only proliferating structures of segregation but also physical violence impeded their movement. Adapting to such threats, one African American show would play "I Wish I Was in Dixie's Land" when moving between the train and the theater to defuse potential white violence. This clever use of "Dixie's Land" illustrates yet another way Southern pastoral music could paradoxically facilitate the movement of Black cultural producers.[56]

It is also important to flag that gender differentiated Black mobility on the ground. Black women faced restrictions on their movement that did not apply to Black men, including the threat of sexual violence. While "The Stage" prominently included Black women alongside Black men as modern travelers and symbols of racial pride, its collective representation of Black artists' travels effaced the gendered differences in mobility individuals experienced. Indeed, Black women performers' gender curtailed not only their general movement throughout US society but also the roles and content they could perform on the stage itself.[57]

Despite its limitations, the portrait of Black mobility sketched in the pages of the *Freeman* countered the perversions and corruptions of sheet music caricatures. Tracing Black entertainers' expansive movements and the economic and popular success of which it was part and parcel, "The Stage" presented Black mobility—especially interurban Black mobility—as frequent, respectable, and thoroughly modern. Indeed, in the pages of "The Stage," Black mobility became a metonym for Black social and economic achievement. The very need to document the widespread travels of Black artists reflected a triumph, albeit a limited one, over racism and segregation in the entertainment industry. The *Freeman* thus served as a community forum in which African American readers were encouraged to take pride in and feel connected to the achievements of Black entertainers, including their mobility. In creating such affinities, the paper fashioned Black artists' geographic movement into a communal experience that suggested such movement was possible for other African American readers.

"The Stage" also revealed the deep contradictions surrounding race and mobility at the core of popular music. While popular song repeatedly broadcast warnings about the unnaturalness of Black mobility and the dangers it posed for white Americans, the desires of audiences—both white and Black—to hear African American performers facilitated the increased movement of Black artists. And while Black artists' renditions of the Southern pastoral furthered the ideological link between Blackness and premodern, agrarian ways, the material circuits they traversed and the entertainment industry they intimately shaped were, of course, inevitably modern. Black cultural producers were in fact woven deep in the sinews of industrial consumer culture, a fact that "The Stage" implicitly highlighted. Contrary to the image of the Black man walking back to his old planation with a stick and handkerchief bundle over his shoulder, African American entertainers were traveling in private pullman cars to cities all over the nation.

Moreover, in its celebration of Black entertainers' mobility, the *Freeman* constructed a narrative that pushed back against the racism so often hampering Black movement. Again, it is important not to discount the very real restrictions African American musicians and performers faced in their travels. But "The Stage" showed that the industrial, urban, and modern structures that popular song insisted African Americans were either absent from or too incompetent and irresponsible to handle were in fact already being deftly navigated by the Black artists performing and producing such songs. The pages of "The Stage" thus shattered popular culture's racial facade, exposing the Black movement upon which it depended.

Nonetheless, the racist onslaught in popular culture was relentless, and Black artists faced a steep hill. As chapter 5 will show, late nineteenth-century popular culture not only attacked Black mobility but also the idea of Black urban space. Well before the residential segregation of neighborhoods emerged in US cities, popular culture erroneously presented exclusively Black urban spaces as factual realities and condemned them as sites of social deviance and criminality. This negative portrayal of fabricated Black city space was yet another way popular culture ideologically funneled white Americans toward Jim Crow residential segregation.

CHAPTER FIVE

Imagining Segregation

Popular Culture and Black Urban Space Before the Ghetto, 1877–1900

While on one of his many tours of the United States in the 1880s and 1890s, the Duke of Newcastle, an upstanding member of the English aristocracy, purchased a perhaps surprising souvenir from the world of American mass entertainment: a complete set of the *Darktown* print series. Racist lithographic prints intended as comedy and featuring caricatures of African Americans, these cultural descendants of blackface minstrelsy proved so delightful to the duke that he bought all one hundred prints available at the time. He was not alone in his appreciation. Over the last two decades of the nineteenth century, hundreds of thousands of Americans bought and laughed at the *Darktown* comic prints, leading the series to become the unquestioned bestseller of printing powerhouse Currier and Ives during the period. First published in the late 1870s, by 1884 the *Darktown* series accounted for one-third of Currier and Ives's output. Festooning the walls of parlors, workplaces, saloons, and shops across the country, the prints enjoyed massive popularity. Each of the *Darktown* prints sold copies in the tens of thousands, and Currier and Ives was soon relying on the series to keep the firm afloat. The duke's purchase of the *Darktown* prints thus gave him a fitting memento of US anti-Black racism and its influential role in American popular culture.[1]

But these immensely popular comic prints did more than just provide racist entertainment—they were part of an emerging steady montage of popular culture images that portrayed homogeneous Black urban space as both commonplace and natural, despite the fact that extensive racial segregation was not the reality in any US cities during the period. African Americans in fact lived in highly mixed neighborhoods throughout the late nineteenth century, and large racially exclusive ghettos did not begin to form until the early twentieth century. And the *Darktown* prints were not alone in presenting exclusive Black urban space as commonplace and natural before such spaces existed. A growing theme in popular culture was the depiction of New York City's Thompson Street as exclusively Black, a representation that was far from accurate.

Examining the *Darktown* print series and representations of Thompson Street from 1877 to 1900, this chapter argues that imagery of all-Black urban spaces in popular culture outpaced segregation on the ground and suggested to audiences not only that homogeneous Black space was an extant reality but also that residential segregation of Black and white Americans was both correct and normal. In disseminating and naturalizing these ideas, such imagery helped foster the development of ghetto segregation and its exclusively Black city neighborhoods at the turn of the twentieth century. Popular culture also persistently crafted Black urban space as fundamentally deviant, dangerous, and inferior, further reinforcing the logic of Jim Crow residential segregation by suggesting that maintaining social order in the city required cordoning off and containing urban African Americans and Black space.

The chapter's first section looks at portrayals of Thompson Street as an exclusively Black space. This street, running south from Washington Square Park down to Canal Street, through the neighborhoods currently known as Greenwich Village and Soho, was home to a sizable Black population in the late nineteenth century. However, it was far from an exclusively Black residential space. Nonetheless, numerous nationally circulating forms of popular culture repeatedly used Thompson Street as a metonym for all-Black space. This chapter not only explores Thompson Street's appearance in cultural objects such as short stories, comic prints, plays, and sheet music but also analyzes contemporary newspaper coverage to help explain how the street acquired its racial meaning. It demonstrates that racialized ideas about Thompson Street cohered in the 1870s and then migrated into popular culture as it became a nationally recognized term for Black urban space. Despite its national reputation, no scholarly work has studied Thompson Street's role in US racial and urban history.[2] This chapter not only brings vital aspects of Thompson Street's racial history to light but also reveals the street's relationship to the development of racial segregation.

The second section analyzes the lithographic print series *Darktown*. Published and sold from 1877 until the early 1900s, the *Darktown* comic series drew heavily from blackface minstrel themes to depict scenes from a fictional all-Black town. Just as with representations of Thompson Street, the *Darktown* prints presented segregated Black space as both a commonplace reality and a site of threatening deviance. Given their popularity, the scholarship on the series is surprisingly scant.[3] This chapter helps correct this lack of attention and illustrates the revealing racial and spatial ideologies at work in the prints.

In analyzing representations of Thompson Street and the *Darktown* comic series, I draw out the ways that ideas about racial mobility informed their visions of Black urban space. Both pathologized and calumniated Black mobility, linking it with criminality, failure to command modern forms of transportation, and a reckless disregard for the rules of the road. Since restricted movement and spatial segregation are inextricably linked, this maligning of Black mobility was directly related to the two forms' portrayal of segregation. In presenting Black mobility as dangerous, they implied that Black movement ought to be curtailed and African Americans immobilized and confined to Black space, safely away from whites. Denigration of Black movement was thus part and parcel of the cultural forms' naturalization of racial segregation.[4]

Race and Residence in Late Nineteenth-Century US Cities

Census enumeration district data from the late nineteenth century reveal that a level of residential segregation existed in US cities in the postbellum period. By 1880, African Americans were constrained to certain neighborhoods regardless of their class standing, as residential segregation at the scale of the house and the block took hold. However, it is imperative to note that with the sole exception of San Francisco's Chinatown, racial segregation at the scale of entire neighborhoods—what scholars have defined as a "ghetto," a definition this book adopts as well—did not develop until the twentieth century.[5] Further, while Black segregation was high on a house-by-house basis, it was not as significant on a street-by-street basis. The isolation index, which measures the extent to which Black residents live next to members of their own race at a given spatial scale, shows that at the building level, Black people were highly isolated (after excluding live-in servants), with isolation indexes of .741 and .725 for New York and Chicago, respectively. However, for both cities, the isolation index was much lower when measured at the scale of the street, dropping to .230 for New York and .328 for Chicago, meaning that most African Americans lived on streets that were predominantly white.[6]

These facts allow us to draw a number of concrete conclusions about segregation in the late nineteenth century. First, it is worth restating that large racially exclusive Black neighborhoods, or ghettos, did not form until the early twentieth century. Geographer John Radford's distinction between micro-segregation, meaning house-by-house or block-by-block segregation, and macro-segregation—the segregation of entire neighborhoods of a city—is helpful here. Macro-segregation was a post-1900 formation. Second, not only were nineteenth-century urban neighborhoods not racially exclusive, but most African Americans lived in majority white neighborhoods. Indeed, on average, Black residents lived in neighborhoods that were overwhelmingly non-Black. Even in the most racially segregated enumeration districts in Chicago in 1880, the Black population was so minimal that whites outnumbered them four to one. Thus, while there was a level of racial segregation prior to 1900, it was primarily at the building level. Segregation at the scale of the block remained much lower and sporadic, and neighborhood segregation was nonexistent.[7]

Finally, and perhaps most basically, while forces of segregation were at work by the last two decades of the nineteenth century, the fact that urban neighborhoods remained mixed-raced spaces meant that the segregationist ideologies and practices leading to and producing the ghetto had to be constructed, elaborated, and extended over time. Segregation and the ghetto were far from inevitable developments; so many of the institutional and legal instruments crucial to creating and maintaining the vast scale of the ghetto, such as racial zoning, racially restrictive covenants, and financial redlining, were not yet invented or employed to any significant degree.[8] These handmaidens to ghettoization needed to be fashioned and developed, and their deployment not only enabled the increased scale of racial segregation across the country after 1900 but also reflected the triumph of residential segregation as an ideology. By naturalizing racially segregated city space, metonymic Thompson Street and the *Darktown* comic series both affirmed the nascent residential segregation of the 1880s and 1890s and acted as ideological agents encouraging the rise of ghettoization at the start of the twentieth century.

Manufacturing Thompson Street as Black Space

The history of New York City's Thompson Street provides valuable insight into the ways in which racialized thinking distorted and obscured extant spatial arrangements. I should note here that I do not offer a complete history of race relations on Thompson Street; rather, I recount how quotidian perceptions and representations of Thompson Street among both New York City residents and white Americans at large came to link the street with Blackness. That Thompson Street would become a nationally recognized symbol for urban Black space by the 1880s and 1890s is hardly apparent from the demographics of the street prior to and during those decades. The census of 1880 shows that Thompson Street—eight blocks long and running south from Washington Square Park to Canal Street—was a thoroughly mixed-race area.

On the whole, Thompson Street was predominantly a mixture of native-born whites and various European immigrants—including French, Irish, German, Swiss, Italian, and English residents—with Black Americans scattered among them. And although enumerated as white in the census, Irish and Italian immigrants often had their racial fitness questioned in the late nineteenth century, lending the street a multiracial air.[9]

On five of Thompson Street's eight blocks, all at its southern end, African Americans made up only between 1 and 10 percent of the residents. However, the two most northern blocks, jutting down from Washington Square Park, had a higher percentage of Black residents, with African Americans composing 28 percent and 20 percent of the population, respectively. Finally, the third block from the park—Thompson between Bleeker and Houston—had the largest Black population, with African Americans making up the majority of residents at 65 percent. But even on this block there was still a sizable white population, which itself was a highly diverse mix of native-born whites and immigrants.

Significantly, African Americans did tend to live in segregated houses and apartment buildings. Precise statistics are a bit elusive—the census recorded data by lot address, but lots could contain more than one building. Landlords commonly constructed multiple tenements on one lot in the late nineteenth century, with additional houses often located behind the original street-adjacent building. Nonetheless, census lot data still provide a fairly detailed picture. On the three northern blocks of Thompson Street—those with the heaviest Black populations—fourteen of the twenty addresses with African American occupants (including both single family and multifamily dwellings) were all, or virtually all, Black, while the remaining six were mixed. However, the street's five southern blocks were a different story. Out of the twenty-one addresses with African American occupants, only five were completely Black, while sixteen were racially mixed.[10] So, while Thompson Street certainly showed signs of nascent segregation, particularly at the building level, it was nonetheless an undeniably mixed-race space. Indeed, as popular narratives about Thompson Street as Black space were taking off in the 1880s, the Black population was in fact shifting from its former concentration in Greenwich Village to the Hell's Kitchen neighborhood in the mid–West Side.[11]

So how did an image of Thompson Street as Black space emerge? To be sure, the racialization of Thompson Street in many ways mirrored the common habit of late nineteenth-century reformers, journalists, and the public in general of labeling certain city neighborhoods where ethnic populations clustered in relatively high numbers "ethnic colonies," such as Little Italy, Little Hungary, and Jewtown. As historians have shown, the residential makeup of these spaces belied their names, as these, too, were heavily mixed in terms of race and ethnicity. But such designations granted native-born whites a sense of racial control. As historian Chad Heap writes, the naming of ethnic enclaves "reflected a desire to contain these racialized groups and their 'alien' ways to particular geographic locations—both on the physical map of the city and, more importantly, in the imaginations of urban residents and visitors."[12] Similarly, scholar Genevieve Carpio points out that all-encompassing racial and ethnic labels for city neighborhoods were "ideological designation[s] aiming to reify race through the myth of spatial fixity, or the falsehood that nonwhite bodies occupied distinct places and that white spaces were wholly homogeneous."[13] Thompson Street was a part of this larger trend, offering whites a stabilizing sense of Black-white relations in the face of New York City's growing Black population over the postbellum decades.

However, the racialization of Thompson Street unfolded on specific historical and ideological terrain that differentiated it from non-Black racial and ethnic enclave designations. The depth of anti-Blackness in the late nineteenth century ensured that white Americans would read representations of Thompson Street differently and that those representations would produce different outcomes from similar designations of European immigrant neighborhoods. Due to European immigrants' relatively privileged place above African Americans in the racial hierarchy, designations such as Little Italy and Little Hungary did not carry the same racial baggage.[14] In this period of virulent anti-Blackness, renderings of Thompson Street as exclusively Black space intersected with preexisting—though still inchoate—ideas and practices of racial segregation in a way that racial ideas about European immigrants did not. These historical contexts thus funneled representations of Thompson Street toward segregationist ends.

Newspaper articles provide insight into racial fabrications about Thompson Street, revealing a process whereby news coverage of crime on the street gradually resulted in its being yoked to Blackness and criminality over the course of the late 1860s and 1870s. This conflation of Thompson Street with criminal Blackness unfolded not only in the New York press but also in newspapers across the country, which reported on the latest headlines and sensational stories coming out of the country's largest metropolis. This national coverage thus spread knowledge of Thompson Street beyond the local New York scene.[15]

Newspapers associated Thompson Street with Black crime in a number of ways. One common news practice of the time was to refer to a crime by the street it occurred on. Headlines like "The Thompson-Street Murder" dotted the press, connecting Thompson Street with crime and increasing its notoriety.[16] That many newspaper reports about Thompson Street, including those emphasizing Black crimes, repeatedly disclosed the street's mixed-race composition exposes the distortionary power of race. In fact, news stories about events taking place on Thompson Street sometimes circulated precisely because they involved cross-racial interactions or cross-racial sex. In many instances, newspapers used stories concerning interracial sex—especially when involving Black men and white women—to decry miscegenation and cast white presence on the street as deviant.[17] However, other news reports simply relayed interracial interactions without comment.[18] Nonetheless, throughout the 1860s and 1870s, news coverage of Black crime on Thompson Street repeatedly descended into racist sensationalism and stereotyping.[19] This stream of stories ensured that Thompson Street remained in the news and connected to Black crime.[20]

By the late 1870s, white New York residents were often referring to sections of the street as "Africa."[21] In this totalizing designation, the street became synonymous with both Blackness and crime. It is likely that some of the reported Black crime stemmed from police persecution. As historians have shown, postbellum police forces—composed almost entirely of white officers—were rife with racist policing and harassment.[22] However, whether the product of racist policing or not, Black crime on Thompson Street continued to be highlighted in the press, both in New York City and nationally. Indeed, the name Thompson Street itself soon became a referent for Blackness.[23] Phrases such as "Africa, otherwise Thompson Street" began to appear in the news and popular magazines.[24] Beginning in the early 1880s, articles from around the country used the phrase "Thompson Street" as a substitute prefix for "Black," registering the degree to which the street had sunk into the popular consciousness.[25] Likewise, the press was dotted with full-length sensationalized exposés that labeled Thompson Street a Black space and portrayed its Black residents as agents of vice and crime.[26]

These lurid and exaggerated accounts continued to ignore the persistent multiracial reality of Thompson Street, a reality still paradoxically documented in other news reports throughout the decade.[27] Indeed, Jacob Riis's immensely popular 1890 muckraking report on New York City's slums, *How the Other Half Lives*, captured Thompson Street's interracial environment in a photograph of one of the street's saloons that showed white and Black men

FIGURE 5.1 Jacob Riis, *A Downtown "Morgue," New York*, photo of a Black-and-tan dive on Thompson Street, 1890.

drinking together (see figure 5.1).[28] But the popular vision of Thompson Street as homogeneous Black space remained impervious to such counterevidence. Instead, newspaper coverage of Thompson Street from 1865 to the mid-1880s unveils a discursive process through which the presence of a minority Black population came to define the street's character. The totalizing logics of race thus produced a counterfeit vision of segregation, first at the scale of the block and then at the scale of the neighborhood. By the early 1880s, representations of Thompson Street in popular culture would join the chorus of voices forging the street's racial reputation and help it become a nationally recognized symbol of Black degeneration in urban space by the late 1880s and 1890s.

(Mis)Representing Thompson Street in Popular Culture

Thompson Street became such a fixture of the American cultural landscape in the last two decades of the nineteenth century that by 1889, the *New York Tribune* would proclaim that Thompson Street was "famed in verse and story throughout the country."[29] It appeared in a diverse array of popular culture forms, including short stories, cartoons, sheet music, and minstrel shows. As early as 1879, it graced the stage in a San Francisco Minstrels' skit titled "Thompson Street Flats." Originally from their namesake city, the San Francisco Minstrels were in fact based in New York City after the Civil War, where they had a lengthy run of success and became one of the most popular minstrel groups of the period. Press coverage of their performance declared that the "Thompson Street Flats" skit was "killing . . . audiences with laughter" and was a huge success. The skit not only assumed audiences would recognize Thompson Street as a Black space but amplified that notion.[30]

Then, in 1883, Thompson Street appeared in the nationally distributed *Life* magazine with the serial publication of the Thompson Street Poker Club stories. Written by Henry Guy Carleton, the white managing editor of *Life*, the stories were short comedic episodes about a fictional Black poker club on Thompson Street. Recycling stock minstrel themes of Black violence, stupidity, and ineptitude in the novel context of weekly poker games, the stories featured a recurring cast of characters—with appropriately humorous names—who cheated, argued, and physically fought with one another. The series proved so popular that in 1884 Carleton published the stories as a book, titled *The Thompson Street Poker Club: From "Life."* The book itself went through multiple editions, with reprints in 1888 and 1889. Carleton continued to write the stories for *Life* throughout the decade, and they were reprinted in newspapers across the country, including in the *Chicago Daily Tribune*, the *New York Times*, the *St. Louis Daily Globe-Democrat*, and the *Atlanta Constitution*.[31]

The Thompson Street Poker Club stories communicated to readers that Black urbanity consisted of crime, financial irresponsibility, and violent confrontation. For example, in "Two Jacks an' a Razzer [Razor]," two members—Tooter Williams and Gus Johnson—face off in a betting war, rapidly raising each other until all their money rides on one hand of cards. Gus finally shows his hand, a straight flush, and asks Tooter, "Whad yo' got den?" Slowly reaching down into his boot, Tooter replies, "Ise jes' got two jacks 'n' a razzer." With a cowed "Dat's good," Gus relinquishes the pot in the face of Tooter's threat. In another story about an "executive session" of the club, a member proposes an amendment to the club's constitution that stipulates, "Members will deposit their razors in the coat room on entering the club, except on occasions when there are guests present from Hoboken." Jokes such as these, which suggested that all Black men carried razors and might use them at any moment, were a common staple of the series.[32]

Other rowdy antics and nods to Black criminality abounded. In one instance, when a regular member fails to show up to a game, another hypothesizes that perhaps "the lateness of the hour had interfered with the securing of bail." In another story, a guest player, the Reverend Dr. Cooppuller, whose name is an allusion to chicken thieving, loses heavily and then hesitates to pay his debt. After another reverend, Thankful Smith, threatens to fight Cooppuller if he refuses to pay, Cooppuller finally relents and hands over a check. It is only after Cooppuller's departure that the members discover the check is from a bank that folded over a year ago and is consequently worthless. Criminality and underhanded, immoral actions are thus the norm for the club's Black members, even for those who are members of the clergy. Over and over, the Thompson Street Poker Club stories recited Black violence and stupidity, constantly ending with a fight or someone being tricked in an obvious way. And while Thompson Street itself was rarely mentioned or discussed in the stories, the title and the standard opening line for each vignette—some version of the phrase "the regular meeting of the Thompson Street Poker Club was held last Saturday evening"—ensured that readers would associate the street with Blackness and the characters' antics.[33]

In 1889, Carleton published a second book, *Lectures Before the Thompson Street Poker Club,* a collection of stories about a lecture series put on by the club in which the members take turns speaking about poker. The book mocks Black intellectual abilities and the members' efforts to imitate refined white society and scientific learning. The lectures are riddled with malapropisms and constantly devolve into arguments and infighting among the members and guests. The success of the original Thompson Street Poker Club stories also spawned the spin-off series the Thompson Street Medical Association and the Thompson Street Bicycle Club, which used the same basic formula to lampoon urban Black society.[34]

By the late 1880s, Thompson Street had made its way into jokes and cartoons in magazines. Printed in popular weeklies like *Puck* and *Judge,* and sometimes reprinted in daily newspapers, these comics and jokes used Thompson Street as a metonym for Black space and Black society in their racist humor. Such was the case in an 1886 witticism from *Puck,* which also exposes the depth of contemporary white anxieties (and exaggerations) about Black demographics in New York City: "Frederick Douglass says there are only seven million free negros [*sic*] in this country to-day. A number must have died or moved away since we last strolled up Thompson Street." An illustrated comic in *Puck* from 1887 likewise testifies to the strong link between Blackness and Thompson Street in popular perceptions. Titled "Thompson Street Echoings," it shows two Black men arguing with each other on a city street about an insult that one has supposedly leveled at the other, all while a young Black boy looks on in amusement from behind. In the illustration, a street sign makes it clear they are standing on Thompson Street. Significantly, the drawing pictures only Black people in the background, completely scrubbing Thompson Street's white population from the ideological frame.[35]

Thompson Street also continued to appear in minstrel shows and seeped into sheet music as well, especially as coon songs about urban African Americans rose in popularity during the late 1880s and 1890s. In 1886, the famed minstrel performer Lew Dockstader developed a sketch called "Thanksgiving in Thompson Street," in which he impersonated a Black preacher fond of chickens. And in 1893, the playwright Edward Harrigan wrote a song called "The Sunny Side of Thompson Street" for his musical *The Woolen Stocking*. Also published as sheet music that same year, the song is an extended disparagement of Black urbanity and explicitly suggests whites must separate themselves from urban African Americans in order to stay safe. Interestingly, it portrays Thompson Street as home to multiple nonwhite races, but with African Americans as the overwhelmingly dominant element:

> If you want to find the people of the colored population,
> Indigo, the Japanese, the black and the brown;
> The greatest place in all the state, oh! yes, in all the nation,
> Is the sunny side of Thompson Street away down town.
> [chorus]
> Now white folk, keep on the shady side when you're trav'ling around;
> Don't talk lo[u]d, but keep your eye on the crow'd on the Sunny side of
>   Thompson Street, away down town.
> Oh, it's when you see a copper chase a coon way up an alley;
> Oh! de nigger seems to grow right out of de ground;
> Oh, when he comes, get on the run, and don't you dilly-dally,
> On the sunny side of Thompson Street, away down town.
> Oh, it's there you'll find a razor with a nigger on de handle,
> Day and night he's full of fight, you can't [keep] him down;
> A yellow wench sits on a bench a making all the scandal,
> On the sunny side of Thompson Street, away down town.

In the song, Black urban space is a carnival of crime, sexual promiscuity, and violence that poses a danger to the physical and moral well-being of whites.

Replete with African American men who elude the "chase" of the police, dangerous Black movement through the city streets is an integral aspect of the Black criminal's "fight" that cannot be kept "down." Confronted with this unrestrained Black presence in the city, whites should themselves "get on the run" and "keep on the shady side" of the street.[36]

Another explicit conflation of Thompson Street with Black crime comes in the song "When Ephraim Plays His Solo on the Drum," from 1899. Ridiculing the Black tradition of Emancipation Day parades, the song debases Black mobility and public assembly. The lyrics set the urban scene and mention Thompson Street by name: "On each Emancipation Day, / From Thompson street to avenue A, / In rain or shine, / These coons they do walk." The lyrics go on to describe the marching band members in the parade as looking like "Zulus" in their outlandish costumes and state that the band and all their spectators are drunk on "good old rum." The song then highlights the criminality that perpetually shadows unrestrained Black movement, warning that if "any man that's white, / Should have the nerve to start a fight," then out of "the pockets of each man a razor comes, / The wool would soon be flying, / And more than one a dying." Dissuading whites from fighting African Americans not because it is morally wrong but because every Black man carries a razor, the song portrays urban Black residents as a physical threat to whites. Indeed, the song implies that Black men are so irrationally and uncontrollably violent that even if a white man provokes the fight it will descend into a melee in which Black men turn on each other, sending "wool . . . flying."[37]

The consistent references to Thompson Street as exclusive Black space in multiple forms of popular culture in the 1880s and 1890s echoed and augmented the racial constructions of the street in the press. Ignoring Thompson Street's actual multiracial and multiethnic demographics, these representations in popular culture disseminated the notion that homogeneous Black urban space existed decades before the actual advent of such racially segregated neighborhoods. Painted in blackface, Thompson Street served as a cultural symbol rendering residential segregation commonsensical and natural. It presented segregation not only as already existing but also, through its images of disorderly, immoral, and dangerous Black urbanity, as implicitly justified. But representations of Thompson Street were not the only way popular culture conveyed such ideas about segregation. Throughout the final decades of the nineteenth century, the extremely popular *Darktown* lithographic prints also contributed to the misrepresentation of urban space and Blackness.

"The Boss of the Road": Images of Segregation and Mobility in the *Darktown* Print Series

Currier and Ives was far and away the leading producer of lithographic prints in the United States during the nineteenth century. By 1900, the firm had published over seven thousand prints, and its sales numbered in the millions. At one point, Currier and Ives accounted for 95 percent of all lithographs in circulation in the United States. In the last two decades of the century, the company's unquestioned bestseller was the *Darktown* comic series, created by white artist Thomas Worth. First published in the late 1870s, these racist prints riffed on themes rooted in blackface minstrelsy and enjoyed massive popularity. Each of the *Darktown* prints sold copies in the tens of thousands, and Currier and Ives was soon relying on the series to keep the firm afloat. By 1884, it accounted for one-third of the firm's total output. Worth conceptualized and illustrated most of the prints, though other Currier and Ives artists produced a portion of them. The drawings proved so popular that businesses and manufacturers even illicitly reprinted and distributed them with superimposed advertisements, further disseminating them throughout the public. In addition to their distribution as advertisements, the cheap cost of the prints and their appearance in barrooms, shops, and firehouses enabled Americans of all classes to buy and view them. Although production of new prints ceased in 1896, Currier and Ives continued to reprint and sell them until 1907, when Americans' changing decorative tastes and the growth of photography forced the company to shutter its doors.[38]

Continuing in the long tradition of blackface minstrelsy, the *Darktown* series ridiculed African Americans and denied them any semblance of social or racial equality. Completely eviscerating the idea of respectable Black social life, the prints found humor in the repeated failure of Darktown's Black residents to mimic white society. They consistently showed Black attempts at refined behavior and middle-class culture ending in chaos, with the heavily caricatured Black participants often coming to physical harm.

As scholars studying the *Darktown* comics have argued, the series and its images of Black social failure formed part of the larger white cultural backlash to emancipation and African American uplift politics in the late nineteenth century. Just as blackface minstrelsy had done decades earlier, the images offered a cultural balm to white Americans threatened by African Americans' push for social and political equality. They also reflected Northern whites' increasing anxieties about growing Black migration to Northern cities during this period. Despite the relatively small size of this migration when compared to later twentieth-century Black migrations, it nonetheless generated outsized concern among whites and spurred desires for racist cultural imagery. Distinguishing it from prior iterations of minstrelsy, the series' more intense racist caricature and violent imagery registered the shift in white supremacy during this period toward more extreme anti-Blackness, a turn heavily informed by the rise of scientific racism.[39] In addition to these factors, I contend that white anxieties about unrestrained Black movement, particularly within urban spaces, drove the popularity of the *Darktown* series. The comics ameliorated these worries by ridiculing Black geographic mobility and Black urban life in general, discursively reasserting racial boundaries and containing the threat free Black movement posed to white social dominance.

Another, more direct influence on the *Darktown* series was Sol Eytinge's *Blackville* cartoons, which first appeared in *Harper's Weekly* in 1874 and ran through the early 1880s. These captioned, single-image drawings ridiculed Black aspirations to upward mobility and social refinement, just like the *Darktown* prints. In fact, some of the *Darktown* comics merely repeated the jokes of the *Blackville* sketches. And, as their titles indicate, *Darktown* took *Blackville*'s basic premise: a fictional all-Black town, which symbolized all of Black life in its mocking humor. The point was that in Blackville or Darktown—that is, in Black society—racial difference rendered class redundant and precluded modern progress, as inherent inequalities prohibited African Americans from attaining whites' level of social development. But of the two series, Worth's *Darktown* was not only more popular and well known but also more virulently racist and demeaning. The *Blackville* series did engage in racist caricature, but it was not as exaggerated and dehumanizing as that of the *Darktown* series. It was also largely free of *Darktown*'s explicitly violent imagery.[40]

The *Darktown* comics were mostly drawn in pairs that featured a "before" and "after" print. The "before" print set up the racist joke by showing African Americans engaged in some activity, often one associated with middle- and upper-class lifestyles or notions of modern society in general. The "after" print ridiculed the Black subjects by having the attempt at the activity end in failure, most often through some violent accident brought on by either chance or the Black subjects' own actions. They thus imparted the overall lesson that African Americans were inept at modernity, urbanity, and freedom. The comics especially targeted the Black middle class for derision, as their material and educational attainments were particularly threatening to white supremacy. Images of the Black middle class stripped of their pretensions and put back in their supposed place were highly gratifying to white viewers worried about their position in the social and racial hierarchy.[41]

Worth's caricatures of the Black body visually encapsulated and symbolized this Black social failure, conceptually merging the social shortcomings illustrated in the scenes with the shortcomings of the Black body. Worth also indicated Black Americans' unfitness for modern life through their overexaggerated or inappropriate clothing. African Americans in the images fail to understand this basic accoutrement of civilization, sometimes wearing rags when finery is required, at other times outlandish versions of contemporary styles. And in direct contrast to Victorian norms about restrained and respectable behavior, the Black characters always overindulge themselves and are unconstrained in their bodily comportment. Excess runs through the whole series—African Americans are constantly overeating, fighting, and being loud.

The print duo *An Ice Cream Racket* exemplifies the series' focus on unrestrained bodily indulgence (see figures 5.2A and 5.2B). In the first print, subtitled *Freezing In*, a Black waiter with a grinning smile and bulging eyes delivers a massive plate of ice cream, almost larger than himself, to a young Black man and woman. The man wears a garish orange suit and gazes intently at the plate, his mouth fixed in an expression of wonder. The woman wears equally loud clothing—a dress with a yellow bodice and a bright red skirt—and is equally transfixed by the ice cream. In her right hand she holds a fan larger than her entire upper body, its enormous size emphasizing African Americans' inept performance of refined customs and the absurdity of Black class pretensions. A caption underneath the illustration reads, "Oh dat lubly cream! seems as I could nebber git enuf!" The print thus portrays African Americans as lacking any control over their own bodily desires and failing to recognize the boundaries of excessive consumption.[42]

In the second print, the unrestrained Black body receives its just deserts. Subtitled *Thawing Out*, it shows the Black woman now at home wrapped in blankets while perched on top of a coal stove, a steaming kettle sitting on her head. Another Black woman, presumably her mother, stands on a stool in front of her and feeds her tonic from a bottle, while an older Black woman rushes toward her carrying two more steaming kettles. A thermometer hangs from the Black woman's hair, its mercury at the bottom of the gauge. Having gorged herself on ice cream, her now frozen body is paying the price. The print mocks her attempt at social refinement not only through her overconsumption but also through its depiction of her run-down apartment—the walls are cracked and bare, save for her massive fan, which hangs upside down

FIGURE 5.2A AND B *An Ice Cream Racket: Freezing In* (New York: Currier and Ives, 1889) and *An Ice Cream Racket: Thawing Out* (New York: Currier and Ives, 1889). Courtesy of the Popular Graphic Arts Collection, Library of Congress.

from a peg. The print thus conveys that beneath the already inadequate facade of Black sophistication lies African Americans' true impoverished racial condition. On the right side of the print, the Black woman's male companion skips out of the room, laughing back at her. The caption below transcribes his parting comment: "Golly! guess you's done got enuf dis time." Black men are thus ungentlemanly, and Black women are incapable of proper feminine restraint. Gratifyingly for white audiences, their futile attempt at social mobility generates its own painful punishment.[43]

Indeed, as with so many of the comics, humor lay in Black bodies experiencing violent pain and injury. The consistent violence and its explicit nature recall Saidiya Hartman's point about the inseparable relationship between violence and pleasure in blackface minstrelsy.[44] Part of the attraction of the series for white audiences was its ritual subjection of the Black body to physical pain and punishment. Repeatedly, firmly, and violently putting Black characters back in their social place, the *Darktown* series engendered enjoyment for whites concerned about their status atop the racial hierarchy.

The *Darktown* comics spoke not only to ideas about race and social place but also to ideas about race and geographic space. As a fictional town, the spatial character of Darktown was fairly nebulous. In some prints, it is a rural town, more farmland than city. In others, it is an urban center of sizable proportions. But these alternating images were not contradictions—Darktown was a concept more than a fleshed-out fictional place, an idea of segregated Black space more than any specific location. It may be that some of the all-Black towns springing up on the western frontier in the late nineteenth century inspired Worth. But given that he heavily based the *Darktown* comics on Eytinge's *Blackville* series, which was first published in the early 1870s, and that the main spate of all-Black town formation in places like Oklahoma and Kansas did not occur until the late 1880s and 1890s, it is unlikely that *Darktown* is a direct reference to these efforts at Black self-determination.[45]

Another potential influence might have been the scattered "contraband" camps that formed in the South during the Civil War and occasionally developed into small all-Black towns during the postbellum years. Likewise, the rapid influx of African Americans from the countryside to Southern cities in the years after the Civil War, as well as the makeshift camps the Freedmen's Bureau organized to care for them on the outskirts of cities, led to the formation of predominantly Black residential "rings" fringing Southern cities. However, all-Black Southern towns were not particularly numerous, and the fact that some of the *Darktown* comics depict significantly built-up urban environments makes it unlikely that audiences would have interpreted

Darktown as solely a reference to these Southern towns and fringe settlements or to Black frontier towns. Instead, Darktown was a flexible segregated space that could encompass small town and city life, the suburban and the urban.[46]

Inextricably linked with the series' depictions of Black social failure, the *Darktown* comics presented Black space as deficient and disorderly. In *A Darktown Tournament: The First Tilt*, a Black woman in an urban environment hangs a sign—riddled with misspellings and backward letters—from her window advertising for a whitewasher, while below her two Black whitewasher men face off with each other in a parody of jousting, their long brushes serving as lances (see figure 5.3A). In the companion print, *A Darktown Tournament: Close Quarters*, the two men have simply descended into an all-out brawl (see figure 5.3B). Their long-handled brushes lie shattered on the ground, and they smack each other with their smaller brushes, sending white paint flying everywhere. In the background, the woman simply laughs at the chaos she has induced, while a Black policeman rushes toward the two, his tiny club and portly caricatured body suggesting he will only add to the confusion rather than resolve it. Meanwhile, the complete absence of white people from the pair of prints establishes the segregated nature of the scene. At a time when Black urban residents had many white neighbors, the lack of white residents contradicted the reality of US urban demographics. Additionally, the very name of the series indicates this is segregated urban space; it is an explicit signpost of an all-Black geography. The prints thus convey to the viewer a fully segregated world, one where disorder reigns and the law is no match for Black violence.[47]

Fisticuffs also rule the day in the pair of prints *A Literary Debate in the Darktown Club*. In the first illustration, two Black men on a stage argue animatedly with each other beneath portraits of George Washington, Abraham Lincoln—misspelled "Linkum"—and Ulysses S. Grant as an audience of attentive Black men look on. In the second, the two men have clearly been fighting—they sit on the stage floor, their clothing torn, furniture and glass bottles broken and scattered about them. One of the men holds his head in pain while the other wears a black eye and a now-broken portrait of Washington around his neck. A banner above Grant's picture with his campaign slogan "Let us have peace" has been ripped in two, suggesting that Black violence, not white violence, fractures the social peace. Meanwhile, a Black policeman pokes his head in from a door to the outside, too late to enforce order. Along with *A Darktown Tournament*, the prints convey that African Americans cannot handle urbanity, whether the everyday service of whitewashing or the

FIGURE 5.3A AND B J. Cameron, *A Darktown Tournament: The First Tilt* (New York: Currier and Ives, 1890) and J. Cameron, *A Darktown Tournament: Close Quarters* (New York: Currier and Ives, 1890). Courtesy of the Popular Graphic Arts Collection, Library of Congress.

FIGURE 5.4A AND B *Horse Car Sports Going to a Chicken Show: All Flush* (New York: Currier and Ives, 1886) and *Horse Car Sports on the Back Track: Dead Broke* (New York: Currier and Ives, 1886). Courtesy of the Popular Graphic Arts Collection, Library of Congress.

higher intellectual pursuit of debate societies. Incapable of resolving conflicts through reason and words, they always resort to physical violence.[48]

In addition to physical altercations, life in Darktown consisted of underhandedness, gambling, and fiscal irresponsibility. The print *Horse Car Sports Going to a Chicken Show* (1886) shows an urban horse-drawn trolley—the "Darktown Fifth Av[e] Line"—moving over a cobblestone street, its front end packed with Black men dressed in lurid suits and conspicuously puffing cigars (see figure 5.4A). One of the men carries a rooster for cockfighting tucked under his arm, and all radiate a buoyant mood. Evidencing Black Americans' insufficient attempt at urban technology, two undersized donkeys pull the trolley rather than horses. Scrawled across the trolley's top are the numbers "4-11-44," African Americans' supposed favorite combination when gambling in illegal lotteries. The second print, *Horse Car Sports on the Back Track*, depicts all the same men, but now riding on the back of the trolley and looking thoroughly dejected (see figure 5.4B). The dead rooster clutched in one of the man's hands explains their depressed spirits—clearly, the fight did not go well. The men have also lost all their money gambling on the contest, failing to save even enough for the trolley fare home, as the irate conductor shaking his fist and pointing to a sign that reads "Niggers wot don't pay will git bounced" testifies.[49]

As part of their larger deprecation of Black space, the *Darktown* comics also repeatedly attacked free Black geographical movement, suggesting that Black mobility produced only disorder and disaster. By deriding Black mobility in addition to Black space, the series bolstered the logics of segregation, telegraphing that Black urban residents had to be spatially contained and separated from white space in order to preserve safety and peace in the city.

Some early prints even portrayed Black mobility as directly harming white people. In *The Boss of the Road* (1884), a Black man riding a tired-looking donkey has run two white men and their horse-drawn carriages off a suburban road (see figure 5.5). The Black man rides smack in the middle of the street and carries a broad tattered sun umbrella over his shoulder, its sharp spokes poking out dangerously. The white men have swerved off the road to avoid the Black man and his umbrella, while the Black man—oblivious to what he has done—simply smiles and stares vacantly in front of him. Behind him, other white men struggle with run-away horses, and a carriage lies upended in the road, all casualties of the Black man's negligent riding. The pristine order of the large suburban houses, with their neat fences and manicured lawns, stands in sharp contrast to the mayhem the Black man's presence has wrought in the neighborhood. The print implies that African Americans are too irresponsible and unaware to follow the rules of the road, and that their unrestricted movement in urban space threatens white residents. Further signaling that the Black man is out of place, he wears a shabby coat and boots to go along with his decrepit umbrella, whereas the white men are all snappily dressed. The Black man also holds a large jug in his left hand, suggesting that alcohol may be partially responsible for his blissfully unaware state.[50]

African Americans with mobility in the *Darktown* comics also threatened each other. Although the word "Darktown" was not included in print titles until the mid-1880s, the early entries made it apparent that they depicted Black space and that African Americans endangered one another there. In *Creating a Sensation* (1881), a young Black male bellhop rides a large-wheeled bicycle recklessly down a town street, leaving chaos in his wake and smiling shamelessly as he gives a side-glance at the disarray his wild riding has caused (see figure 5.6A). In the background, a Black woman has been thrown from the donkey she was riding and lies suspended by her waist from a low-hanging tree branch. Meanwhile, a Black male whitewasher sits spread-eagle on the

FIGURE 5.5 Thomas Worth, *The Boss of the Road* (New York: Currier and Ives, 1884). Courtesy of the Popular Graphic Arts Collection, Library of Congress.

ground, a paint bucket on his head and an expression of anger on his face. His wheelbarrow lies on its side nearby, its wheel snapped off. Once again, the series constructs Black movement as irresponsible and leading to disorder. The print's pair, *Spoiling a Sensation,* enacts the ritual punishment of this reckless mobility through one of Worth's favorite motifs: a bull charge (see figure 5.6B). Coming out of nowhere, a bull rams the bellhop and his bicycle. The bellhop shouts in surprise as he goes for a ride on the bull's back, his legs dangling in the air behind the bull. Rationality thus takes a back seat to the violent punishment of African Americans, with the print failing to provide any clue as to why a bull is running loose on the street. In the background, the woman and the whitewasher laugh heartily at the bellhop's turn of fate, ventriloquizing the satisfaction of white audiences.[51]

Black mobility comes under slightly different fire in *Crossed by "a Milk Train"* and *Wrecked by a Cow Catcher* (1885). In the former, a flimsy patchwork train driven by two Black men makes its way along a ridge. The train has a teapot for a boiler and a dented and bent smokestack—seemingly appropriated from a stove—and is tiny in size, barely larger than the two conductors. All these aspects signal African Americans' inability to create and operate modern technologies of transportation.[52] Despite its small size, it pulls a

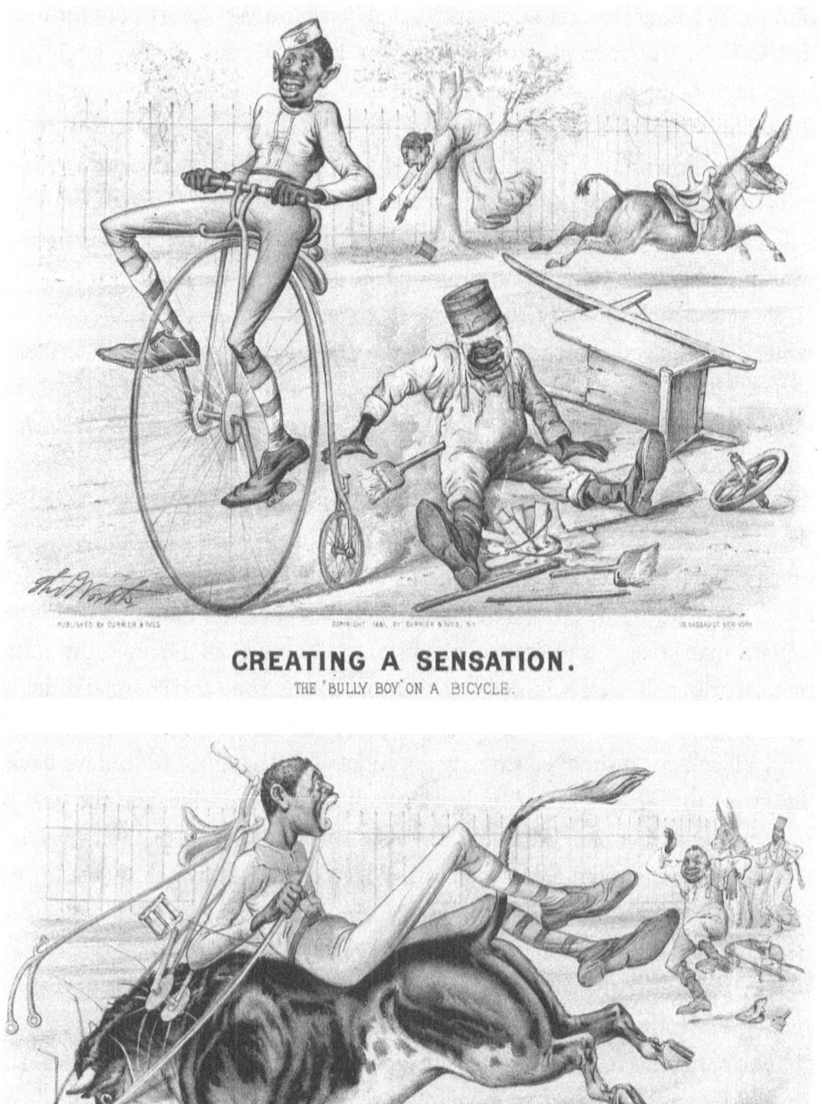

FIGURE 5.6A AND B Thomas Worth, *Creating a Sensation* (New York: Currier and Ives, 1881) and Thomas Worth, *Spoiling a Sensation* (New York: Currier and Ives, 1881). Courtesy of the Popular Graphic Arts Collection, Library of Congress.

number of passenger cars, with caricatured Black heads poking out of the windows. Ahead of the train a cow lounges on the tracks, and the two engineers and the passengers all stare, gripped with fear, as the train steams toward it. In the second print, the train has come off the rails, the passengers screaming as it tumbles down the hill. Still straddling the tracks, the cow looks down angrily from the ridgetop, a piece of the train stuck on one of its horns. Unable to withstand even a cow, the train and its destruction symbolize African Americans' inability to undertake autonomous modern movement and travel.[53]

Bicycles, a technology that greatly expanded the everyday mobility of Americans, played a recurring role in the *Darktown* comics. The late 1880s and 1890s witnessed a bicycle boom as mechanical improvements made them safer and easier to use, and the pair of 1892 prints *The Darktown Bicycle Club* referenced Americans' enthusiasm for bikes while ridiculing Black participation in the craze (see figures 5.7A and 5.7B). The first illustration shows a Black bicycle club "on parade," with Black men and women in gaudy cycling outfits riding proudly down an urban street lined with two- and three-story buildings, while large crowds of Black spectators cheer them on. To the right, a Black man struggles to control a resistant tethered goat. Then, in the companion print subtitled *Knocked Out*, the goat has escaped and charged directly into the parade, causing a large pileup. The lead cyclist now sits on the ground with a black eye, a shocked expression, and a wheel hanging around his neck. The woman riding behind him has also fallen from her bike, and the goat is butting her in the rear. The goat has also obliterated both of their bicycles into tiny pieces strewn about the road. That a goat could wreak such damage is highly unrealistic, but realism, once again, is not the point. Punishing the Black body and Black confidence trumps verisimilitude, and the prints deny Black Americans the ability to occupy public space and engage in urban movement with dignity.[54]

The inhabitants of Darktown likewise could not handle that more advanced technology of urban movement, the trolley, as illustrated in a pair of 1896 prints aptly titled *Darktown Trolley* (see figures 5.8A and 5.8B). In the first, a boxy electric trolley moves down a crowded city thoroughfare. "Darktown" is displayed across its front, and lettering on its side announces it is the "Darktown to Blackville" line. It is full of Black passengers, and a Black driver in a sporty uniform rings a bell and shouts to alert bystanders to the trolley's passing. It is apparently new to the streets of Darktown, as pedestrians and people leaning out nearby windows stare at it in amazement. Foreshadowing tragedy, a Black boy on a bicycle is about to pedal in front of the oncoming trolley, unaware of the danger. And hinting at the disorder of Black space, a

FIGURE 5.7A AND B J. Cameron, *The Darktown Bicycle Club: On Parade* (New York: Currier and Ives, 1892) and J. Cameron, *The Darktown Bicycle Club: Knocked Out* (New York: Currier and Ives, 1892). Courtesy of the Popular Graphic Arts Collection, Library of Congress.

FIGURE 5.8A AND B J. Cameron, *Darktown Trolley: Clar de Track When de Bell Rings* (New York: Currier and Ives, 1896) and J. Cameron, *Darktown Trolley: Through Car in Danger* (New York: Currier and Ives, 1896). Courtesy of the Popular Graphic Arts Collection, Library of Congress.

small dog hangs by its leash from one of the electrical wires above the street.[55]

The second print brings the calamity that inevitably accompanies Black movement in Darktown—out of nowhere, a Black fire brigade rushes across the tracks directly in front of the trolley, setting up an unavoidable collision between it and the brigade's horse-drawn wagon. The firefighters are completely oblivious to the trolley; one of the brigade members even sits in the middle of the wagon strumming a banjo and singing. Even the horses are more conscious of the danger, one rearing up with bulging eyes in the face of the impending crash. From the front of the trolley, the driver yells and throws up his hands in a useless attempt at warning, while behind him the cars are already tilting to one side, about to fly off the tracks completely. The subtext of the prints is not subtle: African Americans are far too irresponsible and unintelligent to handle the demands of modern city life and its technologies of movement. For the residents of Darktown, freedom of mobility is merely a liability, producing physical injury and havoc.[56]

The unruly Black mobility in the *Darktown* comics, which was a key extension of the general disorder characterizing Black space in the series, did not stand alone in Currier and Ives's racial iconography. Imagery of white people in the company's general catalog underscored its derisive representations of Black autonomy and independence. In sharp contrast to the disparagement heaped on Black mobility in the *Darktown* series, Currier and Ives's prints featuring white people routinely presented white mobility as modern, orderly, fast, and efficient.

One of the primary ways such representations of white mobility appeared was in the company's numerous prints about horse racing, which constituted a major portion of Currier and Ives's output. One of the first prints the company produced on the subject, *Ripton* (1850), typifies the genre (see figure 5.9). It shows the racing horse Ripton speedily trotting while pulling a lightweight racing sulky on which an unidentified white man sits. The horse and the man are the clear focus of the print, with Ripton's dark body standing out against a lightly sketched country background. Everything about the pair implies speed and grace. The smooth, curving lines of the horse's body and neck are neat and clean, and its legs and hoofs are suspended above the ground and moving in alternating symmetry, with the left two coming toward each other and the right two extending away. The thin, perfectly straight wooden rods connecting the horse to the sulky descend across the horse's body at a slightly downward angle, mirrored by even thinner reins that stretch above them in a slightly upward trajectory from the bridle to the man's hands,

FIGURE 5.9 *Ripton* (New York: Currier and Ives, 1850). Courtesy of the Popular Graphic Arts Collection, Library of Congress.

which grasp them effortlessly. Perched on an elegant thin seat, the man sits perfectly upright with a stolid expression on his face. Beneath him, two large wheels turn on wooden rims connected to their axels by numerous incredibly fine spokes. Aesthetically pleasing and geometrically neat, the image connotes order and control. In addition, the horse and carriage move at a fast rate, as the dust kicked up beneath them indicates. Completely composed and showing no signs of exertion, the man is fully in command of his body and the horse as they drive along at top speed. The print thus portrays white masculinity as the purveyor of quick but orderly movement—an idea countless Currier and Ives horse-racing lithographs would reinforce throughout the remainder of the century.[57]

But not all Currier and Ives prints construed white mobility as serene. The print *"Trotting Cracks" on the Snow* (1858) highlights the ability of white people to maintain order and control in fast, crowded conditions. A winter scene, *"Trotting Cracks"* depicts a busy snow-covered country road, with horse-drawn sleighs dashing in both directions, all steered by white people. Some of the sleighs are single seaters pulled by a lone horse, while others carry as many as three riders and have multiple horses drawing them. All of the sleighs rush at high speed, horses pulling strenuously on their harnesses. There are no particular lanes, as sleighs heading in either direction are

FIGURE 5.10. J. Cameron, *Speeding on the Avenue* (New York: Currier and Ives, 1870). Courtesy of the Popular Graphic Arts Collection, Library of Congress.

interspersed with one another, but order reigns nonetheless, the sleighs passing each other without a hitch, despite their close proximity and the speed at which they move. One white man even waves his hat to greet an acquaintance zipping in the other direction. One lone agent of chaos, a black dog, chases after a sleigh in the foreground, but despite its best efforts, it does not disrupt the traffic. Unlike the denizens of Darktown, the white drivers in the print are fully capable of navigating thick traffic without collision or loss of speed.[58]

The 1870 print *Speeding on the Avenue* displays whites' ability to handle traffic and adhere to the rules of the road on an even grander scale (see figure 5.10). The print shows an urban scene of dense horse-carriage traffic on a broad dirt avenue. Despite its size, the road is thick with carriages, the traffic extending off into the distance. Although it does not specifically name the avenue, the print potentially depicts the road known as the Harlem River Speedway in New York City, which was a popular horse-carriage track in the late nineteenth century. As the avenue recedes into the distance on the far right, a portion of High Bridge, an aqueduct crossing the Harlem River at 174th Street, is visible. The carriages all rush with evident speed along the avenue—a fact the title of the print makes abundantly clear—and white men drive them all. In fact, women are entirely absent from the image, conveying

FIGURE 5.11 J. Cameron, *Fast Trotters on Harlem Lane N.Y.* (New York: Currier and Ives, 1870). Courtesy of the Popular Graphic Arts Collection, Library of Congress.

the notion that fast driving is a male preserve and inappropriate for women. Despite the heavy traffic, the movement is unimpaired and well-regulated, as those heading north occupy the right side of the road and those headed south ride on the left. A number of carriages are pulled by two horses, and in these instances their legs are perfectly in sync, further suggesting that order and control characterize white movement. In the lower right-hand corner, a man throws a friendly wave at a passing carriage, emphasizing that white men move fast and efficiently in urban space while remaining courteous.[59]

The strong link between white masculinity and quick urban movement also arises in the 1870 print *Fast Trotters on Harlem Lane N.Y.* (see figure 5.11). Harlem Lane was another popular road on which New York's horse enthusiasts exercised and raced their steeds, and this print specifically depicts two of the city's most renowned citizens—railroad magnate Cornelius Vanderbilt and *New York Ledger* owner Robert Bonner—driving carriages in the center foreground, with text below their images listing them and their horses by name. Just as in *Speeding on the Avenue*, the road is bustling with carriages, white men driving them at a rapid clip in both directions. The stream of carriages continues off into the distance and out of sight beyond the left edge of the image, a thick mass completely covering the road, emphasizing the sheer magnitude of modern white mobility. Meanwhile, a clubhouse with stables sits off the road to the right, its porch crowded with white men observing the passing action. A sign just to the right of the clubhouse driveway demarcates a separate "Ladies Entrence [*sic*]," reiterating that this fast-paced scene is the purview of men, and women must be safely separated from its hurried activity. Once again, white men oversee and engage in urban movement that is resolutely ordered and controlled, despite its high volume and speed.[60]

Finally, it is worth noting the differences between the representations of trains in Currier and Ives's general catalog and those in the *Darktown* series. Whereas the trains of Darktown are clumsy and rickety and ultimately meet with destruction, the trains in the general catalog are fast, reliable, and ornate. Indeed, the titles of Currier and Ives train prints repeatedly emphasize speed, including *The Express Train* (1870), *American Railroad Scene: Lightning Express Trains Leaving the Junction* (1874), and *Night Scene at an American Railway Junction: Lightning Express, Flying Mail and Owl Trains, "On Time"* (1876). These prints celebrated trains—the ultimate symbol of modern movement, technological invention, and speed in nineteenth-century Western society—for their contribution to travel and communication and linked them with whiteness. That general Currier and Ives prints represented trains in this way is not particularly surprising, but it drives home the symbolic importance of African Americans' failure to master trains in the *Darktown* series. To fail at trains was to fail at modernity.[61]

Whereas Black mobility on trains was disordered, white train travel was efficient and a key aspect of civilization and urban growth. For example, *Night Scene at an American Railway Junction: Lightning Express, Flying Mail and Owl Trains, "On Time"* draws a visual link between the speed and efficiency of trains and burgeoning urbanity (see figure 5.12). It portrays a busy rail yard at night, with numerous trains pulling in and out, their lanterns shining through the semidark. Despite the lateness of the hour, white workers scurry about the yard, hastening to load freight and otherwise prepare for the arrival and departure of trains. The lit-up windows of the passenger cars reveal they are full of riders, and visible in the background of the image—across a river and beneath a full moon—is the dark skyline of a large unspecified metropolis. With trains at its center, the motion of white urban life never ceases; it is regular and dependable—always "on time."[62]

In the montage of racial imagery streaming out of the Currier and Ives publishing house, the representations of uncontrolled and dangerous Black mobility in the *Darktown* series contrasted starkly with the general catalog's repeated portrayals of white mobility as controlled, fast, and efficient. These

FIGURE 5.12 Parsons and Atwater, *Night Scene at an American Railway Junction: Lightning Express, Flying Mail and Owl Trains, "On Time"* (New York: Currier and Ives, 1876). Courtesy of the Popular Graphic Arts Collection, Library of Congress.

contrasting images of mobility served as prominent markers of racial difference and formed one of the ways the *Darktown* series denigrated and pathologized Black urban space. Furthermore, in traducing Black mobility, the series implicitly conveyed that Black urban movement needed to be restricted in order to uphold peace and social order in the city, thus reinforcing the rationale of residential segregation.

Decades before the advent of large-scale ghetto segregation at the beginning of the twentieth century, the *Darktown* comics and representations of Thompson Street in popular culture propagated the false notion that homogeneous Black urban space was an extant reality, a commonplace and natural outcome of postemancipation life in US cities. In doing so, they completely erased the mixed-race character of the urban neighborhoods in which African Americans actually lived during the late nineteenth century. Circulating nationally, both the *Darktown* prints and representations of Thompson Street reflected and helped naturalize the period's nascent residential segregation, helping drive a process that would bloom into full-blown ghettoization across the country in the early decades of the twentieth century. They legitimized and encouraged this development by presenting their counterfeit visions of Black space as suffused with violence, dangerous mobility, and disorder, suggesting that the segregation and containment of urban African Americans was not only proper but also necessary for the protection of whites.

However, Black movement was not the only form of nonwhite mobility that popular culture attacked in the late nineteenth century. Native American mobility also came under fire in the era's most prominent cultural representation of Native peoples: Buffalo Bill's Wild West show. Perhaps the most famous and popular US entertainment of the late nineteenth century, the Wild West show directly linked Native violence against whites with uncontained Native mobility. What is more, it used the script of dangerous Native mobility to dress up the history of the American West as a tale of white heroism and the triumph of white settled domesticity. The Wild West show proved so popular that one of its producers, Nate Salsbury, went on to bankroll his own show in 1895. But rather than the American West, Salsbury turned to the American South and the Southern pastoral for his new venture, organizing a massive plantation reenactment in New York City dubbed *Black America*. Chapter 6 turns to these two shows, examining not only their racist trappings but also how the Native and Black actors hired to perform in each of them worked to subvert the shows' racist messages and used their employment to further their own economic and geographic mobility.

CHAPTER SIX

Arenas of Mobility

Buffalo Bill's Wild West Show and the Black America *Plantation Reenactment, 1880–1900*

In 1887, the renowned Carlisle Indian Industrial School—a boarding school in Carlisle, Pennsylvania, founded by white reformer Richard Henry Pratt—put on an exhibition in New York City to demonstrate the beneficial effects of boarding school education for Native American children. The evening's program was filled with student speeches, musical recitals, debates, and artwork displays. Among those in attendance were two Native actors from Buffalo Bill's Wild West show, which was then playing in the city, and the show's publicist, John Burke. Whether the two Indian actors requested to attend the Carlisle exhibition or if the show's managers arranged the visit as a means of generating publicity is unclear. Regardless, Native American pupils representing the uplift strategy of white reformers convened in the same urban space that night with Native actors participating in a show that cast Indians as untutored savages. While the actors and the students traveled different paths—both constrained and shaped in different ways by colonial structures—they all arrived in New York City and laid claim to an urban mobility that overturned dominant white stereotypes about Indians and movement.[1]

A year later, an inverse picture presented itself when 175 Carlisle students attended the Wild West show. Many of the students had family members working as performers in the show, and the visit offered a rare opportunity for a reunion of the boarding school pupils and their relatives. A newspaper article commenting on the Carlisle students' attendance mentioned a particularly "joyous meeting" between the actor Blue Horse and his son, who had been at Carlisle for a number of years. Indexing the dislocations of settler colonialism that haunted these moments of Indian mobility and agency, the paper stated that while Blue Horse did not speak English, his son did not know the Sioux language, and therefore the two had to communicate through an interpreter. Further haunting the exchange was the fact that the Wild West show's thematic content presented a vision of Native mobility that helped underwrite the containment of US Indian boarding schools, as well as the larger US reservation policy in general. However, at the same time, the anecdote illustrates the communal possibilities that Native performers' travels with the Wild West show opened up, travels that undermined and contradicted the show's prevailing racial script about Native mobility as antimodern and tied to violence against whites.[2]

This entanglement of the popular and policy, resistance and oppression, forms the subject of this chapter. In particular, the chapter looks at two large-scale performance reenactments to demonstrate that popular performance shows were an arena in which multiple competing visions of race and mobility played out. First, it analyzes Buffalo Bill's Wild West show, which opened in 1883 and played to massive audiences through the end of the century. Next, it examines the highly popular plantation reenactment titled *Black America*, which took place in Brooklyn, New York, in 1895. Both shows fundamentally depended on nonwhite performers. One of the Wild West show's biggest draws was its Native actors, and the producers of *Black America* advertised it as having the largest cast of Black performers ever assembled. As a result, both shows created room for Native and Black resistance despite their overarching racist narratives.

Perhaps the most popular entertainment of the nineteenth century, the Wild West show implicated race and mobility on multiple levels. First, the performance itself foregrounded Native Americans' threatening mobility and painted them as the antithesis of settled domesticity. The show's construction of Indian movement as dangerous and primitive both echoed and justified the carceral conditions of the reservation. Second, white reformers and policymakers in the Office of Indian Affairs engaged in a highly publicized battle to prevent William "Buffalo Bill" Cody from hiring Native American actors off reservations in part because they felt that traveling around the country would rekindle Native actors' racial tendency for nomadism—a tendency reformers felt the reservation was designed to stamp out. These struggles placed the Wild West show at the center of political fights over federal Indian policy. Finally, Native performers used the show to escape the geographical confinement of the reservation. Traveling the continent and sometimes the world, Native actors in the show transcended the spatial boundaries of the reservation and turned the circuits of the entertainment industry into conduits for their autonomous movement. While historians have discussed these various aspects separately, no work has synthesized these aspects of the Wild West show into an encompassing analysis of race and spatial mobility.[3] Doing so illustrates how popular culture was thoroughly enmeshed in the political debates over federal Indian policy and the implementation of the reservation on the ground in the late nineteenth century.

Likewise, competing visions of racial mobility suffused the plantation reenactment *Black America*. Intended as a literal restaging of a Southern plantation in New York City, the show's prevailing theme was Southern pastoralism. It celebrated the rural South as Black Americans' natural home, a home defined by Black contentment. *Black America* thus instantiated the Southern pastoral's spatiality of containment in yet another cultural form, portraying Black bodies rooted in space as the foundation of racial and social harmony. Yet within its Southern pastoralism, the show's Black performers inserted assertions of modern Black urbanity and professional respectability. While created and bankrolled by white producers, *Black America*'s managing producer was the Black performer William "Billy" McClain. McClain exercised particular control over the show's musical segment, which he used to convey a racial progress narrative that situated Black people as modern subjects who were anything but tied down to the plantation. This chapter also discusses how McClain parlayed his considerable success in the entertainment industry, including in *Black America*, into the formation of the Benevolent Order of Colored Professionals (BO of CP), a mutual aid society specifically geared to furthering the careers of Black male entertainers. While its exclusion of Black women performers limited its transgressive potential, the BO of CP nonetheless pushed back against the prevailing racism of the popular culture industry. With chapters in multiple US cities, the BO of CP facilitated Black entertainers' interurban movement across the country, providing both a place to gather on the road and economic aid when in need. Just like the Wild West show, *Black America* was a staging ground for alternative visions of racial mobility.[4]

The Wild West show and *Black America* were linked in deeper ways as well, ways that highlight the entwinements of Greater Reconstruction. It was one of the white producers of the Wild West show, Nate Salsbury, who took the lessons he learned about outdoor arena shows and launched *Black America*. After Cody and Salsbury portrayed the Wild West show as an authentic re-creation that provided audiences with educational instruction through historical and anthropological veracity, Salsbury did the same with *Black America*. This claim to educational value helped imbue both shows with a respectability that unlocked the lucrative middle-class market. Undergirding these conceptual links were material connections. Salsbury had leased land in Ambrose Park, in Brooklyn, New York, for staging and storing the Wild West show, and when the show relocated, he used the land to stage *Black America*. Finally, on a simple but fundamental level, it was the Wild West show's success that paved the financial way for *Black America* by helping provide Salsbury with the necessary capital to start his new venture.

These connections are a reminder that Greater Reconstruction's racial reconstitutions unfolded simultaneously in the late nineteenth century. As US settlers attempted to enclose the West and emancipation destroyed the controlled race relations of slavery, white desires for affirmation of their racial superiority generated popular culture productions pandering to this need. Both the Wild West show and *Black America* latched on to continentally expansive white anxieties about the incorporation of Native and free Black Americans into the US polity, and they posed Native and Black immobility as the solution to those anxieties, echoing and reinforcing Greater Reconstruction's turn to the Indian reservation and Jim Crow segregation. Indeed, Salsbury's neat switch from the Wild West to the Southern pastoral registered the strong grip that white concerns about racial containment held on the cultural imaginary. Before turning to an analysis of the two shows, the next section provides important context concerning US reservation policy, recounting white reformers' growing critiques of the reservation after 1880 and their focus on instituting the even more intensive carceral relations of the Indian boarding school and allotment.

Reforming Confinement

By the 1880s, the reservation system was firmly established as the federal government's reigning Indian policy, and a multitude of reservations dotted the West. But around the end of the 1870s and the beginning of the 1880s, a rising chorus of voices criticizing the reservation emanated from white reformers. For these reformers, the reservation system was failing to produce the desired assimilation of Native Americans. Indians on reservations retained too many of their traditional cultural ways, especially holding lands communally rather than becoming individual property owners devoted to agriculture. Dismayed at the lack of progress, white reformers identified the spatial relations of the reservation as a major part of the problem. But these white reformers did not argue against the confinement of Native peoples; rather, they felt that the reservation did not impose enough confinement. They advocated two new spatial structures to secure Native assimilation, which they envisioned as imposing even stricter restrictions on Indian movement: the off-reservation boarding school for Indian children and the allotment of reservation lands in severalty to force Indians to become settled agriculturalists.

A key aspect of white reformers' rationale for ending the reservation system was the idea that the containment of the reservation had backfired. A long-standing notion stretching back all the way to the early days of the removal policy was that Indians needed to be separated from "bad" whites, since they would invariably adopt their immoral habits. In this view, only white Christian missionaries and benevolent Indian agents should have close contact with Native peoples. This assumption also informed justifications for the reservation.[5] But white reformers now saw the metaphorical walls of the reservation as keeping out not only "bad" whites but also morally upstanding whites. They contended that Native Americans had to intermingle with white society—though in a controlled manner—to benefit from the good example provided by most white Americans.

Former secretary of the interior and zealous reformer Carl Schurz reflected this turn in 1881, when he wrote that on "reservations[,] he [the Indian] lives only among his own kind, excepting the teachers and the few white agency people." Without personally seeing civilization at work directly, Native Americans' assimilation would stall. As a solution, Schurz called for off-reservation boarding schools and land in severalty. Off-reservation boarding schools would ensure that Native children would be away from the influence of their communities and surrounded by "civilized" white society—and strictly supervised and monitored by white teachers, of course. Meanwhile, adult Indians would undergo "individualization in the possession of property by their settlement in severalty upon small farm tracts with a fee simple title." Schurz maintained that "so settled, and hav[ing] become individual property owners," Indians would part with the remainder of reservation lands to whites, ensuring the further development of the country. Schurz's vision thus supplanted the containment of the reservation with the containment of the boarding school and settlement on small farms. Of course, land in severalty had always been the ultimate goal of reservation policy—it was to come at some distant point in the future after the reservation had helped foster Native assimilation. But for Schurz and other white reformers, the point was that the reservation in fact delayed the process and needed to be short-circuited by distributing land in severalty immediately. Rather than an end goal, land in severalty was now a means for achieving assimilation.[6]

Lyman Abbott, one of the most prominent Indian reformers of the time, echoed Schurz's views. Speaking in 1885, Abbott reiterated the right of white Americans to enforce the assimilation of Native Americans by invoking the trope of the wandering Indian. Those who said the US had violated treaties by taking Native Americans' land were incorrect, Abbott asserted, because "the Indians did not occupy this land. A people do not occupy a country simply because they roam over it. . . . The Indians can scarcely be said to have occupied this country more than the bisons [*sic*] and the buffalo they hunted."

White Americans thus had a right and a duty to bring cultivation to Indian lands and a related duty to bring Native peoples into the fold of civilization. According to Abbott, the reservation impeded these duties. "The reservation system," he proclaimed, "runs a fence about a great territory and says to civilization, 'Keep off!'" In addition to keeping white civilization out, the borders of the reservation in fact perpetuated Native peoples' nomadic ways by giving Indians too much land. Native Americans might not be able to cross those borders, but within them they could carry on hunting. As such, he argued that "the reservation barriers should be cast down and the land given to the Indians in severalty." He also praised off-reservation boarding schools but lamented that as long as the reservations existed, graduates would simply return to the problem.[7]

Perhaps one of the most influential reformers of the period was Thomas Morgan, who ascended to the post of commissioner of Indian affairs in 1889 and brought his reforming zeal to the position. He believed the reservation system was antiquated and instead championed allotment. He was also an ardent proponent of off-reservation boarding schools, and his plan for a reformed Indian school system emphasized the need to isolate Indian children from the reservation and place them under the surveillance of white teachers. Once separated in boarding schools, the students would be inculcated with "systematic habits." "The periods of rising and retiring, the hours for meals, times for study, recitation, work and play" would be "fixed and adhered to with great punctiliousness." Placed under surveillance and so disciplined, Indian children would be stripped of the reservation's corrupting influences.[8]

Throughout the last two decades of the nineteenth century, most white reformers remained committed to establishing boarding schools for Indian children and replacing the reservation system with individual allotments. These were two of the most prominent in a raft of reforms that white philanthropists called for, others of which included granting Native Americans citizenship and extending US law over the reservations.[9] As such, white reformers desired to replace the containment of the reservation with the containment of the boarding school and settled, small-proprietor farming.[10] These efforts produced a strong movement for allotment, most notably through the work of Senator Henry Dawes, whose advocacy resulted in the Dawes Act of 1887, which facilitated the division of much Native land into individually owned private plots. Likewise, by 1900, almost eighteen thousand Indian children were enrolled in 153 government-operated boarding schools, twenty-five of which were off-reservation. Privately run boarding schools, the most famous of which was the Carlisle Indian Industrial School in Pennsylvania, also complemented these government schools.[11]

However, the reservation remained the primary structure mediating US-Indian relations for the rest of the century.[12] While allotment was a devastating policy that resulted in significant Native land loss, particularly after 1900, and a major component in the federal government's violent attack on Native lives and territories, it did not supplant the reservation as the primary policy for carrying out US settler-colonial ambitions. In 1934, 65.6 percent of the land owned by Native Americans was still tribally owned reservations.[13] The fact that the reservation continued to be the dominant form for managing relations with the Indigenous tribes was due in no small part to the determined resistance of Native Americans to allotment of their territories. In the face of relentless persecution, Native peoples were able to turn the reservation into a site of cultural and communal preservation.[14]

Of course, many of the coercive and oppressive aspects of the reservation persisted, including sharp curtailments on Native peoples' mobility. Therefore, while some whites began to see the reservation as insufficiently confining Native Americans, Greater Reconstruction's major ideological and material shift to more rigorous containment of Native Americans remained in place and, indeed, continued to be implemented primarily through the reservation. But as white reformers' turn against the reservation illustrates, there were tensions over what constituted the best way to restrict Indian mobility. At the same time, Native peoples consistently strove to exercise control over their own movements. During the 1880s and 1890s, these tensions over Indigenous mobility would fundamentally shape Buffalo Bill's Wild West show.

The Competing Mobilities of the Wild West Show

In 1872, William "Buffalo Bill" Cody decided to capitalize on his minor celebrity as a western buffalo hunter and army scout—enhanced in 1869 by his appearance as a character in one of Ned Buntline's dime novels—and try his luck on the theater stage. He left Nebraska and began touring the Midwest and Northeast with his theater company, the Buffalo Bill Combination, entertaining spectators with plays about fighting Indians and white outlaws. An ingenious self-promoter, Cody's early stage career was highly successful. However, the frontier violence depicted in his plays, especially the combat with Indians and immigrant villains, appealed predominantly to working-class Americans, who made up the bulk of his audiences. But Cody's persistent ambition to attract a more lucrative middle-class audience led him in the late 1870s to tone down the violence and, most significantly, to begin hiring Native American actors to play the Indian roles onstage.

The use of Native American actors tapped into white Americans' widespread desire to see "authentic" premodern Indians in a society undergoing rapid urbanization and industrialization. In addition, many whites felt US western expansion would inevitably lead to the extinction of Native Americans or, at least, any semblance of their traditional way of life, and they wanted a glimpse of premodern savagery before it disappeared. Cody's incorporation of Indian actors not only augmented the success of his theater show and its cross-class appeal but also led him to envision a much more ambitious outdoor arena show in which Native American actors would play a central role.[15]

The Wild West show first opened in 1883 and, after a financially bumpy two years, eventually found firm ground and achieved enormous popularity. In a bid to attract middle-class audiences, particularly middle-class women, Cody leaned on the show's purported authenticity and realism to market it as an educational experience. In 1884, Cody partnered with veteran show manager Nate Salsbury, who had cut his managerial teeth overseeing minstrel troupes. Salsbury and the show's publicist, John Burke, set about helping Cody market the Wild West show as respectable entertainment. They consistently billed it as an edifying re-creation of real life on the western frontier and touted the performers' genuine—if often exaggerated—western roots and experiences. Alongside Native American actors, the show featured white sharpshooters and white and Mexican cowboys who performed various feats of marksmanship, horse riding, bronco busting, and lassoing.

Thus did the consumer power of middle-class women yet again fundamentally shape popular culture, repeating the dynamics of antebellum sheet music and blackface minstrelsy. Claims to authenticity fended off potential public perceptions of the show as merely sensational or frivolous, characterizations that marked other entertainments, such as circuses, as beyond the pale of middle-class respectability.[16] As with blackface minstrel shows, these claims to realism made the Wild West show ideologically insidious, in that under the veil of authenticity coursed deep racial fictions.

As the historian Louis Warren has observed, at the heart of the Wild West show was a narrative about the creation and defense of white homes and white domesticity. In numerous acts throughout its decades-long run, the Wild West show depicted martial, physical white masculinity as clearing the way for the safe establishment of white homes and white female presence in the West. The overarching message of the show was that rough white frontier masculinity and violence were in service of white domesticity and settled civilization.[17] But as Warren also notes, equally central to the show and inextricably bound with its gendered narrative was a tale about race and mobility. The Wild West show glorified white physical movement—in terms of both migration and speed in combat—as heroic and noble, most prominently as the foundation for future white fixity through the production of settled white homes. At the same time, it cast Indians as perpetually mobile, emphasizing their threatening movement and denying them any semblance of fixed domesticity.[18] Thus, like so many other cultural narratives about white western expansion—including those in antebellum popular song, as discussed in chapter 1—the Wild West show attempted to resolve the contradiction of portraying nonwhite movement as uncivilized and white movement as heroic by claiming that white mobility enabled rooted settlement and society.

These racial lessons suffused the show. From the very first act, it highlighted the threat and spectacle of Indian mobility. For most of its existence, the Wild West show opened with the same routine: A group of mounted Native American actors in their traditional dress and body paint would charge out of a partition on the far side of the arena walls, yelling traditional war cries as they rushed toward the audience grandstands. After the Indian charge, white cowboys—and, in later years, soldiers of the US Army Cavalry—would ride in, sometimes preceded by the Mexican actors. The routine thus enacted and (re-)created a racial hierarchy, with the threatening movement and presence of Native Americans and Mexicans ultimately matched—and, by implication, superseded—by martial white mobility.

Newspaper accounts of the show emphasized the sense of danger and racial fascination the Native riders provoked in the opening scene. An article in the *Chicago Daily Tribune* noted that the Indians "raced around the track, whooping and yelling as they went." The *Boston Daily Advertiser* played up not only the screams of the Indian actors but also their exotic dress: "The portals of civilization at the far away end of the quadrangle flopped open, and a bunch of warwhooping Indians, ochre and indigo and cereulean [*sic*] and olive, came careering down the plain, their ponies slaying the grass as they tore." The uncontrolled, fast, and aggressive movement of the "careering" Indians who "slew" the grass stood at the heart of this threatening image. The article continued, "Other bands of Indians came tearing around the corner innocent of garb save paint, a g[ir]dle, moccasins and strings of feathers," further mixing fear and fascination in the description of their fast moving, uncivilized bodies.[19]

Another newspaper report describing the opening act in the *Chicago Daily Inter-Ocean* hit on similar themes, telling readers: "A gate at the lower end of the arena swung open and the first detachment of Indians, headed by High Bear, dashed half way around the ground, and took up their position in front of the grandstand center. Three other bands of Sioux followed, riding in at a furious pace, many of the braves being dressed merely in a breech-clout and bright colored paint." In immediate contrast to these barely clothed Indian actors who stormed in "at a furious pace," a detachment of the US Cavalry rode in directly afterward, "mounted on white horses" and presenting "a fine appearance." The symbolism of the white horses and the paper's emphasis on the contrasting appearance of the riders blatantly signaled the racial and moral superiority of the cavalry for the paper's readership.[20]

The impressions of England's Queen Victoria perhaps best capture white perceptions of the Indian actors' threatening mobility in the opening scene. The queen saw the Wild West show when it traveled to London in 1887 and afterward recorded in her diary: "We sat in a box in a large semi circle. It is an amphitheatre with a large open space, all the seats being under cover. All the different people, wild, painted Red Indians from America, on their wild bare backed horses, of different tribes,—cow boys, Mexicans, &c., all came tearing round at full speed, shrieking & screaming, which had the weirdest effect. . . . The cow boys, are a fine looking people, but the painted Indians, with their feathers, & wild dress (very little of it) were rather alarming looking, & they have cruel faces." In this whirl of motion, it is the "wild bare backed" riding of the Indians that stands out, the term "wild" being applied to the Indians no less than three times in the brief description, and it is they who have "cruel faces," in contrast to the "fine" looking white cowboys. The aggressive staging of the opening act intentionally encouraged and elicited such racialized interpretations of Native Americans as frightening, threatening, and fascinating and clearly established from the outset that the show would be about the competing speed and martial skills of its racial actors.[21]

Subsequent acts kept the focus squarely on mobility. The show's mainstay second act was a horse race, and in its first year it featured as many as ten Native performers racing around the arena, thus reinforcing the link between Indians and movement, as well as highlighting their threatening speed. The next year, the race was expanded to include Indian, Mexican, and white riders, sometimes as many as four from each racial group. This interracial contest neatly encapsulated the show's central theme of race war and racial competition for the West. Unlike the show's mock battles, the victors of the races were not predetermined—any rider could win on any particular day, heightening the drama and stakes of the show's racial contest. Other races appeared throughout the performance, including one that pitted a foot runner (sometimes an Indian actor, sometimes a white actor) against a rider on horseback (sometimes Indian, sometimes white). Thus, what Warren evocatively calls the show's "constant racing of its races" underlined the mobility of nonwhites, particularly Native Americans, and implied that their movement posed a threat that whites always had to be ready to counter. Taken together, the racing scenes "suggested the speed of the Indians—and the necessary speed of settlers in outracing them."[22]

These themes of race and mobility were reprised in heightened form in the Wild West show's famous mock battles. One of the largest crowd-pleasers was "Attack on the Deadwood Coach." In this scene, white actors drove a stagecoach around the arena and then were "attacked" by a group of Indian actors. The stagecoach, which was actually imported from the West by Cody, would take off at high speed with the Native American attackers in hot pursuit, all furiously firing blank cartridges from their rifles. Just when it seemed the Indians were going to overwhelm the stagecoach, Buffalo Bill and a group of white cowboys would rush in and save the day "from the horde of yelling savages," as one newspaper put it. The scene's racial meaning was unambiguous. Mobile, dangerous Indians threatened innocent white settlers, or, as a story in the *Washington Post* summarized the scene, "a group of howling savages pursue a defenseless stage coach."[23]

Cody himself was in fact relatively progressive when it came to white–Indian relations; he paid his Indian actors fair wages, maintained cordial relationships with many of them, and regularly stated to the press that, nine times out of ten, conflicts between whites and Indians in the West resulted from injustices perpetrated by whites. But the Wild West show did not tell a story of white provocation and Indian response. Instead, it depicted Indians as unprovoked and bloodthirsty killers.

In "Attack on the Deadwood Coach," the stagecoach—the symbol of white transportation in the frontier West—came under fire from a swift and inherently violent Indigenous enemy. It took a similarly fast and violent—and eminently justified—white response to secure white travel and progress. As one newspaper article phrased it, Buffalo Bill and the white cowboys would "always dash in at the right time, and punish the marauders of the plains." The word "punish" neatly captures the wayward criminality the show ascribed to Native Americans, and the description of the Indians as "marauders" reveals the centrality of mobility to their identity and threat ("maraud" meaning "to roam about and raid in search of plunder"). Through its simple moral narrative, the scene knitted Indian mobility to danger.[24]

The culmination of the Wild West's message about race and mobility came with the show's most well-known act, "Attack on the Settler's Cabin." Closing out the performance for most of the show's existence, the scene featured a white family cabin that came under siege from a band of mounted Indians. Sometimes white women and children acted in the scene, fleeing indoors at the Indians' approach while their white male family members heroically held off the invaders. Just as in "Attack on the Deadwood Coach," Buffalo Bill and his white cowboys appeared just in the nick of time to rescue the cabin's inhabitants and drive the Indians away. As the last act in the show, "Attack on the Settler's Cabin" capped the gender and racial arc of the performance, assuring audiences that white male mobility and violence were all in service of settled domesticity and the defense of white femininity.[25]

While white mobility ultimately ended with the flowering of fixed settlement, the show denied Native Americans any trace of domesticity and stationary society. As Warren observes, Indians in the Wild West show "were unable to make homes, to settle, to domesticate the land. They represented a kind of *ur*-mobility, the embodiment of nomadism, the opposite of settlement." Native Americans in the show ended where they began—as mobile figures. Mounted on horses, they ruthlessly attacked the cabin and threatened to undo the white home and settled life, all while never creating fixed settlement or domestic life themselves. With "Attack on the Settler's Cabin" and its final white victory over the Indians, the Wild West show emphasized that white western expansion resulted in civilization and settled fixity defeating Native nomadism.[26] The content and narrative structure of the show thus beamed a clear lesson: White movement ended in the sanctity of the home, but Indian movement remained perpetual and it inhibited, or actively destroyed, civilized society.

These racial lessons touting white fixity and denigrating Indian mobility had affinities with, and ramifications for, federal Indian policy and the reservation system. Cody and the show's managers of course assembled the Wild West show within a cultural milieu of hegemonic ideas about Indianness, mobility, and civilization, which they then instantiated in the performance. But more than just reflecting these ideas, the Wild West then rebroadcast and recirculated them, deepening the racial links between Indianness and nomadism, and between Indian mobility and violence. The show implied that in order to protect settled white society and foster its spread, white men had to use their superior physical and marital abilities to contain Indians and prevent their incursion into white western space. In this way, the show ideologically reinforced the reservation policy's central focus on restricting Indian movement, providing "authentic" evidence of its necessity and joining the Wild West to Greater Reconstruction's larger effort to contain the mobility of Indigenous peoples. With its incredible popularity, the Wild West show disseminated this hegemonic racial imagery to millions of Americans from the mid-1880s through the end of the century.[27]

Moving Behind the Scenes

Paradoxically, the Wild West show and its symbolic denunciations of Indian mobility also opened up material channels for Native American movement. Thus, while it ideologically reinforced the structure of the reservation, it simultaneously provided an outlet for Native peoples to escape reservation confines. As multiple historians have discussed, the show facilitated both the geographic and the economic mobility of its Native actors, offering them a chance to physically leave the reservation and its dire economic conditions. In its early years, the show hired Pawnee actors, but then later drew predominantly from the Sioux reservations, including the notable hire of Sitting Bull for one season. For these Native Americans, the show not only paid fair wages, which many saved up and sent back to relatives on their home reservations, but also enabled them to travel the continent—and sometimes the world—with a large body of community members.

Although they had to perpetually suffer fictional defeat at the hands of Cody and his white cowboys, as well as play one-dimensional roles that reduced them to racial threats, Native performers were able to earn a living using their traditional horse-riding skills and were able to wear traditional dress, practices discouraged on reservations. One member of the show, a Lakota Sioux performer named Black Elk, spoke about these tensions for Native actors, saying he enjoyed getting paid to do a job he found exciting, but he did not see why the white cowboys had to win every mock battle. He also thought the show unfairly focused on the skills of the cowboys and not the Indian actors.[28]

Strikingly, because the US public was so fascinated by the idea of Native actors' authentic savagery, newspaper coverage often ironically documented their movements through modern urban landscapes, including in many cases their quotidian participation in city life. In 1890, the *Washington Post* noted that some of the Native performers in the nation's capital attended a play at the Bijou Theater. It observed that "notwithstanding the fact that they [the Native actors] did not understand enough English to keep the run of the dialogue, they followed the pantomime closely enough to retain a lively interest, and their appreciation was manifested every now and then by broad grins." Likewise, during one of the show's residencies in New York City, the *New York Times* reported that some of the Indian actors patronized multiple Brooklyn saloons and drank liquor there, actions technically prohibited by law. That same year, an article covering the Suburban Stakes horse race quietly related that among the diverse group of spectators were "some Indians from Buffalo Bill's Wild West Show." And when the *Philadelphia North American* reported on the large crowds that turned out to witness the arrival of Native American actors at one of the city's train stations, it stated that the Indians arrived in two sleeping coaches, highlighting their experience with modern forms of transport. Stories such as these reveal that despite the Wild West show's simulacrum of Indian savagery, Native actors were in fact regularly moving through modern urban environments, and in ways independent of the controlled tours that the show's managers organized for Native employees in both the United States and Europe, though these too marked Native actors' modern spatial mobility.[29]

Indigenous performers with the Wild West show also seized opportunities for more transgressive geographic and social movement. In 1886, one Native actor in the show eloped with a white woman from Newark, New Jersey, who was reportedly quite wealthy. The two traveled to Philadelphia and got married, then eventually returned to New York after Cody and Salsbury asked them to rejoin the show. Similarly, the Lakota Sioux Standing Bear met and married a white woman, Louise Rieneck, in Austria while recovering from injuries he sustained during the show's 1890 European tour. Standing Bear ended up staying in Austria for over a year before he and his new wife returned to his home on the Pine Ridge reservation in South Dakota. And on one occasion in 1895, Native performers used their cachet as members of the Wild West show and their connection to Cody to secure a meeting with the assistant Indian commissioner, to whom they were able to air their communities' grievances about federal Indian policy. In particular, they stated that if they "told of the unfulfilled promises of the Government to the Indians, the show would have to be postponed, as it would take . . . two days."[30]

Often, when glimpses of modern Indian movement appeared in press coverage of Wild West actors, journalists portrayed the Native Americans as awed by, and unfamiliar with, modern society and technology. In many cases, they also ridiculed their experiences. These accounts safely contained and rewrote Native performers' movements that threatened to disrupt narratives of white superiority, in some instances erasing the fact that many of the actors had years of experience traveling throughout the United States and Europe with the show. For example, when the Wild West show set sail for London in 1887, coverage of the show's steamship departure in the *New York Times* painted the Indian actors as frightened premodern figures. It reported that "the upper deck was crowded with the tall figures of Indians, who, clad in all their finery, seemed to wonder what on earth was going to happen, and when." It also mocked "Mr. and Mrs. Walking Buffalo" for looking into the ship's gong "with devouring curiosity" and then, after it was rung, "start[ing] back in affright and [saying] something about their ancestor's beard in Indian." Meanwhile, "Monsieur and Madame Eagle Horse . . . promenaded the deck like tigers and uttered cunning little whoops, which to the initiated expressed satisfaction tempered with awe." In contrast to these displays of Indian incompatibility and discomfort with modern travel and technology, the paper smugly noted that "the cowboys, riders, shooters, and Mexicans gave no trouble at all," as they spread out over the ship "and talked and laughed in high enjoyment."[31]

Another article in the *Times* denigrated the European travel of the Native performer Charles Pichet Pin. It claimed that Pin had gone overseas with the Wild West show and toured many of Europe's major cities but had since left the show and "wandered up and down the whole face of Europe." In conjuring the stereotype of the wandering Indian, the article implied Pin's travels had been aimless. It went on to emphasize that he was now penniless and reported on his arrival back in the United States with mocking racial stereotypes. The *Philadelphia North American* gave a similar take on Pin's travels. Explicitly articulating the stereotype of the roaming Indian, the paper disparagingly wrote that Pin, "true to the instinct of the American Indian," had decided to leave the Wild West show to "seek new hunting grounds and take a look over the European continent." He did so despite the fact that "his exchequer was low."[32]

Whereas these articles rendered Pin an aimless, incapable wanderer, Pin himself probably understood his experience traveling around Europe much differently. He used the Wild West show as a springboard for travel, leaving the show once he arrived in Europe—purportedly to join a circus for a time—and then journeying on his own about the continent. Further, he wore jewelry and fine clothing upon his return to the United States, indicating that he did not travel in destitution. His story thus speaks to the opportunities for autonomous movement that the Wild West afforded Indian actors.[33]

Indeed, despite the show's investment in the image of premodern Indian performers, Burke had to confess to reporters in 1893 that while many of the Indians with the show "were never off the reservation before," "some of the chiefs are old travelers." He also candidly admitted that even with the actors who had never been east, "we have not yet been able . . . to get them to express surprise or wonder at anything they have seen." Burke's statement speaks broadly to the long history of Native nations' familiarity and interaction with Western societies, and more immediately to the fact that most Indigenous actors with the Wild West returned to their reservation homes after the performance season and told their friends and families of their experiences. Far from naive, culturally isolated peoples, Native Americans had sophisticated understandings of Western society that was informed by travel, including that attained through the Wild West show.[34]

Of course, the Wild West show did not provide its Indian performers with completely unfettered mobility. Cody enforced a level of control over their movements, for he not only ran the show's camp with strict discipline but also designated an Indian police force from among the performers and tasked them with regulating the behavior of their fellow Indian actors. One of the responsibilities of this group was to prevent the other Native actors from leaving the camp at night. That said, Indian actors were often able to leave the camp on their own during the day, no passes required. They were also free to leave their employment with the show whenever they pleased, and they moved about the camp without restriction, including when crowds of spectators were present.[35]

For their part, Cody and the show's managers played up Native actors' travel with the Wild West show as a salutary civilizing agent. Seeing the marvels and manners of Western society, they contended, instilled in Native Americans an appreciation for the ways of white people and helped usher them toward assimilation. Repeating the false notion that Indians were completely culturally isolated, Cody publicly asserted that the Indians received "the greatest benefit from traveling" with the show, since "they had no idea whatever of the world outside of their plains and prairies." Travel, especially international travel, Cody proclaimed, "open[ed] their eyes wonderfully to the earth's magnitude." Likewise, another manager of the show told the press that the white managers took it upon themselves to expose the Indian actors to the "attractions" and "historic buildings" in each city they visited in order "to teach them the lessons of civilization." These pronouncements were acts of publicity designed to bolster the show's image as an educational endeavor and fend off any charges that it was exploiting Indian performers and hindering their progress toward civilization. By the late 1880s and early 1890s, however, white reformers increasingly began to level such charges, invoking an entirely different picture of Indian mobility with the show.[36]

Sparking Old Habits

For white reformers interested in Indian affairs, the Wild West show began to present a problem. As the show's popularity took off in the mid-1880s and inspired numerous spin-offs, reformers claimed that it and its imitators were detrimental to the project of civilizing Native Americans. By the late 1880s, Cody and the show's producers were facing consistent pressure from white reformers and their political allies on a number of fronts. One of reformers' most prominent critiques was that the show presented a misleading image of Native Americans and encouraged anti-Indian sentiment among whites. Rather than display the progress toward Christianity, settled agriculture, and white social habits that reformers felt so many Native Americans had made, the Wild West show merely depicted Indians' traditional—and in reformers' view, barbaric—ways. Reformers felt the show thus lent the impression that all Native peoples were still mired in backwardness and heathenism.[37]

Reformers further argued that the Wild West show harmed Native performers directly. According to the Indian Rights Association, it taught them to "think, dress, [and] act like a savage Indian" and "that what the white man really wants of [Indians] is amusement furnished by exhibitions of picturesque barbarism." As such, the Wild West show and its ilk were "the foster-father of those barbarous customs, modes of life, and habits of thought which Indian education justly aims to destroy." As the white reformer Mary C. Collins put it, when Indians performed with these shows, they "usually [came] back morally degraded."[38]

This conception of the Wild West show as a pernicious influence on Indian actors led white reformers to call on the federal government to prevent the hiring of Indian performers. These efforts to cut off Indian employment in the Wild West show had real political traction. As previously discussed, many federal officials in the Office of Indian Affairs shared reformers' views. At various points throughout the late 1880s and 1890s, politicians and federal officials—including reservation agents and, most notably, Commissioner of Indian Affairs Thomas Morgan—attempted to prohibit the Wild West show and others like it from hiring Indians. Cody was only able to stymie these efforts through a rigorous publicity campaign—which Native performers themselves assisted by testifying publicly that they were content working for the show—and by exercising many of the powerful political connections he had made thanks to his fame.[39]

Crucially, in their campaign to prevent the hiring of Native actors, prominent reformers alleged that the Wild West show's very structure as a traveling performance inhibited Native actors' progress toward assimilation. This claim was in part a response to middle-class Americans' general distrust of traveling entertainers, whom they associated with confidence men and saw as having no stable community to enforce moral norms. In such a morally degraded environment, Indians would pick up bad habits that would pervert the course of Christian citizenship. But reformers' fears ran far deeper. They also felt that the peripatetic nature of the show would reawaken Native performers' racial penchant for wandering, throwing them back into the mobile habits of Indian savagery. As historian L. G. Moses notes, some reformers and federal officials felt that as members of a traveling performance, Native actors were merely engaging in another form of nomadism. The show had simply transposed their wandering ways into a new realm.[40]

Commissioner of Indian Affairs John Oberly aired these racial concerns in 1889, sermonizing that "the effect of traveling all over the country . . . creates a roaming and unsettled disposition" in Indian actors. In so doing, Oberly averred, the Wild West show "educates [them] in a manner entirely foreign and antagonistic to that which has been and now is the policy of the Government." Oberly's view that the Wild West show would spark a tendency to wander in the Indian actors fundamentally informed his negative perception of the show, which he saw as a direct threat to the efforts of reformers and the federal government to restrict Native peoples' movement and impose settled agricultural society. Far from a benign entertainment, the Wild West show carried major policy and humanitarian implications for Indian relations.[41]

While Oberly condemned the Wild West show and similar performances, he believed that the Office of Indian Affairs had no legal mechanism to prevent Indians from working in them, since Indians had a right to individually contract to work off the reservation.[42] However, no such legal qualms plagued his successor as commissioner, Thomas Morgan. Morgan repeatedly tried to use his power as commissioner to prevent Indian employment in these shows, though he was mostly unsuccessful. Like Oberly, Morgan worried that Indian performers' travels with such shows would rekindle their racial tendency to wander. In his annual report of 1890, he asserted that "traveling about the country on these expeditions fosters the roving spirit already so common among them, encourages idleness and a distaste for steady occupation, and during their absence their families often suffer for want of their care and assistance."[43]

In the face of this threat, Morgan pressured federal agents on reservations to discourage employment with the Wild West show and had them stress to

Native peoples "the importance of their remaining at home and devoting their time and energies to building houses, establishing permanent homes, cultivating farms, and acquiring thrifty, industrious habits, thus placing themselves in fit position for absorption into our political and civil life." Many Native Americans living on reservations no doubt ignored Morgan's renewed pressure to devote themselves to fixed agriculture and domesticity, as they were well attuned to the freedom of movement and the economic opportunities the Wild West show offered. But Morgan's critique of the Wild West show and its imitators demonstrates the integral role that ideas about Indianness and movement played in his thinking about such shows and his efforts to regulate them through federal policy.[44]

In 1892, Morgan added a new layer to his arguments about the show's effect on Native peoples' innate disposition to wander. He now claimed the show also had "a tendency to awaken a spirit of restlessness among those that remain behind." For Morgan, the show threatened to spark nomadism not only in the Indian actors themselves but also in those still confined to the reservation who witnessed the actors exercising their mobility. This wrinkle was yet another reason Morgan vowed not to allow Indians to be "lured to vagabondage by 'wild west' shows." Ironically, Morgan and other white reformers correctly recognized the opportunities for movement that the Wild West show provided Native peoples while failing to comprehend that the show's representational thrust reaffirmed the confinement of Indians in the West.[45]

White reformers also insisted that the Wild West show's employment of Indian actors led to the moral corruption of those Indians who remained on the reservation. Performers returning from the road, they argued, infected their home communities with the dissolute habits—drinking, idleness, the desire to roam, sexual impropriety—that they picked up during their travels. And just as Morgan claimed that Indians on the reservation began to pine for the mobility of Indian actors, he also held that the Wild West show and others like it were "injurious to the Indians . . . who remain at home" because, due to "their peculiar status and isolation," they were "influenced in a large degree by those who have been absent on such enterprises." In this ironic turn of logic, the containment of the reservation made Native peoples imminently more susceptible to adopting the bad behaviors that Indian performers learned and brought back from their travels.[46]

In pressing their case against the corrupting influences of the Wild West show, white reformers and federal officials occasionally directly addressed the claim made by Cody and the show's other producers that Indian performers' travel was in fact edifying and hastened their assimilation. Commissioner Morgan, for example, acknowledged this argument. "But travel," he responded, "is not necessarily elevating or profitable." Morgan felt that, for Native actors, travel with the show offered only temporary employment and exposed them to disreputable characters in the entertainment industry. In Morgan's calculus, the negative aspects of Native travel with the show far outweighed any potential uplifting effects.[47]

The recurring clashes between Cody and white reformers and their governmental allies over the use of Indian actors was not confined to the publications and speeches of reformers and policymakers. The contest also played out in the national press. Whether Cody would be able to hire Indians from the reservations was of interest to the general public, and newspapers were littered with stories providing updates on the constantly unfolding drama, especially after Cody employed a group of Sioux Indians in 1891 imprisoned for their activities in the Ghost Dance uprisings, a move that prompted much public criticism. Most of the stories in the mainstream press did not express an opinion about which side was correct but merely reported on the state of the struggle and the views of the adversaries.[48] As such, Americans across the country were well aware of the debate about Indian travel with the Wild West show and the claim of reformers and policymakers that Indians needed to be more rigorously confined to the reservation. Cody's publicity efforts touting travel as beneficial for the Indian actors' assimilation made his contrasting position clear, as did his continued efforts to hire Native performers from reservations. He also explicitly stated in 1891 that he thought it "an outrage to confine" young Native men "to the reservations. They ought to be allowed to go away and work in the mills and shops"—and, he left unstated, in his show.[49]

These repeated stories in the press alerted readers to the political stakes of the Wild West show and its importance as a battleground for competing ideas about Indianness and mobility. Not only did practices and ideologies of racial mobility structure the show's representations and the lived experiences of its performers, but they put the show at the center of political debates about federal Indian policy and Native containment. However, the Wild West show had yet another connection to the politics of racial mobility. Its incredible commercial success enabled one of its white producers, Nate Salsbury, to launch another ambitious performance venture—a massive slave plantation reenactment in Brooklyn, New York, titled *Black America*. With *Black America*, Salsbury offered another hegemonic vision of racial mobility, one based on the Southern pastoral's logic of Black confinement.

Southern Transplant

For its 1894 season, the Wild West show was camped at Ambrose Park in Brooklyn, New York. However, in 1895, the show gave up its residence in the park and traveled across the country by train, performing for brief stretches in different cities. However, Nate Salsbury still held a lease on the land in Ambrose Park, and he wished to put it to use. Drawing on his past experiences as a minstrel show producer and his time with the Wild West show, he conceived of siting a massive plantation re-enactment on the land.[50] Employing the same marketing strategy of authenticity that made the Wild West show so successful, he framed the new show as an accurate re-creation of Black plantation life in the US South. The show's name captured this pretense to ethnography, as well as the grand scale of Salsbury's vision: *Black America*. That the plantation was able to stand in for Black people's "America" demonstrates the hold that the Southern pastoral had over white Americans' understandings of Black life. As a concept, it completely erased Black urban existence. Instead, romanticism of the plantation South thoroughly structured *Black America*, from its imagery to its narrative content to its marketing.

Opening in the summer of 1895, *Black America*'s primary selling point was its size. Advertisements for the show routinely touted that it featured five hundred Black men and women and emphasized its unprecedented size. As part of its facade of authenticity, the show never advertised the Black performers as actors. Instead, they were classified as "representatives" of the Black race—actual Black Southerners who were not acting but were simply living as they did in their Southern homes. Salsbury was adamant on this point in his discussions with the press. In interviews, he stressed that *Black America* was not another minstrel show but rather an accurate re-creation of Southern plantation life. A newspaper advertisement announcing the show's opening captured these aspects with its proclamation that *Black America* was "A NOVEL, NATURAL, NATIONAL, Colossal Afro-America Exhibition . . . A Stupendous Aggregation of Actual Field Hands from the Cotton Belt. A Veritable Invasion from THE SUNNY SOUTH."[51]

The show grounds at *Black America* attempted to live up to these promises. The Black cast members lived in more than one hundred log cabins studding the grounds, and an acre-large cotton field was planted among them. Black actors would pick cotton bolls held to the stalks by wire during performances and then reattach them afterward. Similarly, a working cotton gin was imported from the South, and Black performers would gin and bale cotton for curious onlookers. Of course, this "re-creation" of the plantation merely enacted a Southern pastoral fantasy. Absent were the white slave owner, the white slave overseers, and the torture and violence that undergirded slave labor. Instead, *Black America* presented an Eden of Black joviality and contentment. One newspaper account, noting that the cabins "look as if they had been picked up bodily, contents and all, from some hamlet in southern Tennessee and planted here," played up the show's carefree air. It described how one could "hear a laugh from one end of that camp to the other" when the Black performers played games, and how the men and women visited each other and engaged in "glorious uproar, not for the amusement of the public, but just as they would do if they were back in their own Southern homes."[52]

In addition to physically re-creating the plantation space, *Black America* attempted to psychically conjure it in the show's musical segment. A large amphitheater capable of holding roughly seven thousand people was built on the grounds and decorated with murals depicting stereotypical Southern scenery, including a steamboat and levee and a plantation house with a large veranda. Members of the Black cast would then regale the audience with Southern pastoral songs, especially those of Stephen Foster. For some of the musical numbers, hundreds of cast members would form a massive chorus and sing in unison, an act that newspaper reviews consistently praised as a unique spectacle and one of the show's highlights. In general, news coverage characterized the musical performances as exhibitions of the natural and spontaneous musicality of Southern African Americans and claimed that they added to the show's realism. The music segment thus reinforced and elaborated on the show's Southern pastoralism.[53]

Black America proved immensely popular with New York audiences. It played two shows daily, and by the end of its first four weeks it attracted an estimated 180,000 visitors.[54] The show's huge attendance numbers testify to the Southern pastoral's enduring popularity with white Americans and the centrality of its racial and spatial narratives to US popular culture. In many ways, *Black America* most fully realized the Northern white desires that were latent in the Southern pastoral as a theme—it literally instantiated the racio-spatial relations of the slave South in a Northern city. *Black America* immersed white attendees in its idealized racial landscape, allowing them to wander through a tangible construction of the Southern pastoral fantasy. The very act of re-creating a Southern plantation in the midst of the urban environment speaks volumes about white unease with postemancipation urban life and the strength of white longings for a return to the racial hierarchy of slavery and its rooted Black bodies.

But even as *Black America* enacted the Southern pastoral and its logic of Black containment—a logic then rebroadcast and amplified in newspaper accounts—elements within the show actively undermined its hegemonic force. While the white Salsbury bankrolled the show, a Black man, William "Billy" McClain, managed and directed it. McClain himself had achieved notable success as a minstrel show performer in the 1880s and early 1890s, and had gained managerial experience in the minstrel production *South Before the War* before joining *Black America*. In fact, multiple scholars have claimed that *Black America* was McClain's idea, not Salsbury's. However, the evidence is mixed, and it is certainly possible that both men independently arrived at the general outlines of the show before joining forces. Regardless, through his role as the show's director, McClain injected themes of Black respectability that subverted the power of *Black America*'s more racist aspects. Indeed, recollecting years after the show's close, McClain asserted that *Black America* was "by and for colored people," testifying not only to his perception of the show as geared for Black audiences but also to his creative control over its content.[55]

As scholar Barbara L. Webb notes, in 1894 McClain wrote a script of a play intended to portray the progress of African Americans from slavery to membership in Congress. While *Black America* did not contain a similarly clear progress narrative, McClain did insert alternative visions of Blackness and Black history into the musical portion that exceeded the Southern pastoral's confines. And while it did feature stock traits of the Southern pastoral, the musical performance also included a wide array of Black talents, such as an acrobat, a contortionist, jugglers, and female vocal soloists who performed classical, non-minstrel pieces while dressed in formal attire. The all-Black Ninth Cavalry also performed, putting on drill demonstrations that showcased their disciplined horsemanship and marching skills. The press regularly commented on the skill of the Ninth Cavalry and dubbed them a credit to Black soldiery.[56]

The musical interlude also foregrounded historical accounts of slavery and the Civil War that undercut the romantic trappings of the show's Southern pastoralism. McClain designed the final number as a patriotic spectacle that centered the African American experience in US history. As the Black chorus sang patriotic songs, huge portraits of Abraham Lincoln, Ulysses S. Grant, William Tecumseh Sherman, Harriet Beecher Stowe, Frederick Douglass, and John Brown were displayed in the background. The inclusion of these decidedly antislavery figures radically undermined the romantic racial myths about slavery that the show endorsed elsewhere. This emancipationist focus also appeared in advertisements for the show. For example, one handbill for the show featured images of Harriet Beecher Stowe, Abraham Lincoln, Frederick Douglass, and John Brown along its top and bottom. Such depictions of antislavery luminaries militated against the dominant Southern pastoralism of the show before patrons even arrived on the grounds. Taken together, the musical performances and acts of talent signaled that Black Americans were far from contained within the historical and spatial parameters of the plantation. Rather, they were patriotic citizens who actively participated in modern cultural and national life. The show was thus shot through with resistant aspects, even though the Southern pastoral and its racism predominated.[57]

Professionalizing Black Travel

However, *Black America*'s celebrations of emancipation, Black patriotism, and respectability were not the only way it served as a staging ground for Black resistance. It also formed part of the material foundation for McClain's later efforts at improving the economic and professional standing of Black popular culture performers. Along with other successful theatrical roles, *Black America,* which was arguably the most prominent role of his career, helped make McClain one of the most famous Black performers of the 1890s. McClain then parlayed his reputation and industry standing into the creation of a mutual aid society for Black musicians and actors in 1898 called the Benevolent Order of Colored Professionals. Crucially, in addition to providing financial assistance to members in need, the BO of CP established chapters in cities across the country to grow Black performers' professional networks and offer a gathering place for members traveling on their performance circuits. The BO of CP thus facilitated Black geographic mobility on the ground, building an institutional framework that fostered interurban Black travel while insisting that such travelers were respectable professionals.

Mutual aid societies were prevalent in the United States from the nineteenth century through the mid-twentieth century, and Black Americans have a robust history of forming such groups. Mutual aid societies—also known as fraternal organizations, even though many had both male and female membership—provided their members with insurance against sickness and death as well as a network and space for socializing. Many owned buildings that were used for meetings and social events, known as "lodges." For African Americans, mutual aid societies also often enabled advocacy on social and civil rights issues.[58] The Benevolent Order of Colored Professionals falls squarely within this history, though with a focus on Black presence in the entertainment industry.

McClain founded the BO of CP in February 1898 in Indianapolis, Indiana, his hometown. While McClain conceived of the order and spearheaded its founding, earning him the title of grand organizer, he was assisted by another Black musician, Henderson Smith. Smith was himself a well-known bandleader, and he would help McClain publicize the BO of CP and establish lodges in cities across the country. Significantly, while McClain formed the BO of CP to serve Black musicians and performers, he, Smith, and other BO of CP officers consistently referred to Black entertainers simply as members of "the profession." This use of the term "profession" as shorthand for the entertainment industry reflected and advanced the BO of CP's goal of promoting Black artists as professionals. This goal was also reflected, of course, in the organization's name.[59]

The BO of CP grew rapidly. Membership started strong and increased steadily over the order's first year. By May 1898, there were already several hundred members, including the famous Black performers Bert Williams and George Walker. Even though the first chapter was opened in Indianapolis, applications poured in from all over the country, and plans were quickly put in place to open a chapter in St. Louis. The Black press's consistent coverage of the BO of CP no doubt aided its growth, especially coverage in the Indianapolis *Freeman*, one of the largest Black newspapers of the late nineteenth century. Short press snippets constantly announced the induction of new members, helping advertise the new society. By August, the BO of CP had opened a chapter in Chicago with its own banquet hall and roughly 165 members, including the famous minstrel performer Billy Kersands.

However, it is vital to note that this expanding membership consisted of only Black men. While there were many Black women artists in the popular culture industry at the time, the BO of CP seems never to have contemplated including them as members of "the profession." Black women did attend BO of CP banquets and other celebrations, but they were not members of the order. McClain and the BO of CP's vision of Black entertainment professionalism was thus confined to Black men, excluding Black women performers from the order's benefits and conceptually diminishing them into their male counterparts' shadow. This gender discrimination seriously limited the BO of CP's antiracist potential, excluding the industry's numerous Black women from its material and communal advantages.

Still, the order proved incredibly successful at organizing Black male artists, and membership remained strong through the early 1900s. In addition to

Indianapolis and Chicago, the order opened chapters in New York City, St. Louis, Cincinnati, Toledo, Louisville, and Cairo, Illinois.[60] McClain himself opened the New York City lodge in November 1898, and he oversaw the order's first major fundraising event in June of that year in Indianapolis, a theatrical show featuring many Black performers and musicians.[61] While the BO of CP's chapter network by no means extended to all major US cities, it did cover significant ground and included the country's two largest urban centers: Chicago and New York. This geographic footprint, particularly the presence of BO of CP lodge buildings, would help facilitate Black artists' travel across the country as they moved from city to city for work.

Overall, the BO of CP served multiple functions. For one, it protected its members from economic insecurity. As one news article stated, "In case of sickness, death or many other things that might arise, when being a member of the B. O. [of] C. P. much relief can be secured." Such aid was crucial for those like W. A. Porter, a performer with the minstrel show *Darkest America*. When Porter fell sick for a few weeks and had to leave the show, the BO of CP provided financial assistance until he was able to return to work.[62]

Similarly, if members had any logistical issues during their travels on the performance circuit, local BO of CP chapters would furnish aid. For example, when the musician Charles Johnson missed the train his company was traveling on in Indianapolis, local members of the BO of CP took him "in hand" and made his stay "as pleasant for him as they could" while he waited for a later train. BO of CP members could thus travel with greater ease knowing they had a community to call on should they need help.[63]

Another core purpose of the order was to cultivate a larger social network of Black entertainers. BO of CP chapters regularly organized social events that brought their members together. Many of the chapters had large banquet halls, in which they held elaborate dinners. They also often put on musical and theatrical entertainments, such as one New York City session that featured songs, speeches, and card tricks. Before the festivities, the chapter specifically welcomed visiting members of the minstrel show *Darkest America*, demonstrating the community that the BO of CP offered to Black performers on the road. On another occasion, when Oliver Scott's Minstrels were visiting Toledo, Ohio, the local BO of CP chapter put on such a rousing banquet and musical show that it lasted until three in the morning. Newspaper coverage of such events demonstrates that BO of CP members took pride and delight in performing for their fellow members.[64]

Relatedly, the order also provided Black entertainers a home away from home. The peripatetic nature of Black performers' work fundamentally informed the BO of CP's mission and structure. Henderson Smith made this focus explicit in his praise of McClain as "a man to be honored for his untiring efforts to advance a long needed order of this kind among the traveling public."[65] As the phrase "traveling public" testifies, Black performers understood travel as a core aspect of their profession. As such, the organization's lodge buildings in cities dotting the country were crucial infrastructure for Black artists constantly on the move, offering both a welcome respite and a space to gather as a community. One letter to the Indianapolis *Freeman* even described the lodges as "homes." As the writer put it, a member could disembark from a train and "go directly to the Home where he will find all the comforts and refinements of a private residence." Further, each lodge had a list of all the others, including "what they are doing and where they are."[66] By erecting a network of lodges in multiple cities, the BO of CP facilitated and eased Black performers' interurban travels, as well as laid a claim to urban space. The very physical presence of the lodges symbolically asserted that Black artists were prominent and respectable participants in modern urban society and cultural life.

A significant exchange occurring in 1898 evinces that the BO of CP's efforts to advance the professional image of Black performers registered not only with Black Americans but also with at least some white Americans. At a BO of CP fundraising show in Indianapolis, the order collectively honored McClain for his founding work by presenting him with a jewel. But it was the city's white mayor, Thomas Taggart, who actually presented the jewel to McClain onstage. The mayor also gave a speech touting the advancements that African Americans had made in US society, of which the BO of CP was the immediate example. While certainly not indicative of the views of all white Americans, the event reveals that the BO of CP's efforts did manage to puncture the racist discourse that refused to see Black performers as talented actors and musicians engaged in a professional craft.[67]

The order remained strong through the turn of the century, though by 1900 warning signs began to appear. A news article from June of that year noted that interest in the Chicago chapter had declined "for some unexplained reason." While BO of CP activity nonetheless remained steady in general through 1902, it rapidly declined after that year (the St. Louis chapter was a notable exception—it opened membership to those outside the entertainment industry and became a thriving social club). The reason for the BO of CP's decline is unclear, though it may be that McClain's waning involvement with the order played a role. McClain traveled abroad to Australia and New Zealand from mid-1899 through late 1902 and then went overseas again in 1905 to Europe, where he remained for the rest of the decade. Additionally, while McClain remained involved in theatrical productions when he returned to the United States in 1902, he also became deeply interested in boxing and began managing Black boxers.[68]

Whatever the reason for its decline, the creation of the BO of CP and its early success constituted a direct challenge to the ascendant anti-Black views of the late nineteenth century. The BO of CP insisted that Black male popular entertainers did not fit the degrading stereotypes so often depicted in popular culture imagery but were talented professionals engaged in performance. Such an assertion undercut the racial naturalism that propped up the Southern pastoral and its many iterations, such as *Black America*. More than this, the BO of CP's multicity chapter network helped enable the Black transurban mobility that coursed underneath Black performances of the Southern pastoral. This movement and the professional trappings bestowed on it by the BO of CP directly contradicted the Southern pastoral's spatiality of containment, subverting its imagery that equated social and racial order with immobilized Black bodies.

Black performers thus joined the Native performers in the Wild West show in exceeding the conceptual bounds imposed by white racial regimes. Both defied the logic of containment undergirding Jim Crow segregation and the Indian reservation, respectively, as well as the ideas about racial (im)mobility broadcast in the Wild West show, the Southern pastoral, and *Black America*. They harnessed Greater Reconstruction's cultural forms and turned them to their own ends, forging pathways that advanced their own material and cultural well-being. Even as popular culture reinforced the ideological structures of the reservation and Jim Crow segregation, contributing to their development and maintenance on the ground, Black and Native Americans found ways to slip the constrictions imposed by these racial pillars of Greater Reconstruction. When and where they could, they used popular culture to advocate for and instantiate a more capacious racial vision, one founded on freedom of movement.

Epilogue

Lock My Body, Can't Trap My Mind

Many New York families—White, Black, Hispanic and Asian—have had to give up the pleasure of a leisurely stroll in the Park at dusk, the Saturday visit to the playground with their families, the bike ride at dawn, or just sitting on their stoops—given them up as hostages to a world ruled by the law of the streets, as roving bands of wild criminals roam our neighborhoods, dispensing their own vicious brand of twisted hatred on whomever they encounter.

—Donald Trump, after the arrest of the Central Park Five in 1989[1]

They got me trapped, can barely walk the city streets / without a cop harassin' me, searchin' me, then asking my identity / Hands up, throw me up against the wall, didn't do a thing at all.

—Tupac Shakur, "Trapped" (1991)

Lock my body, can't trap my mind, easily explain why we adapt to crime.

—Jay-Z, "Can I Live" (1996)

In late August 2005, Hurricane Katrina swept through southern Louisiana, causing rising waters that broke through New Orleans's flawed levee system and flooded the city. After the wind and rain of the hurricane receded, residents who had not fled before the storm arrived—predominantly people of color too poor to evacuate—left their devastated homes in search of relief. Many began to stream out of the city on foot. Or at least they tried to. When a large group of predominantly African American residents attempted to walk across the bridge connecting New Orleans to the neighboring town of Gretna, they met a police blockade that brought them to a halt. Despite residents' pleas that they were simply looking for aid, the police insisted they turn around and refused to allow them to enter the predominantly white town of Gretna.[2]

The actions of the police and the comments made by Gretna's white mayor and white police chief loudly testify to the racist and classist roots of the blockade. In the aftermath of the storm, police forces were ordered to seal off Gretna in an effort to, as the mayor characterized it, "contain our borders to make sure that property within it was complete [*sic*]."[3] Regarding the pedestrians attempting to cross the bridge, the mayor asserted that it "was quite evident that a criminal element was contained in a crowd of probably mainly decent people."[4] The police chief echoed this vision of an invading criminal force, justifying the bridge blockade by saying, "Our people had left. Our city was locked down and secured, for the sake of the citizens that left their valuables here to be protected by us."[5] The two white officials thus brashly and unashamedly claimed that protecting property superseded human need and that the Black mobility churned up by the storm had to be contained in the name of preserving law and order. For those behind the blockade, the movement of Black residents had conjured fears of unrestrained criminality. They saw not fellow Americans in need of help but a flood of disorder that had breached the containment of urban segregation and threatened to swamp their neighborhoods.

ON NOVEMBER 20, 2016, Native American protesters fighting the construction of the Dakota Access pipeline attempted to cross the Backwater Bridge in order to reach sacred tribal lands that the US Army now claimed ownership over. The attempt to cross the bridge was part of ongoing protests aimed at stopping the pipeline, the planned path of which ran north of the Standing Rock Sioux reservation in North Dakota and threatened the tribe's water supply and nearby sacred lands. Tensions were therefore already high when the demonstrators once again met police on the bridge. As the protesters began to cross, they encountered a police barricade that was quickly reinforced by tear gas and a water cannon. Unable to overcome the violent police tactics—the water cannon was particularly effective in the frigid 27-degree weather—the protesters were forced to retreat. This was not the first time a clash between protesters and the police had turned violent. At a protest a few weeks earlier, the police had arrested more than 140 demonstrators, most of them Native Americans. Afterward, those arrested claimed that the police had used excessive force and conducted sexually violative searches. The settler-colonial state—in service to capitalist oil interests—thus turned to violent repression and carceral detention to contain Native peoples' attempt to access, occupy, and protect their ancestral homelands.[6]

THESE TWO EVENTS illustrate the ongoing importance of mobility and containment to racial structures in the United States. Free and autonomous Indian and Black movement continues to elicit attempts at carceral restraint and to provoke deep white anxieties, particularly around criminality. Indeed, the Gretna bridge controversy and the Dakota Access pipeline protests highlight that the confinements of ghetto segregation and the Indian reservation remain core aspects of the Black and Native American experience in the United States. But they also reveal new developments. They illustrate the importance of police repression to white social control and, by extension, point to the emergence of mass incarceration as a new regime of racial containment in the late twentieth and early twenty-first centuries. While heavily targeting Black Americans, mass incarceration has increasingly swept Native peoples into its net. Along with African Americans, Native Americans remain vastly overrepresented in the US prison population.[7] Inextricably intertwined with the socioeconomic and spatial conditions of the ghetto and the reservation, mass incarceration marks yet one more iteration in white supremacy's project of containing nonwhite mobility.[8] Systematically locking African Americans and Native Americans in the cages of US prisons, it harshly immobilizes Black and Native bodies and fractures nonwhite communities.[9]

Casting our historical eye backward, we can see that mass incarceration is part of a longer history involving the intersection of race, mobility, and space in the United States. As this book shows, geographic mobility was a fundamental structure of race and racial ideology in the last half of the nineteenth century, and ideas about mobility intimately informed the everyday hegemonic racial imagery coalescing in nineteenth-century popular culture. Whether looking at sheet music, lithographic prints, magazine stories, comics, plantation reenactments, or the Wild West show, nineteenth-century popular culture reflected a national preoccupation with race and movement. Most often, the representations of race and mobility embedded in popular culture reinforced white supremacist views that contrived free and unrestrained Black and Native American movement as a threat to white society and a symbol of savagery. Uncontrolled nonwhite movement, the dominant imagery suggested, facilitated criminality, physical violence, and social and sexual disorder. Conversely, popular culture repeatedly cast white movement as regulated, orderly, and fast, the very pinnacle of modernity. These images thus gestured toward the need to contain Black and Native mobilities in order to ensure white social dominance, white safety, and civilization's progress. In so doing, nineteenth-century popular culture performed a pedagogical function, offering lessons that contributed to upholding the carceral regimes of the Indian reservation and Jim Crow segregation.

National popular culture distribution networks that sent images of race and (im)mobility circulating throughout the country therefore helped stitch together the larger racial transformations of Great Reconstruction. From 1845 to 1900, the flood of settlers into the newly acquired western territories and emancipation in the Civil War presented major challenges to the country's racial order. In response to these challenges, white Americans instituted the carceral regimes of the Indian reservation system and Jim Crow segregation. An overarching project of racial containment thus united North, West, and South in this period, and the increasing mobility of popular culture forms under industrial capitalism facilitated this national turn to containment.

While images in popular culture encouraged and reinforced the development of the reservation, representations of Blackness, mobility, and urban space especially influenced the development of Jim Crow segregation. As negative depictions of free Black movement and felicitous portrayals of Black stasis—always hitched to white social dominance—flooded popular culture in the decades following the Civil War, they offered an ideological road map for white supremacy built on Black segregation and containment. Popular culture thus played a significant role in the development of Jim Crow segregation in the 1890s and 1900s, disseminating racist ideas about Black movement to millions of Americans across the country.

By reconstituting and consolidating the United States on a foundation of racial segregation and containment, Greater Reconstruction laid the historical groundwork for mass incarceration. However, just as during Greater Reconstruction, resistance to efforts at racial containment have proliferated. Like their nineteenth-century counterparts, Black and Native cultural producers continue to seize the circuits of the popular culture industry to further their own freedom of movement and contest the structures and ideologies restricting their mobility. In the late twentieth and early twenty-first centuries, with residential segregation still rampant and mass incarceration flourishing, Black hip-hop artists repeatedly critiqued both forms as instruments of exploitation and oppression. Writing in the 1990s, the rap artist Nas commented not only on the containment of the ghetto but also on the link between ghetto containment and mass incarceration. In his song "N.Y. State of Mind," he raps, "Each block is like a maze / Full of black rats trapped, plus the Island is packed / From what I hear in all the stories when my peoples come back."[10] Likening Black residents to rats trapped in a maze of segregation, unable to escape the streets that seemingly lead to nowhere, Nas connects the spaces of his segregated home in New York City's Queensbridge projects to Riker's Island, the city's notorious jail. The only mobility experienced by Black bodies is a cyclical one between the containment of the ghetto and the containment of prison—both are "packed" with Black residents who shuttle between the two but never break out of their looped circuit.[11]

But in the same song, Nas shows that this bewildering and seemingly overwhelming entrapment does not crush resistance and dreams of a better life. Instead, Nas proclaims, "I just max, I dream I can sit back / And lamp like Capone, with drug scripts sewn / Or the legal luxury life, rings flooded with stones, homes."[12] Whether through legal or illegal means, Nas professes his desire to escape the oppressions of racial confinement. In a society where the law is a source of Black oppression, Nas refashions crime as freedom. This reframing of crime is a consistent theme in hip-hop. Rap artist Jay-Z explicitly connects crime to the carceral geography of inner-city segregation, rhyming, "Lock my body, can't trap my mind, easily explain why we adapt to crime / I'd rather die enormous than live dormant, that's how we on it."[13] Jay-Z's line counters the long-standing racist trope that figures crime as a product of free Black movement, instead revealing it as a response to imposed immobility and inequality, a Black adaptation to the conditions of urban segregation.

While hip-hop artists level serious critiques of residential segregation, they also consistently make claims of communal ownership over ghetto spaces and highlight the enduring social connections that exist there. On the cover of Nas's album *Illmatic* (1994), a large headshot of Nas as a young child, wearing an unsmiling, inscrutable expression, is transparently imposed over a street view of the infamous Queensbridge projects in New York City, where Nas grew up. The transparent effect merges his image with Queensbridge, conveying not only that Nas sees the neighborhood as fundamentally shaping his identity but also that he simultaneously claims it as his own. Nas also articulated this sense of ownership in an interview from 1994, when he described a past arrest for smoking marijuana. An incredulous Nas recounted how he had had to spend a night in jail because a "stupid punk cop wanna tell me I can't smoke weed in my own projects."[14] Nas's description of Queensbridge as his "own," and his assertion that marijuana drug laws did not govern him there, radically subverts both legal jurisdiction and the power relations underlying racial segregation.

Critique joined to expressions of communal pride and ownership also characterize the show *Reservation Dogs* (2021). Created by Native American director and writer Sterlin Harjo, a citizen of the Seminole Nation, and Native Māori writer Taika Waititi, the series follows the lives of four Native teenagers from the fictional reservation town of Okern, Oklahoma. Struggling after the suicide death of one of their friends, the four—self-dubbed the Reservation Dogs—resolve to raise money so they can leave the reservation and its oppressions for California. During this effort, they embark on numerous journeys, both on and off the reservation, that highlight not only the reservation's hardships and the injustices of land dispossession but also how the reservation is a site of Native community and cultural traditions. Over the course of the show's three seasons—which are littered with hip-hop references—the Reservation Dogs come to appreciate the communal support and cultural identity the reservation offers. As one of the Reservation Dogs, Willie Jack, says at the funeral of an uncle, "Some of us will go, some of us are gonna stay here [on the reservation]. But this place, and all you people, live in each one of us, forever."

As all these examples demonstrate, popular culture continues to be a vehicle for resistance to structures of racial containment, with Black and Native artists articulating alternative visions of freedom and racial mobility. As a site of racial struggle, it remains as vital as ever—racialized (im)mobilities continue to be key aspects of white supremacy and the ongoing projects of settler colonialism and racial capitalism. In particular, the growth of mass incarceration over the last fifty years drives home the importance of analyzing histories of race and mobility, especially since mass incarceration is overlaid on, and operates in part through, the containments of the Indian reservation and residential segregation. Greater Reconstruction's racial legacies therefore powerfully endure to this day, and studying this foundational period reveals that the intersections of race and mobility were integral to its transformations. Those transformations established the modern US nation-state and empire on a bedrock of racial segregation and containment, and they have made mobility fundamental to our history of race and racial ideology.

Notes

Introduction

1. Aleem Moqbool, "Ahmaud Arbery: Three US Men Guilty of Murdering Black Jogger," BBC News, Nov. 24, 2021, www.bbc.com/news/world-us-canada-59411030; Pamela Kirkland, Kevin Conlon, and Eric Levenson, "Ahmaud Arbery Would Not Have Been Killed If He Were White, Prosecutors Say in Hate Crimes Trial," CNN, Feb. 14, 2022, www.cnn.com/2022/02/14/us/ahmaud-arbery-hate-crime-trial-opening.

2. By "settler colonialism," I mean "the exploitation of a region['s] or country's resources and labor, plus the forcible resettlement of Indigenous peoples and their replacement by settlers who then move onto their lands and rewrite history in an effort to erase the longevity of their presence, and often their very existence." Alaina E. Roberts, *I've Been Here All the While: Black Freedom on Native Land* (University of Pennsylvania Press, 2021), 2. Since most settler-colonists have been white, settler colonialism also involves an element of racial ideology, most prominently the idea that white dominance of lands and nonwhite peoples is natural. However, one need not be white to be a settler-colonist. Roberts, *I've Been Here All the While*, 2–3. At base, settler colonialism enacts a "logic of elimination," the primary motive for which is "access to territory." Patrick Wolfe, "Settler Colonialism and the Elimination of the Native," *Journal of Genocide Research* 8, no. 4 (2006): 388.

3. A note on terminology: I variously use the terms "Indian," "Native American," and "Native" to refer to Indigenous North Americans. I do so with the awareness that, as scholar David Treuer notes, "these terms have come in and out of favor over the years, and different tribes, not to mention different people, have different preferences." David Treuer, *The Heartbeat of Wounded Knee: Native America from 1890 to the Present* (Riverhead Books, 2019), 1. I have elected to use these terms in recognition of these diverse preferences.

4. I define popular culture as "the widely distributed forms of popular music, publishing, art, design and literature, or the activities of leisure-time and entertainment, which make up the everyday lives of the majority of 'ordinary people.'" Stuart Hall, introduction to *Representation: Cultural Representations and Signifying Practices*, ed. Stuart Hall (Sage, 1997), 2. Although I use this more traditional definition of popular culture—one focused more on objects than processes—my analysis is informed by Stuart Hall's more expansive definition of culture in general, which stresses the import of meanings. As Hall writes, "Primarily, culture is concerned with the production and exchange of meanings—the 'giving and taking' of meaning—between members of a society or group." In other words, "to put it simply, culture is about 'shared meanings.'" Hall, introduction, 1, 2.

5. On the close link between racial mobility and racial segregation, see Genevieve Carpio, *Collisions at the Crossroads: How Place and Mobility Make Race* (University of California Press, 2019), 18, 66.

6. I define "Jim Crow segregation" as the systematic, white-enforced separation—whether by social custom, business policy, law, or some combination of these—of white

and non-enslaved Black individuals in space at various local scales, from public accommodations to city neighborhoods to urban-suburban metropolitan regions. Thus, colonization efforts to transplant African Americans beyond US borders and state laws restricting Black in-migration are segregationist policies but are not Jim Crow segregation, which aims to enforce segregation at smaller geographic scales. As with all ideologies and policies of racial separation, Jim Crow segregation inherently involves, at differing scales, both spatial separation and containment. I follow numerous historians in applying the designation "Jim Crow" to Northern segregation practices. See Brian Purnell and Jeanne Theoharis, introduction to *The Strange Careers of the Jim Crow North: Segregation and Struggle Outside of the South*, ed. Brian Purnell and Jeanne Theoharis, with Komozi Woodard (New York University Press, 2019), 9–10; Davison M. Douglas, *Jim Crow Moves North: The Battle over Northern School Segregation, 1865–1954* (Cambridge University Press, 2005); Douglas J. Flowe, *Uncontrollable Blackness: African American Men and Criminality in Jim Crow New York* (University of North Carolina Press, 2020); Lynn M. Hudson, *West of Jim Crow: The Fight Against California's Color Line* (University of Illinois Press, 2020); Mia Bay, *Traveling Black: A Story of Race and Resistance* (Belknap Press of Harvard University Press, 2021), 107–50, 169–73. For an older work employing the Jim Crow framework to early twentieth-century Chicago, see Allan H. Spear, *Black Chicago: The Making of a Negro Ghetto, 1890–1920* (University of Chicago Press, 1967), 29–49. For a recent study of racism in the antebellum North that uses the Jim Crow framework, see Richard Archer, *Jim Crow North: The Struggle for Equal Rights in Antebellum New England* (Oxford University Press, 2017). Stressing Jim Crow's national scope is not to deny the many local variations characterizing segregation in different parts of the country. But local instantiations of Jim Crow were part of a broader national story that saw segregation emerge as the prevailing racial regime governing Black–white relations in the late nineteenth century.

7. The literature on Jim Crow in the US South is vast. For the seminal work naming interracial political politics as a cause of segregation laws, see C. Vann Woodward, *The Strange Career of Jim Crow*, rev. ed. (Oxford University Press, 1974). For works naming a more assertive Black middle class, increased discourse about Black men as sexual threats to white women, and the impersonal relations of urbanization and modern mass transport as causes of Southern Jim Crow laws, see Clarence A. Bacote, "Negro Proscriptions, Protests, and Proposed Solutions in Georgia, 1880–1908," *Journal of Southern History* 25, no. 4 (1959): 471–72; John W. Cell, *The Highest Stage of White Supremacy: The Origins of Segregation in South Africa and the American South* (Cambridge University Press, 1982), 131–70; Joel Williamson, *The Crucible of Race: Black-White Relations in the American South Since Emancipation* (Oxford University Press, 1984), 224–58; George M. Fredrickson, *The Black Image in the White Mind: The Debate on Afro-American Character and Destiny, 1817–1914*, rev. ed. (Wesleyan University Press, 1987), 256–319; Edward L. Ayers, *The Promise of the New South: Life After Reconstruction*, rev. ed. (Oxford University Press, 2007), 145, 432; Glenda Elizabeth Gilmore, *Gender and Jim Crow: Women and the Politics of White Supremacy in North Carolina, 1896–1920* (University of North Carolina Press, 1996); Leon F. Litwack, *Trouble in the Mind: Black Southerners in the Age of Jim Crow* (Knopf, 1998), especially xiii–xv, 229–70; Jane Dailey, Glenda Elizabeth Gilmore, and Bryant Simon, ed., *Jumpin' Jim Crow: Southern Politics from Civil War to Civil Rights* (Princeton University Press, 2000), 4–5; Christopher Caplinger, "Conflict and Community: Racial Segregation in a New South City, 1860–1914"

(PhD diss., Vanderbilt University, 2003), 76–122, 160–90; Marek Steedman, "How Was Race Constructed in the New South?" *Du Bois Review* 5, no. 1 (2008): 60; Omar H. Ali, *In the Lion's Mouth: Black Populism in the New South, 1886–1900* (University Press of Mississippi, 2010), 129–66; Marek Steedman, *Jim Crow Citizenship: Liberalism and the Southern Defense of Racial Hierarchy* (Routledge, 2012), 81; Jane Dailey, *White Fright: The Sexual Panic at the Heart of America's Racist History* (Basic Books, 2020), 6–30. For the development of segregation on Southern trains, which generated much legal contention, see August Meier and Elliott Rudwick, "The Boycott Movement Against Jim Crow Streetcars in the South, 1900–1906," *Journal of American History* 55, no. 4 (1969); Barbara Y. Welke, "When All the Women Were White, and All the Blacks Were Men: Gender, Class, Race, and the Road to *Plessy*: 1855–1914," *Law and History Review* 13, no. 2 (1995); Blair L. M. Kelley, *Right to Ride: Streetcar Boycotts and African American Citizenship in the Era of* Plessy v. Ferguson (University of North Carolina Press, 2010); Steve Luxenberg, *Separate: The Story of* Plessy v. Ferguson, *and America's Journey from Slavery to Segregation* (W. W. Norton, 2019); Bay, *Traveling Black*, 18–106. For an account that ties Jim Crow, both in the South and the North, to industrial capitalists' need to divide labor, see Cedric Robinson, *Forgeries of Memory and Meaning: Blacks and the Regimes of Race in American Theater and Film Before World War II* (University of North Carolina Press, 2007). On how rising white racism in the North scuttled any federal resistance to the growth of Jim Crow in the South, see Thomas Adams Upchurch, *Legislating Racism: The Billion Dollar Congress and the Birth of Jim Crow* (University of Kentucky Press, 2004), 186–220. On the racist discourse and ideologies buttressing Jim Crow in the early twentieth-century South, see I. A. Newby, *Jim Crow's Defense: Anti-Negro Thought in America, 1900–1930* (Louisiana State University Press, 1965). Historian Grace Hale has written about the culture—broadly defined—of Jim Crow segregation in the South, but she does not examine representations of spatial segregation in popular culture. See Grace Hale, *Making Whiteness: The Culture of Segregation in the South, 1890–1940* (Pantheon, 1998). Similarly, historian Jane Dailey has looked at the importance of everyday interactions, particularly the social customs governing sidewalk use, to postbellum racial tensions in the South. Jane Dailey, "Deference and Violence in the Postbellum Urban South: Manners and Massacres in Danville, Virginia," *Journal of Southern History* 63, no. 3 (1997). For two works looking at the daily interactions constituting Jim Crow segregation in the South after World War II, see Robin D. G. Kelley, *Race Rebels: Culture, Politics, and the Black Working Class*, rev. ed. (Free Press, 1996), 55–75; Stephen A. Berrey, *The Jim Crow Routine: Everyday Performances of Race, Civil Rights, and Segregation in Mississippi* (University of North Carolina Press, 2015).

8. For works naming white fears about growing Black urban migration as the cause of residential segregation, see, for example, St. Clair Drake and Horace R. Cayton, *Black Metropolis: A Study of Negro Life in a Northern City*, rev. ed. (Harcourt, Brace, 1945; University of Chicago Press, 1993), 175–78; Karl E. Taeuber and Alma F. Taeuber, *Negroes in Cities: Residential Segregation and Neighborhood Change* (Aldine, 1965), 55; Gilbert Osofsky, *Harlem: The Making of a Ghetto; Negro New York, 1890–1930* (Harper & Row, 1966; Ivan R. Dee, 1996), 40–42; Thomas Philpott, *The Slum and the Ghetto: Neighborhood Deterioration and Middle-Class Reform, Chicago, 1880–1930* (Oxford University Press, 1978), 119–30; Christopher Silver, "The Racial Origins of Zoning: Southern Cities, from 1910–40," *Planning Perspectives* 6, no. 2 (1991): 191; Douglas Massey and Nancy Denton, *American Apartheid:*

Segregation and the Making of the Underclass (University of Harvard Press, 1993), 26–30; Andrew Wiese, *Places of Their Own: African American Suburbanization in the Twentieth Century* (University of Chicago Press, 2004), 40–41; Todd M. Michney, *Surrogate Suburbs: Black Upward Mobility and Neighborhood Change in Cleveland, 1900–1980* (University of North Carolina Press, 2017), 13; Hudson, *West of Jim Crow*, 176; Lance Freeman, *A Haven and a Hell: The Ghetto in Black America* (Columbia University Press, 2019), 31, 40. For works attributing residential segregation to the general intensification of white racism in this "nadir" of Black-white relations, see Thomas W. Hanchett, *Sorting Out the New South City: Race, Class, and Urban Development in Charlotte, 1875–1975* (University of North Carolina Press, 1998), 116–21; James W. Loewen, *Sundown Towns: A Hidden Dimension of American Racism* (New Press, 2005), 24–44. For a work naming racialized real estate practices as the cause of residential segregation, see Emily Lieb, "The 'Baltimore Idea' and the Cities It Built," *Southern Cultures* 25, no. 2 (2019): 106–7. For works identifying growing Black urban demographics and racialized real estate practices as the causes of large-scale residential segregation, see, for example, Robert C. Weaver, *The Negro Ghetto*, rev. ed. (Russell and Russell, 1967), 25–32, 38–40; Seth M. Scheiner, "The New York City Negro and the Tenement, 1880–1910," *New York History* 45, no. 4 (1964): 309–10, 313; Kenneth L. Kusmer, *A Ghetto Takes Shape: Black Cleveland, 1870–1930* (University of Illinois Press, 1976), 35–47; Arnold R. Hirsch, "With or Without Jim Crow," in *Urban Policy in Twentieth-Century America*, ed. Arnold R. Hirsh and Raymond A. Mohl (Rutgers University Press, 1993), 68–75; Kevin Fox Gotham, *Race, Real Estate, and Uneven Development: The Kansas City Experience, 1900–2000* (State University of New York Press, 2002), 22, 38, 48; Jessica Trounstine, *Segregation by Design: Local Politics and Inequality in American Cities* (Cambridge University Press, 2018), 5, 31–34, 46, 75. For works that name rising white racism and growing Black urban demographics as causal factors, see, for example, Spear, *Black Chicago*, 7–8; Roger L. Rice, "Residential Segregation by Law, 1910–1917," *Journal of Southern History* 34, no. 2 (1968): 180; Paul A. Groves and Edward Muller, "The Evolution of Black Residential Areas in Late Nineteenth-Century Cities," *Journal of Historical Geography* 1, no. 2 (1975): 171; David A. Gerber, *Black Ohio and the Color Line, 1860–1915* (University of Illinois Press, 1976), 288–89; John Kellogg, "Negro Urban Clusters in the Postbellum South," *Geographical Review* 67, no. 3 (1977): 310, 313; John Kellogg, "The Formation of Black Residential Areas in Lexington, Kentucky, 1865–1887," *Journal of Southern History* 48, no. 1 (1982): 21–22. Other combinations of these factors arise in the scholarship as well. See Howard Rabinowitz, *Race Relations in the Urban South, 1865–1890* (Oxford University Press, 1978), 103–5; Don H. Doyle, *New Men, New Cities, New South: Atlanta, Nashville, Charleston, Mobile, 1860–1910* (University of North Carolina Press, 1990), 262, 280–81, 284–85; Caplinger, "Conflict and Community," 125–26; David M. P. Freund, *Colored Property: State Policy and White Racial Politics in Suburban America* (University of Chicago Press, 2007), 14–15, 54–59; Carl H. Nightingale, *Segregation: A Global History of Divided Cities* (University of Chicago Press, 2012), 304–11; N. D. B. Connolly, *A World More Concrete: Real Estate and the Remaking of Jim Crow South Florida* (University of Chicago Press, 2014), 31–47; Andrea Gibbons, *City of Segregation: One Hundred Years of Struggle for Housing in Los Angeles* (Verso, 2018), 12, 19–27; Elizabeth A. Herbin-Triant, *Threatening Property: Race, Class, and Campaigns to Legislate Jim Crow Neighborhoods* (Columbia University Press, 2019), 3, 5; Paige Glotzer, *How the Suburbs Were Segregated: Developers and the Business of Exclusionary Housing, 1890–1960* (Columbia University Press, 2020), 1–2, 46–48. For works stressing school segregation as a factor behind residential segregation's emergence, see Karen Benjamin, "Suburbanizing Jim Crow: The Impact of School Policy on Residential Segregation in Raleigh," *Journal of Urban History* 38, no. 2 (2012): 226–27; Walter C. Stern, *Race and Education in New Orleans: Creating the Segregated City, 1764–1960* (Louisiana State University Press, 2018), 8–9, 50–58; Karen Benjamin, *Good Parents, Better Homes, and Great Schools: Selling Segregation before the New Deal* (University of North Carolina Press, 2025), 2. A number of studies focus on documenting when large-scale residential segregation began to appear in US cities without commenting on historical causes. See, for example, John Blassingame, "Before the Ghetto: The Making of the Black Community in Savannah, Georgia, 1865–1880," *Journal of Social History* 6, no. 4 (1973); David M. Katzman, *Before the Ghetto: Black Detroit in the Nineteenth Century* (University of Illinois Press, 1973), 67–80; John P. Radford, "Race, Residence, and Ideology: Charleston, South Carolina in the Mid-Nineteenth Century," *Journal of Historical Geography* 2, no. 4 (1976). In addition, many important works have looked at early twentieth-century government policies, real estate practices, and white extralegal violence that compounded and spread already-existing residential segregation without discussing segregation's origins. See, for example, Christopher G. Wye, "The New Deal and the Negro Community: Toward a Broader Conceptualization," *Journal of American History* 59, no. 3 (1972); Kenneth T. Jackson, *Crabgrass Frontier: The Suburbanization of the United States* (Oxford University Press, 1987), 190–230; Richard Rothstein, *The Color of Law: A Forgotten History of How Our Government Segregated America* (Liveright, 2017), 17–91. For a foundational study of Black urban life and residential patterns in the late nineteenth century, see W. E. B. Du Bois, *The Philadelphia Negro: A Social Study* (Philadelphia, 1899), 287–321. For a recent historiography of the works on residential segregation, see Eric Avila and Thaïsa Way, introduction to *Segregation and Resistance in the Landscapes of the Americas*, ed. Eric Avila and Thaïsa Way (Dumbarton Oaks, 2023), 1–12.

9. For a work that does examine the appearance of ideas about segregated space in popular culture but in the later era of post–WWII Los Angeles, see Eric Avila, *Popular Culture in the Age of White Flight: Fear and Fantasy in Suburban Los Angeles* (University of California Press, 2004). For an examination of how African Americans have represented Black neighborhoods in post–WWII US popular culture, see Yelena Bailey, *How the Streets Were Made: Housing Segregation and Black Life in America* (University of North Carolina Press, 2020).

10. Excavating the importance of popular culture to the history of Jim Crow also offers a corrective to literature on the history of capitalism, which has emphasized business relations and economic forces in US history at the expense of cultural ones. Historian Paige Glotzer has argued for the "coconstruction of culture and the economy"; however, she makes clear that by "culture" she means "race." Glotzer, *How the Suburbs Were Segregated*, 4. Her excellent book certainly demonstrates the important role of race and racial segregation to the history of capitalism and real estate in the twentieth-century United States, yet it privileges economic actors in its analysis of residential segregation's development, erasing the role of broader cultural forces—other than simply "race" and "racism"—in the history of capitalism and racial segregation. Glotzer does address how African American urban residents influenced the spatial and labor practices of Jim Crow suburbs, but overall her work remains focused on the decisions of business leaders and the actions of real estate companies. I would contend that the rise of residential segregation was due just as much, if not more so, to a broader set of cultural ideas and the everyday beliefs and practices of white

Americans. Business leaders fashioned their tools of residential segregation from an existing milieu of ideas about race, space, and mobility, many of which circulated in popular culture, as I demonstrate here.

11. Philip J. Deloria, *Indians in Unexpected Places* (University of Kansas Press, 2004), 7–11. Historian Robert W. Rydell similarly points out that popular entertainments at the Chicago World's Columbian Exposition in 1893 both embodied and disseminated racial ideals to audiences. Robert W. Rydell, *All the World's a Fair: Visions of Empire at American International Expositions, 1876–1916* (University of Chicago Press, 1984), 5.

12. Stuart Hall, "Gramsci's Relevance for the Study of Race and Ethnicity," in *Stuart Hall: Critical Dialogues in Cultural Studies*, ed. David Morley and Kuan-Hsing Chen (Routledge, 1996). I use the term "ideology" regularly throughout the book. The word has a notoriously slippery meaning. For my purposes, ideology refers to "the mental frameworks—the languages, the concepts, categories, imagery of thought, and the systems of representation—which different classes and social groups deploy in order to make sense of, define, figure out and render intelligible the way society works." Stuart Hall, "The Problem of Ideology: Marxism Without Guarantees," *Journal of Communication Inquiry* 10, no. 2 (1986): 29. This definition includes "the practical as well as the theoretical knowledges which enable people to 'figure out' society, and within whose categories and discourses we 'live out' and 'experience' our objective positioning in social relations." Hall, "Problem of Ideology," 30.

13. Michael Omi, "In Living Color: Race and American Culture," in *Cultural Politics in Contemporary America*, ed. Ian H. Angus and Sut Jhally (Routledge, 1989), 114.

14. Hall, reading the work of Antonio Gramsci, elaborates on how culture is a site of race making and intimately involved in the distribution and maintenance of power. Key to this relationship between culture and race making is Gramsci's notion of "common sense." "Common sense" refers to those ideologies and beliefs that are so engrained in a society that they pervade the everyday, popular thought of the masses. While common-sense ideas are often fragmentary and disjointed, they are "the terrain of conceptions and categories on which the practical consciousness of the masses of the people is actually formed. It is the already formed and 'taken-for-granted' terrain, on which more coherent ideologies and philosophies must contend for mastery." Hall, "Gramsci's Relevance for the Study of Race and Ethnicity," 431. Indeed, as scholar Dick Hebdige observes, "It is here, at the level of 'normal common sense,' that the ideological frames of reference are most firmly sedimented and most effective, because it is here that their ideological nature is most effectively concealed." Dick Hebdige, *Subculture: The Meaning of Style* (Routledge, 1979), 11. Popular culture in particular, with its extreme ubiquity and seemingly innocuous character, contributes to the generation of common sense. Its apparent innocence and levity allow its embedded ideologies to, in Deloria's evocative phrase, "sneak into our minds and down to our hearts when we aren't looking." Deloria, *Indians in Unexpected Places*, 6.

15. Louis Althusser, "Ideology and Ideological State Apparatuses," in *Lenin and Philosophy*, ed. Louis Althusser, rev. ed. (Monthly Review Press, 2001); Stuart Hall, "Race, Articulation, and Societies Structured in Dominance," in *Sociological Theories: Race and Colonialism*, ed. UNESCO (UNESCO, 1980), 334.

16. Deloria, *Indians in Unexpected Places*, 11.

17. West argues that histories of race can particularly benefit from this expanded view. Elliott West, "Reconstructing Race," *Western Historical Quarterly* 34, no. 1 (2003): 14. West contends that the rise of scientific racism was in part a response to the major shifts in race relations occurring during Greater Reconstruction and the attendant exigencies of fashioning a national body politic out of an increasingly racially diverse population. For West's other works employing the Greater Reconstruction framework, see Elliott West, *The Last Indian War: The Nez Perce Story* (Oxford University Press, 2009); Elliott West, *Continental Reckoning: The American West in the Age of Expansion* (University of Nebraska Press, 2023); Elliott West, "Reconstruction in the West," online forum, *Journal of the Civil War Era*, accessed Jan. 31, 2025, www.journalofthecivilwarera.org/forum-the-future-of-reconstruction-studies/reconstruction-in-the-west/. On the influence of West's work, see Stacey Smith, "Beyond North and South: Putting the West in the Civil War and Reconstruction," *Journal of the Civil War Era* 6, no. 4 (2016): 573–74.

18. For the works on Greater Reconstruction, see West, "Reconstructing Race"; West, *Last Indian War*; Joshua Paddison, *American Heathens: Religion, Race, and Reconstruction in California* (University of California Press, 2012); Richard W. Etulain, *Lincoln and Oregon Country Politics in the Civil War* (Oregon State University Press, 2013); Steven Hahn, "Slave Emancipation, Indian Peoples, and the Projects of a New American Nation-State," *Journal of the Civil War Era* 3, no. 3 (2013); Adam Arenson and Andrew R. Graybill, *Civil War Wests: Testing the Limits of the United States* (University of California Press, 2015); Pekka Hämäläinen, "Reconstructing the Great Plains," *Journal of the Civil War Era* 6, no. 4 (2016); Steven Hahn, *A Nation Without Borders: The United States and Its World in an Age of Civil Wars, 1830–1910* (Penguin Books, 2016); West, "Reconstruction in the West"; Richard White, *The Republic for Which It Stands: The United States During Reconstruction and the Gilded Age, 1865–1896* (Oxford University Press, 2017), esp. 103–35; Emma Teitelman, "The Properties of Capitalism: Industrial Enclosures in the South and the West After the American Civil War," *Journal of American History* 106, no. 4 (2020); Manisha Sinha, *The Rise and Fall of the Second American Republic: Reconstruction, 1860–1920* (Liveright, 2024), esp. 307–46; West, *Continental Reckoning*; Nicole Martin, "Reconstructing the American Home: Western Boardinghouses on the Comstock Load," *Journal of American History* 112, no. 2 (2025). For a work looking at race and Reconstruction in a transregional framework, though not through the explicit lens of Greater Reconstruction, see Najia Aarim-Heriot, *Chinese Immigrants, African Americans, and Racial Anxiety in the United States, 1848–82* (University of Illinois Press, 2003).

19. See, for example, Benjamin Weber, *American Purgatory: Prison Imperialism and the Rise of Mass Incarceration* (New Press, 2023); Robert T. Chase, ed., *Caging Borders and Carceral States: Incarcerations, Immigration Detentions, and Resistance* (University of North Carolina Press, 2019). As Elliott West recently notes, contests over movement—especially efforts to control Native Americans' mobility—were crucial to settler colonialism in the West. West, *Continental Reckoning*, 156, 425.

20. Nicholas Guyatt, *Bind Us Apart: How Enlightened Americans Invented Racial Segregation* (Basic Books, 2016). See also Paul Frymer, *Building an American Empire: The Era of Territorial and Political Expansion* (Princeton University Press, 2017); Samantha Seeley, *Race, Removal, and the Right to Remain: Migration and the Making of the United States* (Omohundro Institute, 2021); Samuel M. Davis, "'Here They Are in the Lowest State of Social

Gradation—Aliens—Political—Moral—Social Aliens, Strangers, Though Natives': Removal and Colonization in the Old Northwest, 1815–1870" (PhD diss., Temple University, 2019).

21. Stephanie M. H. Camp, *Closer to Freedom: Enslaved Women and Everyday Resistance in the Plantation South* (University of North Carolina Press, 2004); Ryan A. Quintana, *Making a Slave State: Political Development in Early South Carolina* (University of North Carolina Press, 2018).

22. That both Jim Crow and slavery had a common objective of controlling Black movement discloses that emancipation produced not an absolute break in race relations but rather, as the term "Greater Reconstruction" indicates, a reconstruction and renovation of prior forms of racial oppression and resistance. Historian Stephanie Camp remarks on this connection, stating that Jim Crow segregation was built on the "spatial worries and investments of the old order [of slavery]: placing black and white people in space and society," and "in this light, segregation seems as much tradition in a new form as a modern break from it." Camp, *Closer to Freedom*, 140.

23. West puts the end at 1877, the year that saw the end of federal Reconstruction in the South and the last federal Indian war against the Nez Perce Indian nation. Historian Keith McCall has argued that "the traditional dating of Reconstruction's end to 1877 presents too much of a top-down and static view" that privileges federal policy. Similarly, historian Joshua Paddison, in his work on religion and Greater Reconstruction, expands the chronology of Greater Reconstruction through the 1880s to capture the "knitting together of North, South, and West around a newly robust white Christian identity." Like McCall and Paddison, I assert that we must recognize the more capacious chronology implicated by Reconstruction's, and Greater Reconstruction's, larger cultural and structural shifts. West, *Last Indian War*; Keith D. McCall, "Reconstructing Race, Place, and Population: Post-emancipation Migrations and the Making of the Black South, 1865–1915" (PhD diss., Rice University, 2019), 3; Paddison, *American Heathens*, 5–6.

24. The spatial affinity between the reservation and Jim Crow segregation perhaps suggests that we should not see the two structures as isolated from each other. Two scholars, Steven Hahn and Patrick Wolfe, have commented on the intertwined histories of the Indian reservation and Jim Crow, and their statements offer a platform for thinking through additional connections between the two structures. Hahn, speaking about the white reformist discourse of civilizationism at the end of the nineteenth century, writes that the Greater Reconstruction lens gives us "good reason to think about how the languages of 'civilizationism' and of race and racial prospect resonated with one another and then contributed to the logic and choreography of both reservations and segregation." Hahn, "Slave Emancipation, Indian Peoples, and the Projects of a New American Nation-State," 324. Similarly, Wolfe, ruminating on early twenty-first-century racial arrangements, notes that "today in the US, the blatant racial zoning of large cities and the penal system suggests that, once colonized people outlive their utility, settler societies can fall back on the repertoire of strategies (in this case, spatial sequestration) whereby they have also dealt with the Native surplus." Wolfe, "Settler Colonialism," 404. Following Hahn and Wolfe, the spatial affinities between the two suggest that they may have developed in conversation with each other, the spatial logic of one ideologically reinforcing the other.

25. Henri Lefebvre, *The Production of Space*, trans. Donald Nicholson-Smith (Blackwell, 1997); Doreen Massey, *Space, Place, and Gender* (University of Minnesota Press, 1994); Tim

Cresswell, *On the Move: Mobility in the Modern Western World* (Routledge, 2006); John Urry, *Mobilities* (Polity, 2007); Tim Cresswell, "Towards a Politics of Mobility," *Environment and Planning D: Society and Space* 28, no. 1 (2010); Stephen Greenblatt, *Cultural Mobility: A Manifesto* (Cambridge University Press, 2010), 250–53. This work has influenced other social science scholars. See, for example, Hagar Kotef, *Movement and the Ordering of Freedom: On Liberal Governances of Mobility* (Duke University Press, 2015); Mimi Sheller, *Mobility Justice: The Politics of Movement in an Age of Extremes* (Verso, 2018), esp. 45–67. The "mobilities turn" in geography resulted in the creation of a journal devoted to the subject in 2006, titled *Mobilities*.

26. Michelle Granshaw, *Irish on the Move: Performing Mobility in American Variety Theatre* (University of Iowa Press, 2019), 5.

27. For historical works examining mobility as a social construct that reciprocally interacts with racialization, see Kathleen Franz, "'The Open Road': Automobility and Racial Uplift in the Interwar Years," in *Technology and the African-American Experience: Needs and Opportunities for Study*, ed. Bruce Sinclair (MIT Press, 2004); Mary Ting Yi Lui, *The Chinatown Trunk Mystery: Murder, Miscegenation, and Other Dangerous Encounters in Turn-of-the-Century New York City* (Princeton University Press, 2005), 52–110; Cotten Seiler, *Republic of Drivers: A Cultural History of Automobility in America* (University of Chicago Press, 2008), 105–28; Steedman, "How Was Race Constructed," 58–61; Euan Hague, "'The Right to Enter Every Other State': The Supreme Court and African American Mobility in the United States," *Mobilities* 5, no. 3 (2010); Amy R. Sumpter, "Racial Identity, Spatial Mobility, and Labor in the Non-Plantation Rural South, 1880–1940, *Journal of Historical Geography* 37, no. 4 (2011); Steedman, *Jim Crow Citizenship*, 81–105; Elizabeth Stordeur Pryor, *Colored Travelers: Mobility and the Fight for Citizenship Before the Civil War* (University of North Carolina Press, 2016); Quintana, *Making a Slave State*, 89–115; Carpio, *Collisions at the Crossroads*; Granshaw, *Irish on the Move*; Christine Rizzi, "My Feet Are Chained: Settler Colonialism and Mobility in the Florida Borderlands, 1812–1866" (PhD diss., University of Mississippi, 2019); Genevieve Carpio, Natchee Blu Barnd, and Laura Barraclough, eds., "Mobilizing Indigeneity and Race Within and Against Settler Colonialism," special issue, *Mobilities* 17, no. 2 (2022); Desiree Valadares, "Uneven Mobilities: Infrastructural Imaginaries on the Hope–Princeton Highway," *Radical History Review*, no. 147 (2023); Gabriele Pisarz-Ramirez, "Being Black in the Archipelagic Americas: Racialized (Im)Mobilities in the Autobiographies of James Weldon Johnson and Evelio Grillo," *Atlantic Studies* 20, no. 1 (2023); Aaron W. Marrs, *The American Transportation Revolution: A Social and Cultural History* (Johns Hopkins University Press, 2024), 129–64; John K. Bardes, *Carceral City: Slavery and the Making of Mass Incarceration in New Orleans, 1803–1930* (University of North Carolina Press, 2024). For a study of how mobility interacted with the historical construction of class in the early national and antebellum United States, see Kristin O'Brassill-Kulfan, *Vagrants and Vagabonds: Poverty and Mobility in the Early American Republic* (New York University Press, 2019). A number of other historical works have demonstrated the myriad ways beyond immigration that Americans have fought racial contests over spatial movement, including by showing that freedom of movement was a central aspect of civil rights struggles. While these excellent works show the political stakes of movement in histories of race, they do not examine mobility as a historical construct that itself shapes race. See, for example, William Cohen, *At Freedom's Edge: Black Mobility and the Southern White Quest for*

Racial Control, 1861–1915 (Louisiana State University Press, 1991); Leslie A. Schwalm, *Emancipation's Diaspora: Race and Reconstruction in the Upper Midwest* (University of North Carolina Press, 2009); Yael A. Sternhell, *Routes of War: The World of Movement in the Confederate South* (Harvard University Press, 2012), 115–71; Alisha Hines, "Geographies of Freedom: Black Women's Mobility and the Making of the Western River World, 1814–1865" (PhD diss., Duke University, 2018); Martha S. Jones, *Birthright Citizens: A History of Race and Rights in Antebellum America* (Cambridge University Press, 2018), 89–107; Douglas K. Miller, *Indians on the Move: Native American Mobility and Urbanization in the Twentieth Century* (University of North Carolina Press, 2019); Kate Masur, "State Sovereignty and Migration Before Reconstruction," *Journal of the Civil War Era* 9, no. 4 (2019); McCall, "Reconstructing Race, Place, and Population"; Bay, *Traveling Black*; Seeley, *Race, Removal, and the Right to Remain*; Kate Masur, *Until Justice Be Done: America's First Civil Rights Movement, from the Revolution to Reconstruction* (W. W. Norton, 2021); Kirsten E. Wood, *Accommodating the Republic: Taverns in the Early United States* (University of North Carolina Press, 2023), 28–46; Kevin Kenny, *The Problem of Immigration in a Slaveholding Republic: Policing Mobility in the Nineteenth-Century United States* (Oxford University Press, 2023); Joseph A. Rodriguez, *A Right to the Road: How Marginalized American Motorists Fought to Drive and Park* (Rowman and Littlefield, 2024).

28. Historian Michelle Granshaw has analyzed representations of the Irish and mobility—both in terms of local movement and immigration—in postbellum US variety theater and their relation to Irish Americans' racial, class, and gender formation; historian Nathan Cardon has examined Black bicycle racing in the late nineteenth and early twentieth centuries and explored how the idea of Black bicyclists challenged emerging Jim Crow spatial codes in the US South; and historian Genevieve Carpio has analyzed the intersections of race and mobility in Southern California bicycle racing during the 1890s and in local radio shows of the 1930s. Historian Louis Warren has analyzed representations of Indianness and mobility in the Wild West show, while literary scholar Jean Lee Cole has looked at representations of Black mobility in the serialized fiction of Black antebellum authors. Granshaw, *Irish on the Move*; Nathan Cardon, "Cycling on the Color Line: Race, Technology, and Bicycle Mobilities in the Early Jim Crow South, 1887–1905," *Technology and Culture* 62, no. 4 (2021); Carpio, *Collisions at the Crossroads*, 75–83, 173–79; Louis S. Warren, *Buffalo Bill's America: William Cody and the Wild West Show* (Knopf, 2005); Jean Lee Cole, "Theresa and Blake: Mobility and Resistance in Antebellum African American Serialized Fiction," *Callaloo* 34, no. 1 (2011). Scholar Jayna Brown centers mobility as an analytic in her book *Babylon Girls*, documenting how the travels of late nineteenth-century Black women performers formed the material basis for Black popular dance and, to some extent, how dances reflected such movements. But she does not offer a sustained investigation of the ideological ties between race and mobility and their representations in popular culture. Similarly, scholar Christine Bold shows how Indigenous vaudeville artists in the late nineteenth and early twentieth centuries used popular culture to facilitate their geographic movement and how Native kinship and geographic networks underlay their popular culture travels. See Jayna Brown, *Babylon Girls: Black Women Performers and the Shaping of the Modern* (Duke University Press, 2008); Christine Bold, *"Vaudeville Indians" on Global Circuits, 1880s to 1930s* (Yale University Press, 2022). Historian Davarian Baldwin has examined how Black migration to Northern urban centers in the twentieth century, and

attendant white anxieties about this migration, shaped popular culture. In particular, Baldwin shows that white anxieties about Black migration resulted in the segregation of vice entertainments into Black residential districts and an increase in blackface minstrel imagery and romanticism of the Old South in popular culture. Black migrants, meanwhile, used popular culture as a site to express their own ideas and hopes for freedom in the urban North. Similarly, scholars Marcy Sacks and Lori Brooks have argued that white fears about Black migration in the 1890s led to increased romanticism of the Old South in popular culture. But while Baldwin, Sacks, and Brooks trace the historical links between Black migration and popular culture in the late nineteenth and early twentieth centuries, they do not examine representations of mobility and race in popular culture, as I do. My work here also demonstrates that the link they observe between white anxieties about Black migration and romantic imagery of the South has a longer history, reaching back to the antebellum period. See Marcy S. Sacks, *Before Harlem: The Black Experience in New York City Before World War I* (University of Pennsylvania Press, 2006), 49–54, 70–71; Davarian L. Baldwin, "Our Newcomers to the City: The Great Migration and the Making of Modern Mass Culture," in *Beyond Blackface: African Americans and the Creation of American Popular Culture, 1890–1930*, ed. W. Fitzhugh Brundage (University of North Carolina Press, 2011); Lori Brooks, "Journey to a Land of Cotton: A Slave Plantation in Brooklyn, 1895," *American Studies* 53, no. 1 (2014): 59. Some works have examined representations of race and mobility in US popular culture in other periods. See Hazel V. Carby, "It Just Be's Dat Way Sometime: The Sexual Politics of Women's Blues," *Radical America* 20, no. 4 (1986); Louis Owens, "White for a Hundred Years," in *Reading "The Virginian" in the New West*, ed. Melody Graulich and Stephen Tatum (University of Nebraska Press, 2003); Jacqueline Najuma Stewart, *Migrating to the Movies: Cinema and Black Urban Modernity* (University of California Press, 2005); Daphne Brooks, *Bodies in Dissent: Spectacular Performances of Race and Freedom, 1850–1910* (Duke University Press, 2006), 220; Seiler, *Republic of Drivers*, 105–28; Rivke Jaffe, "Talkin' 'Bout the Ghetto: Popular Culture and Urban Imaginaries of Immobility," *International Journal of Urban and Regional Research* 36, no. 4 (2012); Ho'esta Mo'e'hahne and Alex Trimble Young, "Indigenous Mobility and Settler State Transfer: *The Exiles* in Historical Context," *Transfers* 5, no. 3 (2015); Julia Leyda, *American Mobilities: Geographies of Class, Race, and Gender in US Culture* (Transcript, 2016); Birgit Englert, "Moving Beyond Hip-Hop: Tracing Mobilities in the Work of Franco-Comorian Artists Soprano and Ahamada Smis," in *Mobile Kulturen und Gesellschaften/Mobile Cultures and Society*, ed. Alexandra Ganser and Annegret Pelz (V&R Unipress, 2021).

29. Some geographers have offered more complex definitions of the term "mobility." For example, Tim Cresswell's definition contains three constitutive parts: physical movement, representations of movement (which give physical movement its shared meanings), and practice, or the embodied experience of movement. Cresswell, "Towards a Politics of Mobility," 19. While Cresswell's definition is useful for certain analyses, my basic definition of "mobility" meets the needs of my historical arguments and is less confusing to wider audiences.

30. Peter Adey, "If Mobility Is Everything Then It Is Nothing: Towards a Relational Politics of (Im)Mobilities," *Mobilities* 1, no. 1 (2006): 83–84.

31. Carpio, *Collisions at the Crossroads*, 235.

32. Seiler, *Republic of Drivers*, 107.

33. Carpio, *Collisions at the Crossroads*, 10.

34. Scholars across a range of disciplines have studied the Southern pastoral in various cultural texts, primarily analyzing it as an escapist and nostalgic response to industrialization, urbanization, and, in its late nineteenth- and twentieth-century forms, racial demographic changes. See, for example, Francis Pendleton Gaines, *The Southern Plantation: A Study in the Development and the Accuracy of a Tradition* (Columbia University Press, 1924); Robert Bone, *Down Home: A History of Afro-American Short Fiction from Its Beginnings to the End of the Harlem Renaissance* (G. P. Putnam's Sons, 1975), 9–10; J. Stanley Lemons, "Black Stereotypes as Reflected in Popular Culture, 1880–1920," *American Quarterly* 29, no. 1 (1977); Thomas Cripps, *Slow Fade to Black: The Negro in American Film, 1900–1942* (Oxford University Press, 1977), 26–40; Lucinda Hardwick MacKethan, *The Dream of Arcady: Place and Time in Southern Literature* (Louisiana State University Press, 1980); Robert A. Armour, "History Written in Jagged Lightning: Realistic South vs. Romantic South in *The Birth of a Nation*," in *The South and Film*, ed. Warren French (University Press of Mississippi, 1981); Ida Jeter, "Jezebel and the Emergence of the Hollywood Tradition of a Decadent South," in French, *South and Film*; Edward D. C. Campbell Jr., *The Celluloid South: Hollywood and the Southern Myth* (University of Tennessee Press, 1981), 19–30; Berndt Ostendorf, *Black Literature in White America* (Barnes & Noble, 1982), 80–81; Lewis P. Simpson, *The Dispossessed Garden: The Pastoral and History in Southern Literature* (Louisiana State University Press, 1983); Jack Temple Kirby, *Media-Made Dixie: The South in the American Imagination*, rev. ed. (University of Georgia Press, 1986), 64–78; Jan Bakker, *Pastoral in Antebellum Southern Romance* (Louisiana State University Press, 1989); Sue Rainey, "Images of the South in *Picturesque America* and *The Great South*," in *Graphic Arts and the South: Proceedings of the 1990 North American Print Conference*, ed. Judy L. Larson (University of Arkansas Press, 1993); Nina Silber, *The Romance of Reunion: Northerners and the South, 1865–1900* (University of North Carolina Press, 1993), 78–87; Ed Guerrero, *Framing Blackness: The African American Image in Film* (Temple University Press, 1993), 9–28; Charles Hamm, "Genre, Performance and Ideology in the Early Songs of Irving Berlin," *Popular Music* 13, no. 2 (1994); Susan Key, "Sound and Sentimentality: Nostalgia in the Songs of Stephen Foster," *American Music* 13, no. 2 (1995): 155–57; John M. Grammer, *Pastoral and Politics in the Old South* (Louisiana State University Press, 1996); Lee Glazer and Susan Key, "Carry Me Back: Nostalgia for the Old South in Nineteenth-Century Popular Culture," *Journal of American Studies* 30, no. 1 (1996); Saidiya V. Hartman, *Scenes of Subjection: Terror, Slavery, and Self-Making in Nineteenth-Century America* (Oxford University Press, 1997), 28–32; Matthew R. Martin, "The Two-Faced New South: The Plantation Tales of Thomas Nelson Page and Charles W. Chesnutt," *Southern Literary Journal* 30, no. 2 (1998): 18–19; David W. Blight, *Race and Reunion: The Civil War in American Memory* (Harvard University Press, 2001), 221–31; Lori Brooks, "The Negro in the New World: The Cultural Politics of Race, Nation, and Empire, 1885–1911" (PhD diss., Yale University, 2001); Roger William Hecht, "Nature's 'Cunning Alphabet': Pastoral Landscape and Politics in Nineteenth-Century American Literature" (PhD diss., Syracuse University, 2002); Tara McPherson, *Reconstructing Dixie: Race, Gender, and Nostalgia in the Imagined South* (Duke University Press, 2003); Paul Outka, *Race and Nature from Transcendentalism to the Harlem Renaissance* (Palgrave Macmillan, 2008); Esther J. Terry, "Rural as Racialized Plantation vs. Rural as Modern Reconnection: Blackness and Agency in Disney's *Song of the South* and

The Princess and the Frog," *Journal of African American Studies* 14, no. 4 (2010); Baldwin, "Our Newcomers to the City"; Stephanie Dunson, "Black Misrepresentation in Nineteenth-Century Sheet Music Illustration," in Brundage, *Beyond Blackface*; Karen L. Cox, *Dreaming of Dixie: How the South Was Created in American Popular Culture* (University of North Carolina Press, 2011), 1–5, 25; Brooks, "Journey to a Land of Cotton"; Brian Ward, "Music, Musical Theater, and the Imagined South in Interwar Britain," *Journal of Southern History* 80, no. 1 (2014). A new work on the Southern pastoral by scholar Jason Young, which looks at a group of white writers and artists in Charleston, South Carolina, during the early twentieth century, was published too late in this book's editing process to engage with substantively. See Jason R. Young, *The Mask of Memory: White Racial Fantasy After the Civil War* (University of North Carolina Press, 2026).

Chapter One

1. Louis Ruchames, "Jim Crow Railroads in Massachusetts," *American Quarterly* 8, no. 1 (1956): 62.

2. The two scholars who have studied representations of Indians in nineteenth-century popular music most thoroughly, Jon Finson and Michael Pisani, have both noted that most songs about Native Americans painted them in a sympathetic light, and they are both certainly correct in asserting that aspects of these songs aligned with the logic of removal. However, they have underplayed the prevalence and depth of the critiques leveled at white Americans in popular songs of the antebellum period. Finson does make the general remark that "many authors disapproved" of Europeans' "rapacity," but these criticisms deserve more than a passing mention. Overall, both scholars see popular song as firmly anti-Indian and aligning with removal. See Jon W. Finson, *The Voices That Are Gone: Themes in Nineteenth-Century American Popular Song* (Oxford University Press, 1994), 240–41, 246–49, 269; Michael V. Pisani, *Imagining Native America in Music* (Yale University Press, 2005), 95, 97–101, 110–14.

3. Paul Charosh, "Studying Nineteenth-Century Popular Song," *American Music* 15, no. 4 (1997); Nicholas Tawa, *Sweet Songs for Gentle Americans: The Parlor Song in America, 1790–1860* (Bowling Green University Popular Press, 1980), 6, 21–22.

4. Steven Hahn, *The Political Worlds of Slavery and Freedom* (Harvard University Press, 2009), 1–53. Even after emancipation, Northern state economies were deeply linked with Southern slavery in the early national and antebellum period. See Cedric Robinson, *Black Marxism: The Making of the Black Radical Tradition*, 2nd ed. (University of North Carolina Press, 2000), 204; Sven Beckert, *The Monied Metropolis: New York City and the Consolidation of the American Bourgeoisie, 1850–1896* (Cambridge University Press, 2001), 17–97; Edward Baptist, *The Half Has Never Been Told: Slavery and the Making of American Capitalism* (Basic Books, 2014), 309–95; Sven Beckert, *Empire of Cotton: A Global History* (Knopf, 2015), 98–241; Christy Clark-Pujara, *Dark Work: The Business of Slavery in Rhode Island* (New York University Press, 2016); Sven Beckert and Seth Rockman, eds., *Slavery's Capitalism: A New History of American Economic Development* (University of Pennsylvania Press, 2016).

5. Stephanie M. H. Camp, *Closer to Freedom: Enslaved Women and Everyday Resistance in the Plantation South* (University of North Carolina Press, 2004), 1–34. See also Walter

Johnson, *River of Dark Dreams: Slavery and Empire in the Cotton Kingdom* (Harvard University Press, 2013), 46–72, 209–43; Christine Rizzi, "My Feet Are Chained: Settler Colonialism and Mobility in the Florida Borderlands, 1812–1866" (PhD diss., University of Mississippi, 2019). For the history of slave passes and slave patrols, see Sally E. Hadden, *Slave Patrols: Law and Violence in Virginia and the Carolinas* (Harvard University Press, 2001). Urban slaveholders, particular in New Orleans, also relied on municipal police forces and imprisonment to uphold slavery, constituting another aspect to slavery's carceral relations. John K. Bardes, *Carceral City: Slavery and the Making of Mass Incarceration in New Orleans, 1803–1930* (University of North Carolina Press, 2024), 1–78.

6. Susan O'Donovan, "Writing Slavery into Freedom's Stories," in *Beyond Freedom: Disrupting the History of Emancipation*, ed. David Blight and Jim Downs (University of Georgia Press, 2017), 31; Ryan A. Quintana, *Making a Slave State: Political Development in Early South Carolina* (University of North Carolina Press, 2018), 89–115. See also Aaron W. Marrs, *The American Transportation Revolution: A Social and Cultural History* (Johns Hopkins University Press, 2024), 129–57. For the role of the plantation South's poor road system in upholding slavery's relations of Black (im)mobility, see Aaron Hall, "Bad Roads: Building and Using a Carceral Landscape in the Plantation South," *Journal of American History* 111, no. 3 (2024). Of course, another form of coerced slave movement was the internal slave trade. For works on the significance of the internal slave trade, see Walter Johnson, *Soul by Soul: Life Inside the Antebellum Slave Market* (Harvard University Press, 1999); Steven Deyle, *Carry Me Back: The Domestic Slave Trade in American Life* (Oxford University Press, 2005).

7. Quintana, *Making a Slave State*, 79–88, 116–48; Camp, *Closer to Freedom*, 35–92; Hahn, *Political Worlds of Slavery and Freedom*, 47–49; John D. Cox, *Traveling South: Travel Narratives and the Construction of American Identity* (University of Georgia Press, 2005), 64–65. For more on free and enslaved Black women's use of mobility to contest slavery and the racial order of the antebellum South, see Alisha Hines, "Geographies of Freedom: Black Women's Mobility and the Making of the Western River World, 1814–1865" (PhD diss., Duke University, 2018).

8. John Radford, "Race, Residence, and Ideology: Charleston, South Carolina in the Mid-Nineteenth Century," *Journal of Historical Geography* 2, no. 4 (1976): 331–32. Free Black residents in the South also faced legal and extralegal restrictions on their movements. Adam Malka, *The Men of Mobtown: Policing Baltimore in the Age of Slavery and Emancipation* (University of North Carolina Press, 2018), 112; Martha S. Jones, *Birthright Citizens: A History of Race and Rights in Antebellum America* (Cambridge University Press, 2018), 99; Robert Gamble, "African Americans, Mobility, and the Law," *The Junto: A Group Blog on Early American History*, May 11, 2015, https://earlyamericanists.com/2015/05/11/african-americans-mobility-and-the-law/; Bardes, *Carceral City*, 79–107.

9. Quintana, *Making a Slave State*, 108. Historian Walter Johnson's account of a rumored 1835 slave insurrection in Mississippi also shows that, for planters, spatial order was a key signifier of social order, and that Southern white people saw autonomous Black mobility as a harbinger of slave revolt. Johnson, *River of Dark Dreams*, 46–72. For more on the general importance of mobility to the racial order of the antebellum South and slavery, see Yael Sternhell, "Revolution in Motion: Human Mobility and the Transformation of the South, 1861–1865" (PhD diss., Princeton University, 2008), 10–36; Hines, "Geographies of Freedom," 3, 5, 114–15.

10. Elizabeth Stordeur Pryor, *Colored Travelers: Mobility and the Fight for Citizenship Before the Civil War* (University of North Carolina Press, 2016), 47; Kate Masur, *Until Justice Be Done: America's First Civil Rights Movement, from the Revolution to Reconstruction* (W. W. Norton, 2021), 10–12. For legal efforts to restrict the movement of slaves in New York, including the use of passes and prohibitions against public assembly, see Edwin Olson, "The Slave Code in Colonial New York," *Journal of Negro History* 29, no. 2 (1944): 149, 152–54. Northern whites also rigorously monitored the mobility of enslaved Native Americans. Margaret Ellen Newell, *Brethren by Nature: New England Indians, Colonists, and the Origins of American Slavery* (Cornell University Press, 2015), 115.

11. Pryor, *Colored Travelers*, 6.

12. Pryor, *Colored Travelers*, 4, 44–148. White desires to circumscribe Black mobility stemmed not only from slavery but also from emancipation itself. With the racial curbs of slavery gone, whites saw free African Americans as requiring regulation, and they heavily scrutinized free Black travelers. Pryor, *Colored Travelers*, 6; Marrs, *American Transportation Revolution*, 157–63. See also Malka, *Men of Mobtown*, 5. Indeed, emancipation tended to exacerbate racism in general, as whites attempted to shore up the link between whiteness and citizenship. John Wood Sweet, *Bodies Politic: Negotiating Race in the American North, 1730–1830* (Johns Hopkins University Press, 2003). For two later studies that echo Pryor's argument about the importance of Black mobility to struggles over civil rights and ideas of citizenship in the antebellum period, see Masur, *Until Justice Be Done*, 42–82, 225–66; Mia Bay, *Traveling Black: A Story of Race and Resistance* (Harvard University Press, 2021), 3–4, 13–14, 18–32.

13. Pryor, *Colored Travelers*, 5–6, 44–75, 157–58. Long-standing US views linked the mobility of the poor—both Black and white—with crime and indolence. But white anxieties about transient African Americans were higher than elite white concerns about poor whites and led to unequal legal punishments. See Kristin O'Brassill-Kulfan, *Vagrants and Vagabonds: Poverty and Mobility in the Early American Republic* (New York University Press, 2019), esp. 6–9, 22, 101–4. See also Masur, *Until Justice Be Done*, 42–82.

14. Nicholas Guyatt, *Bind Us Apart: How Enlightened Americans Invented Racial Segregation* (Basic Books, 2016), 1–38, 307–34.

15. Ultimately, white Americans abandoned colonization following the Civil War, due primarily to Black resistance and the ongoing need for Black labor in the South. In a revealing exception, in 1890 Southern white Democrats in Congress proposed an emigration bill to provide for the voluntary transportation of African Americans out of the South—either to Liberia or to the western and northern United States (thus dispersing the Black population and blunting its political force). Crucially, Southern Democrats advocated the bill when agriculture in the South was so depressed that a large surplus of Black labor existed. Thus, planters did not have to worry about labor supply and supported the effort, in contrast to their usual anxieties during episodes of Black emigration. The bill failed to pass due to Republican resistance. See Thomas Adams Upchurch, *Legislating Racism: The Billion Dollar Congress and the Birth of Jim Crow* (University of Kentucky Press, 2004), 23–45.

16. While some historians define "popular culture" as the culture of mass consumption that emerged in the late nineteenth and early twentieth centuries, I follow scholar Eric Lott in identifying antebellum minstrelsy as popular culture. Lott labels minstrelsy one of America's first culture industries and notes that it was the most popular form of entertainment in the

antebellum era. Eric Lott, *Love and Theft: Blackface Minstrelsy and the American Working Class* (Oxford University Press, 1993), 4, 8, 17–18. See also Douglas A. Jones, *The Captive Stage: Performance and the Proslavery Imagination of the Antebellum North* (University of Michigan Press, 2014), 55. On early blackface minstrelsy being partly a response to Black political agitation, see D. A. Jones, *Captive Stage*, 15, 57–58, 62–63; John L. Brooke, *"There Is a North": Fugitive Slaves, Political Crisis, and Cultural Transformation in the Coming of the Civil War* (University of Massachusetts Press, 2019), 39, 45.

17. Antecedents of blackface minstrelsy in Anglo-American culture included blackface characters in plays, "Bobolition" broadsides, and musical acts with Black dialect. For more on the transatlantic roots of blackface minstrelsy, see Kellen Hoxworth, *Transoceanic Blackface: Empire, Race, Performance* (Northwestern University Press, 2024).

18. On early minstrel musical sound and its influences, see Matthew D. Morrison, *Blacksound: Making Race and Popular Music in the United States* (University of California Press, 2024), 42–43, 53–56.

19. Scholars have debated whether early blackface minstrelsy is a transgressive form expressing cross-racial identification and alliance. My position is that while there are certainly racially transgressive aspects to minstrelsy, it ultimately aimed to shore up racial inequalities and reassure whites that Black inferiority was irrefutable. For works arguing that early minstrelsy evidences cross-racial class alliance, see Dale Cockrell, *Demons of Disorder: Early Blackface Minstrels and Their World* (Cambridge University Press, 1997); W. T. Lhamon, *Raising Cane: Blackface Performance from Jim Crow to Hip Hop* (Harvard University Press, 1998); W. T. Lhamon, *Jump Jim Crow: Lost Plays, Lyrics, and Street Prose of the First Atlantic Popular Culture* (Harvard University Press, 2003), 1–92. For a more nuanced argument that early minstrelsy cannot be reduced to racial domination and contains subversive expressions of cross-racial identification and admiration, see Lott, *Love and Theft*. For works contending that early minstrelsy is not racially subversive or that its anti-Blackness subsumes any of its subversive potential, see Robert Toll, *Blacking Up: The Minstrel Show in Nineteenth-Century America* (Oxford University Press, 1974); David Roediger, *The Wages of Whiteness: Race and the Making of the American Working Class* (Verso, 1991); Alexander Saxton, "Blackface Minstrelsy," in *Inside the Minstrel Mask: Readings in Nineteenth-Century Blackface Minstrelsy*, ed. Annemarie Bean, James V. Hatch, and Brooks McNamara (Wesleyan University Press, 1996); Saidiya V. Hartman, *Scenes of Subjection: Terror, Slavery, and Self-Making in Nineteenth-Century America* (Oxford University Press, 1997), 17–48; D. A. Jones, *Captive Stage*; Hoxworth, *Transoceanic Blackface*, 3–90.

20. Elizabeth Stordeur Pryor and Kristin O'Brassill-Kulfan have both noted that "Jim Crow" maligns Black mobility. Pryor points out that Jim Crow wreaks havoc as he crisscrosses the nation and that sexual desire is palpable in his travels. She sees "Jim Crow" as reinforcing white Americans' growing criminalization of Black travelers in this period. Similarly, O'Brassill-Kulfan remarks that "Jim Crow" presented vagrant Black Americans as dangerous and fed into the disproportionate punishment of Black Americans under vagrancy laws in the antebellum period. She also indicates the role of white working-class desires in shaping this image of disorderly Black mobility, stating, "Jim Crow became the stage voice of mobility, articulating the challenges of economic instability and social estrangement, the mobility that was associated with the 'lumpenproletariat.'" However, neither Pryor nor O'Brassill-Kulfan looks at more than one blackface minstrel song—Pryor

looks at "Jim Crow," and O'Brassill-Kulfan looks at T. D. Rice's play *Bone Squash Diavolo* and offers commentary on Jim Crow the character without analyzing the song. Therefore, they do not document how negative images of Black mobility constituted a common theme in early minstrelsy, as I do here. In addition, they fail to note the importance of urban space to representations of disorderly Black movement in "Jim Crow" and other early minstrel songs. Finally, both scholars' analyses of "Jim Crow" are brief. The themes of Black mobility in early minstrelsy warrant the more extended analysis given here. See Pryor, *Colored Travelers*, 31; O'Brassill-Kulfan, *Vagrants and Vagabonds*, 90–91. W. T. Lhamon, discussing early blackface minstrelsy generally, emphasizes its thematic focus on vagabondage and characterizes this focus as a vital aspect of minstrelsy's oppositional class politics. However, Lhamon does not address the racial implications of minstrelsy's preoccupation with itinerancy other than to argue it encouraged cross-racial identifications between working-class white and Black Americans. See Lhamon, *Raising Cain*, 116–50; Lhamon, *Jump Jim Crow*, 15–16, 18, 27–37. Similarly, historian Alexander Saxton notes the centrality of "journeys" to blackface minstrelsy narratives, arguing that these journeys reflected the experiences of the white blackface performers and their audiences. Alexander Saxton, *Rise and Fall of the White Republic: Class Politics and Mass Culture in Nineteenth-Century America* (Verso, 1990), 173.

21. T. D. Rice, *Jim Crow* (New York: Firth and Hall, n.d., ca. 1832).

22. See, for example, Mike Wallace and Edwin Burrows, *Gotham: A History of New York City to 1898* (Oxford University Press, 1999), 489–90; Hartman, *Scenes of Subjection*, 28; Lott, *Love and Theft*, 107; Morrison, *Blacksound*, 44; Alan W. C. Green, "'Jim Crow,' 'Zip Coon': The Northern Origins of Negro Minstrelsy," *Massachusetts Review* 11, no. 2 (1970): 390.

23. George M. Fredrickson, *The Black Image in the White Mind: The Debate on Afro-American Character and Destiny, 1817–1914*, rev. ed. (Wesleyan University Press, 1987), 51–54.

24. For T. D. Rice's development of "Jim Crow" on the Western theater circuit, see Lhamon, *Jump Jim Crow*, 32–42; Lhamon, *Raising Cain*, 116–50. On the national Jacksonian coalition of frontier and urban working-class whites assembled around cultural and class grievances against the "corrupt aristocracy" of the rich, see Sean Wilentz, *The Rise of American Democracy: Jefferson to Lincoln* (W. W. Norton, 2005), 307–11, 359–74. The "Jim Crow" stanzas "I wip my weight in wildcats / I eat an Alligater, / And tear up more groud / Dan kifer 50 load of tater," and "I sit upon a Hornet's nest, / I dance upon my head, / I tie a wiper round my neck / And den I goes my bed" echo Crockett's supposed brag upon taking congressional office in 1827: "I can wade the Mississippi, leap the Ohio, ride a streak of lightning, slip without a scratch down a honey locust, whip my weight in wildcats, hug a bear too close for comfort, and eat any man opposed to Jackson!" Crockett, quoted in Wilentz, *Rise of American Democracy*, 433.

25. On the fundamental importance of race to capitalism, see Robinson, *Black Marxism*; W. E. B. Du Bois, *Black Reconstruction in America, 1860–1880* (Harcourt, Brace, 1935; repr., Free Press, 1998); Dipesh Chakrabarty, *Provincializing Europe: Postcolonial Thought and Historical Difference* (Princeton University Press, 2000); Kenneth Pomeranz, *The Great Divergence: China, Europe, and the Making of the Modern World Economy* (Princeton University Press, 2000); David Roediger and Elizabeth Esch, *The Production of Difference: Race*

and the Management of Labor in U.S. History (Oxford University Press, 2012); Lisa Lowe, *The Intimacies of Four Continents* (Duke University Press, 2015).

26. For the influence of the interracial spaces of the West and North on the development of blackface minstrelsy and the white angst these spaces triggered, see Wallace and Burrows, *Gotham*, 489–90; Lott, *Love and Theft*, 41, 47–49; Lhamon, *Raising Cain*, 1–55; D. A. Jones, *Captive Stage*, 52–56. On Black agency catalyzing minstrelsy's racism, see D. A. Jones, *Captive Stage*, 57.

27. My point here about Black mobility as a structural basis of minstrelsy is indebted to Jones's point that Black resistance helped produce the social and racial upheaval motivating blackface minstrelsy. See D. A. Jones, *Captive Stage*, 57. For the role of Black urban communities in furthering resistance to slavery and consolidating Black political power in the antebellum era, see Hahn, *Political Worlds of Slavery and Freedom*, 30–40.

28. William Clifton, *Jim Brown* (New York: Endicott, 1836); *Sich a Gitting Up Stairs* (Baltimore: Geo. Willig Jr., n.d.); R. W. Pelham, *Ginger Blue* (New York: Firth & Hall, 1841); Dan Emmett, *Old Dan Tucker* (Boston: C. H. Keith, 1843); *De Free Nigger* (New York: Firth & Hall, 1841). An alternative version of "Old Dan Tucker" that takes place entirely in a rural setting reveals by way of comparison the heightened disorder early minstrel songs attributed to urban Black mobility. Whereas in the urban version Dan Tucker immediately instigates a fight and causes a white watchman to repeatedly warn residents to get out of his way, in the rural version, Dan Tucker merely tries to steal a pig and chicken and fails to do so. See *Dan Tucker and Jim Crack Corn* (London: Musical Bouquet, n.d.).

29. C. N. B. *Manners and Customs of Ann Street, or, A North End Frolic* (n.p., n.d., ca. 1830s). A copy of the song sheet is housed in the Library of Congress's America Singing: 19th-Century Song Sheets Collection. While there is no date given on the song sheet itself, a copy appears in an 1840 volume titled *A Collection of American Songs and Ballads, 205 in Number. With a Ms. Index* (n.p., 1840), which is currently housed in the British Library. Historian Brian Roberts dates the song to the late 1820s or early 1830s. Brian Roberts, *Blackface Nation: Race, Reform, and Identity in American Popular Music, 1812–1925* (University of Chicago Press, 2017), 329n15.

30. Roediger, *Wages of Whiteness*, 100–111; David Grimsted, *American Mobbing, 1828–1865: Toward Civil War* (Oxford University Press, 1998).

31. *Billy Barlow* (Philadelphia: J. G. Osbourn, 1836).

32. On the widespread recognition of the Jim Crow pose, see Hoxworth, *Transoceanic Blackface*, 71–72; Peter Reed, *Rogue Performances: Staging the Underclasses in Early American Theatre Culture* (Palgrave MacMillan, 2009), 169–70.

33. *Billy Barlow*.

34. O'Brassill-Kulfan, *Vagrants and Vagabonds*, 6, 89, 101–4.

35. On the segregation of Massachusetts's railways and resistance to it by Black and white abolitionists, see Pryor, *Colored Travelers*, 76–102; Ruchames, "Jim Crow Railroads in Massachusetts"; Steve Luxenberg, *Separate: The Story of Plessy v. Ferguson, and America's Journey from Slavery to Segregation* (W. W. Norton, 2019), 3–23; Bay, *Traveling Black*, 26–28. Massachusetts was not alone in segregating its antebellum railroads; for example, streetcar and railroad companies in New Orleans segregated their cars in the 1830s. Kirt Wilson, *The Reconstruction Desegregation Debate: The Politics of Equality and the Rhetoric of Place, 1870–1875* (Michigan State University Press, 2002), 7; Hilary McLaughlin-Stonham, *From Slavery to*

Civil Rights: On the Streetcars of New Orleans, 1830s–Present (Liverpool University Press, 2020), 25.

36. Samuel Purchas, quoted in Robert F. Berkhofer Jr., *The White Man's Indian: Images of the American Indian from Columbus to the Present* (Vintage Books, 1979), 21. As postcolonial scholars have shown, Europeans and the racial epistemologies they generated, particularly in anthropology, often equated Indigenous populations with the native flora and fauna of the land. Thus, they saw Indigenous peoples as lacking mobility on a continental scale; Indigenous people, they imagined, did not leave their native shores. Radhika Mohanram, *Black Body: Women, Colonialism, and Space* (University of Minnesota Press, 1999); Arjun Appadurai, "Putting Hierarchy in Its Place," *Cultural Anthropology* 3, no. 1 (1988). However, scale is vital to white ideas about Native Americans and mobility. While whites often envisioned Native peoples as lacking mobility on a continental scale, they emphasized Native Americans' mobility on regional and more local scales, making it a fundamental aspect of their racialization. Some scholars have failed to note the differences in views about Natives and mobility at different scales, incorrectly asserting that whites have solely constructed Indigenous peoples as immobile.

37. Roxanne Dunbar-Ortiz, *An Indigenous Peoples' History of the United States* (Beacon Press, 2014), 16–31, 45–47; Edmund Morgan, *American Slavery, American Freedom: The Ordeal of Colonial Virginia* (W. W. Norton, 1975), 51–56, 232; Daniel K. Richter, "'Believing That Many of the Red People Suffer Much for Want of Food': Hunting, Agriculture, and a Quaker Construction of Indianness in the Early Republic," *Journal of the Early Republic* 19, no. 4 (1999): 603, 608–9; Roy Harvey Pearce, *Savagism and Civilization: A Study of the Indian and the American Mind*, rev. ed. (University of California Press, 1988), 68.

38. John Locke, *Two Treatises of Government* (London, 1689; repr., C. and J. Rivington, 1824), 148.

39. Locke, *Two Treatises of Government*, 145–46.

40. Locke, *Two Treatises of Government*, 150. In casting the American continent as empty, Locke recycled a long-standing view held among the English since the Elizabethan era that saw the Americas as open "virgin" land. See Leo Marx, *The Machine in the Garden: Technology and the Pastoral Ideal in America* (Oxford University Press, 2000), 36.

41. Locke, *Two Treatises of Government*, 145.

42. Locke, *Two Treatises of Government*, 151.

43. Locke, *Two Treatises of Government*, 154.

44. Bernard Bailyn, *The Ideological Origins of the American Revolution*, rev. ed. (Harvard University Press, 1992), 27–45; Pearce, *Savagism and Civilization*, 68; Nikhil Pal Singh, *Race and America's Long War* (University of California Press, 2017), 41; Paul Frymer, *Building an American Empire: The Era of Territorial and Political Expansion* (Princeton University Press, 2017), 39. Other political texts widely read by the Revolutionary War generation, such as Emer de Vattel's *The Law of Nations* (1758), echoed Locke's depiction of Native Americans as wandering hunters with no land rights. Pearce, *Savagism and Civilization*, 70–71; Jeffrey Ostler, *Surviving Genocide: Native Nations and the United States from the American Revolution to Bleeding Kansas* (Yale University Press, 2019), 100.

45. Even purchases that appeared legitimate on paper were heavily tainted by uneven bargaining power, as rapidly encroaching white settlement often placed Indian tribes in dire economic straits. Jean M. O'Brien, *Dispossession by Degrees: Indian Land and Identity in*

Natick, Massachusetts, 1650–1790 (Cambridge University Press, 1997); Daniel K. Richter, "Onas, the Long Knife: Pennsylvanians and Indians, 1783–1794," in *Native Americans and the Early Republic*, ed. Frederick Hoxie, Ronald Hoffman, and Peter Albert (University of Virginia Press, 1999); Daniel K. Richter, *Facing East from Indian Country: A Native History of Early America* (Harvard University Press, 2001), 225–36; Stuart Banner, *How the Indians Lost Their Land: Law and Power on the Frontier* (Harvard University Press, 2005); Lindsay G. Robertson, *Conquest by Law: How the Discovery of America Dispossessed Indigenous Peoples of Their Lands* (Oxford University Press, 2005); Blake A. Watson, *Buying America from the Indians: Johnson v. McIntosh and the History of Native Land Rights* (University of Oklahoma Press, 2012); Frymer, *Building an American Empire*, 10, 21–24; Allen Greer, *Property and Dispossession: Natives, Empires and Land in Early Modern North America* (Cambridge University Press, 2018), 1–23, 191–270.

46. Native nations suffered a blow when the French were expelled from the continent in 1763 after the French and Indian War, as the tribes were no longer able to use deft diplomatic skills to play European powers off one another. The Revolutionary War only compounded the problem, as land-hungry colonists no longer had to worry about British policies restraining the seizure of western land. Native peoples knew the invasion of their lands would only intensify. Fred Anderson, *Crucible of War: The Seven Years' War and the Fate of Empire in British North America, 1754–1766* (Vintage Books, 2000); Richter, *Facing East from Indian Country*, 167–71, 189–236.

47. Despite the power Indian nations held and the dignity of visiting Native diplomats, Washington and his cabinet never swayed from a conception of all Indians as nomadic hunters, and they remained deeply commitment to the eventual white settlement of Indian lands in the West. Colin Calloway, *The Indian World of George Washington: The First President, the First Americans, and the Birth of the Nation* (Oxford University Press, 2018), 288, 316–17, 327–29, 338, 365–71, 400–418, 431, 459–60; Reginald Horsman, *Expansion and American Indian Policy, 1783–1812*, 2nd ed. (University of Oklahoma Press, 1992), 53–58; Guyatt, *Bind Us Apart*, 43–60; Richter, "'Believing That Many of the Red People Suffer Much for Want of Food,'" 608–14. For some of the various ways Native peoples used mobility to resist settler colonialism during the seventeenth, eighteenth, and nineteenth centuries, see Douglas K. Miller, *Indians on the Move: Native American Mobility and Urbanization in the Twentieth Century* (University of North Carolina Press, 2019), 13–19; Jon Parmenter, *The Edge of the Woods: Iroquoia, 1534–1701* (Michigan State University Press, 2010); Jace Weaver, *The Red Atlantic: American Indigenes and the Making of the Modern World, 1000–1927* (University of North Carolina Press, 2014), 86–215; Coll Thrush, *Indigenous London: Native Travelers at the Heart of Empire* (Yale University Press, 2016), 68–203; Colin Calloway, *"The Chiefs Now in This City": Indians and the Urban Frontier in Early America* (Oxford University Press, 2021); Daniel H. Usner, "Communicating Sovereignty in *Balbancha*: The Performance of Native American Diplomacy in Early New Orleans," in *Indian Cities: Histories of Indigenous Urbanization*, ed. Kent Blansett, Cathleen D. Cahill, and Andrew Needham (University of Oklahoma Press, 2022); Joshua A. McGonagle Althoff, "Managing Settlers, Managing Neighbors: Renarrating *Johnson v. McIntosh* Through the History of Piankashaw Community Building," *Journal of American History* 110, no. 4 (2024).

48. Calloway, *Indian World of George Washington*, 316–17, 325–40; Horsman, *Expansion and American Indian Policy*, 53–65; Guyatt, *Bind Us Apart*, 50, 58–59; R. Douglas Hurt, *The*

Indian Frontier, 1763–1846 (University of New Mexico Press, 2002), 105–6; Richter, *Facing East from Indian Country*, 226; Frymer, *Building an American Empire*, 34–36, 44–68.

49. Christian B. Keller, "Philanthropy Betrayed: Thomas Jefferson, the Louisiana Purchase, and the Origins of Federal Indian Removal Policy," *Proceedings of the American Philosophical Society* 144, no. 1 (2000); James Ronda, "'We Have a Country': Race, Geography, and the Invention of Indian Territory," *Journal of the Early Republic* 19, no. 4 (1999): 741–44; Guyatt, *Bind Us Apart*, 93–103, 144–45, 232–38, 281–94; Horsman, *Expansion and American Indian Policy*, 106–14; Pearce, *Savagism and Civilization*, 56. On Jefferson's vision of an "empire of liberty" and its racial and settler-colonial trappings, see Justin Leroy, "Empire and the Afterlife of Slavery: Black Anti-Imperialisms of the Long Nineteenth Century" (PhD diss., New York University, 2014), 13–51.

50. John Quincy Adams, *An Oration, Delivered at Plymouth, December 22, 1802, At the Anniversary Commemoration of the First Landing of Our Ancestors, At That Place* (Boston, 1802), 23–24; Johnson v. M'Intosh, 21 U.S. 543, 590 (1823). For more invocations of the wandering Indian stereotype in the Johnson v. M'Intosh decision, see *Johnson*, 590–91; see also Cherokee Nation v. Georgia, 30 US 1, 23, 27 (1831).

51. For more examples demonstrating the ubiquity of the wandering Indian stereotype in the early nineteenth century, see Banner, *How the Indians Lost Their Land*, 152–55.

52. Claudio Saunt, *Unworthy Republic: The Dispossession of Native Americans and the Road to Indian Territory* (W. W. Norton, 2020), 27–49; Ostler, *Surviving Genocide*, 206–8; Pearce, *Savagism and Civilization*, 70–71. On the seizure of Indian land for the expansion of slavery, see Jodi A. Byrd, *Transit of Empire: Indigenous Critiques of Colonialism* (University of Minnesota Press, 2011), 12; Saunt, *Unworthy Republic*, 189–96, 308–15; Ostler, *Surviving Genocide*, 248.

53. Guyatt, *Bind Us Apart*, 300–302, 316–17; Saunt, *Unworthy Republic*, 53–83; Michael Morris, "Georgia and the Conversation over Indian Removal," *Georgia Historical Quarterly* 91, no. 4 (2007): 403–4; Mary Hershberger, "Mobilizing Women, Anticipating Abolition," *Journal of American History* 86, no. 1 (1999): 15; Ostler, *Surviving Genocide*, 209–12.

54. Anthony F. C. Wallace, *The Long, Bitter Trail: Andrew Jackson and the Indians* (Hill and Wang, 1993), 54–56, 65–66; Guyatt, *Bind Us Apart*, 302–3; Morris, "Georgia and the Conversation over Indian Removal," 403–4. Jackson's defense of removal to Congress echoed these arguments. Andrew Jackson, "Annual Message to Congress, Communicated December 7, 1830," in *Annual Messages, Veto Messages, Protest, &c. of Andrew Jackson, President of the United States* (Baltimore, 1835), 59–61. For a more generous account of Jackson's views on Indians and removal, see Wilentz, *Rise of American Democracy*, 322–27.

55. Hershberger, "Mobilizing Women, Anticipating Abolition." See also Wilentz, *Rise of American Democracy*, 324; Morris, "Georgia and the Conversation over Indian Removal," 403–14.

56. Tiya Miles, "'Circular Reasoning': Recentering Cherokee Women in the Antiremoval Campaigns," *American Quarterly* 61, no. 2 (2009); Christian Michael Gonzales, "Cultural Colonizers: Persistence and Empire in the Indian Antiremoval Movement, 1815–1859" (PhD diss., University of California San Diego, 2010); Ostler, *Surviving Genocide*, 264–67, 274–86.

57. Gonzales, "Cultural Colonizers," 58–94; Hershberger, "Mobilizing Women, Anticipating Abolition," 18–24; Francis Paul Prucha, *The Great Father: The United States Government*

and the Indians (University of Nebraska Press, 1984), 1:201–8. Native Americans who worked with white reformers to protest removal selectively appropriated US cultural and economic practices in order to preserve their traditional cultures. See Gonzales, "Cultural Colonizers."

58. Prucha, *Great Father,* 191–269; John P. Bowes, *Land Too Good for Indians: Northern Indian Removal* (University of Oklahoma Press, 2016); Saunt, *Unworthy Republic,* 53–322.

59. Guyatt, *Bind Us Apart*; Patrick Wolfe, *Traces of History: Elementary Structures of Race* (Verso, 2016), 164.

60. Berkhofer, *White Man's Indian,* 88; Brian W. Dippie, *The Vanishing American: White Attitudes and U.S. Indian Policy,* rev. ed. (University of Kansas Press, 1991); Rebecca Jaroff, "Opposing Forces: (Re)Playing Pocahontas and the Politics of Indian Removal on the Antebellum Stage," *Comparative Drama* 40, no. 4 (2006–7); Jill Lepore, *The Name of War: King Philip's War and the Origins of American Identity* (Vintage Books, 1998), 191–226; B. Donald Grose, "Edwin Forrest, *Metamora,* and the Indian Removal Act of 1830," *Theatre Journal* 37, no. 2 (1985). Historian Scott C. Martin argues that *Metamora* contains some critiques of white colonists, thus echoing my arguments about ambivalence here. See Scott C. Martin, "Interpreting *Metamora*: Nationalism, Theater, and Jacksonian Indian Policy," *Journal of the Early Republic* 19, no. 1 (1999).

61. Finson, *Voices That Are Gone,* 241; David Monod, *The Soul of Pleasure: Sentiment and Sensation in Nineteenth-Century Mass Entertainment* (Cornell University Press, 2016); Nicholas E. Tawa, *High-Minded and Low-Down: Music in the Lives of Americans, 1800–1861* (Northeastern University Press, 2000), 48–49.

62. Finson, *Voices That Are Gone,* 240–69, quotations on 241 and 255; Pisani, *Imagining Native America in Music,* 98–116, 126–31; Berkhofer, *White Man's Indian,* 86–88.

63. Finson, *Voices That Are Gone,* 268–69; Pisani, *Imagining Native America in Music,* 115. Indeed, the prevalence of romantic treatments of Indians in popular song has led both Jon Finson and Michael Pisani—two scholars who have thoroughly studied representations of Native Americans in nineteenth-century popular music—to mistakenly state that there were virtually no overtly negative or violent images of Native Americans in popular song during the antebellum era. Finson states that he found only one song from the nineteenth century that "attributes a violent act to Native Americans." Finson, *Voices That Are Gone,* 269, 269n29. Pisani says that of the fifty-nine songs published between 1835 and 1860 that he examined, only two of the noninstrumental songs were not sentimental. Pisani, *Imagining Native America in Music,* 114–15. However, in my research, I located six songs with lyrics that portrayed Native Americans as violent—two pieces of sheet music and four song sheets—at least four of which were published in the period Pisani examined. It may be that Finson and Pisani failed to look at song sheets, which, given their predominantly working-class audience, proved more conducive to violent images. However, I concur with their overarching point that sheet music and song sheets predominantly romanticized Native Americans. For songs portraying Native Americans as violent, see Henry R. Bishop, *Yes Tis the Indian Drum* (London: Goulding, D'Almaine, n.d., ca. 1823); *Battle of Stonington, and the Banks of the Ohio* (Boston: L. Deming, n.d.); Henry Russell and George P. Morris, *The Soldier and His Bride* (New York: Firth and Hall, 1841); *Bold Northwestman and Wandering Boys of Switzerland* (Boston: L. Deming, n.d.); *American Perry* (Boston: L. Deming, n.d.); *Hunt the Buffalo, or The Banks of the Pleasant Ohio* (New York: Andrews, n.d.).

64. Finson, *Voices That Are Gone*, 240–41, 246–49, 269; Pisani, *Imagining Native America in Music*, 95, 97–101, 110–14.

65. Numerous literary scholars have also raised this point in discussing romanticism and race generally. See, for example, Shirley Samuels, ed., *The Culture of Sentiment: Race, Gender, and Sentimentality in Nineteenth-Century America* (Oxford University Press, 1992); Lora Romero, *Home Fronts: Domesticity and Its Critics in the Antebellum United States* (Duke University Press, 1997), 35–51; Sara Romeyn, "A Sentimental Empire: White Women's Responses to Native American Policy, 1824–1894" (PhD diss., George Washington University, 2003); Elizabeth Barnes, *Love's Whipping Boy: Violence and Sentimentality in the American Imagination* (University of North Carolina Press, 2011). Scholar Cari Carpenter argues that Native women authors incorporated elements of sentimentality into their texts to articulate and invoke anger about the dispossession of Native peoples' lands. Cari M. Carpenter, *Seeing Red: Anger, Sentimentality, and American Indians* (Ohio State University Press, 2008).

66. In my review of song sheets featuring Native Americans, eight offered sentimental and sympathetic depictions, and four presented Indians as hostile. Although publishers in the antebellum era predominantly geared sheet music toward middle-class audiences and song sheets toward working-class audiences, both often circulated across class and gender lines. The content of song sheets also overlapped a great deal with that of sheet music, and songs often appeared in both forms. Charosh, "Studying Nineteenth-Century Popular Song."

67. *Bold Northwestman.*

68. For the events of McCrea's death, see Woody Holton, *Liberty Is Sweet: The Hidden History of the American Revolution* (Simon and Schuster, 2021), 310.

69. Russell and Morris, *Soldier and His Bride*. For another example of Indian violence in sheet music, see Henry Bishop, *Yes Tis the Indian Drum* (n.p., ca. 1823). The song was from the 1823 play *Cortez; or, The Conquest of Mexico. An Historical Drama. In Three Acts.*

70. As previously mentioned, of the forty-two songs significantly about Indians (those with multiple lyrics about Indians) that I have been able to identify in my research, eleven, or over 25 percent, feature images of Indian mobility.

71. Eliza Cook and Henry Russell, *The Indian Hunter* (New York: Jas. L. Hewitt, n.d., ca. 1837).

72. Cook and Russell, *Indian Hunter*. I agree with Finson that by presenting Indians as uncivilized, "The Indian Hunter" indirectly justifies removal. Finson, *Voices That Are Gone*, 246–48. This practice of using the "noble savage" stereotype as a foil to critique white society was a common motif in white representations of Native Americans. Berkhofer, *White Man's Indian*, 74–75. For another song that critiques the avarice of whites and portrays Indians as innately mobile, see Samuel Lover, *Give Me My Arrows and Give Me My Bow* (New York: Firth, Pond, 1849).

73. J. E. Carpenter and Stephen Glover, *The Indian Hunter's Bride* (London: Willey, n.d.). For other examples of critiques of white society folded into the "tragic lovers" theme, see, for example, George P. Morris and Francis H. Brown, *The Indian and His Bride* (New York: Firth, Hall, and Pond, 1844); W. D. Gallagher and W. C. Peters, *The Spotted Fawn* (Cincinnati: Peters, 1845).

74. D. Loughery and Jas. E. Magruder, *The Indian Captive, or, The Absent Lover* (New York: Firth, Pond, 1854). Strenuous castigations of Indian captivity also appeared in "The

Indian's Prayer" (1846) and an alternative version of the song titled "The Indian Hunter" (c. 1846). In "The Indian Hunter" version, the narrator proclaims his desire to hunt, as the title suggests. The song's critique of Indian captivity thus remains glued to the idea of Indians as nomadic hunters. I. B. Woodbury, *The Indian's Prayer* (Boston: C. Bradlee, 1846); *The Indian Hunter* (Baltimore: F. D. Benteen, n.d.). For another song critiquing Native captivity, see *The Indian Student* (New Orleans: P. P. Werlein, 1851).

75. Owen G. Warren and Herrman S. Saroni, *The Pequot Brave* (New York: W. H. Geib, 1844).

76. Another robust defense of Indian violence comes in "The Death of Osceola," published in 1847. The song details the fate of Osceola, one of the leaders of the Seminole resistance to removal in the 1830s who was betrayed by the US Army when it captured him under a flag of truce in 1837. The song harshly condemns Osceola's capture through US duplicity. S. S. Steele and B. F. Baker, *The Death of Osceola* (Boston: Henry Tolman, 1847). On the US Army's capture of Osceola under a flag of truce—a tactic the army used at other times in the conflict with the Seminoles—see David Silverman, *Thundersticks: Firearms and the Violent Transformation of Native America* (Belknap Press of Harvard University Press, 2016), 215–16. For the Second Seminole War in general, see Silverman, *Thundersticks*, 190–220; C. S. Monaco, *The Second Seminole War and the Limits of American Aggression* (Johns Hopkins University Press, 2018).

77. Marshall S. Pike, *The Indian Warrior's Grave* (Boston: J. P. Ordway, 1850). For another example of a song that heavily aligned with the logic of removal, see T. Wood, *Thye Are Gone, They Are Gone, or The Red Man's Requiem* (New York: Horace Waters, 1855).

78. One exception worth noting is "The Indian Mother's Lullaby," which presented a counternarrative to the racial fiction of the innately mobile Indian. Written in 1855 by white poet and songwriter James G. Clark, the song portrays Indian mobility as a product of white violence, land dispossession, and persecution. See James G. Clark, *The Indian Mother's Lullaby* (Boston: Henry Tolman, 1855). For another song that attributes Indian mobility to white encroachment and coercive force but also justifies removal as inevitable and resulting in more productive land uses, see W. B. Farwell and Frank Howard, *The Indian's Dream* (Boston: S. W. Marsh, 1848).

79. Tony Ballantyne, "Mobility, Empire, Colonization," *History Australia* 11, no. 2 (2014): 27; Genevieve Carpio, Natchee Blu Barnd, and Laura Barraclough, "Introduction to the Special Issue: Mobilizing Indigeneity and Race Within and Against Settler Colonialism," *Mobilities* 17, no. 2 (2022): 5–6. Perhaps the best-known and most fully developed articulation of the myth of white western movement begetting fixity and civilization is Frederick Jackson Turner's "frontier thesis," which he expounded at the 1893 Chicago World's Columbian Exposition. See Alan Trachtenberg, *The Incorporation of America: Culture and Society in the Gilded Age*, rev. ed. (Hill and Wang, 2007), 13–17.

80. Using history to expose the irrationalities and fabrications of race is, as scholar Cedric Robinson notes, vital to defusing race's power: "Race presents all the appearance of stability. History, however, compromises this fixity. Race is mercurial—deadly and slick. And since race is presumably natural, the intrusion of convention shatters race's relationship to the natural world." Cedric Robinson, *Forgeries of Memory and Meaning: Blacks and the Regimes of Race in American Theater and Film Before World War II* (University of North Carolina Press, 2007), 4.

81. Tim Cresswell, *The Tramp in America* (Reaktion Books, 2001); Kenneth Kusmer, *Down and Out, On the Road: The Homeless in American History* (Oxford University Press, 2002); Todd DePastino, *Citizen Hobo: How a Century of Homelessness Shaped America* (University of Chicago Press, 2003); O'Brassill-Kulfan, *Vagrants and Vagabonds*.

82. Charles E. Horn and Georgia P. Morris, *A Western Refrain: Westward Ho!* (New York: Davis and Horn, 1839). This pattern was consistent. The song sheet for "Banks of the Ohio" (c. 1830) made it abundantly clear that white men did not have to worry about movement affecting their property rights or racial standing. It coupled images of white hunters with stock celebrations of white male mastery over nature and highlighted the rewards of white migration. It opened with the call "Come all you young men, who have a mind for to range, / Into the western country, your station for to change," before stating " 'Tis a garden of Eden in North America, / Come along my lively lads, and we'll altogether go, / And we'll settle on the banks of the Pleasant Ohio." Once there, white men could not only "plough, reap and sow" but also take advantage of "all kinds of game there, besides the buck and doe," and "range through the wild woods and hunt the buffalo." Once again, white mobility proves compatible with the ownership and development of western land, as the lyrics laud white hunting—though in conjunction with the practice of agriculture. Such rosy views of life in the West read as virtual propaganda for western land speculators trying to stir up excitement for white settlement. *Battle of Stonington, and the Banks of the Ohio* (Boston: L. Deming, n.d.). For other similar examples, see *Hunters of Kentucky, or Half Horse and Half Alligator* (Boston: William Rutter, n.d.); E. A. Hosmer and Alfred B. Street, *Happy Are We Hunters Free* (Boston: G. P. Reed, 1848). Leonard Deming was a Boston bookseller and printer between 1829 and 1840 according to the Library of Congress. "Deming, Leonard, 1787–1853," Library of Congress Authorities, https://lccn.loc.gov/nr91010991, accessed June 14, 2022. See also "Text Context," Isaiah Thomas Broadside Ballads Project, American Antiquarian Society, www.americanantiquarian.org/thomasballads/textcontext, accessed June 14, 2022. For other songs lionizing the West, see *To the West* (Philadelphia: G. S. Harris, n.d., ca. late 1850s); *Parody on To the West* (New York: Andrews, n.d.); *Land of the West* (New York: H. De Marsan, n.d.). I date "To the West" circa late 1850s because the song sheet lists the printer's address in Philadelphia as 4th and Vine, and George S. Harris moved his shop to that address in 1854. "Harris, George S., Geo. S. Harris & Son, Geo. S. Harris & Sons," The Library Company of Philadelphia, https://digital.librarycompany.org/islandora/object/digitool%3A79266/print, accessed June 15, 2022. Gender played a prominent role in these idealized narratives of whiteness and western migration. In "The Pioneer's Home" (1858), the "true and honest" white pioneer and his labor in the untouched "wildwood" produce fixed habitation—it is "his sturdy stroke" that "grew" a cabin on the land, gesturing toward the idea, with all its sexual connotations, that white male cultivation results not just in crops but also in society and civilization. The song thus reflects and re-creates the fundamental racialization of whites as both mobile and fixed, while its description of the land as "virgin soil" provides the requisite erasure of Native American cultivation. The role of women in such songs was purely domestic. In "Banks of the Ohio," women are the overseers of domestic production: Those who can "card, knit, and spin" will be "rewarded" for accompanying men westward. In "The Pioneer's Home," they appear merely as the "smiling wife" inhabiting the home the male pioneer has built. *Battle of Stonington, and the Banks of the Ohio*; T. E. Garrett and F. Woolcott, *The Pioneer's Home* (St. Louis: G. Fritz, 1958).

83. As previously discussed, the 1836 song "Billy Barlow" cast aspersions on poor white urban mobility. But this was one of the few negative examples of white mobility in popular song, and its urban setting and focus on poor whites speaks to the specific geographical and class ideas at play in such representations.

Chapter Two

1. "Music," *Frank Leslie's Illustrated*, Jan. 5, 1856, 50.

2. Petra Meyer-Frazier, "Music, Novels, and Women: Nineteenth-Century Prescriptions for an Ideal Life," *Women and Music: A Journal of Gender and Culture* 10 (2006): 46–47.

3. Jon W. Finson, *The Voices That Are Gone: Themes in Nineteenth-Century American Popular Song* (Oxford University Press, 1994), 241; Robert F. Berkhofer Jr., *The White Man's Indian: Images of the American Indian from Columbus to the Present* (Vintage Books, 1979), 86–88; Nicholas E. Tawa, *High-Minded and Low-Down: Music in the Lives of Americans, 1800–1861* (Northeastern University Press, 2000), 48–49. On the impact of melodrama—a genre that greatly overlapped with sentimentalism—on mid-nineteenth-century popular culture, see Elisabeth R. Anker, *Orgies of Feeling: Melodrama and the Politics of Freedom* (Duke University Press, 2014), 77–84.

4. I use the term "redface" here to refer to non-Indians' enactment of and identification with a fabricated Native identity and experience in order to express their own emotional and ideological longings as well as racial antipathies. For the history of redface, and an elaboration of its overlaps with and differences from blackface, see Bethany Hughes, *Redface: Race, Performance, and Indigeneity* (New York University Press, 2024).

5. On the middle-class culture of sentimentalism in the mid-nineteenth century and its influence on minstrelsy, including minstrel artists' use of sentimentality to appeal to middle-class audiences, see David Monod, *The Soul of Pleasure: Sentiment and Sensation in Nineteenth-Century Mass Entertainment* (Cornell University Press, 2016); Robert Nowatzki, *Representing African Americans in Transatlantic Abolitionism and Blackface Minstrelsy* (Louisiana State University Press, 2010), 13–14. For minstrelsy's middle-class turn in the 1840s, see Stephanie Dunson, "The Minstrel in the Parlor: Nineteenth-Century Sheet Music and the Domestication of Blackface Minstrelsy" (PhD diss., University of Massachusetts, Amherst, 2004).

6. In writing about the South, I follow scholar Jennifer Rae Greeson's observation that "'the South' is, first and foremost, an ideological concept rather than a place." Jennifer Rae Greeson, *Our South: Geographic Fantasy and the Rise of National Literature* (Harvard University Press, 2010), 10; see also W. Fitzhugh Brundage, introduction to *A New History of the American South*, ed. W. Fitzhugh Brundage (University of North Carolina Press, 2023), xv–xxv. Therefore, I do not settle on one geographic definition of the South but instead employ the term with the recognition that contemporary understandings and uses were not necessarily uniform. However, in general, contemporary invocations of the South in popular culture referred to the antebellum slave states.

7. George M. Fredrickson, *The Black Image in the White Mind: The Debate on Afro-American Character and Destiny, 1817–1914*, rev. ed. (Wesleyan University Press, 1987), 133–35; Kate Masur, *Until Justice Be Done: America's First Civil Rights Movement, from the Revolution to Reconstruction* (W. W. Norton, 2021), 225–66.

8. Finson, *Voices That Are Gone,* 266; Michael V. Pisani, *Imagining Native America in Music* (Yale University Press, 2005), 81.

9. Cherokee Nation v. Georgia, 30 U.S. 1, 2 (1831).

10. As mentioned in chapter 1, of the forty-two songs significantly about Native Americans that I have been able to identify in my research on sheet music and song sheets, eleven—over 25 percent—feature overt images of Indians as inherently mobile. Of that eleven, six explicitly cast a Native American female narrator as mobile.

11. M. D. Sullivan, *The Blue Juniata* (Boston: Oliver Ditson, 1844). For the song's massive popularity, see Finson, *Voices That Are Gone,* 262–63.

12. E. A. Hosmer, *Dark Eyed Ulalee, or Indian Maiden of Echo Lake* (Boston: G. P. Reed, 1855).

13. Shirley Brooks, *The Wigwam: A Burletta* (London: W. S. Johnson, 1847).

14. For a work looking at the very different subject of Bollywood cinema but exploring how musical interludes open up more expansive gender and sexual politics and subversive flashes opposed to the traditional, dominant ideas expressed in the narrative plot, see Gayatri Gopinath, *Impossible Desires: Queer Diasporas and South Asian Public Cultures* (Duke University Press, 2005), 93–130.

15. Shirley Brooks and Alexander Lee, *Cora: The Indian Maiden's Song* (New York: Firth, Pond, 1851).

16. J. M. Smith Jr. and Charles E. Horn, *The American Indian Girl* (New York: Firth, Pond, 1835). For two other songs presenting Native women as inherently mobile, see Edward J. Porter and F. Romani, *The Indian Bride's Farewell* (Baltimore: F. D. Benteen, 1844); G. H. Bohannan, *The Hunters [sic] Bride* (New York: Firth, Pond, 1850).

17. On the ideology of separate spheres and women's resistance and accommodation to it, see Tiya Miles, *Wild Girls: How the Outdoors Shaped the Women Who Challenged a Nation* (W. W. Norton, 2023); Nancy F. Cott, *The Bonds of Womanhood: "Woman's Sphere" in New England, 1780–1935,* rev. ed. (Veritas, 2020); Carroll Smith-Rosenberg, *Disorderly Conduct: Visions of Gender in Victorian America* (Oxford University Press, 1985); Jeanne Boydston, *Home and Work: Housework, Wages, and the Ideology of Labor in the Early Republic* (Oxford University Press, 1990); Elizabeth Maddock Dillon, *The Gender of Freedom: Fictions of Liberalism and the Literary Public Sphere* (Stanford University Press, 2004); Amy Kaplan, "Manifest Domesticity," *American Literature* 70, no. 3 (1998); Sarah Deutsch, *Women and the City: Gender, Space, and Power in Boston, 1870–1940* (Oxford University Press, 2000); Jessica Ellen Sewell, *Women and the Everyday City: Public Space in San Francisco, 1890–1915* (University of Minnesota Press, 2011).

18. Nicholas Tawa, *Sweet Songs for Gentle Americans: The Parlor Song in America, 1790–1860* (Bowling Green University Popular Press, 1980), 33–35, 38–40; Tawa, *High-Minded and Low-Down,* 71, 155–58, 161–62; Katherine C. Grier, *Culture and Comfort: Parlor Making and Middle-Class Identity, 1850–1930,* 2nd ed. (Smithsonian Books, 2010); Petra Meyer-Frazier, "American Women's Roles in Domestic Music Making as Revealed in Parlor Song Collections: 1820–1870" (PhD diss., University of Colorado at Boulder, 1999), 7–15, 44–72; Dunson, "Minstrel in the Parlor," 4, 25–30. On the cross-class popularity of sheet music, see Tawa, *Sweet Songs for Gentle Americans,* 6, 21–22.

19. Dunson, "Minstrel in the Parlor," 85; see also 36–38, 87–129.

20. Robin D. G. Kelley, "Notes on Deconstructing 'the Folk,'" *American Historical Review* 97, no. 5 (1992): 1406.

21. This opposition to domesticity did not mean Indian women in sheet music did not embody other feminine ideals accompanying the rise of separate spheres; sheet music often painted Indian women as empathetic and dedicated lovers and, on occasion, as deeply caring mothers in accordance with the antebellum "cult of motherhood." (See the previous examples of Indian sheet music, as well as Sara Romeyn, "A Sentimental Empire: White Women's Responses to Native American Policy, 1824–1894" [PhD diss., George Washington University, 2003].) However, their dominant representation as mobile embodiments of the wilderness overrode any images that might suggest a connection between Indian women and the domestic sphere.

22. Philip J. Deloria, *Playing Indian* (Yale University Press, 1998). This tension between gender subversion and racial oppression found in sheet music featuring Indian women echoes the tension around race and gender that Dunson identifies in blackface minstrel sheet music. Dunson, "Minstrel in the Parlor," 108.

23. Sheet music featuring Indian women's potential function as an outlet for rebellious urges against separate spheres echoes Frederick Douglass's characterization of the annual Christmas celebrations on slave plantations as "safety-valves" that released some of the pressure resulting from slavery's violent oppression, thus dampening the likelihood of slave revolts. Frederick Douglass, *Narrative of the Life of Frederick Douglass: An American Slave* (First Avenue Editions, 2014), 79. For an elaboration on Douglass's point, see Saidiya Hartman, *Scenes of Subjection: Terror, Slavery, and Self-Making in Nineteenth-Century America* (Oxford University Press, 1997), 43–48. For a work pushing back on Hartman's characterization of slave celebrations as dominated by oppressive forces, see Walter Johnson, "On Agency," *Journal of Social History* 37, no. 1 (2003).

24. Finson, *Voices That Are Gone*, 23, 41; Meyer-Frazier, "American Women's Roles in Domestic Music Making," 42–43; Meyer-Frazier, "Music, Novels, and Women," 47.

25. Henry Bishop and John Howard Payne, *Home, Sweet Home!* (New York: Firth and Hall, 1830). A close examination of the illustration reveals that just discernible in the shadows of the cottage door is another female figure. The figure is hard to make out, and one could argue that it is impossible to determine its sex. However, the figure's clothing billows out around it, suggesting a women's dress.

26. Annette Kolodny, *The Lay of the Land: Metaphor as Experience and History in American Life and Letters* (University of North Carolina Press, 1975); Gillian Rose, *Feminism and Geography: The Limits of Geographical Knowledge* (University of Minnesota Press, 1993), 92–99. Rose recognizes that such imagery presents women as rooted to the ground, but she does not develop this point further. Historian Nina Silber notes that romantic depictions of the postbellum South in travel literature equated Southern white women with the landscape, but she does not investigate the geographic implications of this rhetorical move. Nina Silber, *The Romance of Reunion: Northerners and the South, 1865–1900* (University of North Carolina Press, 1993), 84–86.

27. Melani McAlister, *Epic Encounters: Culture, Media, and U.S. Interests in the Middle East Since 1945*, 2nd ed. (University of California Press, 2005), 6.

28. *Bonja Song* (New York: A. Geib, n.d., ca. 1811). While the sheet music for "Bonja Song" does not list a publication date, scholar Sarah Meredith dates the song to circa 1811, though she does not provide the evidence leading her to this conclusion. The National Library of Australia's online catalog dates the song to circa 1811–12. However, historian Karina

Williamson claims the song was published earlier, around 1802, but also does not explain how she arrived at this date. See Sarah Meredith, "With a Banjo on Her Knee: Gender, Race, Class, and the American Classic Banjo Tradition, 1880–1915" (PhD diss., Florida State University, 2003), 14n20; "Bonga Song [music]: A Favorite Negro Air for the Piano Forte," 1811–12, Collection of Jamie and Michael Kassler, National Library of Australia, https://catalogue.nla.gov.au/Record/5366601; Karina Williamson, *Contrary Voices: Representations of West Indian Slavery, 1657–1834* (University of the West Indies Press, 2008), 491–92.

29. Leo Marx, *The Machine in the Garden: Technology and the Pastoral Ideal in America* (Oxford University Press, 2000), 3, 6, 9–10.

30. Roger William Hecht, "Nature's 'Cunning Alphabet': Pastoral Landscape and Politics in Nineteenth-Century American Literature" (PhD diss., Syracuse University, 2002), 4–5, 114–15; Thomas Jefferson, *Notes on the State of Virginia*, 8th ed. (Boston, 1801). For more on the pastoralism of Jefferson's *Notes on the State of Virginia*, see Marx, *Machine in the Garden*, 116–41.

31. Lewis P. Simpson, *The Dispossessed Garden: The Pastoral and History in Southern Literature* (Louisiana State University Press, 1983), 20–64; Hecht, "Nature's 'Cunning Alphabet,'" 114–15. See also John M. Grammer, *Pastoral and Politics in the Old South* (Louisiana State University Press, 1996), 11–12, 20–97. For more on the Southern pastoral in literature, see Lucinda Hardwick MacKethan, *The Dream of Arcady: Place and Time in Southern Literature* (Louisiana State University Press, 1980); Jan Bakker, *Pastoral in Antebellum Southern Romance* (Louisiana State University Press, 1989); Hecht, "Nature's 'Cunning Alphabet,'" 110–56.

32. See, for example, Marx, *Machine in the Garden*, 5, 7, 9; Herbert Gutman, *Work, Culture and Society in Industrializing America: Essays in American Working-Class and Social History* (Vintage Books, 1977), 3–32.

33. Elliott West, "Reconstructing Race," *Western Historical Quarterly* 34, no. 1 (2003): 8–9; James Brewer Stewart, *Holy Warriors: The Abolitionists and American Slavery* (Hill and Wang, 1976), 119; Sean Wilentz, *The Rise of American Democracy: Jefferson to Lincoln* (W. W. Norton, 2005), 585, 594–632; Eric Foner, *Free Soil, Free Labor, Free Men: The Ideology of the Republican Party Before the Civil War* (Oxford University Press, 1995), 60, 124–25, 188–90; John L. Brooke, *"There Is a North": Fugitive Slaves, Political Crisis, and Cultural Transformation in the Coming of the Civil War* (University of Massachusetts Press, 2019), 13, 55–63.

34. On the increased activity of Black and white abolitionists in response to the Fugitive Slave Act of 1850 and most Northern whites' acceptance of the law and antagonism to abolitionist activity, see Wilentz, *Rise of American Democracy*, 649–50, 652; Brooke, *"There Is a North,"* 65–88; Stanley Harrold, *American Abolitionism: Its Direct Political Impact from Colonial Times Into Reconstruction* (University of Virginia Press, 2019), 115, 124, 127. On the general uptick in abolitionist sentiment and militant abolitionist rhetoric and resistance in the 1850s, see Harrold, *American Abolitionism*, 136, 151–52, 154; James Brewer Stewart, *Abolitionist Politics and the Coming of the Civil War* (University of Massachusetts Press, 2008), 3–6, 21–31; Brooke, *"There Is a North,"* 65–294; Stewart, *Holy Warriors*, 97–177, esp. 123, 136. For the actions of Northern Black activists in particular, see Stephen Kantrowitz, *More Than Freedom: Fighting for Black Citizenship in a White Republic, 1829–1889* (Penguin Press, 2012), 175–262. For two studies showing the incredible popularity of Stowe's *Uncle Tom's Cabin*

and how it permeated American culture in the 1850s, see Robin Bernstein, *Racial Innocence: Performing American Childhood from Slavery to Civil Rights* (New York University Press, 2011), 92–145; Sarah Meer, *Uncle Tom Mania: Slavery, Minstrelsy, and Transatlantic Culture in the 1850s* (University of Georgia Press, 2005).

35. Stuart Hall, *The Hard Road to Renewal: Thatcherism and the Crisis of the Left* (Verso, 1988), 8.

36. Literary scholar Paul Outka argues that this conflation renders Black Americans natural resources available for white exploitation, and scholar Roger William Hecht—examining the antebellum period—sees the move as an attempt on the part of Southern whites to justify slavery. Historian Nina Silber likewise notes that pastoral images in post-bellum Southern travel literature presented African Americans as part of the landscape, palliating white oppression of Southern African Americans and its threat as a divisive sectional issue. Paul Outka, *Race and Nature: From Transcendentalism to the Harlem Renaissance* (Palgrave Macmillan, 2008), 3, 93, 170; Hecht, "Nature's 'Cunning Alphabet,'" 119–20, 132–37; Nina Silber, *Romance of Reunion*, 78–81.

37. In analyzing these increasingly elaborate pastoral images, we must therefore expand on scholar Saidiya Hartman's insight about antebellum minstrel songs symbolically returning Black bodies to their "proper place" by foregrounding the songs' larger spatial stakes. Hartman writes that pastoral minstrel songs featuring former slaves reminiscing about the plantation enact a logic of return and proper placement that soothed white fears about free Black Americans by returning them to their proper place in the social and racial hierarchy. Hartman, *Scenes of Subjection*, 28–30. However, pastoral renderings of the plantation did not simply play on white desires to return free African Americans to the racial stability of slavery; they also reflected deep-seated fears about Black movement, conceptually rooting Black bodies to the plantation landscape and presenting a hegemonic vision of Black containment.

38. For example, the cover illustration for a two-song series published in 1844 called the Georgia Melodies, consisting of the songs "Old Virginia State" and "Jolly Raftsman," shows a bucolic and sweeping vista of what is supposedly Georgia. However, the scenery is more reminiscent of Mediterranean Europe than the American South. Significantly, neither of the songs in the series features lyrics romanticizing the South. *The Georgia Melodies: No. 1 Old Virginia State; No. 2 Jolly Raftsman* (Boston: Henry Prentiss, 1844). Likewise, the cover for another series of minstrel songs published in 1844, called Carter's Melodies, also reveals the inconsistencies of these early forays into the Southern pastoral. While the cover illustration's scenery more closely resembles what one might envision as the American South—palm trees stand over a run-down wooden hut beside a river, with a number of lush trees and bushes nearby—the smiling Black man in the foreground playing a banjo is more similar to the urban dandy stereotype than a plantation slave. He wears long striped pants and has a tie around his neck, a formal top hat on his head, and shiny black shoes on his feet—unlikely attire for a rural slave. *Carter's Melodies* (Boston: Keith's Music, 1844).

39. One of the first minstrel groups to consciously tailor their act to middle-class audiences, Christy's Minstrels—led by E. P. Christy—was the most influential minstrel group of the antebellum period. Monod, *Soul of Pleasure*, 63–69.

40. Thos. Vaughn, *My Lovely Virginia Gal* (New York: Jaques and Brother, 1847).

41. The song's author is difficult to say with certainty. Some versions attribute the song to Charles White, while others name Christy's Minstrels as the originators. All the published versions of the sheet music I have reviewed contain essentially the same lyrics, with only minor discrepancies and alternative titles. See Charles White, *De Floating Scow of Old Virginia* (Philadelphia: Lee and Walker, 1847); E. P. Christy, *Carry Me Back to Old Virginia* (New York: Jaques and Brother, 1847); *Oh! Carry Me Back, as Sung by Christy's Minstrels* (New York: C. Holt Jr., 1848).

42. Steven Deyle, *Carry Me Back: The Domestic Slave Trade in American Life* (Oxford University Press, 2005), 243. Deyle briefly discusses this genre of songs but mistakenly characterizes all the antebellum versions as portraying slaves sold to the Deep South as wishing to return to their former plantations in the border South. A fair number do feature the domestic slave trade as a plot device, most notably Stephen Foster's "My Old Kentucky Home, Goodnight" (1853). But many have the Black narrator ambiguously "wandering" from the plantation or escaping to the North, placing the blame for the narrator's subsequent unhappiness on their own independent mobility.

43. White, *De Floating Scow of Old Virginia.*

44. White, *De Floating Scow of Old Virginia.*

45. Marshall S. Pike, *I Hab Leff Alabama* (Boston: A. and J. P. Ordway, 1849).

46. See, for example, Outka, *Race and Nature*, 86–87, 93; Jessica Adams, *Wounds of Returning: Race, Memory, and Property on the Postslavery Plantation* (University of North Carolina Press, 2007), 17.

47. Outka, *Race and Nature*, 171.

48. Stephen C. Foster, *Massa's in de Cold Ground* (New York: Firth, Pond, 1852). The song "Meet Me in Heaven, or The Night Funeral of a Slave" (1854) inverts this theme, with a dying slave asking his master to meet him in heaven. Charlie C. Converse, *Meet Me in Heaven, or The Night Funeral of a Slave* (Boston: Oliver Ditson, 1854).

49. The number of copies sold comes from Danny Oliver Crew, "Political Discourse and American Published Sheet Music: A Commentary of Four Published Works" (PhD diss., University of Sunderland, 2024), 14. For Stephen Foster's vast impact on popular music in the nineteenth century, see Susan Key, "Sound and Sentimentality: Nostalgia in the Songs of Stephen Foster," *American Music* 13, no. 2 (1995); Ken Emerson, *Doo-Dah! Stephen Foster and the Rise of American Popular Culture* (New York: Simon & Schuster, 1997); Brooke, *"There Is a North,"* 176–82; Stephen Saunders, "The Social Agenda of Stephen Foster's Plantation Melodies," *American Music* 30, no. 3 (2012); Ken Emerson, "Stephen Foster and American Popular Culture," *American Music* 30, no. 3 (2012); Emily Bingham, *My Old Kentucky Home: The Astonishing Life and Reckoning of an Iconic American Song* (New York: Knopf, 2022).

50. A spin-off of Foster's song titled "Where Am Massa" (1852) also connected African Americans and the landscape by equating the sorrow of the slaves with the plantation environment: "Oh, de mocking bird am silent, / And de robin's silent too; . . . / Oh, de grove am bery lonely, / And de trees am bending low; / Not a sound to make us happy, / How de bitter tear drops flow!" Frank Spencer, *Where Am Massa* (New York: Horace Waters, 1852).

51. Nowatzki, *Representing African Americans*; Meer, *Uncle Tom Mania*, 12–13, 19–50. On the slave trade as a weakness in Southern polemical defenses of slavery, see Deyle, *Carry Me Back*, 174–244.

52. Marshall S. Pike and G.S.P., *The Little White Cottage, or Gentle Nettie More* (Boston: Oliver Ditson, 1857). For more examples, see Stephen Foster, *Farewell My Lilly Dear* (New York: Firth, Pond, 1851); Peter Swift and Ole Bull Jr., *Juney at the Gate* (Philadelphia: J. C. Smith, 1850).

53. Saunders, "Social Agenda of Stephen Foster's Plantation Melodies," 284–85.

54. Stephen C. Foster, *My Old Kentucky Home, Good Night* (New York: Firth, Pond, 1853).

55. "Old Folks at Home" sold around forty thousand copies in its first eleven months. James H. Stone, "The Merchant and the Muse: Commercial Influences on American Popular Music Before the Civil War," *Business History Review* 30, no. 1 (1956): 14.

56. Stephen C. Foster, *Old Folks at Home* (New York: Firth, Pond, 1851).

57. G. Friedrich Wurzel [George Frederick Root], *Old Folks Are Gone* (New York: William Hall, 1852); Charles P. Dare, *"I Long for My Home in Kentuck"* (Philadelphia: Willm. H. Shuster, 1852); Frank Spencer and Hattie Livingston, *The Young Folks at Home* (New York: T. S. Berry, 1852).

58. R. S. M. and Stewart Macaulay, *Old River Farm, or The Darkey's Regret* (Baltimore: Henry McCaffrey, 1853). On this point, song sheets of the period were often far more overtly political than sheet music. The cheaper publication costs of song sheets meant that publishers would have had to worry less about reaching a broader audience, making overtly proslavery and antiabolitionist politics more economically viable. For examples of proslavery song sheets, see *Old John Brown, a Song for Every Southern Man* (n.p., n.d.); *Aunty Sarah Rowe* (Philadelphia: Johnson's Printing, n.d.). This last song was a direct response to Harriet Beecher Stowe's *Uncle Tom's Cabin*, a fact confirmed by another version featuring "Aunt Ha'iet Becha Stowe" rather than "Aunty Sarah Rowe." This version, originally printed in the *Baltimore Aegis*, was sung by George Kunkel's minstrel group. "Now and Then—an Old Song," *New York Evangelist*, Jan. 17, 1884, 2.

59. Coleman Hutchinson, "Whistling 'Dixie' for the Union (Nation, Anthem, Revision)," *American Literary History* 19, no. 3 (2007): 603, 607.

60. Trenchantly illustrating the song's popularity across sectional lines, when a Union military band played "Dixie's Land" within earshot of both Confederate and Union camps in Virginia in 1862, soldiers on both sides cheered the song. Maureen Manjerovic and Michael J. Budds, "More Than a Drummer Boy's War: A Historical View of Musicians in the American Civil War," *College Music Symposium* 42, (2002): 125.

61. Eric Foner, *The Fiery Trial: Abraham Lincoln and American Slavery* (W. W. Norton, 2010), 128, 231–36, 239–40, 244, 259–61.

62. Dan Emmett, *I Wish I Was in Dixie's Land* (New York: Firth, Pond, 1860).

63. Steven Hahn, *The Political Worlds of Slavery and Freedom* (Harvard University Press, 2009), 1–53.

64. Paul Finkelman, "Prelude to the Fourteenth Amendment: Black Legal Rights in the Antebellum North," *Rutgers Law Journal* 17, nos. 3–4 (1986): 437–42; Gerald L. Neuman, "The Lost Century of Immigration Law (1776–1875)," *Columbia Law Review* 93, no. 8 (1993): 1866–69 and accompanying footnotes; William G. Thomas III, Richard G. Healey, and Ian Cottingham, "Reconstructing African-American Mobility After Emancipation, 1865–67," *Social Science History* 41, no. 4 (2017): 693; William D. Green, "Race and Segregation in St. Paul's Public Schools, 1846–69," *Minnesota History* 55, no. 4 (1996): 142; Kirt Wilson, *The Reconstruction Desegregation Debate: The Politics of Equality and the Rhetoric of*

Place, 1870–1875 (Michigan State University Press, 2002), 5; Wilentz, *Rise of American Democracy*, 652; Leon Litwack, *North of Slavery: The Negro in the Free States, 1790–1860* (University of Chicago Press, 1961), 68–70; Paul Frymer, *Building an American Empire: The Era of Territorial and Political Expansion* (Princeton University Press, 2017), 236–37; Masur, *Until Justice Be Done*, 225–66. For African Americans' resistance to state laws restricting their migration in the 1850s, see Kate Masur, "State Sovereignty and Migration Before Reconstruction," *Journal of the Civil War Era* 9, no. 4 (2019): 601–4; Masur, *Until Justice Be Done*, 225–66.

65. Quoted in Masur, *Until Justice Be Done*, 229.

66. Abraham Lincoln, "Second Annual Message," Dec. 1, 1862, Miller Center, University of Virginia, transcript, https://millercenter.org/the-presidency/presidential-speeches/december-1-1862-second-annual-message.

67. For more on Northern whites' widespread fears about potential Black migration to the North in the early years of the Civil War, see Frymer, *Building an American Empire*, 237–60. Fears about Black mobility also manifested in another realm of the law: the Supreme Court's *Dred Scott* decision. As geographer Euan Hague has demonstrated, the 1857 *Dred Scott* ruling is "fundamentally concerned with the mobility of African Americans and the spatiality of slavery." Euan Hague, "'The Right to Enter Every Other State': The Supreme Court and African American Mobility in the United States," *Mobilities* 5, no. 3 (2010): 336. The *Dred Scott* decision was thus one more shot in the salvo against free Black mobility during the 1850s.

68. Additionally, to the extent that earlier minstrel songs such as "Jim Crow" continued to be played and performed, they worked in tandem with the Southern pastoral to offer a powerful racial lesson for white audiences. While the more raucous early minstrel songs associated peripatetic Black male characters with social calamity and violence, Southern pastorals increasingly showed the pacified, immobile Black body as integral to white social dominance. Taken together, each genre sharpened and reinforced the spatial message of the other. While it is difficult to determine the exact degree to which Americans continued to listen to and play older minstrel sheet music, songs with a mobile Black narrator raising havoc continued to be published sporadically throughout the 1850s, though they were certainly nowhere near as common as in previous decades. See, for example, Chas. White, *Old Bob Ridley* (New York: Firth, Pond, 1855); Austin Hart, *A Little More Cider* (Boston: Oliver Ditson, 1853).

69. Popular song echoed long-standing ideas about racial hierarchy that placed Native Americans above African Americans on the racial ladder. Ideas about race and mobility in popular song conformed to this tradition, becoming another modality through which whites conveyed and enforced differences in racial worth. Thomas Jefferson's *Notes on the State of Virginia* is an early example exemplifying this current in American racial thought. Jefferson ascribed intellectual creativity and linguistic ability to Native Americans but denied African Americans any such skills. Invoking Indians' independence from whites, another link with popular song, Jefferson stated that Indians, without the benefit of white example, "will often carve figures on their pipes not destitute of design and merit. They will crayon out an animal, a plant, or a country, so as to prove the existence of a germ in their minds which only wants cultivation." Jefferson, *Notes on the State of Virginia*, 207. In a preview of so many of popular songs' racial themes, Jefferson associated Indians with

nature—they drew animals and plants and were intimately familiar with the landscape. In what may have been an intentional reference to Enlightenment philosophy's characterization of Indians as undeveloped, Jefferson claimed the merit Indians possessed required "cultivation." Nonetheless, Jefferson still granted Indians a degree of respect. He also praised Indians' linguistic abilities, writing, "They also astonish you with strokes of the most sublime oratory; such as prove their reason and sentiment strong, their imagination glowing and elevated." Jefferson, *Notes on the State of Virginia*, 207. In contrast, Jefferson reported, "Never yet could I find a black that had uttered a thought above the level of plain narration; never see even an elementary trait of painting or sculpture." Jefferson, *Notes on the State of Virginia*, 207. For more on Jefferson's racial comparison of African Americans and Indians in *Notes on the State of Virginia*, see Peter Onuf, "'To Declare Them a Free and Independent People': Race, Slavery, and National Identity in Jefferson's Thought," *Journal of the Early Republic* 18, no. 1 (1998): 26; Justin Leroy, "Empire and the Afterlife of Slavery: Black Anti-Imperialisms of the Long Nineteenth Century" (PhD diss., New York University, 2014), 13–25.

70. For example, see Theodore Schallehn, *Hiawatha Schottisch* (New York: G. B. Demarest, 1856); Francis H. Brown, *Minnehaha or Laughing Water Polka* (New York: William Hall, 1856); Charles Pape, *Minnehaha Schottisch* (Baltimore: Miller and Beacham, 1856); D. Wood, *On Away! On Away! Beautiful Song from Hiawatha* (Philadelphia: Beck and Lawton, 1857); C. C. Converse, *The Death of Minnehaha* (Boston: Oliver Ditson, 1866).

71. Songs leveling serious critiques of white dealings with Native Americans did still appear from time to time, but they were uncommon. See Henry Clay Work, *The Song of the Red Man* (Cleveland: Brainard's Sons, 1868); G. F. Howard and H. P. Pierce, *Mount Hope* (Boston: White, Smith, and Perry, 1872). However, songs like the "Sioux March and Waltz" (1856), with its cover image of plains Indians fighting the US Army, and "Ten Little Injuns" (1868), replete with violent misfortunes befalling Indian boys, were more the norm. In the 1870s, multiple odes to General Custer appeared as sympathy for Indians in popular song receded even further. See Louis Wallis, *Sioux March and Waltz* (St. Louis: Balmer and Weber, 1856); Sep. Winner, *Ten Little Injuns* (Philadelphia: Lee and Walker, 1868); Charles Glover, *Requiem to the Memory of Gen. Geo. A. Custer* (New York: Wm. A. Pond, 1876); A. R. Milner, *General Custer's Last March* (Canal Dover, OH: A. Milner, 1879). Other sheet music songs, like "Clear the Way! or Song of the Wagon Road" (1856) and "Kansas Pacific Grand March" (1872), made it clear that the advance of white civilization and technology in the West was pushing Indians on the plains aside, and that this displacement was a good thing. Stephen C. Massett, *Clear the Way! or Song of the Wagon Road* (San Francisco: Stephen C. Massett, 1856); Geo. Schleiffarth, *Kansas Pacific Grand March* (St. Louis: Kunkel Brothers, 1872).

72. For overviews of the immense violence whites inflicted on Native peoples in the West post-1850, see Manisha Sinha, *The Rise and Fall of the Second American Republic: Reconstruction, 1860–1920* (Liveright, 2024), 307–46; Elliott West, *Continental Reckoning: The American West in the Age of Expansion* (University of Nebraska Press, 2023).

73. Scholar Sally Jones details a similar dynamic affecting white Americans' receptions of the play *Metamora*, with hardening anti-Indian racism among whites following US expansion across the Mississippi fueling negative responses to the play. Sally L. Jones, "The First but Not the Last of the 'Vanishing Indians': Edwin Forrest and Mythic Re-Creations of the

Native Population," in *Dressing in Feathers: The Construction of the Indian in American Popular Culture*, ed. S. Elizabeth Bird (Westview Press, 1996), 22.

74. As sentimentalized Indians in song declined, so did the critiques of white society so often adhering to them. As noted previously, these critiques and their transgressive potential were always deeply limited. Nonetheless, flawed as they were, they still offered a degree of resistance to white dispossession of Indian territories and violence against Native peoples, opening up avenues for thinking about alternative policies to removal and the reservation. The near absence of these critiques in popular music after 1855 further cleared the way for western expansion and reflected a more punitive turn in Americans' views of Native Americans.

Chapter Three

1. Nell Irvin Painter, *Exodusters: Black Migration to Kansas After Reconstruction* (Knopf, 1976), 247–49; Douglass, quoted in Painter, *Exodusters*, 248. On the Black debate over emigration to Kansas, see Steven Hahn, *A Nation Under Our Feet: Black Political Struggles in the Rural South from Slavery to the Great Migration* (Belknap Press of Harvard University Press, 2003), 341–45.

2. While he did not overtly mention Native Americans in conjunction with the exodus, at other times Douglass explicitly articulated stereotypes about Native American savagery in his political thought. See Rodger C. Henderson, "The Native American Experience According to Frederick Douglass (1818–1895)," *NAAAS Conference Proceedings* (National Association of African American Studies, 2005).

3. Two scholars, Marcy Sacks and Lori Brooks, have connected the popularity of the Southern pastoral to white anxieties about Black demographic growth in the North in the 1880s and 1890s. However, neither contends that white fears about Black movement, on both the regional and the local scale, propelled the Southern pastoral. Further, neither notes that these white fears drove the Southern pastoral's popularity from emancipation in the Civil War until the end of the century, nor that such fears were national and not restricted to Northern whites. See Marcy S. Sacks, *Before Harlem: The Black Experience in New York City Before World War I* (University of Pennsylvania Press, 2006), 49–54, 70–71; Lori Brooks, "Journey to a Land of Cotton: A Slave Plantation in Brooklyn, 1895," *Journal of American History* 53, no. 1 (2014): 59.

4. *Chicago Tribune* and Lyman Trumbull, quoted in Eric Foner, *The Fiery Trial: Abraham Lincoln and American Slavery* (W. W. Norton, 2010), 221–22. Dire predictions about Black migration had been common in the press leading up to Lincoln's victory in the election of 1860, as Northern newspapers across the region warned that emancipation would produce a flood of former slaves into the North and widespread vagabondage. On Northern whites' widespread fears about Black migration to the North following emancipation, see Richard Newman, "The Grammar of Emancipation: Putting Final Freedom in Context," in *Beyond Freedom: Disrupting the History of Emancipation*, ed. David Blight and Jim Downs (University of Georgia Press, 2017), 14–15; Leslie A. Schwalm, "'Overrun with Free Negroes': Emancipation and Wartime Migration in the Upper Midwest," *Civil War History* 50, no. 2 (2004); Paul Frymer, *Building an American Empire: The Era of Territorial and Political Expansion* (Princeton University Press, 2017), 237–60. Southern whites also dreaded free

Black mobility, particularly planters, who feared mass labor shortages. See William Cohen, *At Freedom's Edge: Black Mobility and the Southern White Quest for Racial Control, 1861–1915* (Louisiana State University Press, 1991), 23–43.

5. On Northern Democrats stoking white fears about Black freedom, see Foner, *Fiery Trial*, 234–35; Schwalm, "'Overrun with Free Negroes,'" 160.

6. *Epitaph* (n.p, n.d.). Though there is no publishing date on the broadside, it states that Cox's speech was given on June 6, 1862, and thus was probably published that year or early in 1863. Cox did indeed give a speech on June 6, 1862, titled "Emancipation and Its Results." See Samuel S. Cox, *Eight Years in Congress, from 1857–1865: Memoir and Speeches* (New York: D. Appleton, 1865), 236–59.

7. William G. Thomas III, Richard G. Healey, and Ian Cottingham, "Reconstructing African American Mobility After Emancipation, 1865–67," *Social Science History* 41, no. 4 (2017): 689.

8. *The New Jim Crow Song, About the Darkies and the War* (n.p., 1862).

9. Quoted in Leslie A. Schwalm, *Emancipation's Diaspora: Race and Reconstruction in the Upper Midwest* (University of North Carolina Press, 2009), 82.

10. Schwalm, *Emancipation's Diaspora*, 84.

11. D[an]. D. Emmett, *I'm Going Home to Dixie* (New York: Firth, Pond, 1861). For another song exemplifying heightened postbellum racism, see Dan. D. Emmett, *High Daddy* (New York: Wm. A. Pond, 1863).

12. *Carry Me Back to Tennessee; or, Ellie Rhee* (Philadelphia: Winner, 1865).

13. See, for example, Henry Clay Work, *Kingdom Coming* (Chicago: Root and Cady, 1863); Henry Clay Work, *Babylon Is Fallen* (Chicago: Root and Cady, 1863); Henry Clay Work, *Wake Nicodemus* (Chicago: Root and Cady, 1864); Benjamin Russell Hanby, *Ole Shady, or, the Song of the Contraband* (Boston: Oliver Ditson, 1861); Kate Crayon and J. M. Hubbard, *Who Comes Dar?* (Chicago: Root and Cady, 1865); Eastburn, *The Contraband's Song of Freedom* (Philadelphia: W. R. Smith, 1865); George F. Root, *Glory! Glory! or, The Little Octoroon* (Chicago: Root and Cady, 1865).

14. Examples include A. Jones, *The Ham Fat Man* (Cincinnati: John Church Jr., 1863); Billy Emerson, *The Happy Contraband* (New Orleans: A. E. Blackmar, 1864); Eugene Raymond, *Take Me Home* (New Orleans: A. E. Blackmar, 1865); *Gay and Festive Boy from the South* (New Orleans: A. E. Blackmar, 1866); John S. Murphy, *The Freed Man's Lament* (Detroit: J. Henry Whittemore, 1868).

15. Jas. M. Stewart, *Get Along Old Mule, or, "Plowing the Field Where the Sugar Cane Grew"* (Boston: White, Smith, and Perry, 1870). The title "Get Along Old Mule" also potentially references the "forty acres and a mule" policy developed by General William Tecumseh Sherman during the war and later proposed, but not passed, as a law in Congress by Radical Republicans. General Sherman instituted the "40 acres and a mule" policy as an expedient to manage the large number of Black slaves fleeing to Union lines. Jeffrey Kerr-Ritchie, "Forty Acres, or, An Act of Bad Faith," *Souls* 5, no. 3 (2003); Claude F. Oubre, *Forty Acres and a Mule: The Freedmen's Bureau and Black Land Ownership* (Louisiana State University Press, 1978), esp. 1–21. While Northern whites never widely supported redistributing land to the previously enslaved, the former slaves themselves were deeply committed to redistribution and consistently pushed for it throughout Reconstruction. Eric Foner, *Reconstruction: America's Unfinished Revolution, 1863–1877*, rev. ed. (Harper Perennial, 2014),

70–71, 104–6, 374–76; Hahn, *A Nation Under Our Feet*, 128–46; Richard White, *The Republic for Which It Stands: The United States During Reconstruction and the Gilded Age, 1865–1896* (Oxford University Press, 2017), 42–45. For another sympathetic portrayal of African Americans and a critique of slavery in song, see Ed Harrigan and Dave Braham, *Slavery Days* (New York: Wm. Pond, 1876).

16. Stephanie Dunson, "Black Misrepresentation in Nineteenth-Century Sheet Music Illustration," in *Beyond Blackface: African Americans and the Creation of American Popular Culture, 1890–1930*, ed. W. Fitzhugh Brundage (University of North Carolina Press, 2011), 56.

17. Lucinda Hardwick MacKethan, *The Dream of Arcady: Place and Time in Southern Literature* (Louisiana State University Press, 1980), 8. For a sampling of works romanticizing the South in the postbellum period by Southern writers, see David W. Blight, *Race and Reunion: The Civil War in American Memory* (Harvard University Press, 2001), 221–31.

18. On reconciliation and romanticism of the South in popular literature, see Blight, *Race and Reunion*, 216–17; Robert Bone, *Down Home: Origins of the Afro-American Short Story* (Columbia University Press, 1975), 9; MacKethan, *Dream of Arcady*, 37. Historian Nina Silber attributes the popularity of such literature not only to Northern white desires for sectional reconciliation but also to growing class and gender tensions in the North, which made images of suffering but noble Southern planters, their loyal Black labor force, and traditionally feminine Southern white women more attractive to middle-class whites. Nina Silber, *The Romance of Reunion: Northerners and the South, 1865–1900* (University of North Carolina Press, 1993), 105–23. For Southern pastoral popular music as a response to white desires for reconciliation, see J. Stanley Lemons, "Black Stereotypes as Reflected in Popular Culture, 1880–1920," *American Quarterly* 29, no. 1 (1977): 109–11.

19. Some scholars have questioned the extent of desires for reconciliation in the late nineteenth century, arguing instead that many Northern and Southern whites continued to blame their regional counterparts for the war. These scholars also emphasize the constructed nature of regional identity and the historical processes that created a "New South" and a new sectional relationship in the late nineteenth century, belying any simple story of reunion. For these scholars, desires for reconciliation lack explanatory power for the increased popularity of cultural works romanticizing the South. Caroline E. Janney, *Remembering the Civil War: Reunion and the Limits of Reconciliation* (University of North Carolina Press, 2013), 9, 200, 210–11; K. Stephen Prince, *Stories of the South: Race and the Reconstruction of Southern Identity, 1865–1915* (University of North Carolina Press, 2014), 9, 146, 181. For a review of the scholarly debate about sectional reconciliation and a rejoinder to the position advanced by Janney and Prince, see Nina Silber, "Reunion and Reconciliation, Reviewed and Reconsidered," *Journal of American History* 103, no. 1 (2016).

20. C. Vann Woodward, *Origins of the New South, 1877–1913* (Louisiana State University Press, 1951), 107–74.

21. Most scholars studying the Southern pastoral, regardless of whether they examine its appearance in the nineteenth or twentieth century, make this point about Americans reacting to modernity, urbanization, and industrialism. See, for example, Bone, *Down Home*, 10; Wayne Mixon, *Southern Writers and the New South Movement, 1865–1913* (University of North Carolina Press, 1980), 31–47; Richard Gray, *Writing the South: Ideas of an American Region* (Cambridge University Press, 1986), 90–91; MacKethan, *Dream of Arcady*, 8–10;

Silber, *Romance of Reunion*, 82, 106; Lee Glazer and Susan Key, "Carry Me Back: Nostalgia for the Old South in Nineteenth-Century Popular Culture," *Journal of American Studies* 30, no. 1 (1996): 6–7, 22–23; Blight, *Race and Reunion*, 222; Krystyn R. Moon, *Yellowface: Creating the Chinese in American Popular Music and Performance, 1850s–1920s* (Rutgers University Press, 2005), 120; John Strausbaugh, *Black Like You: Blackface, Whiteface, Insult and Imitation in American Popular Culture* (Penguin Books, 2008), 118; Janney, *Remembering the Civil War*, 211; Prince, *Stories of the South*, 146, 181. Scholar Cedric Robinson sees the "plantation genre" at the beginning of the twentieth century as both industrial capital's response to a "vast but disparate labor force which required cultural discipline, social habituation, and political regulation" and white desires for sectional reconciliation. Literary scholar Jeremy Wells contends that Southern pastoral literature of the 1880s helped whites combat Black demands for civil rights. Similarly, scholar Jessica Adams posits that romanticism of the "Old South" served as "a bulwark against encroachments of blackness into post-Emancipation 'mainstream' culture." Cedric Robinson, *Forgeries of Memory and Meaning: Blacks and the Regimes of Race in American Theater and Film Before World War II* (University of North Carolina Press, 2007), 91–92, 141; Jeremy Wells, *Romances of the White Man's Burden: Race, Empire, and the Plantation in American Literature, 1880–1936* (Vanderbilt University Press, 2011), 2–3, 107; Jessica Adams, *Wounds of Returning: Race, Memory, and Property on the Postslavery Plantation* (University of North Carolina Press, 2007), 21. Scholars Gavin Jones and Michael North have also attributed the dialect writing found in "local color" literature to elite fears about cultural and linguistic contamination in an age of immigration and race mixing. For Jones and North, dialect writings represented elites' attempt to categorize and rank linguistic cultures and thus impose order on the social upheavals of industrialism. Gavin Jones, *Strange Talk: The Politics of Dialect Literature in Gilded Age America* (University of California Press, 1999), 11, 210; Michael North, *The Dialect of Modernism: Race, Language, and Twentieth-Century Literature* (Oxford University Press, 1994), 15, 22.

22. For example, one of the most popular songs of 1874, "The Alabama Blossoms," made young Black men its primary characters. The Black men are nicknamed "Blossoms," forging a direct connection between Black bodies and the environment. Frank Dumont, *The Alabama Blossoms* (New York: J. L. Peters, 1874). For the song's popularity, see Julius Mattfeld, *Variety Music Cavalcade, 1620–1969: A Chronology of Vocal and Instrumental Music Popular in the United States*, 3rd ed. (Prentice-Hall, 1971), 146, www.loc.gov/collections/american-sheet-music-1870-to-1885/articles-and-essays/greatest-hits-1870–85-variety-music-cavalcade/.

23. C. A. White, *The Old Home Ain't What It Used to Be* (Boston: White, Smith, 1872). Although not a carry-me-back, "The Little Old Cabin in the Lane"—one of the biggest hits of 1871—also depicts Black flight from the plantation as interrupting the pastoral. Will S. Hays, *The Little Old Cabin in the Lane* (Boston: Oliver Ditson, 1871). For the song's popularity, see Mattfeld, *Variety Music Cavalcade*, 136.

24. Arthur French and Charles Blake, *Trabling Back to Georgia* (Boston: G. D. Russell, 1874). "Trabling Back to Georgia" was one of the biggest hits of 1874. See Mattfeld, *Variety Music Cavalcade*, 146. It is also highly significant that the labor described in the song is that of hoeing, as the hoe, and often the spade, signaled the menial and subservient labor performed by Black slaves. For another Southern pastoral symbolizing Black subservience

through hoeing, see Edward A. Sloane, *God Bless the Old Plantation* (Montgomery, AL: Edward A. Sloane, 1877).

25. The cover of one version of the song states, "Over 500,000 of the song already sold." The fact that it had multiple printings with different cover illustrations lends credence to this claim, and an 1891 newspaper article covering a "Southern Ball" in New York City notes that the song was played at the party and called it "the popular song without which no Southern assembly here now seems complete." "Topics in New York: Large and Brilliant Southern Ball at Sherry's," *Baltimore Sun*, Jan. 28, 1891, 3. For the version with the number of sales on the cover, see C. A. White, *I'se Gwine Back to Dixie* (New York: White, Smith, 1874). For the alternative cover, see C. A. White, *I'se Gwine Back to Dixie* (Boston: White, Smith, 1874).

26. Henry Newman, *Dem Good Ole Times* (Boston: White, Smith, 1877).

27. See, for example, Raymond, *Take Me Home* (Boston: Oliver Ditson, 1877); John T. Rutledge, *I'm Going Back to Alabam' to Die* (East Liverpool, OH: W. L. Thompson, 1878). The song "The Cabin on the Mississippi Shore" (1883) reduces the Black body to the Southern landscape even more literally, with its sketched style blurring the image of a Black man with the surrounding terrain. The illustration thus makes him visually synonymous with the landscape, anchoring him in space and reassuring the viewer he will "forever . . . remain" on his cabin plot and "never roam again," as the lyrics put it. Gussie L. Davis, *The Cabin on the Mississippi Shore* (Cincinnati: J. C. Groene, 1883).

28. James Bland, *My Old Home in Mississippi* (Boston: John F. Perry, 1879). For another cover illustration expressing Black disillusionment with the city, see Thomas Westendorf, *I'll Nebber Leave Old Dixie Land Again* (Philadelphia: W. F. Shaw, 1882).

29. Sam Dennison, *Scandalize My Name: Black Imagery in American Popular Music* (Garland, 1982), 260; Mattfeld, *Variety Music Cavalcade*, 159.

30. J. Brent Morris, *Dismal Freedom: A History of the Maroons of the Great Dismal Swamp* (University of North Carolina Press, 2022); Marcus P. Nevius, *City of Refuge: Slavery and Petit Marronage in the Great Dismal Swamp, 1763–1856* (University of Georgia Press, 2020); Michael Bennett, "Anti-Pastoral, Frederick Douglass, and the Nature of Slavery," in *Beyond Nature Writing: Expanding the Boundaries of Ecocriticism*, ed. Karla Armbruster and Kathleen R. Wallace (University of Virginia Press, 2001); Michael J. Beilfuss, "Ironic Pastorals and Beautiful Swamps: W. E. B. Du Bois and the Troubled Landscapes of the South," *Interdisciplinary Studies in Literature and Environment* 22, no. 3 (2015): 486, 494–503.

31. James Bland, *Carry Me Back to Old Virginny* (Boston: Oliver Ditson, 1878). My findings here about the veiled antislavery and antiracist content of "Carry Me Back to Old Virginny" align with the work of William Hullfish, who has found encoded antislavery themes in a number of Bland's other songs. See William Hullfish, "James A. Bland: Pioneer Black Songwriter," *Black Music Research Journal* 7 (1987).

32. For more examples of carry-me-backs from this period (though hardly an exhaustive list), see Frank Dumont and James Stewart, *I Want to See the Old Home* (St. Louis: J. L. Peters, 1873; repr., Boston: Oliver Ditson, 1884); H. P. Danks, *My Ole Home in Alabama 'Fo' de War* (Boston: G. D. Russell, 1875); C. A. White, *The Old Log Cabin in the Dell* (Boston: White, Smith, 1875); Herbert Hersey, *Dear Old Home* (Boston: John F. Perry, 1875); Frank Dumont, *Since I Saw de Cotton Grow* (Boston: John F. Perry, 1876); John T. Rutledge, *Happy Times in Dixie Fo' de War* (Cincinnati: John Church, 1878); S. N. Mitchell and

William A. Huntley, *I'm Going Home to Clo* (Philadelphia: W. F. Shaw, 1879); H. P. Danks and Ida Scott Taylor, *De Cabin on de Mississippi Shore* (New York: H. P. Danks, 1879); Frank Dumont and James Stewart, *That Old Cabin Home Upon the Hill* (Boston: Oliver Ditson, 1880); Bro. Gardner and C. Alixa, *Old Joe's Dream* (Boston: J. M. Russell, 1881); Mannie Friend and James A. Bland, *Traveling Back to Alabam* (New York: William J. A. Lieder, 1881); H. P. Danks, *My Dear Savannah Home* (Boston: Oliver Ditson, 1881); Jas. A. Putnam, *My Home in Alabam* (Boston: John F. Perry, 1881); O. R. Beers and L. M. French, *I Lost My Massa When Dey Set Me Free* (Savannah: Ludden and Bates, 1882).

33. Arthur W. French and Chas. D. Blake, *Down Among de Sugar Cane* (New York: Wm. A. Pond, 1875); Wallace A. A. Fernandez, *My Mississippi Home* (Brooklyn: Frank P. Anderson, 1882). For other similar examples, see James Bland, *In the Evening by the Moonlight* (New York: Hitchcock's Music, 1880); Billy Radcliffe, *The Little Old Log Cabin by de Stream* (Cincinnati: Geo. D. Newhall, 1880). For a song employing the Southern pastoral as a vehicle for sentimental courtship and featuring the immobile Black body as its staging ground, see Edgar B. Smith, *Creole Love Song* (Boston: Oliver Ditson, 1889).

34. Robert Trennert Jr., *Alternative to Extinction: Federal Indian Policy and the Beginnings of the Reservation System, 1846–51* (Temple University Press, 1975), vii, 23, 29–31. See also Robert M. Utley, *The Indian Frontier of the American West, 1846–1890* (University of New Mexico Press, 1984), 46, for a virtually identical definition of the reservation.

35. In 1681, the colony ordered Indians confined to just three of the towns, and any Native peoples found outside them were to be sent to houses of correction or prisons. Yasu Kawashima, "Legal Origins of the Indian Reservation in Colonial Massachusetts," *American Journal of Legal History* 13, no. 1 (1969): 42–44. See also Jean M. O'Brien, *Dispossession by Degrees: Indian Land and Identity in Natick, Massachusetts, 1650–1790* (Cambridge University Press, 1997), 60–62, 87–90; Lisa Brooks, *Our Beloved Kin: A New History of King Philip's War* (Yale University Press, 2018), 175; Stuart Banner, *How the Indians Lost Their Land: Law and Power on the Frontier* (Harvard University Press, 2005), 229–30. Native Americans in New England continually resisted these efforts at physical—as well as economic and social—containment. See Brooks, *Our Beloved Kin*, 175.

36. For example, as US Indian agent for the Indiana Territory, William Wells sketched out some of the core ideas of the later reservation system in 1807, linking spatial confinement to both the procurement of Native lands and assimilation. Nicholas Guyatt, *Bind Us Apart: How Enlightened Americans Invented Racial Segregation* (Oxford University Press, 2016), 103.

37. Elliott West, *Continental Reckoning: The American West in the Age of Expansion* (University of Nebraska Press, 2023), 165–67; Ryan Hall, "Patterns of Plunder: Corruption and the Failure of the Indian Reservation System, 1851–1887," *Western Historical Quarterly* 55, no. 1 (2024): 25; Elliott West, "Reconstructing Race," *Western Historical Quarterly* 34, no. 1 (2003): 11–12; Trennert, *Alternative to Extinction*, vii, 18, 29. Historians Frederick Hoxie and Philip Deloria have similarly argued that after 1860, the spread of white settlement across the trans-Mississippi West and US military victories over armed Indian resistance led white Americans to reimagine Native peoples as an "internal" population, fully encircled and pacified by white settlement. Frederick E. Hoxie, *A Final Promise: The Campaign to Assimilate the Indians, 1880–1920*, rev. ed. (Cambridge University Press, 1989), xii–xiii, 2–4; Philip J. Deloria, *Indians in Unexpected Places* (University of Kansas Press, 2004), 63.

38. West, *Continental Reckoning,* 75–76; Trennert, *Alternative to Extinction,* 29–31; Utley, *Indian Frontier,* 46; Francis Paul Prucha, *American Indian Policy in Crisis: Christian Reformers and the Indian, 1865–1900* (University of Oklahoma Press, 1976), 104–5.

39. Trennert, *Alternative to Extinction,* 31–32, 39; Elliott West, "Reconstruction in the West," *Journal of the Civil War Era,* forum, accessed Apr. 19, 2022, www.journalofthecivilwarera.org/forum-the-future-of-reconstruction-studies/reconstruction-in-the-west/.

40. On the development and implementation of the reservation policy as the primary means of managing relations with Native Americans in the 1850s, as well as its characteristics of confinement, see Trennert, *Alternative to Extinction,* vii, 47–48, 50–51, 54–60, 127–30, 158, 187–91; Robert F. Berkhofer Jr., *The White Man's Indian: Images of the American Indian from Columbus to the Present* (Vintage Books, 1978), 165; West, *Continental Reckoning,* 166–67; Hall, "Patterns of Plunder," 25.

41. Megan Kate Nelson, *The Three-Cornered War: The Union, the Confederacy, and Native Peoples in the Fight for the West* (Scribner, 2020).

42. Utley, *Indian Frontier,* 72–86; Francis Paul Prucha, *The Great Father: The United States Government and the Indians* (University of Nebraska Press, 1984), 1:437–57, 544; West, *Continental Reckoning,* 167–69. As Lincoln's commissioner of Indian affairs, William P. Dole, put it, "The plan of concentrating Indians and confining them to reservations may now be regarded as the fixed policy of the government." Quoted in David Nichols, *Lincoln and the Indians: Civil War Policies and Politics,* rev. ed. (University of Illinois Press, 2000), 154. As historian Francis Paul Prucha notes, "The ultimate goal of the [US Army and the Indian Office] was the same; to locate the Indians on reservations with set boundaries, where they could be educated and trained for American citizenship." Prucha, *Great Father,* 1:544; see also West, *Continental Reckoning,* 166–67.

43. Prucha, *Great Father,* 1:487–96, 535–44; Elliott West, *The Last Indian War: The Nez Perce Story* (Oxford University Press, 2009). Not all Indian reservations were established and secured by military force. For example, in 1868, the Ute Nation in what is now Colorado used diplomacy to secure a reservation, as Ute leaders saw the acceptance of a reservation as the best means of preserving their lands and traditional way of life in the face of western expansion. In this way, Native Americans attempted to invert the reservation from a mechanism of territorial expropriation to one of land security. However, increasing US expansionist pressure and military force later compelled the Ute Nation to accept reductions of their land. Ned Blackhawk, *Violence over the Land: Indians and Empires in the Early American West* (Harvard University Press, 2006), 218–24.

44. Sherman, quoted in Prucha, *American Indian Policy in Crisis,* 75 (emphasis in the original).

45. Schofield, quoted in Richard Perry, *Apache Reservation: Indigenous Peoples and the American State* (University of Texas Press, 1993), 116. Similarly, after the Sioux carried out raids on white Montana settlements and railroad surveyors in 1875, US Army commanders sent a message stating that any members of the tribe not on reservation land would be considered active enemies and returned to the reservation by force. Prucha, *American Indian Policy in Crisis,* 93.

46. Of course, some civilians echoed the martial views of the military brass. Senator Thomas Tipton of Nebraska, speaking before Congress in 1870, called for "reservations guarded around by bayonets; reservations over the limits of which the Indians shall not

pass . . . reservations with walls as high as necessary, and with pitfalls as deep as necessary." Tipton, quoted in C. Joseph Genetin-Pilawa, *Crooked Paths to Allotment: The Fight over Federal Indian Policy After the Civil War* (University of North Carolina Press, 2012), 105. But in general, most federal officials and white reformers cast the reservation system as a pedagogical tool for the education and assimilation of Native Americans—however insincere such professions may have been on the part of federal officials. For more on the assimilationist functions of the reservation, see West, *Continental Reckoning*, 367–69.

47. Welsh, quoted in Banner, *How the Indians Lost Their Land*, 233.

48. Welsh, quoted in Genetin-Pilawa, *Crooked Paths to Allotment*, 96–97.

49. Francis Amasa Walker, "The Indian Question," *North American Review* 116, no. 239 (1873): 375–76. In keeping with this logic, Walker praised military enforcement of reservation boundaries as acts of discipline rather than acts of war. Walker, "Indian Question," 354. This characterization, along with the statements of white reformers and policymakers in general about the use of force as necessary to impose "civilization" on Indians, lends verisimilitude to scholar Nikhil Pal Singh's argument that white Americans carried out and justified a long-standing race war by reducing imperial acts of warfare to "police actions" necessary to correct the misguided and wayward actions of racial others. See Nikhil Pal Singh, *Race and America's Long War* (University of California Press, 2017).

50. Douglas K. Miller, *Indians on the Move: Native American Mobility and Urbanization in the Twentieth Century* (University of North Carolina Press, 2019), 26–27; Francis Paul Prucha, *Great Father*, 2:719; Perry, *Apache Reservation*, 129; Louis S. Warren, *Buffalo Bill's America: William Cody and the Wild West Show* (Knopf, 2005), 361.

51. On the importance of white hunting in the West to the weakening of Native American tribes and the establishment of the reservation system, see Utley, *Indian Frontier*, 47; Prucha, *Great Father*, 1:561; Steven Hahn, *A Nation Without Borders: The United States and Its World in an Age of Civil Wars, 1830–1910* (Penguin Random House, 2016), 382.

52. Valerie Sherer Mathes and Richard Lowitt, *The Standing Bear Controversy: Prelude to Indian Reform* (University of Illinois Press, 2003), 13–16; James A. Lake Sr., "Standing Bear! Who?," *Nebraska Law Review* 50, no. 3 (1981): 454, 457–59.

53. Lawrence A. Dwyer, *Standing Bear's Quest for Freedom: The First Civil Rights Victory for Native Americans* (University of Nebraska Press, 2019), 27–44; Joe Starita, *"I Am a Man": Chief Standing Bear's Journey for Justice* (St. Martin's Press, 2008), 52–58, 64–65; Mathes and Lowitt, *Standing Bear Controversy*, 17–23, 29, 34–36; Lake, "Standing Bear! Who?," 460–69. On the financial motives behind the removal, see Mathes and Lowitt, *Standing Bear Controversy*, 32; Lake, "Standing Bear! Who?," 461.

54. Dwyer, *Standing Bear's Quest*, 43, 45; Starita, *"I Am a Man,"* 65–78, 87–91, 98–99; Mathes and Lowitt, *Standing Bear Controversy*, 36–38; Lake, "Standing Bear! Who?," 469–71.

55. Dwyer, *Standing Bear's Quest*, 45–46; Lake, "Standing Bear! Who?," 471–72. For more on Standing Bear's flight from Indian Territory, see Starita, *"I Am a Man,"* 105–11.

56. Dwyer, *Standing Bear's Quest*, 47, 53–68; Valerie Sherer Mathes, "Boston, the Boston Indian Citizenship Committee, and the Poncas," *Massachusetts Historical Review* 14 (2012): 122.

57. Quoted in Lake, "Standing Bear! Who?," 476. For more on the trial, see Dwyer, *Standing Bear's Quest*, 69–107; Lake, "Standing Bear! Who?," 474–76.

58. United States ex rel. Standing Bear v. Crook, 5 Dill. 453, 25 F. Cas. 695, 699–700 (1879).

59. Speaking to the courage of the Ponca's decision, a similar flight by a group of 350 Northern Cheyenne from Indian Territory to their homelands in Montana in late 1878 and early 1879 had ended very differently, with many dying in skirmishes with pursuing soldiers. James N. Leiker and Ramon Powers, *The Northern Cheyenne Exodus in History and Memory* (University of Oklahoma Press, 2011), 12–13.

60. Mathes, "Boston, the Boston Indian Citizenship Committee, and the Poncas," 119–20, 123–24; Mathes and Lowitt, *Standing Bear Controversy*, 84–85. Tibbles played a large role in organizing and executing the lecture tour, but in order to highlight the agency of Standing Bear and La Flesche, I do not use Tibbles's name in my characterizations of the tour's authorship, instead naming just Standing Bear and La Flesche.

61. Angela G. Ray, *The Lyceum and Public Culture in the Nineteenth-Century United States* (Michigan State University Press, 2005), 2–3, 6, 176–78; Donald M. Scott, "The Popular Lecture and the Creation of a Public in Mid-Nineteenth-Century America," *Journal of American History* 66, no. 4 (1980): 791–92, 800; Tom F. Wright, introduction to *The Cosmopolitan Lyceum: Lecture Culture and the Globe in Nineteenth-Century America*, ed. Tom F. Wright (University of Massachusetts Press, 2013), 4; Angela G. Ray, "How Cosmopolitan Was the Lyceum, Anyway?" in Wright, *Cosmopolitan Lyceum*, 28. For more on the history of the lecture circuit, see Carl Bode, *The American Lyceum: Town Meeting of the Mind* (Oxford University Press, 1956), and the essays in Tom F. Wright, ed., *Cosmopolitan Lyceum*.

62. Schurz, quoted in Lake, "Standing Bear! Who?," 479n83.

63. "Standing Bear," *Boston Post*, Oct. 30, 1879, 3; "Our Ponca Guests," *Boston Globe*, Oct. 30, 1879, 4. For detailed accounts of the lecture tour, see Starita, *"I Am a Man,"* 177–202; Mathes and Lowitt, *Standing Bear Controversy*, 83–98; Stanley Clark, "Ponca Publicity," *Mississippi Valley Historical Review* 29, no. 4 (1943): 498–508.

64. "Standing Bear's Complaint," *New York Herald*, Dec. 9, 1879, 10; Clark, "Ponca Publicity," 508; Lake, "Standing Bear! Who?," 492n102.

65. "The Indian's Story," *Chicago Inter-Ocean*, Oct. 18, 1879, 3; Lake, "Standing Bear! Who?," 494n107.

66. Susette La Flesch, untitled lecture (1880), in the "Thomas Henry Tibbles Papers—Bright Eyes, Susette La Flesche: Speeches, 1880," Smithsonian National Museum of the American Indian Archives Center. For further details of La Flesche's experience on the tour and the content of her speeches, see Dorothy Clarke Wilson, *Bright Eyes: The Story of Susette La Flesche, an Omaha Indian* (McGraw-Hill, 1974), 211–60.

67. H. H., "An Appeal for the Indians," *New York Tribune*, Dec. 9, 1879, 5. The article, most likely written by Helen Hunt Jackson, also emphasized that La Flesche was subject to arrest by US authorities at any moment for being off her reservation without permission. For Jackson's likely authorship, see Wilson, *Bright Eyes*, 234.

68. Wilson, *Bright Eyes*, 15–26, 31–32, 66–67, 211–60; Sarah Pripas-Kapit, "'We Have Lived on Broken Promises': Charles A. Eastman, Susan La Flesche Picotte, and the Politics of American Indian Assimilation During the Progressive Era," *Great Plains Quarterly* 35, no. 1 (2015): 55; Frank Kelderman, "Writing Omaha Children: Susette La Flesche and the Politics of American Indian Guardianship," *American Quarterly* 74, no. 1 (2022): 28–30.

69. Erin E. Pedigo, "'The Gifted Pen': The Journalism Career of Susette La Flesche Tibbles (1854–1903)" (master's thesis, University of Nebraska, 2011), 66. For more on

the ambivalences of La Flesche's assimilationism, see Kelderman, "Writing Omaha Children."

70. Lake, "Standing Bear! Who?," 493n105; Mathes and Lowitt, *Standing Bear Controversy*, 162–63, 165–66.

71. Painter, *Exodusters*, 185–88, 234–40, 252–53; Heather Cox Richardson, *The Death of Reconstruction: Race, Labor, and Politics in the Post–Civil War North, 1865–1901* (Harvard University Press, 2001), 156–82; Robert G. Athearn, *In Search of Canaan: Black Migration to Kansas, 1879–80* (Regents Press of Kansas, 1978), 139–41; Keith D. McCall, "Reconstructing Race, Place, and Population: Postemancipation Migrations and the Making of the Black South, 1865–1915" (PhD diss., Rice University, 2019), 170–96. On the political considerations motivating Republican support for Southern African Americans, see Desmond King and Stephen Tuck, "De-Centering the South: America's Nationwide White Supremacist Order After Reconstruction," *Past and Present* 194, no. 1 (2007): 240–43. On Black movement after the Civil War and Southern white efforts to contain it, in large part to control Black labor, see W. E. B. Du Bois, *Black Reconstruction in America, 1860–1880* (Harcourt, Brace, 1935; repr., Free Press, 1998), 166–80; Foner, *Reconstruction*, 198–200, 208–9, 225, 244; White, *Republic for Which It Stands*, 53–55, 66; Cohen, *At Freedom's Edge*, 8–12, 30, 34; Yael A. Sternhell, "Revolution in Motion: Human Mobility and the Transformation of the South, 1861–1865" (PhD diss., Princeton University, 2008), 115–171; Edward L. Ayers and Scott Nesbit, "Seeing Emancipation: Scale and Freedom in the American South," *Journal of the Civil War Era* 1, no. 1 (2011): 3–24; Cicero Fain, "Early Black Migration and the Post-Emancipation Black Community in Cabell County, West Virginia, 1865–1871," *West Virginia History* 5, no. 2 (2011): 29–58; Yael A. Sternhell, *Routes of War: The World of Movement in the Confederate South* (Harvard University Press, 2012), 93–154; Abigail Cooper, "'Away I Goin' to Find My Mamma': Self-Emancipation, Migration, and Kinship in Refugee Camps in the Civil War Era," *Journal of African American History* 102, no. 4 (2017); Thomas, Healey, and Cottingham, "Reconstructing African American Mobility After Emancipation"; McCall, "Reconstructing Race, Place, and Population," 14–110. For Southern white fears—stemming from ideas about race and climate—that Black migration to, and concentration in, the "tropical" Deep South would lead to Black social and political dominance in that region, see McCall, "Reconstructing Race, Place, and Population," 111–69.

72. Foner, *Reconstruction*, 409, 587–601; David M. Oshinsky, *"Worse Than Slavery": Parchman Farm and the Ordeal of Jim Crow Justice* (Free Press, 1996); Douglas A. Blackmon, *Slavery by Another Name: The Re-Enslavement of Black Americans from the Civil War to World War II* (Anchor Books, 2008); John K. Bardes, *Carceral City: Slavery and the Making of Mass Incarceration in New Orleans, 1803–1930* (University of North Carolina Press, 2024), 209–36. Importantly, convict leasing and sharecropping both operated in part by immobilizing Black populations. Amy R. Sumpter, "Racial Identity, Spatial Mobility, and Labor in the Non-Plantation Rural South, 1880–1940," *Journal of Historical Geography* 37, no. 4 (2011): 460. In this, they echoed earlier Southern white efforts to reinstate slavery's geography of containment after the Civil War through the Black Codes and, of course, the spatial restrictions of Jim Crow segregation. On the Black Codes, see Du Bois, *Black Reconstruction*, 166–80; Foner, *Reconstruction*, 198–200, 208–9, 225, 244; R. White, *Republic for Which It Stands*, 53–55.

73. The migration numbers here come from Painter, *Exodusters*, 147, 184. Black migration to Kansas was in fact larger in aggregate over the years 1870–1878, with about 9,500 Black

Americans heading into the state. As historian Nell Irvin Painter comments, these figures show that the exodus garnered attention vastly out of proportion to its numbers. Painter, *Exodusters*, 147. This outsized attention both epitomized white Americans' tendency to exaggerate and catastrophize about Black migration and presaged Northern whites' panic over the relatively small Black migration to the urban North in the 1880s and 1890s. Nonetheless, the number of migrants involved in the Kansas Exodus was significant.

74. Painter, *Exodusters*, 77, 101, 193.

75. Painter, *Exodusters*, 153–59, 196, 199–200; Hahn, *Nation Under Our Feet*, 334–37.

76. Painter, *Exodusters*, 196–201.

77. Thos. P. Westendorf, *Going from de Cotton Fields* (Philadelphia: W. F. Shaw, 1879).

78. Geo. M. Vickers, *Am Dis Kansas?* (New York: S. T. Gordon, 1880). For other songs denigrating the Kansas Exodus, see Samuel N. Mitchell and H. P. Danks, *Down Among de Orange Blossoms* (New York: S. T. Gordon, 1878); Thomas Westendorf, *De Little Cabins All Am Empty Now* (Boston: Thompson and Odell, 1881). While "Down Among de Orange Blossoms" does not mention Kansas by name and predates the most publicized migrations of 1879–80, it nonetheless alludes to Black migration to the western plains.

79. Richardson, *Death of Reconstruction*, 156–82.

80. On the prevalence of Northern white animosity toward the exodus, see Athearn, *In Search of Canaan*, 139–41. It is worth noting that at least one song about the Kansas Exodus displayed a pro-Exodus position. "Whar de Shot Gun Rules No Mo'e" (1880), written anonymously by "A Native Hoosier," catalogs the violence inflicted on African Americans by Southern whites during Reconstruction, including by the Ku Klux Klan, and makes this violence the cause of African Americans' decision to leave the South for Kansas. See *Whar de Shot Gun Rules No Mo'e* (n.p., 1880).

81. Historian Elliott West asserts that the Exoduster movement is best understood through the Greater Reconstruction framework, stating that the Exodusters' "move from South to West was, paradoxically, both a rejection of, and an aggressive claim to, a traditional racial order," with African Americans participating in settler colonialism to escape racial persecution in the South. West, "Reconstructing Race," 14; see also West, *Continental Reckoning*, 125–35. Of course, many of the Native tribes that the US government forcibly relocated across the Mississippi to Indian Territory in the 1830s, including the Cherokee, Creek, Choctaw, Chickasaw, and Seminole, also carried their Black slaves with them and used their enslaved peoples' labor to remake and profit from western land. On the imbrications of African American and Native American histories, see Quintard Taylor, *In Search of the Racial Frontier: African Americans in the American West, 1528–1990* (W. W. Norton, 1998), 62–71; Tiya Miles, *Ties That Bind: The Story of an Afro-Cherokee Family in Slavery and Freedom* (University of California Press, 2005); Tiya Miles, "Beyond a Boundary: Black Lives and the Settler-Native Divide," *William and Mary Quarterly* 76, no. 3 (2019); Alaina E. Roberts, *I've Been Here All the While: Black Freedom on Native Land* (University of Pennsylvania Press, 2021).

Chapter Four

1. "Letter from Clifford D. Brooks," *Freeman*, Dec. 24, 1898, 7.

2. There is evidence of residential segregation of city streets beginning as early as the 1880s, but the residential segregation of entire neighborhoods, or ghettoization, did not

begin until the 1900s. Douglas Massey and Nancy Denton, *American Apartheid: Segregation and the Making of the Underclass* (Harvard University Press, 1993); Lance Freeman, *A Haven and a Hell: The Ghetto in Black America* (Columbia University Press, 2019); Trevon D. Logan and John M. Parman, "The National Rise in Residential Segregation," *Journal of Economic History* 77, no. 1 (2017); John R. Logan, Weiwei Zhang, Richard Turner, and Allison Shertzer, "Creating the Black Ghetto: Black Residential Patterns Before and During the Great Migration," *Annals of the American Academy of Political and Social Science* 660, no. 1 (2015).

3. While the *Freeman* was not the only African American newspaper to cover Black entertainers in the late nineteenth century, its standing as one of the largest Black publications in the country, with a national circulation, made it one of the most prominent voices in the Black public sphere. It therefore constitutes an ideal source for exploring Black views on popular culture and the entertainment industry. See Lynn Abbott and Doug Seroff, *Out of Sight: The Rise of African American Popular Music, 1889–1895* (University Press of Mississippi, 2002), xii.

4. See, for example, David Krasner, *Resistance, Parody, and Double Consciousness in African American Theatre, 1895–1910* (St. Martin's Press, 1997); Lori Brooks, "The Negro in the New World: The Cultural Politics of Race, Nation and Empire, 1885–1911" (PhD diss., Yale University, 2001); Barbara L. Webb, "Authentic Possibilities: Plantation Performance of the 1890s," *Theatre Journal* 56, no. 1 (2004); Daphne Brooks, *Bodies in Dissent: Spectacular Performances of Race and Freedom, 1850–1910* (Duke University Press, 2006); Karen Sotiropoulos, *Staging Race: Black Performers in Turn of the Century America* (Harvard University Press, 2006); Davarian L. Baldwin, *Chicago's New Negroes: Modernity, the Great Migration, and Black Urban Life* (University of North Carolina Press, 2007); Adam Green, *Selling the Race: Culture, Community, and Black Chicago, 1940–1955* (University of Chicago Press, 2007); Jayna Brown, *Babylon Girls: Black Women Performers and the Shaping of the Modern* (Duke University Press, 2008); Marvin McAllister, *Whiting Up: Whiteface Minstrels and Stage Europeans in African American Performance* (University of North Carolina Press, 2011), 73–109; W. Fitzhugh Brundage, ed., *Beyond Blackface: African Americans and the Creation of American Popular Culture, 1890–1930* (University of North Carolina Press, 2011); Erin D. Chapman, *Prove It on Me: New Negroes, Sex, and Popular Culture in the 1920s* (Oxford University Press, 2012); Amy Absher, *The Black Musician and the White City: Race and Music in Chicago, 1900–1967* (University of Michigan Press, 2014); Allyson Nadia Field, *Uplift Cinema: The Emergence of African American Film and the Possibility of Black Modernity* (Duke University Press, 2015); David Gilbert, *The Product of Our Souls: Ragtime, Race, and the Birth of the Manhattan Musical Marketplace* (University of North Carolina Press, 2015); Einav Rabinovitch-Fox, "Fabricating Black Modernity: Fashion and African American Womanhood During the First Great Migration," *International Journal of Fashion Studies* 6, no. 2 (2019).

5. Nicholas E. Tawa, *The Way to Tin Pan Alley: American Popular Song, 1866–1910* (Schirmer Books, 1990), 3, 38–53; Kenneth Hartvigsen, "Patriotism, Race, and Gender Bending Through American Song: Cover Illustrations of Popular Music from the Civil War to World War I" (PhD diss., Boston University, 2014), 14–20; Danny Oliver Crew, "Political Discourse and American Published Sheet Music: A Commentary of Four Published Works" (PhD diss., University of Sunderland, 2014), 29, 29n100.

6. Karl Hagstrom Miller, *Segregating Sound: Inventing Folk and Pop Music in the Age of Jim Crow* (Duke University Press, 2010), 38; Tawa, *Way to Tin Pan Alley*, 162–206. It is important to note that Tin Pan Alley and the music publishing business were not entirely top-down phenomenon; consumers had a large role in shaping the content that publishing companies produced, especially audiences in the leisure sites of New York City, which were the proving grounds for Tin Pan Alley songwriters and publishers. Samuel Backer, "The Best Songs Came from the Gutters: Tin Pan Alley and the Birth of Manhattan Mass Culture," *Journal of the Gilded Age and Progressive Era* 22, no. 4 (2023).

7. Hattie Starr, *Little Alabama Coon* (New York: Willis Woodward, 1893). For the song's popularity, see Frank L. Boyden, *Popular American Composers* (New York, 1902), 47. Indeed, Starr's song was so popular that a short story initially printed in the London newspaper the *St. James Budget* and later reprinted in a Maine magazine referenced it. See "A Case of Plagiarism," *Maine Farmer*, Jan. 10, 1895, 6.

8. Tara McPherson, *Reconstructing Dixie: Race, Gender, and Nostalgia in the Imagined South* (Duke University Press, 2003), 58–59.

9. For additional examples, see Sam Dennison, *Scandalize My Name: Black Imagery in American Popular Music* (Garland, 1982), 394–97.

10. Lee Johnson, *Mammy's Carolina Twins* (San Francisco: Lee Johnson, 1899).

11. G. M. Blandford, *Honey in the Cornfield* (Boston: Vivian, 1899). For an earlier example of a Southern pastoral song taking young Black men as its primary subject, see Frank Dumont, *The Alabama Blossoms* (New York: J. L. Peters, 1874). For more Southern pastoral sheet music that reduced African Americans to the landscape in the 1890s, see, for example, G. L. Lansing and L. Isabelle Giles, *The Darkies Dream* (Boston: L. B. Gatcomb, 1891); *Folio of Plantation Melodies and Comic Songs* (Chicago: National, 1891); Monroe H. Rosenfeld, *The Cotton Field Dance* (Chicago: National, 1891); William H. Gardner and Stanley Clayton, *It Doan Seem as It Used To* (Chicago: National, 1894); Margaret Caroline Denny and S. J. Anderson, *The Cabin Where I Was Born* (New York: K. Dehnhoff, 1895); Jos. W. Wheeler, *Hush My Little Coon* (Boston: Geo. W. Setchell, 1895); Chas. W. Arnold and Dave Fitzgibbon, *Go 'Way Trouble* (New York: M. Witmark, 1896); Chas. Gilbert and E. W. Dustin, *Doan Give Me No Golden Harp* (St. Louis: Thiebes-Stierlin, 1898); Clara Scott and Paul B. Armstrong, *Way Down in the Old Palmetto State* (Chicago: Frank K. Root, 1898); Geo. W. Gage, *I Wants Ter See Mah Chloe* (Chicago: Bowen, 1899); Hattie Starr, *Ma Little Yalla Daisy* (Chicago: Windsor, 1899); Chas. S. Tarbox, *The Cotton Pickers* (Chicago: McKinley, 1899).

12. See, for example, "A Confederate Camp Fire," *New Orleans Daily Picayune*, Nov. 30, 1890, 7; "Topics in New York," *Baltimore Sun*, Jan. 28, 1891, 3; "An Event in Brooklyn Society," *New York Times*, May 28, 1891, 5; "In Social Spheres: Notes and Personals," *Los Angeles Times*, Oct. 11, 1891, 12; "Pumped Lemonade," *St. Paul Daily News*, Aug. 26, 1893, 1; "Aiding Southern Needy," *New Orleans Daily Picayune*, Oct. 31, 1893, 7; "At the Grand," *Atlanta Constitution*, Sept. 13, 1894, 5; "The Original Words of 'Dixie,'" *New York Times*, Oct. 7, 1894, 24; "Songs of Olden Time," *Chicago Daily Tribune*, Feb. 18, 1895, 6; "Four Centuries of American Song," *Chicago Daily Tribune*, Feb. 26, 1895, 8; "An Old-Time Cake Walk," *New York Times*, Mar. 2, 1895, 6; "Southern Song and Sweetest Story," *New Orleans Daily Picayune*, May 28, 1895, 8; "About the Theaters: Lounger in the Lobby," *Los Angeles Times*, Aug. 11, 1895, 21; "Confederate Songs," *Baltimore Sun*, Dec. 11, 1895, 10; "Merry Piper Girls," *Chicago*

Daily Inter-Ocean, Dec. 16, 1895, 7; "The Thirteen Club's Dinner," *New York Times*, Mar. 14, 1897, 5; "Music of the Negro," *Washington Post*, Sept. 6, 1897, 7; "Beauty Spots of the South," *New York Times*, Dec. 4, 1897, 7; "Old Plantation Melodies," *New York Tribune*, Apr. 29, 1898, 7; "Joy Among Philomatheans," *New York Tribune*, June 22, 1898, 7; "Five Theaters Filled: Isham's Octoroons at the Academy," *Washington Post*, Feb. 20, 1898, 22; "Guests at Dixie Dinner," *Chicago Daily Tribune*, Mar. 5, 1899, 2; "Souvenir Hatchets for Children," *New York Tribune*, Feb. 23, 1900, 7; Harry T. Finch, "Some Popular Songs," *Current Literature* 25, no. 3 (1900): 217.

13. "New York Southern Society's Ninth Annual Dinner, February 22d, 1895, Sherry's," program, Buttolph Collection of Menus, New York Public Library, https://digitalcollections.nypl.org/items/510d47db-27e8-a3d9-e040-e00a18064a99.

14. Dennison, *Scandalize My Name*, 354; Sotiropoulos, *Staging Race*, 89; James H. Dormon, "Shaping the Popular Image of Post-Reconstruction American Blacks: The 'Coon Song' Phenomenon of the Gilded Age," *American Quarterly* 40, no. 4 (1988): 453.

15. Dennison, *Scandalize My Name*, 354; Dormon, "Shaping the Popular Image," 451–53; Eileen Southern, *The Music of Black Americans: A History* (W. W. Norton, 1971), 314.

16. Dennison, *Scandalize My Name*, 394, 397.

17. Joel Williamson, *The Crucible of Race: Black-White Relations in the American South Since Emancipation* (Oxford University Press, 1984); Rayford W. Logan, *The Negro in American Life and Thought: The Nadir, 1877–1901* (Dial Press, 1954). See also Robert W. Rydell, *All the World's a Fair: Visions of Empire at American International Expositions, 1876–1916* (University of Chicago Press, 1984), 5, chaps. 1–3; George M. Fredrickson, *The Black Image in the White Mind: The Debate on Afro-American Character and Destiny, 1817–1914*, rev. ed. (Wesleyan University Press, 1987), 228–319; Nell Irvin Painter, *The History of White People* (W. W. Norton, 2010), 190–244; Ann Fabian, *The Skull Collectors: Race, Science, and America's Unburied Dead* (University of Chicago Press, 2010), esp. 165–220; Michael Omi and Howard Winant, *Racial Formation in the United States* (Routledge, 2015), 109–17.

18. Dormon, "Shaping the Popular Image," 455.

19. Dennison, *Scandalize My Name*, 394. See also Dormon, "Shaping the Popular Image," 452–64.

20. Susan Curtis, "Black Creativity and Black Stereotype: Rethinking Twentieth-Century Popular Music in America," in Brundage, *Beyond Blackface*, 126–36.

21. Regarding men's increased piano playing, the author of an 1875 *Christian Union* article wrote, "I can remember very well the early prejudices against educating boys in music. . . . The piano was regarded as a feminine instrument, to be studied chiefly by the girls of the wealthy. . . . What a radical change has taken place in this period, every one knows." Horatio C. King, "The Songs of the People," *Christian Union*, May 12, 1875, 387. Nonetheless, women remained the primary target audience of sheet music in the late nineteenth century. Miller, *Segregating Sound*, 37–38. For the debate over coon songs, see, for example, "The Popular Song," *Chicago Daily Inter-Ocean*, Oct. 11, 1896, 32; "Cheers for 'Coon' Songs," *Chicago Daily Tribune*, Aug. 25, 1898, 3; "The Drama," *Chicago Daily Tribune*, Aug. 28, 1898, 30; "The Invasion of the Tough Coon Song and Its Effect on Decency—a Homily and a Protest," *Denver Evening Post*, Nov. 14, 1899, 10; *Arkansas Democrat*, Oct. 27, 1899, 2; "Form Plans to Suppress Music," *Chicago Daily Tribune*, Dec. 25, 1899, 9.

22. Hartvigsen, "Patriotism, Race, and Gender," 148. For more on barbering's economic importance to Black communities and its racialized meanings in the nineteenth century, see Quincy T. Mills, *Cutting Along the Color Line: Black Barbers and Barber Shops in America* (University of Pennsylvania Press, 2013).

23. William F. Quown and Sam Lucas, *De Coon Dat Had de Razor* (Boston: White, Smith, 1885).

24. In his analysis of coon songs, Hartvigsen comments on the prevalence of "the street" as a setting and describes African Americans in coon songs as "[un]contained—they were fictional embodiments of white fears stalking the city streets." Hartvigsen, "Patriotism, Race, and Gender," 133–36. Similarly, historian James H. Dormon has stated that coon songs connoted African Americans as "dangerous not only in the way that animals are dangerous if allowed to roam unrestrained, but dangerous as well to white bourgeois culture itself." Dormon, "Shaping the Popular Image," 466. However, neither scholar expatiates on their statements other than to say that coon songs represented African Americans as general threats to the social and racial order who required disciplining.

25. Carl Stowe and L. Mauran Bloodgood, *I'm the Toughest, Toughest Coon* (Boston: Walter Jacobs, 1904); Charles E. Trevathan, *May Irwin's "Bully" Song* (Boston: White-Smith Music, 1896). For prime examples of these themes in cover art, see Harry MacDonough, *Don't Fool, Dat Black Gal's Mine* (New York: T. B. Harms, 1897); Al Johns, *I Thought I Heard Somebody Calling Me (Jim and Gin Sounded So Much the Same)* (New York: F. A. Mills, 1898).

26. Lori Brooks, "'To Be Black Is to Be Funny': 'Coon Shouting' and the Melancholic Production of the White Comedienne," *Women and Performance* 25, no. 1 (2015): 2. On the vogue for female coon shouters, see Miller, *Segregating Sound*, 125–28; L. Brooks, "'To Be Black Is to Be Funny'"; Sharon Ammen, *May Irwin: Singing, Shouting, and the Shadow of Minstrelsy* (University of Illinois Press, 2017), esp. 110.

27. Quoted in Miller, *Segregating Sound*, 127.

28. Edward Harrigan and Dave Braham, *The Sunny Side of Thompson Street (Away Down Town)* (New York: Wm. A. Pond, 1893).

29. Massey and Denton, *American Apartheid*, 28.

30. For information on early Black migrants to the North, see Allan H. Spear, *Black Chicago: The Making of a Negro Ghetto, 1890–1920* (University of Chicago Press, 1967); William M. Tuttle Jr., *Race Riot: Chicago in the Red Summer of 1919* (Atheneum, 1970), 112–13, 160–61; Marcy S. Sacks, *Before Harlem: The Black Experience in New York City Before World War I* (University of Pennsylvania Press, 2006); Douglas J. Flowe, *Uncontrollable Blackness: African American Men and Criminality in Jim Crow New York* (University of North Carolina Press, 2020). On the use of African Americans as strikebreakers, see Joe William Trotter Jr., *Workers on Arrival: Black Labor in the Making of America* (University of California Press, 2019), 65–66. On the racial fitness of newly arriving immigrants during this period, see Thomas A. Guglielmo, *White on Arrival: Italians, Race, Color, and Power in Chicago, 1890–1945* (Oxford University Press, 2003); David R. Roediger, *Working Toward Whiteness: How America's Immigrants Became White; The Strange Journey from Ellis Island to the Suburbs* (Basic Books, 2005), esp. 57–92; Matthew Frye Jacobson, *Whiteness of a Different Color: European Immigrants and the Alchemy of Race* (Harvard University Press, 1998), 13–90, 137–85, 203–22.

31. Sacks, *Before Harlem*, 45–47, 70. For more on white residents' fears about Black migration to Northern cities in the 1890s, see L. Brooks, "Negro in the New World," 151–59; Khalil Gibran Muhammad, *The Condemnation of Blackness: Race, Crime, and the Making of Modern Urban America* (Harvard University Press, 2010), 53–54.

32. John W. Cell, *The Highest Stage of White Supremacy: The Origins of Segregation in South Africa and the American South* (Cambridge University Press, 1982), 133; David R. Goldfield, *Cotton Fields and Skyscrapers: Southern City and Region, 1607–1980* (Louisiana State University Press, 1982), 105; Edward L. Ayers, *The Promise of the New South: Life After Reconstruction*, rev. ed. (Oxford University Press, 2007), 68; Howard Rabinowitz, "The Conflict Between Blacks and the Police in the Urban South, 1865–1900," *Historian* 39, no. 1 (1976): 62–65.

33. Dormon, "Shaping the Popular Image," 464–66; Sacks, *Before Harlem*, 49–54, 70–71.

34. Fredrickson, *Black Image in the White Mind*, 51–54, 260. See also Krasner, *Resistance, Parody, and Double Consciousness*, 24. For a contemporary expression of this dyad, see Thomas Nelson Page, "The Negro Question," in *The Old South: Essays Social and Political*, ed. Thomas Nelson Page (New York: Charles Scribner's Sons, 1892), 312, 325, 326; Thomas Nelson Page, *The Negro: The Southerner's Problem* (New York: Charles Scribner's Sons, 1904), 163, 165–66, 170, 194–95, 203–4. It is important to note that not all coon songs depicting African Americans as dangerous or deviant are set in the city; some are set in the country, such as those about stealing chickens, and others are set in the South, though they do not employ the pastoral. However, the dichotomy between peaceful African Americans in the Southern pastoral and dangerous African Americans in nonpastoral coon songs still holds in general for these songs. See, for example, Sam Lucas, *Coon's Salvation Army* (Boston: Charles D. Blake, 1884); Charles S. O'Brien, *Ma Angeline* (San Francisco: Zeno Mauvais, 1896).

35. For scholarship stressing the indeterminacy of Southern segregation and the improvement of Black–white relations in the North and West from 1865 to 1900, see C. Vann Woodward, *The Strange Career of Jim Crow*, rev. ed. (Oxford University Press, 1974), 25–65; Dale A. Somers, "Black and White in New Orleans: A Study in Urban Race Relations, 1865–1900," *Journal of Southern History* 40, no. 1 (1974); Eric Foner, *Reconstruction: America's Unfinished Revolution, 1863–1877*, rev. ed. (Harper Perennial, 2014), 372, 470–71; Mia Bay, *Traveling Black: A Story of Race and Resistance* (Harvard University Press, 2021), 32–37; Kirt Wilson, *The Reconstruction Segregation Debate: The Politics of Equality and the Rhetoric of Place, 1870–1875* (Michigan State University Press, 2002), 10; Steven Hahn, *A Nation Without Borders: The United States and Its World in an Age of Civil Wars, 1830–1910* (Penguin Random House, 2016), 480. See also Cell, *Highest Stage of White Supremacy*, 134–35, 169–70. Historian Edward Ayers succinctly summarizes the point: "The segregation begun in the decade following the end of the Civil War did not spread inexorably and evenly across the face of the South. The 1880s saw much uncertainty and much bargaining, many forays and retreats." Ayers, *Promise of the New South*, 137. While some scholars, most notably Howard Rabinowitz, contend that segregation in the South was entrenched soon after the Civil War, even Rabinowitz acknowledges that it is "clear that something highly significant happened in southern race relations during the 1890s," and he agrees with C. Vann Woodward's seminal argument that the passage of segregation laws in that decade marked an important development in the history of Jim Crow segregation. Howard Rabinowitz, "More Than the

Woodward Thesis: Assessing *The Strange Career of Jim Crow*," *Journal of American History* 75, no. 3 (1988): 849. See also Howard Rabinowitz, *Race Relations in the Urban South, 1865–1890* (Oxford University Press, 1978); W. Fitzhugh Brundage, introduction to *The Folly of Jim Crow: Rethinking the Segregated South*, ed. Stephanie Cole and Natalie J. Ring (Texas A&M University Press, 2012), 5–7.

36. Two scholars have loosely connected coon songs and the Southern pastoral to Jim Crow segregation. Scholar James Dormon has argued that the popularity of coon songs stemmed from white Americans' need to justify the Jim Crow institutions solidifying in the South during the 1890s. Relatedly, historian Marcy Sacks notes that taken together, songs romanticizing the South and nonpastoral coon songs reflected white fears about Black social deviance in the city and licensed Northern whites' racist treatment of African Americans—treatment that ultimately manifested in segregation. Dormon, "Shaping the Popular Image," 464–66; Sacks, *Before Harlem*, 49–54, 70–71; see also Brooks, "Journey to a Land of Cotton," 59. While the racist content of nonpastoral coon songs and Southern pastoral sheet music certainly did justify Jim Crow segregation, as Dormon and Sacks claim, the relation of the two genres to segregation—in the North, West, and South—goes deeper than the broad ideological convergence these two scholars identify. Likewise, the two genres express more than just white fears about changing racial demographics and Black degeneracy in city space, per Sacks. As I have shown here, Southern pastoral sheet music and nonpastoral coon songs implicate race and geographic mobility in a more immediate and direct way. White fears about Black movement crystallized directly in representations of Black (im)mobility in these popular culture forms. Furthermore, sheet music imagery excoriating Black movement and celebrating Black fixity indicted Black mobility at multiple scales. Southern pastorals preached against interregional Black migration, and both coon songs about urban African Americans and Southern pastoral music assailed more local quotidian forms of Black movement—in the case of Southern pastorals, through felicitous images of the rooted Black body; in that of coon songs, through images of dangerous urban Black residents stalking the city streets.

37. Two studies have also highlighted the important role of spatial mobility to Black cultural producers' experiences and expressions of modernity in this period. Scholar Jayna Brown's *Babylon Girls* documents the travels of Black women entertainers at the turn of the century and argues that their travels contravened the dominant trope of African Americans as premodern agricultural laborers. Brown, *Babylon Girls*, esp. 10. Similarly, scholar Daphne Brooks shows how Black artists Bert Williams and George Walker's 1902 musical *In Dahomey* offered a mélange of Black mobilities through its rapidly shifting international settings and its focus on Black emigration. As Brooks contends, William and Walker's musical "created a space where black patrons were able to *imagine* themselves moving through time and space, across land and nation, from costume to costume." D. Brooks, *Bodies in Dissent*, 220 (emphasis in the original). "The Stage" echoed this function of a collective space for imagining Black mobility that Brooks identifies in *In Dahomey*.

38. Edwin G. Burrows and Mike Wallace, *Gotham: A History of New York City to 1898* (Oxford University Press, 1999), 487–88. Exceptions to Black exclusion from popular entertainment included a few all-Black minstrel troupes and the renowned Black dancer William Henry Lane, also known as Master Juba, who performed in Manhattan drinking establishments for mixed-race audiences and later performed at New York's Vauxhall

Gardens under P. T. Barnum's direction. However, at Vauxhall, Lane wore blackface paint and Barnum passed him off as a white minstrel performer. Douglas Jones, "'The Black Below': Minstrelsy, Satire, and the Threat of Vernacularity," *Theatre Journal* 73, no. 2 (2021): 131; Matthew D. Morrison, *Blacksound: Making Race and Popular Music in the United States* (University of California Press, 2024), 33–36, 65–79.

39. Krasner, *Resistance, Parody, and Double Consciousness*; Sotiropoulos, *Staging Race*.

40. See, for example, Cedric Robinson, *Forgeries of Memory and Meaning: Blacks and the Regimes of Race in American Theater and Film Before World War II* (University of North Carolina Press, 2007), 127–79; Krasner, *Resistance, Parody, and Double Consciousness*; Sotiropoulos, *Staging Race*; McAllister, *Whiting Up*, 73–109; Thomas L. Riis, *Just Before Jazz: Black Musical Theater in New York, 1890–1915* (Smithsonian Institute Press, 1989), 52–53; Patricia R. Schroeder, "Passing for Black: Coon Songs and the Performance of Race," *Journal of American Culture* 33, no. 2 (2010).

41. Krasner, *Resistance, Parody, and Double Consciousness*, 4.

42. Bob Cole and Billy Johnson, *No Coons Allowed* (New York: Howley, Haviland, 1897). Both David Krasner and Karen Sotiropoulos analyze the subversive content of this song. Krasner, *Resistance, Parody, and Double Consciousness*, 33–37; Sotiropoulos, *Staging Race*, 95.

43. Miller, *Segregating Sound*, 41, 45; "Decline of Rag Time Music," *Iowa State Bystander*, Nov. 24, 1899, 1; editorial, *Kansas Plaindealer*, July 28, 1899, 2.

44. *Leavenworth Herald*, Feb. 1, 1896, 3.

45. John S. Durham, "The Artist and His Art," *American Citizen*, Aug. 26, 1898, 1; R. C. Ransom, "The Border Land of Dreams," *Freeman*, Jan. 28, 1899, 6; "An Aristocratic Cake Walk," *Freeman*, Jan. 29, 1898, 4.

46. Darrel E. Bigham, "The Black Press in Indiana, 1879–1985," in *The Black Press in the Middle West, 1865–1985*, ed. Henry Lewis Suggs (Greenwood Press, 1996), 53–57; Frank E. Dobson Jr., "Indianapolis Freeman," in *Encyclopedia of African American History 1896 to the Present*, ed. Paul Finkelman (Oxford University Press, 2009); Andreá N. Williams, "Cultivating Black Visuality: The Controversy over Cartoons in the Indianapolis *Freeman*," *American Periodicals: A Journal of History and Criticism* 25, no. 2 (2015): 124–25.

47. "The Stage," *Freeman*, Nov. 29, 1890, 7; "The Stage," *Freeman*, Nov. 21, 1891, 3.

48. "The Stage," *Freeman*, July 16, 1892, 6.

49. On the fad for Black female concert singers, see Sonya R. Gable-Wilson, "Let Freedom Sing! Four African-American Concert Singers in Nineteenth-Century America" (PhD diss., University of Florida, 2005), 28–29, 77–110; Abbott and Seroff, *Out of Sight*, 205–72.

50. "The Stage," *Freeman*, Apr. 17, 1897, 5; "The Stage," *Freeman*, Nov. 20, 1897, 5.

51. "The Stage," *Freeman*, Oct. 24, 1896, 6.

52. "The Stage," *Freeman*, June 12, 1897, 6; "The Stage," *Freeman*, Feb. 26, 1898, 5.

53. "The Stage," *Freeman*, Nov. 20, 1897, 5; "The Stage," *Freeman*, Feb. 15, 1896, 3.

54. "The Stage," *Freeman*, June 12, 1897, 6.

55. "The Stage," *Freeman*, Nov. 19, 1898, 5.

56. "The Stage," *Freeman*, Dec. 10, 1898, 5; Miller, *Segregating Sound*, 31–33.

57. On Black women's geographies in the United States, see Stephanie M. H. Camp, *Closer to Freedom: Enslaved Women and Everyday Resistance in the Plantation South* (University of North Carolina Press, 2004); Glenda Elizabeth Gilmore, *Gender and Jim Crow:*

Women and the Politics of White Supremacy in North Carolina, 1896–1920 (University of North Carolina Press, 1996); Katherine McKittrick, *Demonic Grounds: Black Women and the Cartographies of Struggle* (University of Minnesota Press, 2006). For analyses of space and women in general, see Gillian Rose, *Feminism and Geography: The Limits of Geographical Knowledge* (University of Minnesota Press, 1993); Doreen Massey, *Space, Place, and Gender* (University of Minnesota Press, 1994). On gender and late nineteenth-century urban space, see Sarah Deutsch, *Women and the City: Gender, Space, and Power in Boston, 1870–1940* (Oxford University Press, 2000); Jessica Ellen Sewell, *Women and the Everyday City: Public Space in San Francisco, 1890–1915* (University of Minnesota Press, 2011).

Chapter Five

1. Harry T. Peters, *Currier and Ives: Printmakers to the American People* (Doubleday, 1942), 23; Michael D. Harris, *Colored Pictures: Race and Visual Representation* (University of North Carolina Press, 2003), 62; Joshua Brown, illus. ed., "Countersigns," in *Forever Free: The Story of Emancipation and Reconstruction*, by Eric Foner (Vintage, 2005), 181–88. It should be noted here that the title of the series itself, *Darktown*, is offensive and racist, let alone the images it contains.

2. A number of works have mentioned Thompson Street in relation to African Americans but only as one in a list of streets where Black residents disproportionately resided in the last half of the nineteenth century. See Seth M. Scheiner, *Negro Mecca: A History of the Negro in New York City, 1865–1920* (New York University Press, 1965), 16, 18, 25; Gilbert Osofsky, *Harlem: The Making of a Ghetto, Negro New York, 1890–1930* (Ivan R. Dee, 1996), 11; Roi Ottley and William J. Weatherby, *The Negro in New York: An Informal Social History, 1626–1940* (Praeger, 1967), 131; Edwin G. Burrows and Mike Wallace, *Gotham: A History of New York City to 1898* (Oxford University Press, 1998), 854; Marcy S. Sacks, *Before Harlem: The Black Experience in New York City Before World War I* (University of Pennsylvania Press, 2006); Sule Greg C. Wilson, "Little Africa," in *The Encyclopedia of New York City*, ed. Kenneth T. Jackson (Yale University Press, 2010), 757; Gerald W. McFarland, *Inside Greenwich Village: A New York City Neighborhood, 1898–1918* (University of Massachusetts Press, 2001), 12, 24, 47; Chad Heap, *Slumming: Sexual and Racial Encounters in American Nightlife, 1885–1940* (University of Chicago Press, 2009), 117, 119; John Strausbaugh, *The Village: A History of Greenwich Village, 400 Years of Beats and Bohemians, Radicals and Rouges* (HarperCollins, 2013), 66; Douglas J. Flowe, *Uncontrollable Blackness: African American Men and Criminality in Jim Crow New York* (University of North Carolina Press, 2020), 212n62.

3. Most works mentioning the *Darktown* comics provide only brief descriptions and analysis. See Morton Cronin, "Currier and Ives: A Content Analysis," *American Quarterly* 4, no. 4 (1952): 327–28; Francis John Martin Jr., "The Image of Black People in American Illustration from 1825 to 1925" (PhD diss., University of California, Los Angeles, 1986), 403–30; Bryan F. Le Beau, "African Americans in Currier and Ives's America: The Darktown Series," *Journal of American and Comparative Cultures* 23, no. 1 (2000); Michael Hatt, "'Making a Man of Him': Masculinity and the Black Body in Mid-Nineteenth-Century American Sculpture," *Oxford Art Journal* 15, no. 1 (1992): 32–34; Harris, *Colored Pictures*, 62–63; Brown, "Countersigns," 182–83; Sacks, *Before Harlem*, 55–56; Melanie Hernandez, "Border Crossings: Passing and Other(ed) Strategic Performances of Race in African American and

Chicana/o Literatures" (PhD diss., University of Washington, 2014), 42–66; Robert J. Turpin, *Black Cyclists: The Race for Inclusion* (University of Illinois Press, 2024), 81–84.

4. On the close link between racial mobility and racial segregation, see Genevieve Carpio, *Collisions at the Crossroads: How Place and Mobility Make Race* (University of California Press, 2019), 18, 66.

5. Extreme anti-Chinese violence following the rapid influx of Chinese immigrants to San Francisco after 1850 forced Chinese immigrants to concentrate in the city's Chinatown neighborhood after 1870. The neighborhood therefore had a high level of racial segregation in the late nineteenth century. However, San Francisco's Chinatown was the exception in this regard, as Chinatowns in other US cities were mixed-race spaces. Charlotte Brooks, *Alien Neighbors, Foreign Friends: Asian Americans, Housing, and the Transformation of Urban California* (University of Chicago Press, 2009), 11–38; Hannah Melissa Postel, "Records of Exclusion: Chinese Immigration in Historical Perspective" (PhD diss., Princeton University, 2022), 5–32.

6. Recent work showing the development of residential segregation in the 1880s revises the arguments of scholars such as Douglas Massey and Nancy Denton, who date the beginnings of residential segregation to the 1900s. While this new work shows that residential segregation of city streets began as early as the 1880s, there nonetheless remains a consensus in the scholarship that residential segregation of entire neighborhoods, or ghettoization, did not begin until the 1900s. See Douglas Massey and Nancy Denton, *American Apartheid: Segregation and the Making of the Underclass* (Harvard University Press, 1993), esp. 17, 19; Lance Freeman, *A Haven and a Hell: The Ghetto in Black America* (Columbia University Press, 2019), 11–40; John R. Logan, Weiwei Zhang, and Miao David Chunyu, "Emergent Ghettos: Black Neighborhoods in New York and Chicago, 1880–1940," *American Journal of Sociology* 120, no. 4 (2015); John R. Logan et al., "Creating the Black Ghetto: Black Residential Patterns Before and During the Great Migration," *Annals of the American Academy of Political Science* 660, no. 1 (2015); John R. Logan and Isabelle R. Notter, "Residential Segregation Under Jim Crow: Whites, Blacks, and Mulattoes in Southern Cities, 1880–1920," *City and Community* 21, no. 1 (2022). The isolation index figures come from Logan et al., "Emergent Ghettos," 1082. The recent studies on segregation support the claims of a number of earlier scholars who argued that significant racial segregation began prior to 1900, as Logan, Zhang, and Chunyu acknowledge in their piece. Logan et al., "Emergent Ghettos," 1056. For examples of such earlier works, see Paul A. Groves and Edward K. Muller, "The Evolution of Black Residential Areas in Late Nineteenth-Century Cities," *Journal of Historical Geography* 1, no. 2 (1975); John Radford, "Race, Residence, and Ideology: Charleston, South Carolina in the Mid-Nineteenth Century," *Journal of Historical Geography* 2, no. 4 (1976); John Kellogg, "Negro Urban Clusters in the Postbellum South," *Geographical Review* 67, no. 3 (1977); Howard Rabinowitz, *Race Relations in the Urban South, 1865–1890* (Oxford University Press, 1978); Thomas Philpott, *The Slum and the Ghetto: Neighborhood Deterioration and Middle-Class Reform, Chicago 1880–1930* (Oxford University Press, 1978); Edward L. Ayers, *The Promise of the New South: Life After Reconstruction*, rev. ed. (Oxford University Press, 2007), 67–68. The muckraking journalist Jacob Riis, writing in 1890, corroborates the picture of rising segregation at the house-by-house level. Jacob Riis, *How the Other Half Lives: Studies Among the Tenements of New York* (New York: Charles Scribner's Sons, 1890), 150–52. For another work discussing the existence of

racial discrimination in the late nineteenth-century New York City housing market, see Seth M. Scheiner, "The New York City Negro and the Tenement, 1880–1910," *New York History* 45, no. 4 (1964). Instances of racial discrimination in housing were not new in the late nineteenth century; the question was how widespread that discrimination was. For references to anti-Black housing discrimination in the eighteenth century, see Jane Ptomely, "Our Native Soil: Philadelphian Quakers and Geographies of Race, 1780–1838" (PhD diss., Yale University, 2013), 107; Ibram X. Kendi, *Stamped from the Beginning: The Definitive History of Racist Ideas in America* (Bold Type Books, 2016), 170. For a foundational early study of Black urban life and residential patterns in the late nineteenth century, see W. E. B. Du Bois, *The Philadelphia Negro: A Social Study* (Philadelphia, 1899), 287–321.

7. Radford, "Race, Residence, and Ideology," 330; Logan et al., "Emergent Ghettos," 1072; Freeman, *Haven and a Hell*, 29–30.

8. For histories of the institutional and legal instruments facilitating ghettoization, see, for example, Arnold R. Hirsch, *Making the Second Ghetto: Race and Housing in Chicago, 1940–1960*, rev. ed. (University of Chicago Press, 2021); Kenneth T. Jackson, *Crabgrass Frontier: The Suburbanization of the United States* (Oxford University Press, 1987), 190–218; Christopher Silver, "The Racial Origins of Zoning: Southern Cities, from 1910–40," *Planning Perspectives* 6, no. 2 (1991); Arnold R. Hirsch, "With or Without Jim Crow," in *Urban Policy in Twentieth-Century America*, ed. Arnold R. Hirsh and Raymond A. Mohl (Rutgers University Press, 1993), 68; Thomas J. Sugrue, *The Origins of the Urban Crisis: Race and Inequality in Postwar Detroit* (Princeton University Press, 1996), 41–55; Kevin Fox Gotham, *Race, Real Estate, and Uneven Development: The Kansas City Experience, 1900–2000* (State University of New York Press, 2002), 27–74; David M. P. Freund, *Colored Property: State Policy and White Racial Politics in Suburban America* (University of Chicago Press, 2007); Richard Rothstein, *The Color of Law: A Forgotten History of How Our Government Segregated America* (Liveright, 2017); Andrea Gibbons, *City of Segregation: One Hundred Years of Struggle for Housing in Los Angeles* (Verso, 2018), 19–63; Elizabeth A. Herbin-Triant, *Threatening Property: Race, Class, and Campaigns to Legislate Jim Crow Neighborhoods* (Columbia University Press, 2019); Emily Lieb, "The 'Baltimore Idea' and the Cities It Built," *Southern Cultures* 25, no. 2 (2019); Paige Glotzer, *How the Suburbs Were Segregated: Developers and the Business of Exclusionary Housing, 1890–1960* (Columbia University Press, 2020).

9. On the racial fitness of Southern and Eastern European immigrants during this period, see Thomas A. Guglielmo, *White on Arrival: Italians, Race, Color, and Power in Chicago, 1890–1945* (Oxford University Press, 2003); David R. Roediger, *Working Toward Whiteness: How America's Immigrants Became White; The Strange Journey from Ellis Island to the Suburbs* (Basic Books, 2005), esp. 57–92; Matthew Frye Jacobson, *Whiteness of a Different Color: European Immigrants and the Alchemy of Race* (Harvard University Press, 1998), 13–90, 137–85, 203–22.

10. The statistics of Thompson Street's racial demographics come from my own compilation of data from 1880 census maps created by the Urban Transition Historical GIS Project at Brown University. Urban Transition Historical GIS Project, *Brown University*, accessed Apr. 16, 2022, https://s4.ad.brown.edu/Projects/UTP/query.htm. For more on the project, see John R. Logan, Jason Jindrich, Hyoungjin Shin, and Weiwei Zhang, "Mapping America in 1880: The Urban Transition Historical GIS Project," *Historical Methods* 44, no. 1 (2011).

11. Burrows and Wallace, *Gotham*, 993.

12. Heap, *Slumming*, 118. See also Mary Ting Yi Lui, *The Chinatown Trunk Mystery: Murder, Miscegenation, and Other Dangerous Encounters in Turn-of-the-Century New York City* (Princeton University Press, 2005), 17–51.

13. Genevieve Carpio, *Collisions at the Crossroads: How Place and Mobility Make Race* (University of California Press, 2019), 71.

14. For European immigrants' positioning above African Americans in the racial hierarchy, see Guglielmo, *White on Arrival*; Cybelle Fox and Thomas A. Guglielmo, "Defining America's Racial Boundaries: Blacks, Mexicans, and European Immigrants, 1890–1945," *American Journal of Sociology* 118, no. 2 (2012).

15. On the national reach of New York City news, see Richard White, *The Republic for Which It Stands: The United States During Reconstruction and the Gilded Age, 1865–1896* (Oxford University Press, 2017), 195–96. For examples of national coverage of Thompson Street, see "By Telegraph: From New York," *Boston Daily Advertiser*, Dec. 31, 1866, 1; "Telegraphic to the Whig and Courier," *Bangor Daily Whig and Courier*, Feb. 27, 1867; "A Brutal Murder in the Negro Quarter of New York," *Boston Daily Advertiser*, May 19, 1873; "Affairs in New York," *Baltimore Sun*, May 19, 1873, 1; "New York: The Thompson Street Tragedy," *Chicago Tribune*, May 21, 1873, 1.

16. See, for example, "The Thompson-Street Murder," *New York Times*, Jan. 1, 1867, 3; "The Thompson-Street Murder," *New York Times*, Jan. 4, 1867, 8.

17. See, for example, "Horrible Murder," *Milwaukee Daily Sentinel*, Nov. 10, 1868; "Atrocious Murder," *New York Times*, Nov. 4, 1868, 5; "The Thompson-Street Murder," *New York Times*, Nov. 5, 1868, 2.

18. For stories in the late 1860s and early 1870s documenting the interracial makeup of Thompson Street without editorializing, including those reporting on white residents as victims of Black crime and stories broadcasting the occurrence of white-on-white crime, see "Local News," *New York Times*, July 30, 1866, 4; "Shooting Affray in the Eighth Ward—a Policeman Wounded," *New York Times*, July 28, 1868, 8; "Sharp Treatment of Criminals by Judge Bedford," *New York Times*, Apr. 20, 1870, 2; "A Probable Murder," *New York Times*, Jan. 10, 1873, 8; "Minor Crimes and Casualties," *New York Times*, Jan. 17, 1872, 3; "A Bold Arrest," *New York Times*, Sept. 4, 1874, 8; "Robbery in Thompson Street," *New York Times*, Oct. 28, 1874, 9; "Highway Robbery in Thompson Street," *New York Times*, Oct. 31, 1874, 8.

19. See, for example, "Atrocious Murder," *New York Times*, Nov. 4, 1868, 5; "The Thompson-Street Murder," *New York Times*, Nov. 5, 1868, 2; "Stabbing Affray in Thompson-Street," *New York Times*, July 8, 1869, 5; "One Negro Murdered and Another Fatally Stabbed," *New York Times*, July 19, 1875, 8; "Later—Identification of the Murdered Man," *New York Times*, July 19, 1875, 8; "A Baltimore Negro Commits Murder in New York," *Baltimore Sun*, July 20, 1875, 4; "Sunday's Deeds of Violence," *New York Tribune*, July 20, 1875, 5; "Current Events," *New York Evangelist*, July 22, 1875, 8.

20. For additional coverage of Black crime on Thompson Street in the 1870s, see "Affray in Thompson Street—a Woman's Skull Fractured with a Stove Lid," *New York Times*, Dec. 30, 1872, 8; "Fatal Result of a Fracas—Fires and Street Accidents," Crimes and Casualties, *New York Times*, Jan. 20, 1873, 2; "A Probable Murder," *New York Times*, Jan. 10, 1873, 8; "A Brutal Murder in the Negro Quarter of New York," *Boston Daily Advertiser*, May 19, 1873;

"Affairs in New York," *Baltimore Sun*, May 19, 1873, 1; "New York: The Thompson Street Tragedy," *Chicago Tribune*, May 21, 1873, 1; "General Sessions: Sentences Yesterday—the Thompson Street Tragedy," *New York Times*, July 16, 1873, 2; "A Colored Highway Man Arrested," *New York Times*, Oct. 12, 1874, 8; "A Colored Highway Man," *New York Times*, Jan. 9, 1875, 3; "Robbed in a Negro Den," *New York Times*, Jan. 24, 1875, 2; "The Eighth Ward Murder," *New York Times*, July 21, 1875, 8; "Local Miscellany," *New York Tribune*, July 21, 1875, 10; "A Colored Outlaw's Crime," *New York Times*, Aug. 23, 1875, 8; "Local Miscellany: The Thompson Street Tragedy," *New York Times*, Sept. 3, 1875, 8; "The Sorrell Manslaughter Case," *New York Times*, Oct. 15, 1875, 2; "Reckless Use of Firearms," *New York Times*, Jan. 2, 1876, 12; "A Check to Criminals," *New York Times*, Jan. 29, 1876, 5; "Latest News Items," *San Francisco Daily Evening Bulletin*, Feb. 9, 1876; "Shooting Affray at a Negro Ball," *New York Times*, Feb. 22, 1877, 2; "A Mulatto Murdered," *New York Times*, Apr. 21, 1877, 5; "Highway Robbers Sentenced," *New York Times*, Aug. 15, 1877, 3; "Breaking Up Disorderly Houses," *New York Times*, Aug. 19, 1877, 5; "A Policeman Beaten by a Woman," *New York Times*, Sept. 11, 1877, 8; "A Disgusted Hebrew," *New York Times*, Jan. 23, 1878, 3; "New-York," *New York Times*, Feb. 4, 1878, 8; "A Desperate Negro Highwayman," *New York Times*, May 7, 1878, 8; "A Policeman's Skull Broken," *New York Times*, Sept. 7, 1878, 5; "Robbed of His Clothes," *New York Times*, Nov. 26, 1878, 3; "A Colored Virago," *New York Times*, Jan. 6, 1879, 2; "Highway Robbery in the Eighth Ward," *New York Times*, June 10, 1879, 8.

21. "Trouble in Thompson-Street," *New York Times*, Sept. 22, 1877, 3; "'Big Africa' Vanishing," *New York Times*, Sept. 24, 1877, 8.

22. Adam Malka, *The Men of Mobtown: Policing Baltimore in the Age of Slavery and Emancipation* (University of North Carolina Press, 2018), 217–46; Flowe, *Uncontrollable Blackness*, 28, 33, 35, 52; Marcy S. Sacks, "'To Show Who Was in Charge': Police Repression of New York City's Black Population at the Turn of the Twentieth Century," *Journal of Urban History* 31, no. 6 (2005); Howard Rabinowitz, "The Conflict Between Blacks and the Police in the Urban South, 1865–1900," *Historian* 39, no. 1 (1976); Khalil Gibran Muhammad, *The Condemnation of Blackness: Race, Crime, and the Making of Modern Urban America* (Harvard University Press, 2010), 49; Sam Mitrani, *The Rise of the Chicago Police Department: Class and Conflict, 1850–1894* (University of Illinois Press, 2013). New York City did not have a Black police officer until 1911, though some cities in the postbellum South had a small number of Black officers when Republicans were able to gain control of municipal governments. Flowe, *Uncontrollable Blackness*, 52; Rabinowitz, "Conflict Between Blacks and the Police in the Urban South," 64–68.

23. "The Black Doctor," *St. Louis Daily Globe-Democrat*, June 20, 1877, 2; "Life in Thompson-Street," *New York Times*, June 27, 1878, 3.

24. "Midnight Pictures," *National Police Gazette*, Jan. 31, 1880, 16. The *National Police Gazette* was highly popular with its target male audience in the late nineteenth century. Guy Reel, *The "National Police Gazette" and the Making of the Modern American Man, 1879–1906* (Palgrave Macmillan, 2006).

25. "A Blind Man's Love Story," *Chicago Daily Inter-Ocean*, Sept. 14, 1880, 9; "New York Topics," *Atlanta Constitution*, Mar. 30, 1884, 1; "Chicago Responsible: For an Aged Darky's New Hat and Thompson Street Activity," *St. Louis Daily Globe-Democrat*, June 8, 1884; "Bishop [L]yman Talks," *Galveston Daily News*, Mar. 21, 1890, 2; "The Race Question," *New Orleans Daily Picayune*, Mar. 21, 1890.

26. "New York: Dusky Woman Pugilists," *Milwaukee Sentinel*, Feb. 1, 1884, 2; "Witchcraft in New York," *St. Louis Daily Globe-Democrat*, Oct. 15, 1884, 4; "The Cholera in Paris," *New York Tribune*, Nov. 17, 1884, 1; "New York Niggertown," *Washington Post*, Aug. 15, 1886, 6; "New York Slums," *Milwaukee Sentinel*, Aug. 15, 1886, 10; "New York Letter," *Milwaukee Journal*, Jan. 27, 1888. For similar sensationalized news stories about Black disorder on Black-owned riverboat tours and resorts on the Potomac River, see Andrew Kahrl, "'The Slightest Semblance of Unruliness': Steamboat Excursions, Pleasure Resorts, and the Emergence of Segregation Culture on the Potomac River," *Journal of American History* 94, no. 4 (2008): 1121–27.

27. Examples of newspaper reports attesting to the multiracial and multiethnic demographics of Thompson Street in the 1880s include "Tragedy in a Tenement House," *Baltimore Sun*, Aug. 12, 1880, 4; "Quarrel in Thompson-Street," *New York Times*, Aug. 25, 1880, 2; "Discovered Under a Bed—Stoned by a Thief—Former Friends Fighting," Thefts and Burglaries, *New York Times*, Mar. 14, 1881, 2; "Westchester County," *New York Times*, May 11, 1881, 8; "New York: A Horrible Double Murder by a Jealous Italian Husband," *Chicago Tribune*, Dec. 10, 1881, 6; "An Indian Skirmish," *New York Times*, Dec. 11, 1881, 13; "A Week of Murders," *National Police Gazette*, Dec. 24, 1881, 7; "An Unfortunate Prisoner's Plea," *New York Times*, June 20, 1883, 8; "Shot by His Cousin," *New York Times*, Aug. 9, 1883, 8; "A Murder Prevented by Italians," *New York Times*, Aug. 20, 1884, 8; "A Dance House Raided," *New York Times*, Aug. 3, 1885, 8; "A Dog's Race Prejudice," *New York Times*, Aug. 28, 1885, 5; "The Italian Banker's Creditors," *New York Times*, Apr. 9, 1888, 1; "Blind but Not a Beggar," *New York Times*, Feb. 3, 1889, 16; "A Detective Roughly Handled," *New York Times*, Apr. 5, 1889, 5. For the highly mixed racial demographics of the Greenwich Village neighborhood in general in 1900, see McFarland, *Inside Greenwich Village*, 8–11, 13–16, 36.

28. Riis, *How the Other Half Lives*, 214.

29. Quoted in Scheiner, *Negro Mecca*, 18.

30. Sharon D. McCoy, "'The Trouble Begins at Eight': Mark Twain, the San Francisco Minstrels, and the Unsettling Legacy of Blackface Minstrelsy," *American Literary Realism* 41, no. 3 (2009): 233; "Matinees Today," *New York Times*, Nov. 27, 1879, 5; "The Theaters," *Puck*, Dec. 10, 1879, 652; "The Theaters," *Puck*, Dec. 24, 1879, 685.

31. Henry Guy Carleton, *The Thompson Street Poker Club: From "Life"* (London: George Routledge and Sons, 1884; repr. New York: White and Allen, 1888, 1889). Citations refer to the George Routledge and Sons edition. For the widespread popularity of the stories, see Martin, "Image of Black People in American Illustration," 442–44. For newspaper reprints of Carleton's stories, see, for example, "The Thompson Street Poker Club," *St. Louis Daily Globe Democrat*, Mar. 19, 1884, 5; "'No 'Sideration for de Secks,'" *Chicago Daily Tribune*, Sept. 11, 1884, 8; "The Thompson-St Poker Club," *New York Times*, Aug. 22, 1885, 5; "A Colored Jack-Pot," *Chicago Daily Tribune*, July 19, 1886, 5; "The Thompson-St Poker Club," *New York Times*, Aug. 1, 1886, 4; "Mr. Tooter Williams in Trouble," *Chicago Daily Tribune*, Dec. 22, 1887, 12; "Toot Williams Resigns," *Chicago Daily Tribune*, Apr. 30, 1888, 10; "Mr. Williams Turns Informer," *Chicago Daily Tribune*, May 11, 1888, 6. The *Atlanta Constitution* featured a blatant rip-off of the series, featuring "possibl[e] members of the Thompson Street Poker Club." See "Colored Poker," *Atlanta Constitution*, July 7, 1885, 4.

32. Carleton, *Thompson Street Poker Club*, 7–9; "The Thompson-St Poker Club," *New York Times*, Aug. 15, 1886, 7.

33. "The Thompson-St Poker Club," *New York Times*, Aug. 1, 1886, 4; Carleton, *Thompson Street Poker Club*, 16–19.

34. Henry Guy Carleton, *Lectures Before the Thompson Street Poker Club* (New York: White and Allen, 1889). For the spin-offs, see "The War of Medical Ethics," *Life*, Nov. 8, 1883, 230; "Thompson Street Bicycle Club Meets," *Chicago Daily Tribune*, May 18, 1896, 8; "Thompson Street Bicycle Club," *Rocky Mountain News*, May 30, 1897, 24.

35. Mrs. James Brown Potter, "Tips on Topmost Topics," *Puck*, Dec. 8, 1886, 241; "Thompson Street Echoings," *Puck*, Mar. 9, 1887, 31. Other such jokes abounded. See "He Didn't Come Back," *Puck*, Nov. 30, 1887, 222; "Moving in Thompson Street," *Chicago Daily Tribune*, July 31, 1887, 18; "Thompson Street Luxury," *Chicago Daily Tribune*, July 10, 1887, 14.

36. "Dockstader's," *New York Times*, Nov. 24, 1886, 5; "New York 'First Nights,'" *Philadelphia North American*, Oct. 10, 1893, 6; Edward Harrigan and Dave Braham, *The Sunny Side of Thompson Street (Away Down Town)* (New York: Wm. A. Pond, 1893).

37. John H. Kerr, *When Ephraim Plays His Solo on the Drum* (Milwaukee: Chas. K. Harris, 1899). For other songs linking the street with Black vice and crime, see Lew Sully, *I Don't Love Nobody* (New York: Howley, Haviland, 1896); T. Barrett McMahon, *Take Me Back Babe* (Boston: G. W. Setchell, 1898).

38. Bernard F. Reilly Jr., introduction to *Currier and Ives: A Catalogue Raisonné*, ed. Gale Research Company (Gale Research, 1984), xxvii–xxx; Bryan F. Le Beau, "Art in the Parlor: Consumer Culture and Currier and Ives," *Journal of American Culture* 30, no. 1 (2007): 20–25, 35; Le Beau, "African Americans in Currier and Ives's America," 71, 74; Hernandez, "Border Crossings," 42; Michael D. Harris, "Memories and Memorabilia, Art and Identity: Is Aunt Jemima Really a Black Woman?," *Third Text* 12, no. 44 (1998): 27; Sacks, *Before Harlem*, 55. Two standard catalogs of Currier and Ives's prints exist: Gale Research Company, ed., *Currier and Ives: A Catalogue Raisonné* (Gale Research, 1984), and Frederick A. Conningham, *Currier and Ives Prints: An Illustrated Checklist* (Crown, 1983).

39. Hernandez, "Border Crossings," 43; Hatt, "'Making a Man of Him,'" 34; Sacks, *Before Harlem*, 55–56.

40. Hernandez, "Border Crossings," 42; Shawn Michelle Smith, *Photography on the Color Line: W. E. B. Du Bois, Race, and Visual Culture* (Duke University Press, 2004), 82–86.

41. Indeed, laughter was a highly effective remedy for white anxieties. Portraying racial equality as ludicrous undermined Black demands for civil and political rights, and the humor allowed whites to laugh at what they saw as the very real threat of Black ambition, literally helping calm their fears. This point about the role of humor is indebted to scholar Sharon Ammen's analysis of white coon shouter May Irwin. See Sharon Ammen, *May Irwin: Singing, Shouting, and the Shadow of Minstrelsy* (University of Illinois Press, 2017), 110.

42. *An Ice Cream Racket: Freezing In* (New York: Currier and Ives, 1889).

43. *An Ice Cream Racket: Thawing Out* (New York: Currier and Ives, 1889). Some important qualifications are necessary when analyzing physical violence and race in the *Darktown* comics. Worth's humor ran toward the violent in general, as he did a number of other comic prints outside the *Darktown* series that depicted white individuals experiencing pain or harm. See, for example, Thomas Worth, *A Very Warm Corner* (New York: Currier and Ives, 1883); Thomas Worth, *We Parted on the Hillside, amid the Winter's Snow* (New York: Currier and Ives, 1880); Thomas Worth, *A Swell Sport on a Buffalo Hunt* (New York: Currier and Ives, 1882); Thomas Worth, *A Swell Sport Stampeded* (New York: Currier and Ives, 1882).

Still, while Worth occasionally employed violent humor and caricature in cartoons about whites, he reserved the most extreme caricature and violent imagery for the residents of Darktown. Although not solely motivated by Worth's racism, the violent humor in the *Darktown* comics cannot be separated from race.

44. Saidiya Hartman, *Scenes of Subjection: Terror, Slavery, and Self-Making in Nineteenth-Century America* (Oxford University Press, 1997), 31.

45. Mozell C. Hill, "The All-Negro Communities of Oklahoma: The Natural History of a Social Movement," *Journal of Negro History* 31, no. 3 (1946); Norman L. Crockett, *The Black Towns* (University of Kansas Press, 1979); David J. Organ, "The Historical Geography of African-American Frontier Settlement" (PhD diss., University of California, Berkeley, 1995), 85–97; David Chang, "From Indian Territory to White Man's Country: Race Nation, and the Politics of Land Ownership in Eastern Oklahoma, 1880–1940" (PhD diss., University of Wisconsin, 2002), 130–35; Quintard Taylor, "The Black Towns," in *Encyclopedia of African-American Culture and History*, ed. Colin A. Palmer, vol. 1 (Gale, 2006), 280–86.

46. Joe A. Mobley, "In the Shadow of White Society: Princeville, a Black Town in North Carolina, 1865–1915," *North Carolina Historical Review* 63, no. 3 (1986); Taylor, "Black Towns," 281; Rabinowitz, *Race Relations in the Urban South*, 99–100; Andrew Wiese, *Places of Their Own: African American Suburbanization in the Twentieth Century* (University of Chicago Press, 2004), 17–19. Another possible influence may be the "freedom colonies" of Black farmers squatting in remote lands within the South, especially Texas, which had formed by the 1870s. However, these communities had highly scattered residential patterns and were often barely noticed by the white Southerners living closest to them. See Thad Sitton and James H. Conrad, *Freedom Colonies: Independent Black Texans in the Time of Jim Crow* (University of Texas Press, 2005), esp. 3–4.

47. J. Cameron, *A Darktown Tournament: The First Tilt* (New York: Currier and Ives, 1890); J. Cameron, *A Darktown Tournament: Close Quarters* (New York: Currier and Ives, 1890).

48. Thomas Worth, *A Literary Debate in the Darktown Club: Settling the Question* (New York: Currier and Ives, 1885); Thomas Worth, *A Literary Debate in the Darktown Club: The Question Settled* (New York: Currier and Ives, 1885).

49. *Horse Car Sports Going to a Chicken Show: All Flush* (New York: Currier and Ives, 1886); *Horse Car Sports Going to a Chicken Show: Dead Broke* (New York: Currier and Ives, 1886).

50. Thomas Worth, *The Boss of the Road* (New York: Currier and Ives, 1884). This 1884 comic is a revision of an 1877 print by Worth with the same fundamentals but set in a more rural environment. A similar lesson about Black disregard for the rules of the road inheres in Thomas Worth, *Bound to Shine!!* (New York: Currier and Ives, 1877); Thomas Worth, *Bound to Smash!!* (New York: Currier and Ives, 1877).

51. Thomas Worth, *Creating a Sensation* (New York: Currier and Ives, 1881); Thomas Worth, *Spoiling a Sensation* (New York: Currier and Ives, 1881).

52. For more on the importance of white perceptions of technological competence to the creation and justification of racial hierarchies, see Michael Adas, *Machines as the Measure of Men: Science, Technology, and Ideologies of Western Dominance*, rev. ed. (Cornell University Press, 2014), esp. 133–342; Cotten Seiler, *Republic of Drivers: A Cultural History of Automobility in America* (University of Chicago Press, 2008), 109.

53. *Crossed by a "Milk Train"* (New York: Currier and Ives, 1885); *Wrecked by a Cow Catcher* (New York: Currier and Ives, 1885).

54. J. Cameron, *The Darktown Bicycle Club: On Parade* (New York: Currier and Ives, 1892); J. Cameron, *The Darktown Bicycle Club: Knocked Out* (New York: Currier and Ives, 1892). On the late nineteenth-century bicycle craze, see Gary Allan Tobin, "The Bicycle Boom of the 1890s: The Development of Private Transportation and the Birth of the Modern Tourist," *Journal of Popular Culture* 7, no. 4 (1974): 838–49. On the challenge Black bicyclists and their mobility posed to the racial and spatial arrangements of the Jim Crow South, see Nathan Cardon, "Cycling on the Color Line: Race, Technology, and Bicycle Mobilities in the Early Jim Crow South, 1887–1905," *Technology and Culture* 62, no. 4 (2021): 973–1002.

55. J. Cameron, *Darktown Trolley: Clar de Track When de Bell Rings* (New York: Currier and Ives, 1896).

56. J. Cameron, *Darktown Trolley: Through Car in Danger* (New York: Currier and Ives, 1896). For more *Darktown* examples depicting the inadequacy of Black mobility and its subsequent dangers, see Thomas Worth, *The Darktown Tally Ho: Tangled Up* (New York: Currier and Ives, 1889); Thomas Worth, *The Darktown Tally Ho: Straightened Out* (New York: Currier and Ives, 1889); *The Darktown Riding Class: The Trot* (New York: Currier and Ives, 1890); *The Darktown Riding Class: The Gallop* (New York: Currier and Ives, 1890).

57. *Ripton* (New York: Currier and Ives, 1850). For another example of Currier and Ives's portrayal of dignified and disciplined white mobility, see O. Knirsch, *The Road: Winter* (New York: Currier and Ives, 1853).

58. L. Maurer, *"Trotting Cracks" on the Snow* (New York: Currier and Ives, 1858).

59. J. Cameron, *Speeding on the Avenue* (New York: Currier and Ives, 1870).

60. J. Cameron, *Fast Trotters on Harlem Lane N.Y.* (New York: Currier and Ives, 1870). Currier and Ives prints did not write white women out of its images of urban movement completely. Rather, white women occupied a prominent place in depictions of the slower upper-class tradition of driving through Central Park. Whereas African Americans' reckless and disorderly movement revealed the absurdity of their class ambitions, the promenading of elite white men and women in Currier and Ives prints substantiated their class status. See Thomas Worth, *Fashionable "Turn-Outs" in Central Park* (New York: Currier and Ives, 1869); *The Grand Drive, Central Park N.Y.* (New York: Currier and Ives, 1870).

61. *The Express Train* (New York: Currier and Ives, 1870); Charles R. Parsons and Lyman Atwater, *American Railroad Scene: Lightning Express Trains Leaving the Junction* (New York: Currier and Ives, 1874); Charles R. Parsons and Lyman Atwater, *Night Scene at an American Railway Junction: Lightning Express, Flying Mail and Owl Trains, "On Time"* (New York: Currier and Ives, 1876). On trains as the preeminent symbol of modernity in the nineteenth century, see Eric Hobsbawm, *The Age of Revolution, 1789–1848* (Vintage, 1996), 44.

62. Parsons and Atwater, *Night Scene at an American Railway Junction*. For another print linking white mobility with modern civilization through the mobility of trains, see Parsons and Atwater, *American Railroad Scene*.

Chapter Six

1. "Not Wild West Indians Exactly," *New York Tribune*, Feb. 5, 1887, 5.

2. "Buffalo Bill's Wild West," *Philadelphia North American*, Aug. 21, 1888.

3. Historian Louis Warren has written about the significance of mobility as a theme in the performances of the Wild West show, and historian L. G. Moses has noted that white reformers thought the show would spark nomadic urges in Indian actors. Louis S. Warren, *Buffalo Bill's America: William Cody and the Wild West Show* (Knopf, 2005); L. G. Moses, *Wild West Shows and the Images of American Indians, 1883–1933* (University of New Mexico Press, 1996). Likewise, prior historians, including Moses, have pointed out that the show offered Indian actors an escape from the geographical and economic containments of the reservation. Much great work has been done on this topic. Moses, *Wild West Shows*, 21–128; Warren, *Buffalo Bill's America*, 194, 358–89; David R. M. Beck, *Unfair Labor? American Indians and the 1893 World's Columbian Exposition in Chicago* (University of Nebraska Press, 2019), 158–66; Philip J. Deloria, *Indians in Unexpected Places* (University of Kansas Press, 2004), 68–71; Sam A. Maddra, *Hostiles? The Lakota Ghost Dance and Buffalo Bill's Wild West* (University of Oklahoma Press, 2006), 63–121, 156–75; Kevin Meethan, "Touring the Other: Buffalo Bill's Wild West in Europe," *Journal of Tourism History* 2, no. 2 (2010); Ryan E. Burt, "'Sioux Yells' in the Dawes Era: Lakota 'Indian Play,' the Wild West, and the Literatures of Luther Standing Bear," *American Quarterly* 62, no. 3 (2010); Linda Scarangella McNenly, *Native Performers in Wild West Shows: From Buffalo Bill to Euro Disney* (University of Oklahoma Press, 2012), intro, chaps. 1–2; Melissa Rinehart, "To Hell with the Wigs! Native American Representation and Resistance at the World's Columbian Exposition," *American Indian Quarterly* 36, no. 4 (2012): 419–22. For a discussion of similar dynamics with Native vaudeville performers, see Christine Bold, *"Vaudeville Indians" on Global Circuits, 1880s to 1930s* (Yale University Press, 2022). No work has yet provided a synthesis of these various aspects, nor do Warren and Moses uncover all the ways in which mobility suffused the show's content and motivated the critiques of white reformers. Warren does briefly note that "the emergence of Indians as show performers . . . compounded their essential savagery with a veneer of 'gypsy-ness'" in the eyes of white reformers, but he does not connect this observation to the history of Indians' racialization as perpetual nomads. See Warren, *Buffalo Bill's America*, 366.

4. A number of scholars have examined *Black America*, and a few, most notably Barbara L. Webb and Josephine Lee, have highlighted how the show contained elements of Black resistance and claims on modernity. However, no scholar has connected *Black America* and McClain's work in the show to the formation of the BO of CP. See Robert Toll, *Blacking Up: The Minstrel Show in Nineteenth-Century America* (Oxford University Press, 1974), 262–63; Roger Allan Hall, "*Black America*: Nate Salsbury's 'Afro-American Exhibition,'" *Educational Theatre Journal* 29, no. 1 (1977); Thomas L. Riis, *Just Before Jazz: Black Musical Theater in New York, 1890–1915* (Smithsonian Institution Press, 1989), 22–24; Eric J. Sundquist, *To Wake the Nations: Race in the Making of American Literature* (Belknap Press of Harvard University Press, 1993), 288; David Krasner, *Resistance, Parody, and Double Consciousness in African American Theatre, 1895–1910* (St. Martin's Press, 1997), 22–25; Barbara L. Webb, "Authentic Possibilities: Plantation Performance of the 1890s," *Theatre Journal* 56, no. 1 (2004); Karen Sotiropoulos, *Staging Race: Black Performers in Turn of the Century America* (Harvard University Press, 2006), 22–23; Jayna Brown, *Babylon Girls: Black Women Performers and the Shaping of the Modern* (Duke University Press, 2008), 138–42; Bill Reed, *Hot from Harlem: Twelve African American Entertainers, 1890–1960* (McFarland, 2010), 43–45, 50–51; Bethany D. Holmstrom, "Producing Memories: Staging the Civil War

in US Culture, 1867–1908" (PhD diss., City University of New York, 2013), 148–52; Lori Brooks, "Journey to a Land of Cotton: A Slave Plantation in Brooklyn, 1895," *American Studies* 53, no. 1 (2014): 57–78; Dorothy Berry, "*Black America, 1895*," *Public Domain Review*, Feb. 24, 2021, https://publicdomainreview.org/essay/black-america-1895; Josephine Lee, *Oriental, Black, and White: The Formation of Racial Habits in American Theater* (University of North Carolina Press, 2022), 166–69.

5. Nicholas Guyatt, *Bind Us Apart: How Enlightened Americans Invented Racial Segregation* (Basic Books, 2016), 110–11, 225–45, 281–305; Francis Paul Prucha, *American Indian Policy in Crisis: Christian Reformers and the Indian, 1865–1900* (University of Oklahoma Press, 1976), 193–94.

6. Carl Schurz, "Present Aspects of the Indian Problem," *North American Review* 133, no. 296 (1881): 6, 12–14, 17.

7. Lyman Abbott, "Criticism of the Reservation System," in *Americanizing the American Indians: Writings by the "Friends of the Indian," 1880–1900*, ed. Francis Paul Prucha (Harvard University Press, 1973), 33–35. Such complaints were common among prominent reformers of the period, such as Charles C. Painter. See, for example, Charles C. Painter, "The Indian and His Property," in Prucha, *Americanizing the American Indians*, 115; Charles C. Painter, "Our Indian Policy as Related to the Civilization of the Indian," in Prucha, *Americanizing the American Indians*, 72–73.

8. Thomas J. Morgan, "Statement on Indian Policy," in Prucha, *Americanizing the American Indian*, 75; Thomas J. Morgan, "Supplemental Report on Indian Education," in Prucha, *Americanizing the American Indian*, 230–31, 234–35.

9. Prucha, *American Indian Policy in Crisis*, 224–352; Frederick E. Hoxie, *A Final Promise: The Campaign to Assimilate the Indians, 1880–1920*, rev. ed. (Cambridge University Press, 1989), 53–81; Jon Reyhner and Jeanne Eder, *American Indian Education: A History* (University of Oklahoma Press, 2004), 132–67; John W. Troutman, *Indian Blues: American Indians and the Politics of Music, 1879–1934* (Oklahoma University Press, 2009), 7; Larry E. Burgess, "What Is a Woman Worth?" in *The Women's National Indian Association: A History*, ed. Valerie Sherer Mathes (University of New Mexico Press, 2015), 1–8. On the essential consensus between government officials and the Indian Rights Association and the Women's National Indian Association regarding Indian policy, see David Wallace Adams, *Education for Extinction: American Indians and the Boarding School Experience, 1875–1928* (University of Kansas Press, 1995), 9–24; Valerie Sherer Mathes et al., conclusion to Mathes, *Women's National Indian Association*.

10. On boarding schools as confinement, see Douglas K. Miller, *Indians on the Move: Native American Mobility and Urbanization in the Twentieth Century* (University of North Carolina Press, 2019), 11, 13; Genevieve Carpio, *Collisions at the Crossroads: How Place and Mobility Make Race* (University of California Press, 2019), 35–37; Robert T. Chase, introduction to *Caging Borders and Carceral States: Incarcerations, Immigration Detentions, and Resistance*, ed. Robert T. Chase (University of North Carolina Press, 2019), 20–21; Douglas K. Miller, "The Spider's Web: Mass Incarceration and Settler Custodialism in Indian Country," in Chase, *Caging Borders and Carceral States*, 390–91; Tiya Miles, *Wild Girls: How the Outdoors Shaped the Women Who Challenged a Nation* (W. W. Norton, 2023), 70–112. On allotment of land in severalty as confinement, see C. Joseph Genetin-Pilawa, *Crooked Paths to Allotment: The Fight over Federal Indian Policy After the Civil War* (University of North

Carolina Press, 2012), 113; Warren, *Buffalo Bill's America*, 361; Elliott West, *Continental Reckoning: The American West in the Age of Expansion* (University of Nebraska Press, 2023), 371–72. Despite the surveillance and control of Indian mobility by whites at boarding schools, Native American students regularly seized opportunities to direct their own movements and repurposed boarding school practices toward the end of preserving and rebuilding their communities and cultures. Miller, *Indians on the Move*, 16; Kevin Whalen, *Native Students at Work: American Indian Labor and Sherman Institute's Outing Program, 1900–1945* (University of Washington Press, 2016).

11. Prucha, *Indian Policy in Crisis*, 227–91; Brian W. Dippie, *The Vanishing American: White Attitudes and U.S. Indian Policy* (Wesleyan University Press, 1982), 171–76; Troutman, *Indian Blues*, 113. Attesting to the ideological and material links between military conquest, incarceration, and the Indian boarding school, Carlisle Indian Industrial School founder Richard Henry Pratt was inspired to create a boarding school for Native Americans while he was an army officer assigned to teach Great Plains Indians imprisoned at Fort Marion in St. Augustine, Florida, in 1875. Reyhner and Eder, *American Indian Education*, 133.

12. Frederick E. Hoxie, *This Indian Country: American Indian Activists and the Place They Made* (Penguin Press, 2012), 394–98.

13. Hoxie, *Final Promise*, 44, 78; Francis Paul Prucha, *The Great Father: The United States Government and the American Indian* (University of Nebraska Press, 1984), 2:864, 2:896.

14. Peter Iverson and Wade Davies, *"We Are Still Here": American Indians Since 1890*, 2nd ed. (Wiley Blackwell, 2015), 3–4; David Treuer, *The Heartbeat of Wounded Knee: Native America from 1890 to Present* (Riverhead Books, 2019); Hoxie, *This Indian Country*, chaps. 5–8, afterword; Nick Estes, *Our History Is the Future: Standing Rock Versus the Dakota Access Pipeline, and the Long Tradition of Indigenous Resistance* (Verso, 2019), esp. 1–65; Edmund Jefferson Danziger Jr., *Great Lakes Indian Accommodation and Resistance During the Early Reservation Years, 1850–1900* (University of Michigan Press, 2009); Thomas Carter, Edward Chappell, and Timothy McCleary, "In the Lodge of the Chickadee: Architecture and Cultural Resistance on the Crow Indian Reservation, 1884–1920," *Perspectives in Vernacular Architecture* 10 (2005).

15. Bethany Hughes, *Redface: Race, Performance, and Indigeneity* (New York University Press, 2024), 135–59; Joy S. Kasson, *Buffalo Bill's Wild West: Celebrity, Memory, and Popular History* (Hill and Wang, 2000), 23–25; Warren, *Buffalo Bill's America*, 187–95, 210.

16. Press accounts of the show in its early days bear the stamp of these publicity efforts. See, for example, "The 'Wild West' Show," *Milwaukee Sentinel*, Oct. 15, 1883, 5.

17. Warren argues that it was this narrative arc that made the Wild West show so successful with middle-class audiences, particularly middle-class women. The masculine feats of combat and mastery over nature (horses, buffalo, and, in the racist narrative of the show, Indians) resonated with a gathering backlash against the cult of domesticity, yet repeated allusions to the importance of the home and domestic space tempered such displays, gesturing to the continued importance of women in American life. So did the inclusion of white female sharpshooter Annie Oakley, who in public interviews repeatedly stressed her domestic skills alongside her shooting skills. This mixed imagery allowed the show to walk a fine line that reflected many of the gender tensions of the period. Warren, *Buffalo Bill's America*, 215–18, 238–47. On the symbolic importance of home for late nineteenth-century Americans, see Richard White, *The Republic for Which*

It Stands: The United States During Reconstruction and the Gilded Age, 1865–1896 (Oxford University Press, 2017), 5, 136–71.

18. Warren, *Buffalo Bill's America*, 238–53.

19. "The Wild West," *Chicago Daily Tribune*, Oct. 18, 1883, 8; "Buffalo Bill," *Boston Daily Advertiser*, May 25, 1897, 2.

20. "World's Fair Doings," *Chicago Daily Inter-Ocean*, Apr. 27, 1893, 7.

21. Queen Victoria, quoted in Moses, *Wild West Shows*, 54.

22. Warren, *Buffalo Bill's America*, 222, 238, 244. Warren's phrase "constant racing of its races" is a play on the title "Race of Races," which the Wild West Show program gave to the racing act in 1899. See Jonathan D. Martin, "'The Grandest and Most Cosmopolitan Object Teacher': *Buffalo Bill's Wild West* and the Politics of American Identity, 1883–1899," *Radical History Review* 66 (1996): 115.

23. "The 'Wild West' Show," *Milwaukee Sentinel*, Oct. 13, 1883, 5; "Plenty of 'Wild West' Enthusiasm," *Washington Post*, June 23, 1885, 1.

24. "A Gray Abroad," *Atchison Daily Globe*, Feb. 25, 1885; *Merriam-Webster Dictionary*, "maraud," accessed May 28, 2025, www.merriam-webster.com/dictionary/maraud.

25. Warren, *Buffalo Bill's America*, 252–53.

26. Warren, *Buffalo Bill's America*, 238, 250, 253. Historian Paul Reddin echoes Warren's more extended discussion of the show's focus on mobility, writing, "Rapid movement; a kaleidoscope of color; smells of earth, animals, and gunpowder; and noise—all these set the mood of the Wild West show. Everything moved fast: horses always galloped and riders burst suddenly into view from behind scenery." Paul Reddin, *Wild West Shows* (University of Illinois Press, 1999), 67.

27. Cody himself echoed many white reformers in calling for land in severalty and criticizing the reservation system as not imposing enough geographic containment. As he remarked in 1888, the reservation was counterproductive to civilizing efforts since it gave "a tribe an immense tract to roam over." "Buffalo Bill upon the Indian Question," *Harper's Weekly*, July 14, 1888.

28. Moses, *Wild West Shows*, 21–128; Warren, *Buffalo Bill's America*, 194, 358–89; Beck, *Unfair Labor?*, 158–66; Deloria, *Indians in Unexpected Places*, 68–71; McNenly, *Native Performers in Wild West Shows*, 3–70; Reddin, *Wild West Shows*, 79.

29. "Buffalo Bill's Sioux," *Washington Post*, Nov. 15, 1890, 6; "'Round About New-York," *New York Times*, June 15, 1894, 8; "A Suburban for Ramapo," *New York Times*, June 22, 1894, 3; "A Hundred Indians in Town," *Philadelphia North American*, Apr. 16, 1895, 5.

30. Reddin, *Wild West Shows*, 81; Warren, *Buffalo Bill's America*, 390–91; "Won a White Bride," *New York Times*, Aug. 19, 1886, 3; "Got a Wife in Austria," *Chicago Daily Tribune*, Feb. 17, 1891, 2; "The Indian Did A-Courting Go," *New York Tribune*, Feb. 17, 1891, 12; "Miscellaneous News of Gotham," *Chicago Daily Tribune*, Oct. 28, 1892, 5; "Indians Make Their Complaints," *New York Times*, Oct. 4, 1895, 9; "At the National Capital," *New York Tribune*, Oct. 4, 1895, 11.

31. "Buffalo Bill's Good-Bye," *New York Times*, Apr. 1, 1887, 8.

32. "Red Cow Comes Home," *New York Times*, Mar. 1, 1889, 8; "Welcome Home, 'Red Cow,'" *Philadelphia North American*, Mar. 1, 1889, n.p.

33. "Red Cow Comes Home," *New York Times*, Mar. 1, 1889, 8; "Welcome Home, 'Red Cow,'" *Philadelphia North American*, Mar. 1, 1889, n.p.

34. "Build Their Tepees," *Chicago Daily Tribune*, Apr. 20, 1893, 1. On the long history of Indigenous peoples' travel within US settler-colonial society, see, for example, Joshua A. McGonagle Althoff, "Managing Settlers, Managing Neighbors: Renarrating *Johnson v. McIntosh* Through the History of Piankashaw Community Building," *Journal of American History* 110, no. 4 (2024); Colin Calloway, *"The Chiefs Now in This City": Indians and the Urban Frontier in Early America* (Oxford University Press, 2021); Colin Calloway, *The Indian World of George Washington: The President, the First Americans, and the Birth of the Nation* (Oxford University Press, 2018); Miller, *Indians on the Move*; Coll Thrush, *Native Seattle: Histories from the Crossing-Over Place* (University of Washington Press, 2007).

35. "The Stage and the Ring," *Baltimore Sun*, Aug. 29, 1887, 1; McNenly, *Native Performers in Wild West Shows*, 67; Warren, *Buffalo Bill's America*, 371.

36. "Cowboys in Old Verona," *New York Times*, May 18, 1890, 17; "Buffalo Bill's Sioux," *Washington Post*, Nov. 14, 1890, 2.

37. As alleged by the prominent white reform group the Indian Rights Association, the Wild West show and its imitators taught whites "false ideas about the present condition of the Indians; they represent him only as a savage, and convey no idea of the progress he has made in civilized pursuits." Reformers believed that this imagery justified white prejudice against Native Americans and provided encouragement to those seeking to deny Indians legal rights under US law. They preferred, and thought far more accurate, representations like the Carlisle Indian Industrial School's exhibition, which documented the many strides Native Americans had made toward civilization. Indian Rights Association, "Condemnation of Wild West Shows," in Prucha, *Americanizing the American Indian*, 314; Prucha, *American Indian Policy in Crisis*, 319–27; Warren, *Buffalo Bill's America*, 366–72; Moses, *Wild West Shows*, 60–79; Reddin, *Wild West Shows*, 115.

38. Indian Rights Association, "Condemnation of Wild West Shows," 314; "Lo's Place Is at Home," *Chicago Daily Tribune*, Mar. 17, 1891, 2.

39. Moses, *Wild West Shows*, 65, 92–104, 108; Warren, *Buffalo Bill's America*, 367–72, 387; Reddin, *Wild West Shows*, 115–16. See also "Buffalo Bill After More Redskins," *Chicago Daily Tribune*, Feb. 28, 1891, 5; "Buffalo Bill's Protégé," *Philadelphia North American*, Nov. 1, 1893, 2.

40. Moses, *Wild West Shows*, 68.

41. Oberly, quoted in Prucha, *American Indian Policy in Crisis*, 320.

42. Moses, *Wild West Shows*, 69–70.

43. Thomas J. Morgan, "Wild West Shows and Similar Exhibitions," in Prucha, *Americanizing the American Indian*, 311.

44. Morgan, "Wild West Shows and Similar Exhibitions," 312. Morgan doubled down on his assessment that Wild West shows reinvigorated Indians' inherent nomadism in his 1892 annual report. See Thomas J. Morgan, *Sixty-First Annual Report of the Commissioner of Indian Affairs to the Secretary of the Interior* (Washington: Government Printing Office, 1892), 105–6.

45. Morgan, *Sixty-First Annual Report of the Commissioner of Indian Affairs* (Washington: Government Printing Office, 1892), 105–6, 138. Other reformers and federal officials reiterated the point that Native performers' mobility undermined the fragile progress toward agricultural fixity achieved on reservations. See the statements in "Indian Affairs," *Friends' Review*, Mar. 27, 1890, 557, and *Annual Reports of the Department of the Interior for the Fiscal Year Ended June 30, 1899: Report of the Commissioner of Indian Affairs*, pt. 1 (Washington:

Government Printing Office, 1899), 42, as well as the quotes of reformer Herbert Welsh in Moses, *Wild West Shows*, 131.

46. Morgan, "Wild West Shows and Similar Exhibitions," 310.

47. Morgan, "Wild West Shows and Similar Exhibitions," 310–11. Relatedly, a federal Indian agent writing in 1899 argued that Indian actors with the Wild West had traveled so much that they exhausted the show's beneficial potential and should now remain on the reservation. *Annual Reports of the Department of the Interior*, 42. See also the critiques in H. D. Gallagher, "Report of Pine Ridge Agency," in *Fifty-Eighth Annual Report of the Commissioner of Indian Affairs to the Secretary of the Interior* (Washington: Government Printing Office, 1889), 153.

48. For newspaper articles covering Cody's struggle to procure Indian actors, see, for example, "Buffalo Bill Will Lose His Indians," *Chicago Daily Tribune*, Dec. 5, 1889, 1; "Buffalo Bill's Sioux," *Washington Post*, Nov. 14, 1890, 2; "Buffalo Bill's Sioux," *Washington Post*, Nov. 15, 1890, 6; "'Buffalo Bill' Indians Well Treated," *New York Tribune*, Nov. 16, 1890, 4; "Indians for Cody's Show," *Atchison Daily Champion*, Mar. 8, 1891, 8; "Buffalo Bill Engages Indians," *San Francisco Daily Bulletin*, Mar. 7, 1891, 3; "Washington Notes," *Los Angeles Times*, Mar. 7, 1891, 5; "Will Accompany 'Buffalo Bill,'" *Chicago Daily Tribune*, Mar. 14, 1891, 6; editorial, *New York Times*, Mar. 14, 1891, 4; "Sioux Prisoners," *Bismarck Daily Tribune*, Mar. 14, 1891; "Legal Murders in Cuba," *Chicago Daily Tribune*, Mar. 15, 1891, 17; "The Hostile Sioux," *Los Angeles Times*, Mar. 15, 1891, 5; "Day's Objections," *Bismarck Daily Tribune*, Mar. 19, 1891; "Philadelphia Affairs," *Baltimore Sun*, Mar. 31, 1891, 1; "Miscellaneous News of Gotham," *Chicago Daily Tribune*, Oct. 28, 1892, 5; "Buffalo Bill and His Indians," *Chicago Inter-Ocean*, Apr. 15, 1892, 7; "The United States and the Show Business," *Christian Union*, May 14, 1892, 927; "Buffalo Bill Gets His Indians," *Emporia Daily Gazette*, Apr. 14, 1893; "Capital Notes," *New Orleans Daily Picayune*, Apr. 14, 1893, 2; "For the World's Fair," *Milwaukee Sentinel*, Apr. 14, 1893, 1; "Cody's Wild West Show," *Denver Daily News*, Apr. 14, 1893, 2; "Buffalo Bill's Protégé," *Philadelphia North American*, Nov. 1, 1893, 2; "Washington Notes," *Milwaukee Sentinel*, Mar. 27, 1894, 8; "Indians for Buffalo Bill," *Milwaukee Journal*, Mar. 27, 1893, 2; "Washington," *Minneapolis Penny Press*, Apr. 2, 1894, 2.

49. "Buffalo Bill After More Redskins," *Chicago Daily Tribune*, Feb. 28, 1891, 5.

50. Hall, "*Black America*," 56–57.

51. Advertisement for *Black America*, *New York Tribune*, May 19, 1895, 9.

52. "Strange Exhibition," *Indianapolis Journal*, June 25, 1895, 4.

53. "*Black America*," *Brooklyn Times Union*, May 24, 1895, 10; "*Black America*," *Cleveland Plain Dealer*, June 16, 1895, 17; "Strange Exhibition," *Indianapolis Journal*, June 25, 1895, 4; "A Negro Camp," *Boston Post*, July 18, 8; Hall, "*Black America*," 49, 52; Brooks, "Journey to a Land of Cotton," 62.

54. Hall, "*Black America*," 60.

55. McClain, quoted in interview by Zeke Blossom, clipping, Billy McClain folder, Billy Rose Theatre Division, New York Public Library. For scholars attributing *Black America*'s authorship to McClain, see Webb, "Authentic Possibilities," 74; Sotiropoulos, *Staging Race*, 22–23; Tom Fletcher, *The Tom Fletcher Story: 100 Years of the Negro in Show Business* (Burdge, 1954; repr., Da Capo Press, 1984), 91, 94.

56. Webb, "Authentic Possibilities," 76–78; "*Black America*," *Brooklyn Times Union*, May 24, 1895, 10; "*Black America*," *Brooklyn Citizen*, May 24, 1895, 4; "Wild Negro Chants

and Dances," *New York Times*, May 25, 1895, 9; "*Black America* Is Here," *Brooklyn Citizen*, May 26, 1895, 2.

57. "Black America on View," *Brooklyn Daily Eagle*, May 24, 1895, 7; Webb, "Authentic Possibilities," 65, 74–81.

58. For the history of Black mutual aid societies, see Theda Skocpol and Jennifer Lynn Oser, "Organization Despite Adversity: The Origins and Development of African American Fraternal Associations," *Social Science History* 28, no. 3 (2004); Theda Skocpol, Ariane Liazos, and Marshall Gans, *What a Mighty Power We Can Be: African American Fraternal Groups and the Struggle for Racial Equality* (Princeton University Press, 2006). For an overview of the history of fraternal organizations in the nineteenth-century United States in general, see David T. Beito, *From Mutual Aid to the Welfare State: Fraternal Societies and Social Services, 1890–1967* (University of North Carolina Press, 2000), 5–16.

59. "Organization of the B.O. of C.P.," *Freeman*, Feb. 26, 1898, 8; "Race Gleanings," *Freeman*, Mar. 5, 1898, 2; "In the Glare of Footlights," *Colored American*, Mar. 19, 1898, 7; "Mr. Wm. M'Clain," *Freeman*, Dec. 24, 1898, 8; "The Stage," *Freeman*, Mar. 11, 1899, 5. One letter to the Indianapolis *Freeman* mentions that the BO of CP had grown so much that not only "professional men but men of every vocation" were members, suggesting that the order was open to those outside the entertainment business. "Mr. Wm. M'Clain," *Freeman*, Dec. 24, 1898, 8. However, I have found no other evidence to corroborate this. Regardless, the BO of CP at its founding was geared toward Black entertainers.

60. "The Stage," *Freeman*, Mar. 12, 1898, 5; "The Stage," *Freeman*, May 7, 1898, 5; "The Stage," *Freeman*, May 14, 1898, 5; "The Stage," *Freeman*, Aug. 6, 1898, 5; "The Stage," *Freeman*, Aug. 13, 1898, 5; "The Stage," *Freeman*, Nov. 12, 1898, 5; "Race Echoes," Des Moines *Bystander*, Dec. 23, 1898, 8; "The Stage," *Freeman*, Jan. 21, 1899, 5; "The Stage," *Freeman*, Apr. 1, 1899, 5; "The Stage," *Freeman*, Apr. 15, 1899, 5; "Spicy News," *Freeman*, June 17, 1899, 4; "The Buffaloes," *Freeman*, July 1, 1899, 5; "The Stage," *Freeman*, Sept. 2, 1899, 5; "The Buffaloes' Anniversary," *Freeman*, Feb. 10, 1900, 8; "Revival Meetings!" *Freeman*, Nov. 29, 1902, 1.

61. "Moore Lodge, B.O. of C.P.," *Colored American*, Nov. 12, 4; "The Stage," *Freeman*, June 11, 1898, 5. One of the artists performing at the fundraising event was McClain's wife, Cordelia McClain.

62. "Race Gleanings," *Freeman*, Mar. 5, 1898, 2; "The Stage," *Freeman*, Dec. 10, 1898, 5; see also "Town Talk," *Freeman*, Sept. 10, 1898, 8.

63. "The Stage," *Freeman*, Feb. 26, 1898, 5.

64. "The Stage," *Freeman*, Aug. 6, 1898, 5; "The Stage," *Freeman*, Mar. 4, 1899, 5; "The Stage," *Freeman*, May 6, 1899, 5.

65. "Mr. Wm. M'Clain," *Freeman*, Dec. 24, 1898, 8.

66. "Mr. Wm. M'Clain," *Freeman*, Dec. 24, 1898, 8.

67. "The Stage," *Freeman*, June 11, 1898, 5.

68. Reed, *Hot from Harlem*, 45–47. For the continued vitality of the St. Louis chapter, see, for example, "The Buffalos' Ball and Banquet a Success in Every Respect," *St. Louis Palladium*, Feb. 3, 1906, 1. Other organizations soon sprang up to fill the void created by the BO of CP's demise, including the New Amsterdam Musical Association (1904), the Frogs (1906), and the Colored Vaudeville Benevolent Association (1909). Sotiropoulos, *Staging Race*, 197–207; David Gilbert, *The Product of Our Souls: Ragtime, Race, and the Birth of the Manhattan Musical Marketplace* (University of North Carolina Press, 2015), 94–95; Fletcher, *100 Years*, 172–76.

Epilogue

1. Jan Ransom, "Trump Will Not Apologize for Calling for Death Penalty over Central Park Five," *New York Times*, June 18, 2019, www.nytimes.com/2019/06/18/nyregion/central-park-five-trump.html.

2. John Burnett, "Evacuees Were Turned Away at Gretna, La.," *National Public Radio*, Sept. 20, 2005, www.npr.org/-templates/story/story.php?storyId=4855611; Angela A. Allen-Bell, "Bridge over Troubled Waters and Passageway on a Journey to Justice: National Lessons Learned About Justice from Louisiana's Response to Hurricane Katrina," *California Western Law Review* 46, no. 2 (2010): 266–72; "Crescent City Connection Blockade After Hurricane Katrina Wasn't Illegal, US Justice Department Says," *Nola.com*, Oct. 1, 2011, www.nola.com/news/politics/article_e62c0621-1b07-590e-b1b0-03b24cc061d2.html. The incident spawned numerous lawsuits and a federal investigation by the Department of Justice, but in the end, the DOJ declined to pursue legal action and the courts denied the various lawsuits of private citizens.

3. Brock N. Meeks, "Gretna Mayor Defends Bridge Blockade," NBC News, Sept. 21, 2005, www.nbcnews.com/id/wbna9427111.

4. Quoted in Allen-Bell, "Bridge over Troubled Waters," 270.

5. Quoted in Allen-Bell, "Bridge over Troubled Waters," 269.

6. Nigel Duara, "Pipeline Protesters Clash with Police in North Dakota," *Los Angeles Times*, Nov. 20, 2016, www.latimes.com/nation/la-na-north-dakota-protest-20161120-story.html; Sam Levin, "Dakota Access Pipeline: Native Americans Allege Cruel Treatment," *Guardian*, Oct. 30, 2016, www.theguardian.com/us-news/2016/oct/29/dakota-access-pipeline-native-american-protesters.

7. For example, in South Dakota, Native Americans make up only 9 percent of the population, but Native men account for 29 percent of incarcerated males. The disparity for Native women is even higher, as they make up 35 percent of the adult women imprisoned in the state. Douglas K. Miller, "The Spider's Web: Mass Incarceration and Settler Custodialism in Indian Country," in *Caging Borders and Carceral States: Incarcerations, Immigration Detentions, and Resistance*, ed. Robert T. Chase (University of North Carolina Press, 2019), 386.

8. Mass incarceration of Native Americans has arisen on historical terrain intimately shaped by settler-colonial violence. Years of warfare, land dispossession, racism, and the reservation system's economic hardships all created the poverty and weakened political power that allowed mass incarceration to take root in Native communities. Subject to the dislocations and deprivations of settler colonialism, Native peoples made vulnerable targets for mass incarceration's race- and class-based tactics. Miller, "Spider's Web," 388.

9. For works examining the history of mass incarceration, see, for example, Ruth Wilson Gilmore, *Golden Gulag: Prisons, Surplus, Crisis, and Opposition in Globalizing California* (University of California Press, 2007); Michelle Alexander, *The New Jim Crow: Mass Incarceration in the Age of Colorblindness* (New Press, 2010); Kelly Lytle Hernández, Khalil Gibran Muhammad, and Heather Ann Thompson, "Introduction: Constructing the Carceral State," *Journal of American History* 102, no. 1 (2015); Elizabeth Hinton, *From the War on Poverty to the War on Crime: The Making of Mass Incarceration in America* (Harvard University Press, 2016); James Forman Jr., *Locking Up Our Own: Crime and Punishment in Black*

America (Farrar, Straus and Giroux, 2017); Kelly Lytle Hernández, *City of Inmates: Conquest, Rebellion, and the Rise of Human Caging in Los Angeles, 1771–1965* (University of North Carolina Press, 2017); Christopher Clements, "'There Isn't No Trouble At All If the State Law Would Keep Out': Indigenous People and New York's Carceral State," *Journal of American History* 108, no. 2 (2021).

10. Nas, "N.Y. State of Mind," *Illmatic* (Columbia Records, 1994).

11. Loïc Wacquant, "Deadly Symbiosis: When Ghetto and Prison Meet and Mesh," *Punishment and Society* 3, no. 1 (2001).

12. Nas, "N.Y. State of Mind."

13. Jay-Z, "Can I Live," *Reasonable Doubt* (Roc-A-Fella Records, 1996).

14. Jon Shecter, "The Second Coming," *The Source*, April 1994, 46.

Index

Italic page numbers refer to illustrations.

www.ingramcontent.com/pod-product-compliance
Lightning Source LLC
LaVergne TN
LVHW090833031026
849361LV00018B/163